WORKING WITH
OFFENDERS

For Ray Cochrane, who offered the opportunity

WORKING WITH OFFENDERS

Psychological Practice in Offender Rehabilitation

Edited by

Clive R. Hollin

School of Psychology
University of Birmingham
and
Youth Treatment Service, Birmingham, UK

JOHN WILEY & SONS

Chichester • New York • Brisbane • Toronto • Singapore

Other Wiley Editorial Offices

John Wiley & Sons, Inc., 605 Third Avenue,
New York, NY 10158-0012, USA

Jacaranda Wiley Ltd, 33 Park Road, Milton,
Queensland 4064, Australia

John Wiley & Sons (Canada) Ltd, 22 Worcester Road,
Rexdale, Ontario M9W 1L1, Canada

John Wiley & Sons (SEA) Pte Ltd, 37 Jalan Pemimpin #05-04,
Block B, Union Industrial Building, Singapore 2057

Library of Congress Cataloging-in-Publication Data

Working with offenders : psychological practice in offender
  rehabilitation / edited by Clive R. Hollin
       p.   cm.
    Includes bibliographical references (p.   ) and index.
    ISBN 0-471-95776-3 (cased : alk. paper). – ISBN 0-471-95349-0
(pbk. : alk. paper)
      1. Criminals – Rehabilitation – United States. 2. Criminal
psychology – United States. I. Hollin, Clive R.
HV9304.W64   1996
364.3–dc20   95-32340
                                                            CIP

British Library Cataloguing in Publication Data

A catalogue record for this book is available from the British Library

ISBN 0-471-95776-3 (cased)
ISBN 0-471-95349-0 (paper)

Typeset in 10/12pt Times by Mayhew Typesetting, Rhayader, Powys
Printed and bound in Great Britain by Biddles Ltd, Guildford

This book is printed on acid-free paper responsibly manufactured from sustainable forestation, for
which at least two trees are planted for each one used for paper production.

CONTENTS

ABOUT THE EDITOR

Clive R. Hollin
School of Psychology, University of Birmingham, and Youth Treatment Service, Birmingham
Clive Hollin spent 4 years working as a prison psychologist before taking academic posts at the University of Leicester and the University of Birmingham. His current appointment is to the joint posts of Director of Research and Development in the Youth Treatment Service and Senior Lecturer in Psychology at the University of Birmingham. He is a Fellow of the British Psychological Society. His publication list includes over 100 academic articles and 14 books, among which are *Psychology and Crime* (Routledge, 1989); *Clinical Approaches to Sex Offenders and Their Victims* (co-edited with Kevin Howells, Wiley, 1991); and *Managing Behavioural Treatment: Policy and Practice with Delinquent Adolescents* (with David Kendrick & Kevin Epps, Routledge, 1995). He is co-editor of the journal *Psychology, Crime and Law*.

CONTRIBUTORS

Ronald Blackburn
Ashworth Hospital, Liverpool
Ronald Blackburn has been involved with problems of mentally disordered offenders for much of his professional career as practitioner, teacher and researcher. After graduating from Cambridge University in 1961, he trained as a clinical psychologist in Leicester, and subsequently held posts for several years in the psychology departments of Broadmoor and Rampton special hospitals. In 1974, he moved to the University of Aberdeen to head post-graduate training for clinical psychologists, but returned to the special hospital system as Chief Psychologist at Park Lane (now Ashworth) hospital in 1981. Since 1993, he has been Professor of Clinical and Forensic Psychological Studies at the University of Liverpool and Director of Research at Ashworth hospital. His interests centre on violent offenders and the assessment and treatment of personality disorders. He has written extensively on these topics, and is the author of *The Psychology of Criminal Conduct* (Wiley, 1993).

Kevin Browne
School of Psychology, University of Birmingham
Dr Kevin Browne has been researching family violence and child abuse for fifteen years and has published extensively on the subject. He is Chair of the Research Committee of the International Society for the Prevention of Child Abuse and Neglect (ISPCAN) and Co-Editor (with Dr Margaret Lynch) of *Child Abuse Review*, Journal of the British Association for the Study and Prevention of Child Abuse and Neglect (BAPSCAN). As a Chartered Psychologist and a Chartered Biologist, he is currently employed by the School of Psychology at the University of Birmingham, as a Senior Lecturer in Clinical Criminology and Research Coordinator for the Youth Treatment Service at the Glenthorne Centre, Birmingham. His publications include: Browne, K., Davies, C., and Stratton, P., *Early Prediction and Prevention of*

Child Abuse (1988) and Browne, K., and Herbert, M., *Preventing Family Violence* (1995), both published by Wiley.

Kevin Epps
Glenthorne Youth Treatment Centre, Birmingham

Kevin Epps is a forensic clinical psychologist with over twelve years experience of working with offenders in residential, community and psychiatric settings. Currently he is Principal Psychologist at Glenthorne Centre, Birmingham. This is one of two centres operating under the auspices of the Youth Treatment Service (YTS), offering care, education and treatment to some of Britain's most difficult young people. He has developed a particular interest in the management and treatment of sexual offenders, an interest reflected in his clinical, teaching and research activities. He has also represented the YTS on several national committees and working groups concerned with the treatment of sexually aggressive adolescents. Among his publications he is co-author, with Clive Hollin and David Kendrick, of *Managing Behavioural Treatment: Policy and Practice with Delinquent Adolescents* (Routledge, 1995)

David P. Farrington
Institute of Criminology, University of Cambridge

Dr David P. Farrington is Professor of Psychological Criminology, University of Cambridge, where he has been on the staff since 1969, and Acting Director of the Institute of Criminology. His major research interest is in the longitudinal study of delinquency and crime, and he is Director of the Cambridge Study in Delinquent Development, a prospective longitudinal survey of over 400 London males aged from 8 to 40, funded by the Home Office. He is also co-Principal Investigator of the Pittsburgh Youth Survey, a prospective longitudinal study of over 1500 Pittsburgh males from 7 to 20. In addition to over 170 published papers on criminological and psychological topics, he has published 14 books, one of which, *Understanding and Controlling Crime* (1986), won the prize for distinguished scholarship of the American Sociological Association Criminology Section. He is President-elect of the European Association of Psychology and Law, a member of the advisory boards of the U.S. National Juvenile Court Data Archive and The Netherlands Institute for the Study of Criminality and Law Enforcement, joint editor of the Cambridge University Press book series on Research in Criminology and on Criminal Behaviour and Mental Health, and a member of the editorial boards of several journals. He has been President of the British Society of Criminology, Chair of the Division of Criminological and Legal Psychology of the British Psychological Society, Vice-Chair of the U.S. National Academy of Sciences Panel on Violence, a member of the U.S. National Academy of Sciences Committee on Law and Justice, a member of the U.S. National Academy of

Sciences Panel on Criminal Career Research, and a member of the national Parole Board for England and Wales. He is a Fellow of the British Psychological Society and of the American Society of Criminology. He received BA, MA and PhD degrees in psychology from the University of Cambridge, and the Sellin-Glueck Award of the American Society of Criminology for international contributions to criminology.

Gisli H. Gudjonsson
The Maudsley Hospital, Institute of Psychiatry, London
Gisli Gudjonsson is a Reader in Forensic Psychology, Institute of Psychiatry, University of London, and the Head of Forensic Psychology Services at the Maudsley and Bethlem Royal Hospitals. His research has been primarily in the area of forensic and criminological psychology. He has published over 130 journal articles and 30 book chapters. He is the author of *The Psychology of Interrogations, Confessions and Testimony* (Wiley) and a co-author (with Hans Eysenck) of *The Causes and Cures of Criminality* (Plenum Press). Dr Gudjonsson has acted as an expert witness in many criminal trials, including the Court of Appeal cases of Judith Ward and Engin Raghip, which resulted in major legal precedent, the case of the UDR Four in Northern Ireland, and the Ashworth Inquiry, 1992. He testified in 1989 at the arbitration of "test cases" concerning the Zeebrugge disaster. In 1993 Dr Gudjonsson gave evidence in a military court in Israel against the General Security Service.

Kevin Howells
Reaside Clinic, Birmingham
Kevin Howells is a chartered clinical and forensic psychologist. He has worked in a range of clinical and academic environments. He worked for some years at Broadmoor Hospital and has occupied a post as Top Grade Psychologist at the Reaside Clinic since 1992. He has held academic appointments at Leicester University and Birmingham University. At Birmingham he was Director of the clinical psychology postgraduate course and was appointed Professor of Clinical Psychology in 1991. He is currently a Visiting Fellow at Edith Cowan University in Perth, Western Australia, where he is involved in postgraduate training in forensic and clinical psychology. His current interests include the psychology of anger and public perceptions of mentally disordered offenders, topics on which he has published widely, including *Clinical Approaches to the Mentally Disordered Offender* (co-edited with Clive Hollin, Wiley, 1993).

Cynthia McDougall
Home Office, Prison Department, London
Cynthia McDougall is Head of Prison Service Psychology in England and Wales. She was awarded a psychology degree by Newcastle upon Tyne

University, and a D Phil by York University for research into anger control. Before joining the Prison Service she worked in industry, and as a Probation Officer for five years. Cynthia McDougall joined the Prison Service in 1979 working initially in an area team providing psychological services to a range of prison establishments, including those for young offenders, women and adult males from the lower security categories, to high-risk and life-sentence prisoners. She has been involved in individual and group work with offenders, including development of anger management and sex offender programmes, and initiated development of a risk assessment model for life-sentence and other long-term prisoners. While working in prison establishments, she also advised on regime development, population profiling and hostage negotiation. She has worked over a number of years with a range of prison staff from all backgrounds and professions. She has published widely and presented papers regularly to psychological conferences. She is currently Membership Officer of the European Association of Psychology and Law. In 1994, in addition to her role as Head of Prison Service Psychology, she was appointed Head of Prison Service Personnel Services.

James McGuire

James McGuire is a Senior Lecturer in Forensic Clinical Psychology at the University of Liverpool and works as a clinical psychologist in Ashworth Hospital. He obtained degrees from the Universities of Glasgow, Leicester and Leeds, and has carried out research in prisons, probation services, adolescent units and special hospitals on a number of aspects of offender rehabilitation and evaluation of services. He has worked at the Universities of Edinburgh, Hong Kong and London and was also for some years involved independently in training, staff development and consultation in criminal justice agencies. Among his publications, he is editor of the book *What Works: Effective Methods to Reduce Reoffending* (Wiley, 1995)

Mary McMurran

Rampton Hospital, Nottinghamshire
Mary McMurran is Director of Psychological Services at Rampton Hospital, a secure psychiatric hospital for mentally disordered offenders. She is a former prison psychologist and spent 10 years working with young offenders. Her main research interest is alcohol and crime, and she has published widely in this area. She is co-author with Clive Hollin of *Young Offenders and Alcohol-Related Crime: A Practitioner's Guidebook* (Wiley, 1993) and author of *The Psychology of Addiction* (Taylor & Francis, 1994).

PREFACE

As well as working with (mainly young) offenders, I have, I suppose, read a great deal about working with offenders: I have read passionate arguments for working with offenders, and equally strident arguments against; I have read studies about successes and studies about failures; I have read empirical and non-empirical studies; I have read highly specialized texts on ways of working; and detailed texts on working with specific types of offender. On top of all this, I have edited several books on the topic, and in my own writing I've made my own modest contribution to other people's reading. So, why this book?

The idea for this book was, as we have learned to say in the 1990s, driven by the market. Often students and professional colleagues ask me for references on working with offenders and I happily supply them with lists as long as their arms. All well and good, but the reply kept coming back, "why isn't there one text with the basic information?" Well, why not? In our Series *Clinical Approaches to Criminal Behaviour*, Kevin Howells and I had attempted the very same thing, with some degree of success, albeit on rather more specialist lines. So, why not a general text on the topic of working with offenders?

In planning this book my first step was to work out what the main topics should be and then decide who should be asked to do the writing. In terms of topics, I decided that three areas were important in a sourcebook that aimed to provide a synopsis of the field. First, an overview of criminological and legal psychology to familiarize readers with the theoretical and practical necessities needed to work with offenders. Second, a review of the areas of service provision to show the diversity of settings in which rehabilitative work takes place. Third, reviews of working with different offender groups to present information on what is known of the effectiveness of rehabilitative work with offenders. In terms of selection of authors I made a conscious decision to follow the editorial lead of Robert Holdstock and Christopher Priest in compiling my own *Stars of Albion*.[1] Acknowledging the undoubted importance of the contribution of practitioners and researchers from many countries, I feel that this is an area of psychology in which we British can justly hold our heads high. I am grateful therefore to the publishers for having the nerve to back my judgement. The list of authors does, I believe, stand comparison with anything else currently in print.

For the opening section of the book, I have been fortunate in gaining contributions from two leading figures. David Farrington is, of course, a leading researcher in the field of criminological psychology; while Gisli Gudjonsson is not only a prolific writer and researcher but, in terms of court appearances, also one of the most experienced legal psychologists in the country. The two authors on service provision are both vastly experienced in the practical and organizational aspects of working with offenders. James McGuire, equally at home as academic, trainer, and practitioner, has achieved the rare distinction for a psychologist of being seen as an important figure in the work of the Probation Service. It is difficult to imagine that there is any psychologist more qualified to write on community work with offenders. Alongside our north-eastern roots, Cynthia McDougall and I share a common heritage: in 1980 we both joined the ranks of prison psychologists, and spent many a weary hour role playing our way through countless training courses. I got early release, but Cynthia has risen to the position of professional head of psychological services in the Prison Department: there can be few psychologists as well qualified to write on the topic of working in institutions.

The first four of the five chapters on working with offenders are written by psychologists who can justly claim, through both research and practice, to know their topic. Ron Blackburn is, of course, best known for his work on psychopathy but, as shown by his chapter here, he is equally knowledgeable about mentally disordered offenders in general. I have published elsewhere with Kevin Epps (Hollins, Epps & Kendrick, 1995) and can testify at first hand to his abilities as a clinician. Kevin is steadily building a reputation for his work with adolescent sex offenders, while his chapter here shows his full grasp of the intricacies of working with the broad population of sex offenders. Kevin Browne has already established a position in the field of prevention of child abuse; while Kevin Howells has an established reputation for his work on the role of anger in violent behaviour. In their chapter they offer a concise overview of the issues in working with a range of violent offenders. Mary McMurran is another psychologist with whom I have had the pleasure of

---

[1]   See the Epilogue.

publishing a full length work (McMurran & Hollin, 1993). I am delighted to have here her chapter on drugs, alcohol and working with offenders. My own piece on young offenders draws proceedings to a close.

There are, as always, other people to thank: Rita Granner for typing letters, making telephone calls, and sending faxes; Tracey Swaffer for her help with the referencing of my chapter; family and friends, for all the usual reasons.

Clive R. Hollin

REFERENCES

Hollin, C.R., Epps, K.J. & Kendrick, D.J. (1995) *Managing Behavioural Treatment.* London: Routledge.
McMurran, M. & Hollin, C.R. (1993) *Young Offenders and Alcohol-Related Crime.* Chichester: Wiley.

CRIMINOLOGICAL AND LEGAL PSYCHOLOGY

CRIMINOLOGICAL PSYCHOLOGY: INDIVIDUAL AND FAMILY FACTORS IN THE EXPLANATION AND PREVENTION OF OFFENDING

David P. Farrington

The main aims of this chapter are to review evidence about the role of individual and family factors in offending, to review psychological theories of crime that focus on individual and family factors, and to review methods of preventing and treating offending based on individual and family factors. More than other types of theories, psychological explanations of crime focus on individual difference factors such as personality, impulsivity and intelligence, and on family features such as parental supervision and discipline. In this chapter, I will discuss the various kinds of individual and family influences sequentially, since many psychological theories are essentially multiple-factor explanations that assume that offending depends on the sum total of all these different influences acting together. There is not space in this chapter to review peer, school or situational factors, or more sociological research on socio-economic, demographic, neighbourhood, community and society features that influence offending (see e.g. Farrington, 1993b,c).

Working with Offenders: Psychological Practice in Offender Rehabilitation.
Edited by C.R. Hollin. © 1996 John Wiley & Sons Ltd.

Psychologists believe that, like other types of behaviour, criminal behaviour results from the interaction between a person (with a certain degree of criminal potential or antisocial tendency) and the environment (which provides criminal opportunities). Some people will be consistently more likely to commit offences than others in different environments, and conversely the same person will be more likely to commit offences in some environments than in others. A major problem in psychological theories is to explain the development of individual differences in criminal potential, or conversely in the strength of internal inhibitions against offending.

Psychologists view offending as a type of behaviour, similar in many respects to other types of antisocial or deviant behaviour. Hence, the theories, methods and knowledge of other types of antisocial behaviour can be applied to the study of crime. Generally, psychologists are committed to the scientific study of human behaviour (e.g. Farrington, 1984a, 1991c), with its emphasis on theories that can be tested and falsified using empirical, quantitative data, controlled experiments, systematic observation, valid and reliable measures, replications of empirical results, and so on.

Psychologists usually concentrate on the types of offences that dominate the official criminal statistics in Western countries, principally theft, burglary, robbery, violence, vandalism and drug abuse. There is less concern with "white-collar" crime or with crimes by organizations. Most research has concentrated on offending by males, since this is generally more frequent and serious than offending by females (e.g. Farrington, 1987a). Psychologists are also interested in biological factors that may underlie psychological constructs.

Psychologists argue that officially recorded offenders and non-offenders (or, in self-report studies, more and less serious offenders) are significantly different in numerous respects, before, during and after their offending careers. This is basically because of consistent individual differences in underlying criminal potential or antisocial tendency. Generally, the worst offenders according to self-reports (taking account of frequency and seriousness) tend also to be the worst offenders according to official records (Farrington, 1973; Huizinga & Elliott, 1986). The correlates of official and self-reported offending are very similar (Farrington, 1992c). Hence, conclusions about individual characteristics of offenders can be drawn validly from both convictions and self-reports. In this chapter, "offenders" will refer to officially recorded offenders, unless otherwise stated.

Psychologists have made many contributions to knowledge about offending, and it is only possible to mention a small number of these in this chapter, focusing on individual and family factors. Wilson & Herrnstein (1985), Hollin

(1989, 1992) and Blackburn (1993) have published more extensive reviews of psychological research on crime. In discussing influences on offending, I will refer especially to knowledge gained in the Cambridge Study in Delinquent Development, which is a prospective longitudinal survey of over 400 London males from age 8 to age 32 (Farrington & West, 1990). Similar results have been obtained in similar studies elsewhere in England (Kolvin et al., 1988, 1990), in the United States (McCord, 1979; Robins, 1979), in the Scandinavian countries (Pulkkinen, 1988; Wikstrom, 1987) and in New Zealand (Moffitt & Silva, 1988a).

Criminal career research has been important in establishing basic knowledge about the development of offending and antisocial behaviour from childhood to adulthood (Blumstein et al., 1986; Blumstein, Cohen & Farrington, 1988; Farrington, 1992a). Generally, offenders are versatile, committing not only many different types of crimes but also many different types of antisocial acts. The prevalence of most types of offending increases to a peak in the teenage years, and then decreases in the twenties and thirties (Farrington, 1986a). However, there is also considerable continuity in offending over time, since the worst offenders at any given age tend also to be the worst offenders at other ages (Farrington, 1989b, 1990a). It is plausible to suggest that there is continuity over time in an underlying construct such as criminal potential or antisocial personality, which has different behavioural manifestations at different ages (Farrington, 1991a). For example, the antisocial child may be troublesome and disruptive in school, the antisocial teenager may steal cars and burgle houses, and the antisocial adult male may beat up his wife and neglect his children.

Loeber & Dishion (1983) and Loeber & Stouthamer-Loeber (1987) extensively reviewed the predictors of male offending. The most important predictors were poor parental child management techniques, childhood antisocial behaviour, offending by parents and siblings, low intelligence and educational attainment, and separation from parents. All of these influences will be reviewed in this chapter. In contrast, low socio-economic status was a rather weak predictor, in agreement with other research casting doubt on the importance of this factor (e.g. Hindelang, Hirschi & Weis, 1981).

INDIVIDUAL INFLUENCES

PERSONALITY

Robins' (1979) explanation of offending suggests that there is an "antisocial personality" that arises in childhood and persists into adulthood, and this idea is embodied in the DSM-IV diagnosis of antisocial personality disorder (American Psychiatric Association, 1994). According to Robins, the antisocial adult male generally fails to maintain close personal relationships with anyone else, tends to perform poorly in his jobs, tends to be involved in crime, fails to support himself and his dependents without outside aid, and tends to change his plans impulsively and to lose his temper in response to minor frustrations. As a child, he tended to be restless, impulsive and lacking in guilt, performed badly in school, truanted, ran away from home, was cruel to animals or people, and committed delinquent acts. Robins and Ratcliff (1978) documented the continuity between childhood and adult antisocial behaviour.

Psychologists have carried out a great deal of research on the relationship between different personality factors and offending. However, the personality scales that correlate most reliably with offending (the psychopathic deviate scale of the Minnesota Multiphasic Personality Inventory and the socialization scale of the California Psychological Inventory: see Tennenbaum, 1977) are probably measuring much the same antisocial personality construct that underlies offending itself. Hence, these personality constructs are unlikely to be causes of offending.

One of the best known theories linking personality and offending was proposed by Eysenck (1977). He viewed offending as natural and even rational, on the assumption that human beings were hedonistic, seeking pleasure and avoiding pain. He assumed that delinquent acts such as theft, violence and vandalism were essentially pleasurable or beneficial to the offender. In order to explain why everyone was not a criminal, Eysenck suggested that the hedonistic tendency to commit crimes was opposed by the conscience, which was viewed as a conditioned fear response. The likelihood of people committing crimes depended on the strength of their conscience.

Eysenck proposed that the conscience was built up in childhood. Each time a child committed a disapproved act and was punished by a parent, the pain and fear aroused in the child tended to become associated with the act by the process of classical conditioning. After children had been punished several times for the same act, they felt fear when they next contemplated it, and this fear tended to stop them committing it. According to the theory, this conditioned fear response was the conscience, and it would be experienced subjectively as guilt if the child committed a disapproved act.

On the Eysenck theory, people who commit offences are those who have not built up strong consciences, mainly because they have inherently poor conditionability. Poor conditionability is linked to Eysenck's dimensions of personality. People who are high on extroversion (E) build up conditioned responses less well, because they have low levels of cortical arousal. People who are high on neuroticism (N) condition less well, because their high resting level of anxiety interferes with the conditioning. Also, since neuroticism acts as a drive, reinforcing existing behavioural tendencies, neurotic extroverts should be particularly criminal. Eysenck also predicts that people who are high on psychoticism (P) will tend to be offenders, because the traits included in his definition of psychoticism (emotional coldness, low empathy, high hostility, inhumanity) are typical of criminals. It seems likely that psychopathy may be a more accurate label than psychoticism for Eysenck's P scale.

Farrington, Biron & Le Blanc (1982) reviewed studies relating Eysenck's personality dimensions to official and self-reported offending. They concluded that high N (but not E) was related to official offending, while high E (but not N) was related to self-reported offending. High P was related to both, but this could have been a tautological result, since many of the items on the P scale are connected with antisocial behaviour or were selected in the light of their ability to discriminate between prisoners and non-prisoners (Eysenck & Eysenck, 1976, pp. 39, 47). In the Cambridge Study, those high on both E and N tended to be juvenile self-reported offenders, adult official offenders and adult self-reported offenders, but not juvenile official offenders. Furthermore, these relationships held independently of other variables such as low family income, low intelligence and poor parental child-rearing behaviour. However, when individual items of the personality questionnaire were studied, it was clear that the significant relationships were caused by the items measuring impulsivity (e.g. doing things quickly without stopping to think). Hence, it was concluded that research inspired by the Eysenck theory, like other projects, had identified a link between impulsivity and offending.

HYPERACTIVITY AND IMPULSIVITY

Hyperactivity is an important psychological construct that predicts later delinquency. It usually begins before age 5 and often before age 2, and it tends to persist into adolescence (Taylor, 1986). It is associated with restlessness, impulsivity and a short attention span, and for that reason has been termed the "hyperactivity–impulsivity–attention deficit" or HIA syndrome (Loeber, 1987). Related concepts include a poor ability to defer gratification (Mischel, Shoda & Rodriguez, 1989) and a short future time perspective (Stein, Sarbin & Kulik, 1968). Pulkkinen (1986) has usefully reviewed the various concepts and measures of hyperactivity and impulsivity.

HIA may be an early stage in a causal or developmental sequence leading to offending. For example, in the Cambridge Study, Farrington et al. (1990)

showed that HIA at age 8–10 significantly predicted juvenile convictions independently of conduct problems at age 8–10. Hence, it might be concluded that HIA is not merely another measure of antisocial tendency. Other studies have also concluded that hyperactivity and conduct disorder are different constructs (Taylor et al., 1986; Blouin et al., 1989). Similar constructs to HIA, such as sensation seeking, are also related to offending (Farley & Sewell, 1976; White, Labouvie & Bates, 1985). In the Cambridge Study, the rating of daring or risk-taking at age 8–10 by parents and peers significantly predicted convictions up to age 32 independently of all other variables (Farrington, 1990b, 1993a), and poor concentration or restlessness was the most important predictor of convictions for violence (Farrington, 1994).

It has been suggested that HIA might be a behavioural consequence of a low level of physiological arousal (Ellis, 1987). Offenders have a low level of arousal according to their low alpha frequency (brain) waves on the electro-encephalogram (EEG), or according to autonomic nervous system indicators such as heart rate, blood pressure or skin conductance, or they show low autonomic reactivity (Venables & Raine, 1987). For example, violent offenders in the Cambridge Study had significantly low heart rates (Farrington, 1987b). The causal links between low autonomic arousal, consequent sensation seeking and offending are brought out explicitly in Mawson's (1987) theory of transient criminality.

In the Cambridge Study, being shy, nervous or withdrawn was the main factor that protected boys from criminogenic backgrounds against becoming offenders (Farrington et al., 1988a,b). In Boston, Kagan, Reznick & Snidman (1988) classified children as inhibited (shy, fearful, socially avoidant) or uninhibited at age 2 on the basis of observations of how they reacted to unfamiliar people or objects. This classification of inhibited or uninhibited children remained significantly stable up to age 7 and was independent of social class and intelligence. Furthermore, the inhibited children had a higher resting heart rate and a greater increase in their heart rate in the unfamiliar situation. Hence, just as low arousal may be conducive to impulsivity, sensation-seeking and offending, high arousal may be conducive to shyness and may act as a protective factor against offending.

INTELLIGENCE AND MORALITY

As Hirschi & Hindelang (1977) showed in their review, intelligence is an important correlate of offending: at least as important as social class or race. In the Cambridge Study, West and Farrington (1973) found that twice as many of the boys scoring 90 or less on a non-verbal intelligence test (Raven's

Progressive Matrices) at age 8–10 were convicted as juveniles than of the remainder. Low non-verbal intelligence was highly correlated with low verbal intelligence (vocabulary, word comprehension, verbal reasoning) and with low school attainment, and all of these measures predicted juvenile convictions to much the same extent. In addition to their poor school performance, delinquents tended to be frequent truants, to leave school at the earliest possible age (which was then 15) and to take no school examinations.

Low non-verbal intelligence was especially characteristic of the juvenile recidivists and those first convicted at the earliest ages (10–13). Furthermore, low non-verbal intelligence predicted juvenile self-reported offending to almost exactly the same degree as juvenile convictions, suggesting that the link between low intelligence and delinquency was not caused by the less intelligent boys having a greater probability of being caught. Also, measures of intelligence predicted measures of offending independently of other variables such as family income and family size. Similar results have been obtained in other projects (Lynam, Moffitt & Stouthamer-Loeber, 1993; Wilson & Herrnstein, 1985; Moffitt & Silva, 1988a). It has also been argued that high intelligence is a protective factor against offending for children from high-risk backgrounds (Kandel et al., 1988; White, Moffitt & Silva, 1989). Delinquents often do better on non-verbal performance tests, such as object assembly and block design, than on verbal tests (Walsh, Petee & Beyer, 1987), suggesting that they find it easier to deal with concrete objects than with abstract concepts.

Intelligence may lead to delinquency through the intervening factor of school failure, as Hirschi & Hindelang (1977) suggested. However, a more plausible explanatory factor underlying the link between intelligence and offending is the ability to manipulate abstract concepts. People who are poor at this tend to do badly in intelligence tests such as the Matrices and in school attainment, and they also tend to commit offences, mainly because of their poor ability to foresee the consequences of their offending and to appreciate the feelings of victims (i.e. their low empathy). Certain family backgrounds are less conducive than others to the development of abstract reasoning. For example, lower class, poorer parents tend to live for the present and to have little thought for the future, and tend to talk in terms of the concrete rather than the abstract, as Cohen (1955) pointed out many years ago. A lack of concern for the future is also linked to the concept of impulsivity.

Modern research is studying not just intelligence but also detailed patterns of cognitive and neuropsychological deficit. For example, in a New Zealand longitudinal study of over 1000 children from birth to age 15, Moffitt & Silva (1988b) found that self-reported offending was related to verbal, memory and visual–motor integration deficits, independently of low social class and family adversity. Neuropsychological research might lead to important advances in knowledge about the link between brain functioning and delinquency. For example, the "executive functions" of the brain, located in the frontal lobes, include sustaining attention and concentration, abstract reasoning and concept formation, anticipation and planning, self-monitoring of behaviour, and inhibition of inappropriate or impulsive behaviour (Moffitt, 1990). Deficits in these executive functions are conducive to low measured intelligence and to offending. Moffitt & Henry (1989) found deficits in these executive functions especially for delinquents who were both antisocial and hyperactive.

The importance of abstract reasoning and thinking is also emphasized in other psychological theories of offending, for example in the moral development theory of Kohlberg (1976). According to Kohlberg, people progress through different stages of moral development as they get older: from the pre-conventional stage (where they are hedonistic and only obey the law because of fear of punishment) to the conventional stage (where they obey the law because it is the law) to the post-conventional stage (where they obey the law if it coincides with higher moral principles such as justice, fairness and respect for individual rights). The pre-conventional stage corresponds to rather concrete thinking, whereas abstract thinking is required to progress to the post-conventional stage. Clearly, the developing moral reasoning is related to the developing intelligence.

The key idea of moral reasoning theory is that moral actions depend on moral reasoning (Kohlberg & Candee, 1984). Specifically, it is argued that offenders have retarded powers of moral reasoning and are mainly stuck in the pre-conventional stage. There is a good deal of evidence that offenders indeed show lower levels of moral reasoning than non-offenders (Thornton, 1987a; Smetana, 1990), and some institutional treatment programmes have been designed to improve moral reasoning ability (Scharf & Hickey, 1976; Duguid, 1981; Arbuthnot & Gordon, 1988). However, while moral reasoning is important independently of intelligence, it is unclear whether it is a cause of offending or merely another symptom of an underlying antisocial personality.

ENVIRONMENTAL INFLUENCES

Even in psychological theories focusing on individual difference factors, there is a great deal of concern with family influences. Loeber & Stouthamer-Loeber (1986) completed an exhaustive review of family factors as correlates and predictors of juvenile conduct problems and delinquency. They found that poor parental supervision or monitoring, erratic or harsh parental discipline, parental disharmony, parental rejection of the child, and low parental involvement in the child's activities (as well as antisocial parents and large family size) were all important predictors of offending. Similar conclusions were drawn by Snyder & Patterson (1987) in another detailed review. Utting, Bright & Henricson (1993) have provided perhaps the most recent extensive review of the literature on family factors in offending.

PARENTAL SUPERVISION, DISCIPLINE AND ATTITUDE

In the Cambridge–Somerville study in Boston, McCord (1979) reported that poor parental supervision was the best predictor of both violent and property crimes. Parental aggressiveness (which included harsh discipline, shading into child abuse at the extreme) and parental conflict were significant precursors of violent but not property crimes, while the mother's attitude (passive or rejecting) was a significant precursor of property but not violent crimes. Robins (1979), in her long-term follow-up studies in St Louis, also found that poor supervision and discipline were consistently related to later offending, and Shedler & Block (1990) in San Francisco reported that hostile and rejecting mothers when children were aged 5 predicted their children's frequent drug use at age 18.

Other studies also show the link between supervision and discipline and delinquency. In a Birmingham survey, Wilson (1980) followed up nearly 400 boys in 120 large intact families, and concluded that the most important correlate of convictions, cautions and self-reported delinquency was lax parental supervision at age 10. In their English national survey of juveniles aged 14–15 and their mothers, Riley & Shaw (1985) found that poor parental supervision was the most important correlate of self-reported delinquency for girls, and that it was the second most important for boys (after delinquent friends). Also, in their follow-up of nearly 700 Nottingham children in intact families, the Newsons reported that physical punishment by parents at ages 7 and 11 predicted later convictions (Newson & Newson, 1989).

In the Cambridge Study, West & Farrington (1973) found that harsh or erratic parental discipline, cruel, passive or neglecting parental attitude, poor supervision and parental conflict, all measured at age 8, all predicted later juvenile convictions. Generally, the presence of any of these adverse family background features doubled the risk of later juvenile conviction. Furthermore, poor parental child-rearing behaviour (a combination of discipline, attitude and conflict) and poor parental supervision both predicted juvenile self-reported as well as official offending (Farrington, 1979b). Poor parental child-rearing behaviour was related to early rather than later offending, and it predicted early convictions between ages 10 and 13 independently of all other factors (Farrington, 1984b, 1986b). However, it was not characteristic of those first convicted as adults (West & Farrington, 1977). In contrast, poor parental supervision predicted both juvenile and adult convictions (Farrington, 1992b).

Offenders tend to have difficulties in their personal relationships. The juvenile offenders tended to be in conflict with their parents at age 18. Both juvenile and adult offenders tended to have a poor relationship with their wife or cohabitee at age 32, or had assaulted her, and they also tended to be divorced and/or separated from their children (Farrington, 1992c).

There seems to be significant intergenerational transmission of aggressive and violent behaviour from parents to children, as McCord's (1979) research suggested. This is also demonstrated in Widom's (1989) retrospective study of over 900 abused children in Indianapolis. Children who were physically abused up to age 11 were significantly likely to become violent offenders in the next 15 years. Similarly, harsh discipline and attitude of parents when the boys were aged 8 significantly predicted later violent as opposed to non-violent offenders up to age 21 in the Cambridge Study (Farrington, 1978). More recent research (Farrington, 1991b) showed that harsh discipline and attitude predicted both violent and persistent offending up to age 32. Of course, the mechanisms underlying the intergenerational transmission of violence could be genetic as well as environmental (DiLalla & Gottesman, 1991).

BROKEN HOMES

Inspired by psychoanalytic ideas (discussed later), Bowlby (1951) popularized the theory that broken homes cause delinquency. In his research, he found that delinquents were significantly more likely than comparison children to have suffered a complete and prolonged separation from their mothers during their first five years of life. He argued that mother love in infancy and childhood was just as important for mental health as were vitamins and proteins for physical health. He thought that it was essential that a child should experience a warm, loving and continuous relationship with a mother figure. If a child suffered a prolonged period of maternal deprivation during the first five years of life, this would have irreversible negative effects, including delinquency. Such deprived children tended to become "affectionless characters", failing to develop loving ties with other children or with adults, and hence having no close friendships and no deep emotional feelings in their relationships.

Later researchers (Andry, 1960; Rutter, 1981) have emphasized the complexity of the concept of maternal deprivation and the importance of separation from the father as well as from the mother. Many of the children identified as suffering maternal deprivation in Bowlby's research and other early studies were children who had been brought up in institutions. They had suffered not only maternal but also paternal deprivation, and they had also had a constantly changing stream of caretakers. The development of affectionless characters and delinquency may have more to do with the lack of a continuous, unbroken, loving relationship with one person than with the loss of the mother specifically. It is important to distinguish separation from a biological or operative parent after a loving relationship has been built up, attributable to different causes such as death or parental disharmony, from the complete lack of contact with a biological parent. Modern research, inspired by Bowlby's work, on offending and childhood conduct disorder focuses especially on the attachment of the child to the mother (Erickson et al., 1985; Sroufe, 1986).

Most studies of broken homes have focused on the loss of the father rather than the mother, simply because the loss of a father is much more common. In the Newcastle Thousand Family Study, Kolvin et al. (1988) reported that marital disruption (divorce or separation) in a boy's first five years predicted his later convictions up to age 32. McCord (1982) in Boston carried out an interesting study of the relationship between homes broken by loss of the natural father and later serious offending. She found that the prevalence of offending was high for boys reared in broken homes without affectionate mothers (62%) and for those reared in united homes characterized by parental conflict (52%), irrespective of whether they had affectionate mothers. The prevalence of offending was low for those reared in united homes without conflict (26%) and, importantly, equally low for boys from broken homes with affectionate mothers (22%).

These results suggest that it is not so much the broken home which is criminogenic as the parental conflict which often causes it. They also suggest that a loving mother might in some sense be able to compensate for the loss of a father. The importance of the cause of the broken home is also shown in the English national longitudinal survey of over 5000 children born in one week of 1946 (Wadsworth, 1979). Illegitimate children were excluded from this survey, so all the children began life with two married parents. Boys from homes broken by divorce or separation had an increased likelihood of being convicted or officially cautioned up to age 21, in comparison with those from homes broken by death or from unbroken homes. Homes broken while the boy was between birth and age 4 especially predicted delinquency, while homes broken while the boy was between age 11 and age 15 were not particularly criminogenic. Remarriage (which happened more often after divorce or separation than after death) was also associated with an increased risk of delinquency, suggesting a possibly negative effect of step-parents. The meta-analysis by Wells & Rankin (1991) also shows that broken homes are more strongly related to delinquency when they are caused by parental separation or divorce rather than by death.

In the Cambridge Study, both permanent and temporary (more than one month) separations before age 10 (usually from the father) predicted convictions and self-reported delinquency, providing that they were not caused by death or hospitalization (Farrington, 1992c). However, homes broken at an early age (under age 5) were not unusually criminogenic (West & Farrington, 1973). Separation before age 10 predicted both juvenile and adult convictions (Farrington, 1992b) and predicted convictions up to age 32 independently of all other factors such as low family income or poor school attainment (Farrington, 1990b, 1993a).

In a survey of over 1000 adults carried out by NOP for the *Sunday Times* (14 November 1993), the majority (63%) thought that it was vital for a child to grow up with both a mother and a father. Indeed, growing up in a single-parent, female-headed household has predicted offending in American research (e.g. Ensminger, Rellam & Rubin, 1983). In Canada, the large-scale Ontario Child Health Study of 3300 children aged 4–16 reported that single-parent families tended to have conduct-disordered and substance-abusing children (Boyle & Offord, 1986; Blum, Boyle & Offord, 1988). However, the researchers found it difficult to disentangle the effects of single-parent families from the effects of low income families, because most single-parent families were living in poverty. The analyses of Morash & Rucker (1989) suggest that teenage childbearing combined with a single-parent female-headed household is particularly conducive to later offending by children. Wadsworth (1979) also found a link between teenage marriage and later delinquency.

PARENTAL CRIMINALITY

Criminal, antisocial and alcoholic parents also tend to have delinquent sons, as Robins (1979) found. Robins, West & Herjanic (1975) followed up over 200 black males in St Louis and found that arrested parents (her subjects) tended to have arrested children, and that the juvenile records of the parents and children showed similar rates and types of offences. McCord (1977), in her 30-year follow-up of about 250 treated boys in the Cambridge–Somerville study, also reported that convicted sons (her subjects) tended to have convicted fathers. Whether there is a specific relationship in her study between types of convictions of parents and children is not clear. McCord found that 29% of fathers convicted for violence had sons convicted for violence, in comparison with 12% of other fathers, but this may reflect the general tendency for convicted fathers to have convicted sons rather than any specific tendency for violent fathers to have violent sons. Wilson (1987) in Birmingham also showed that convictions of parents predicted convictions and cautions of sons; more than twice as many sons of convicted parents were themselves convicted.

In the Cambridge Study, the concentration of offending in a small number of families was remarkable. West & Farrington (1977) discovered that less than 5% of the families were responsible for about half of the criminal convictions of all members (fathers, mothers, sons and daughters) of all 400 families. West & Farrington (1973) showed that having convicted mothers, fathers and brothers by a boy's tenth birthday significantly predicted his own later convictions. Furthermore, convicted parents and delinquent siblings were related to self-reported as well as to official offending (Farrington, 1979b).

Unlike most early precursors, a convicted parent was related less to offending of early onset (age 10–13) than to later offending (Farrington, 1986b). Also, a convicted parent predicted which juvenile offenders went on to become adult criminals and which recidivists at age 19 continued offending rather than desisted (West & Farrington, 1977), and predicted convictions up to age 32 independently of all other factors (Farrington, 1990b, 1993a). As many as 59% of boys with a convicted parent were themselves convicted up to age 32 (Farrington, 1990b).

It is not entirely clear why criminal parents tend to have delinquent children. In the Cambridge Study, there was no evidence that criminal parents directly encouraged their children to commit crimes or taught them criminal techniques. On the contrary, criminal parents were highly critical of their children's offending; for example, 89% of convicted men at age 32 disagreed with the statement that "I would not mind if my son/daughter committed a criminal offence". Also, it was extremely rare for a parent and a child to be convicted for an offence committed together (Reiss & Farrington, 1991).

There was some evidence that having a convicted parent increased a boy's likelihood of being convicted, over and above his actual level of misbehaviour (West & Farrington, 1977). However, the fact that a convicted parent predicted self-reported offending as well as convictions shows that the labelling of children from known criminal families was not the only reason for the intergenerational transmission of criminality. It is possible that there is some genetic factor in this transmission (Mednick, Gabrielli & Hutchings, 1983). However, the main link in the chain between criminal parents and delinquent children that we could discover in the Cambridge Study was the markedly poor supervision by criminal parents.

Just as early family factors predict the early onset or prevalence of offending, later family factors predict later desistance. For example, it is often believed that male offending decreases after marriage, and there is some evidence in favour of this (Bachman, O'Malley & Johnston, 1978). In the Cambridge Study, there was a clear tendency for convicted males who got married at age 22 or earlier to be reconvicted less in the next two years than comparable convicted males who did not get married (West, 1982). However, in the case of both the males and their fathers, convicted males tended to marry convicted females, and convicted males who married convicted females continued to offend at the same rate after marriage as matched unmarried males. Offenders who married convicted females incurred more convictions after marriage than those who married unconvicted females, independently of their conviction records before marriage. Hence, it was concluded that the reformative effect of marriage was lessened by the tendency of male offenders to marry females who were also offenders. Rutter (1989) has drawn attention to the importance of studying turning points in people's lives, such as marriage. These are rarely included in psychological theories.

OTHER FAMILY FEATURES

Many studies show that large families predict delinquency (Fischer, 1984). For example, in the National Survey of Health and Development, Wadsworth (1979) found that the percentage of boys who were officially delinquent increased from 9% for families containing one child to 24% for families containing four or more children. The Newsons in their Nottingham study also concluded that large family size was one of the most important predictors of offending (Newson, Newson & Adams, 1993).

In the Cambridge Study, if a boy had four or more siblings by his tenth birthday, this doubled his risk of being convicted as a juvenile (West & Farrington, 1973). Large family size predicted self-reported delinquency as well as convictions (Farrington, 1979b), and adult as well as juvenile convictions (Farrington, 1992b). Large family size was the most important independent predictor of convictions up to age 32 in a logistic regression analysis (Farrington, 1993a); 58% of boys from large families were convicted up to this age.

There are many possible reasons why a large number of siblings might increase the risk of delinquency. Generally, as the number of children in a family increases, the amount of parental attention that can be given to each child decreases. Also, as the number of children increases, the household will tend to become more overcrowded, possibly leading to increases in frustration, irritation and conflict. In the Cambridge Study, large family size did not predict delinquency for boys living in the least crowded conditions, with two or more rooms than there were children (West & Farrington, 1973). More than 20 years earlier, Ferguson (1952) drew a similar conclusion in his study of over 1300 Glasgow boys, suggesting that an overcrowded household might be an important intervening factor between large family size and delinquency.

In a study of delinquent boys and girls in Ottawa, Jones, Offord & Abrams (1980) proposed that there was male potentiation and female suppression of delinquency by boys. This theory was intended to explain why they found that male delinquents had many more brothers than sisters. However, this result was not obtained in the Cambridge Study, where the number of sisters was just as closely related to a boy's delinquency as his number of brothers (West & Farrington, 1973).

A final suggestion that will be mentioned is that a lack of parental involvement in the child's activities is conducive to delinquency. In Nottingham, the Newsons found that low participation by the father in a child's activities at ages 7 and 11 predicted the child's later convictions (Lewis, Newson & Newson, 1982). In the Cambridge Study, having a father who never joined in the boy's leisure activities when he was aged 12 doubled his risk of a juvenile conviction (West & Farrington, 1973). Having a father who rarely or never joined in the boy's leisure activities at age 12 was an important predictor of convictions for violence and of self-reported violence at age 32 (Farrington, 1989a), and it was the most important independent predictor of persistence in offending, as opposed to desistance, after age 21 (Farrington & Hawkins, 1991).

PSYCHOLOGICAL THEORIES OF OFFENDING

Some important psychological theories of crime have already been discussed, such as the personality theory of Eysenck (1977), the moral development theory of Kohlberg (1976) and the maternal deprivation theory of Bowlby (1951). Several others are reviewed in this section.

PSYCHOANALYTIC THEORIES

Historically, psychoanalytic theories were important in explaining the link between child rearing, personality development and criminal behaviour (Kline, 1987; McDaniel, Balis & Strahan, 1990). These theories suggested that there were three major personality mechanisms: the id, ego and superego. The id contained the instinctual, unconscious desires (especially sexual and aggressive) with which a child was born. It was governed by the pleasure principle, seeking to achieve pleasure and avoid pain. The ego developed out of the id by about age 3. This was the seat of consciousness, and it tried to achieve the desires of the id while taking account of the reality of social conventions. Hence, the ego was governed by the reality principle, and it could delay immediate gratification in favour of long-term goals, think ahead, and reduce the desires of the id through fantasy. Children would only develop a strong ego if they had a close emotional relationship with their parents.

The superego developed out of the ego by about age 5, and contained two functions, the conscience and the ego-ideal. The conscience acted to suppress or divert instinctual desires that violated social rules, while the ego-ideal was the internal representation of parental standards. In the formation of the conscience, punishment of the child by the parent aroused the child's aggressive energy towards the parent. However, because the child was punished even more if the aggression was expressed against the parent, children became self-punitive and turned their aggression against themselves. The verbal prohibitions of the parents became the superego. In the formation of the ego-ideal, children incorporated into themselves the emotionally charged images of their parents, thinking, feeling and acting like them. This process was called introjection, and it also depended on children having loving relationships with their parents.

According to psychoanalytic theories, offending resulted from a weak ego or a weak superego. The weak ego meant that people had a poor ability to control their instinctual desires (to balance the demands of the id and the superego) and a poor ability to defer gratification. The weak superego meant that people had a weak conscience or an undesirable ego-ideal. Since both depended on children having loving relationships with their parents, it followed that cold, unloving, rejecting parents tended to have delinquent children. Also, since the conscience depended on consistent discipline, parents who were inconsistent tended to have children with weak consciences; and the ego-ideal was undesirable to the extent that children had criminal or deviant parents. Generally, psychoanalytic theories can explain empirical relationships between family factors and crime.

LEARNING THEORIES

Most of the modern psychological theories that aim to explain the link between child-rearing methods and criminal behaviour are social learning theories. They focus on learning not to offend rather than on learning to offend. According to these theories, children learn to inhibit their antisocial tendencies and build up internal inhibitions against offending in a conditioning or social learning process as a result of the way their parents react to their transgressions. Conditioning theories focus on reinforcement and punishment, whereas social learning theories focus on modelling and thinking processes as well.

One of the most influential conditioning theories was propounded by Trasler (1962). This suggests that, when a child behaves in a socially disapproved way, the parent will punish the child. This punishment causes an anxiety reaction, or an unpleasant state of physiological arousal. After a number of pairings of the disapproved act and the punishment, the anxiety becomes classically conditioned to the act, and conditioned also to the sequence of events preceding the act. Consequently, when the child contemplates the disapproved act, the conditioned anxiety automatically arises and tends to block the tendency to commit the act, so the child becomes less likely to do it. Also, the anxiety generalizes to similar acts, so the child tends to feel anxious when contemplating similar acts. Hence, as Eysenck (1977) also argued, conscience is essentially a conditioned anxiety response.

However, whereas Eysenck emphasized individual, constitutional differences in conditionability, Trasler emphasized differences in parental child-rearing behaviour as the major source of differences in criminal tendencies (conditioned anxiety). Children are unlikely to build up the link between disapproved behaviour and anxiety unless their parents supervise them closely, use punishment consistently, and make punishment contingent on disapproved acts. Hence, poor supervision, erratic or inconsistent discipline and conflict between parents are all conducive to offending by children. It is also important for parents to explain to children why they are being punished, so that they can discriminate precisely the behaviour that is disapproved.

Trasler argued that middle class parents were more likely to explain to children why they were being punished and were more likely to be concerned with long-term character-building and the inculcation of general moral principles. This was linked to the greater facility of middle class parents with language and abstract concepts. In contrast, lower class parents supervised their children less closely and were more inconsistent in their use of discipline. Generally, middle class parents used love-oriented discipline, relying on withdrawal of love as the main sanction, whereas lower class parents used much more physical punishment. Trasler contended that lower class children committed more crimes because lower class parents used less effective methods of socialization.

More recent learning theories tend to be cognitive social learning theories which emphasize the role of modelling, instruction, thought processes and interpersonal problem-solving strategies (Bandura, 1977; Sarason, 1978; Nietzel, 1979). The individual is viewed as an information processor whose behaviour depends on cognitive (thinking, problem-solving) processes as well as the history of rewards and punishments. Ross & Ross (1988) explicitly linked offending to cognitive deficits, arguing that offenders tended to be impulsive, egocentric, concrete rather than abstract in their thinking, and poor at interpersonal problem solving because they failed to understand how other people were thinking and feeling (Chandler, 1973). Many other scholars have argued that offenders are deficient in their thinking processes (e.g. Guerra, 1989). Whether they are also deficient in interpersonal social skills is less clear (Dishion et al., 1984; Tisdelle & St Lawrence, 1986; Hollin, 1990).

THE WILSON–HERRNSTEIN THEORY

In many ways, Wilson & Herrnstein's (1985) theory is a typical psychological explanation of crime, incorporating propositions seen in several other psychological theories. They suggested that people differed in their underlying criminal tendency, and that whether a person chose to commit a crime in any situation depended on whether the expected benefits of offending outweighed the expected costs. The benefits of offending, including material gain, peer approval and sexual gratification, tended to be contemporaneous with the crime. In contrast, many of the costs of offending, such as the risk of being caught and punished, and the possible loss of reputation or employment, were uncertain and long-delayed. Other costs, such as pangs of conscience (or guilt), disapproval by onlookers and retaliation by the victim, were more immediate.

As in many other psychological theories, Wilson and Herrnstein emphasized the importance of the conscience as an internal inhibitor of offending, and suggested that it was built up in a process of classical conditioning according to parental reinforcement or punishment of childhood transgressions. Nevertheless, the key individual difference factor in the Wilson–Herrnstein theory is the extent to which people's behaviour is influenced by immediate as opposed to delayed consequences. As in other theories, they suggested that individuals varied in their ability to think about or plan for the future, and that this was linked to intelligence. The major determinant of offending was a person's impulsivity. More impulsive people were less influenced by the likelihood of future consequences and hence were more likely to commit crimes.

THE GOTTFREDSON–HIRSCHI THEORY

Gottfredson & Hirschi's (1990) theory is both similar to the Wilson–Herrnstein theory and typical of psychological explanations of crime. Gottfredson & Hirschi (1990) castigated criminological theorists for ignoring the fact that people differ in underlying criminal propensities and that these differences appeared early in life and remained stable over much of the life course. The key individual difference factor in their theory is low self-control, which refers to the extent to which individuals are vulnerable to the temptations of the moment. People with low self-control are impulsive, take risks, have low cognitive and academic skills, are egocentric, have low empathy, and have short time horizons. Hence, they find it hard to defer gratification and their decisions to offend are insufficiently influenced by the possible future painful consequences of offending.

Gottfredson and Hirschi argued that crimes were part of a larger category of deviant acts (including substance abuse, heavy smoking, heavy drinking, heavy gambling, sexual promiscuity, truanting and road accidents) which were all behavioural manifestations of the key underlying theoretical construct of low self-control. They conceded that self-control, as an internal inhibitor, was similar to the conscience, but preferred the term self-control because the idea of the conscience was less applicable to some of the wider category of acts that they were concerned with (e.g. accidents). Their theory easily explains the considerable versatility of antisocial behaviour.

They argued that between-individual differences in self-control were present early in life (by age 6–8), were remarkably stable over time, and were essentially caused by differences in parental child-rearing practices. Much parenting was concerned with suppressing impulsive behaviour, with making children consider the long-range consequences of their acts, and with making them sensitive to the needs and feelings of others. Poor parental supervision contributed to low self-control, and poor parental supervision was more common in large families, with single parents, or with criminal parents. Ambitiously, Gottfredson and Hirschi aimed to present a theory that applied to all kinds of crimes in all kinds of cultures.

PREVENTION AND TREATMENT

PREVENTION OF OFFENDING

The most important implications of the research and theories reviewed here on individual and family factors are for the early prevention of offending. Hence, in reviewing implications for prevention and treatment, I will focus on the efficacy of prevention programmes in the community. Gordon & Arbuthnot (1987), Kazdin (1985, 1987) and McCord & Tremblay (1992) have provided more extensive reviews of this topic. My focus is on randomized experiments with reasonably large samples and with outcome measures of offending, since the effect of any intervention on offending can be demonstrated most convincingly in such experiments (Farrington, 1983; Farrington, Ohlin & Wilson, 1986). Many interesting experiments are not randomized (Jones & Offord, 1989), or do not have outcome measures of offending (Kazdin et al., 1987, 1989), or are based on very small samples (Shore & Massimo, 1979).

INDIVIDUAL DIFFERENCE FACTORS

Impulsivity and other personality characteristics of offenders might be altered using the set of techniques variously termed cognitive–behavioural interpersonal skills training, which has proved to be quite successful (e.g. Michelson, 1987). For example, the methods used by Ross to treat juvenile delinquents (see Ross, Fabiano & Ewles, 1988; Ross & Ross, 1988) were solidly based on some of the known individual characteristics of offenders: impulsivity, concrete rather than abstract thinking, low empathy and egocentricity.

Ross believed that delinquents could be taught the cognitive skills in which they were deficient, and that this could lead to a decrease in their offending. His reviews of delinquency rehabilitation programmes (Gendreau & Ross, 1979, 1987) showed that those which were successful in reducing offending generally tried to change the offender's thinking. Ross carried out his own "Reasoning and Rehabilitation" programme in Canada, and found (in a randomized experiment) that it led to a significant decrease in reoffending for a small sample in a nine-month follow-up period. His training was carried out by probation officers, but he believed that it could be carried out by parents or teachers.

Ross's programme aimed to modify the impulsive, egocentric thinking of delinquents, to teach them to stop and think before acting, to consider the consequences of their behaviour, to conceptualize alternative ways of solving interpersonal problems, and to consider the impact of their behaviour on other people, especially their victims. It included social skills training, lateral thinking (to teach creative problem solving), critical thinking (to teach logical reasoning), value education (to teach values and concern for others), assertiveness training (to teach non-aggressive, socially appropriate ways to obtain desired outcomes), negotiation skills training, interpersonal cognitive problem solving (to teach thinking skills for solving interpersonal problems), social perspective training (to teach how to recognize and understand other people's feelings), role playing and modelling (demonstration and practice of effective and acceptable interpersonal behaviour).

The successful social skills training programme carried out by Sarason (1978) in Tacoma, Washington, is also worth mentioning here, although it was conducted in a juvenile institution. Nearly 200 male first offenders were randomly allocated to modelling, discussion or control groups. The modelling and discussion groups focused on prosocial ways of achieving goals, coping with frustrations, resisting temptation and delaying gratification. A five-year follow-up showed that the proportion of recidivists was halved in the modelling and discussion groups compared with the control group.

If low intelligence and school failure are causes of offending, then any programme that leads to an increase in school success should lead to a decrease in offending. One of the most successful delinquency prevention programmes was the Perry pre-school project carried out in Michigan by Schweinhart & Weikart (1980). This was essentially a "Head Start" pro-gramme targeted on disadvantaged black children, who were allocated (approximately at random) to experimental and control groups. The experimental children attended a daily pre-school programme, backed up by weekly home visits, usually lasting two years (covering ages 3–4). The aim of the programme was to provide intellectual stimulation, to increase cognitive abilities, and to increase later school achievement.

More than 120 children in the two groups were followed up to age 15, using teacher ratings, parent and youth interviews, and school records. As demonstrated in several other Head Start projects, the experimental group showed gains in intelligence that were rather short-lived. However, they were significantly better in elementary school motivation, school achievement at 14, teacher ratings of classroom behaviour at 6 to 9, self-reports of classroom behaviour at 15 and self-reports of offending at 15. Furthermore, a later follow-up of this sample by Berrueta-Clement et al. (1984) showed that, at age 19, the experimental group was more likely to be employed, more likely to have graduated from high school, more likely to have received college or vocational training, and less likely to have been arrested. These benefits persisted up to age 27 (Schweinhart, Barnes & Weikart, 1993). Hence, this pre-school intellectual enrichment programme led to decreases in school failure and to decreases in offending.

The Perry project is admittedly only one study based on relatively small numbers. However, its results become more compelling when viewed in the context of 10 other similar American Head Start projects followed up by the Consortium for Longitudinal Studies (1983) and other pre-school programmes (e.g. Horacek et al., 1987). With quite impressive consistency, all studies show that pre-school intellectual enrichment programmes have long-term beneficial effects on school success, especially in increasing the rate of high school graduation and deceasing the rate of special education placements. The Perry project was the only one to study offending, but the consistency of the school success results in all projects suggests that the effects on offending might be replicable.

FAMILY FACTORS

If poor parental supervision and erratic child-rearing behaviour are causes of delinquency, it seems likely that parent training might succeed in reducing offending. Many different types of family therapy have been used (Tolan, Cromwell & Brasswell, 1986; Kazdin, 1987), but the behavioural parent management training developed by Patterson (1982) in Oregon is one of the most hopeful approaches. His careful observations of parent–child interaction showed that parents of antisocial children were deficient in their methods of child rearing. These parents failed to tell their children how they were expected to behave, failed to monitor the behaviour to ensure that it was desirable, and failed to enforce rules promptly and unambiguously with appropriate rewards and penalties. The parents of antisocial children used more punishment (such as scolding, shouting or threatening), but failed to make it contingent on the child's behaviour.

Patterson attempted to train these parents in effective child-rearing methods, namely noticing what a child is doing, monitoring behaviour over long periods, clearly stating house rules, making rewards and punishments contingent on behaviour, and negotiating disagreements so that conflicts and crises did not escalate. His treatment was shown to be effective in reducing child stealing and antisocial behaviour over short periods in small-scale studies (Patterson, Chamberlain & Reid, 1982; Patterson, Reid & Dishion, 1992; Dishion, Patterson & Kavanagh, 1992).

Another parenting intervention, termed functional family therapy, was evaluated by Alexander and his colleagues (Alexander & Parsons, 1973; Alexander et al., 1976; Klein, Alexander & Parsons, 1977). This aimed to modify patterns of family interaction by modelling, prompting and reinforcement, to encourage clear communication between family members of requests and solutions, and to minimize conflict. In a detailed review of behavioural treatment programmes in the community, Farrington (1979a, p. 359) noted that:

> By most standards, this [Alexander & Parsons] study was based on very small numbers (a total of 86 in the four groups). By the standards of the behaviour modification literature, it is one of the most methodologically adequate studies that has ever been done.

Essentially, all family members were trained to negotiate effectively, to set clear rules about privileges and responsibilities, and to use techniques of reciprocal reinforcement with each other. This technique halved the recidivism rate of status offenders in comparison with other approaches (client-centred or psychodynamic therapy). Its effectiveness with more serious offenders was confirmed in a replication study using matched groups (Barton et al., 1985).

A combination of interventions may be more effective than a single method. For example, Kazdin, Siegel & Bass (1992) found that a combination of parent management training and problem-solving skills training was more effective in reducing self-reported delinquency than either method alone. Also, more complex individualized techniques including several different elements may be effective. For example, Henggeler, Melton & Smith (1992) and Henggeler et al. (1993) showed that "multi-systemic therapy", targeting the relationships between children and families, peers and schools, was effective in reducing rearrests in a two-year follow-up period, compared with the usual probation.

One of the most important recent longitudinal experimental intervention studies was carried out in Montreal by Tremblay et al. (1991, 1992). They identified about 250 disruptive boys at age 6 for a prevention experiment. Between ages 7 and 9, the experimental group received training to foster social skills and self-control, while their parents were trained using Patterson's techniques. By age 12, the experimental boys committed less burglary and theft, and were less likely to get drunk, than the controls. Interestingly, the differences in antisocial behaviour between experimental and control boys increased as the follow-up progressed.

Another important experiment was carried out in Seattle by Hawkins, Von Cleve & Catalano (1991) and Hawkins et al. (1992). This combined parent training, teacher training and skills training. About 500 first grade children in 21 classes in eight schools were randomly assigned to be in experimental or control classes. The children in the experimental classes received special treatment at home and school which was designed to increase their attachment to their parents and their bonding to the school. Their parents were trained to notice and reinforce socially desirable behaviour in a programme called "Catch 'em being good". Their teachers were trained in classroom management, for example to provide clear instructions and expectations to children, to reward children for participation in desired behaviour, and to teach children prosocial methods of solving problems.

In an evaluation of this programme 18 months later, when the children were in different classes, Hawkins, Von Cleve & Catalano (1991) found that the boys who received the experimental programme were significantly less aggressive than the control boys, according to teacher ratings. This difference was particularly marked for white boys rather than black boys. The experimental girls were not significantly less aggressive, but they were less self-destructive, anxious and depressed. By the fifth grade, the experimental children were less likely to have initiated delinquency and alcohol use. It might be expected that a combination of interventions might in general be more effective than a single technique, although combining interventions makes it harder to identify the active ingredient.

Finally, it is worth mentioning a very early prevention programme, the Syracuse (New York) Family Development Research Programme (Lally, Mangione & Honig, 1988). The researchers began with a sample of pregnant women and gave them weekly help with child-rearing, health, nutrition and other problems. In addition, their children received free day care, designed to develop intellectual abilities, up to age 5. This was not a randomized experiment, but a matched control group was chosen when the children were aged 3. The treated children had significantly higher intelligence than the controls at age 3 but were not different at age 5. Ten years later, about 120 treated and control children were followed up to about age 15. Significantly fewer of the treated children (2% as opposed to 17%) had been referred to the juvenile court for delinquency offences, and the treated girls showed better school attendance and school performance. Hence, this omnibus programme in the first few years of life was successful in preventing later delinquency.

CAN OFFENDING BE PREVENTED AND TREATED SUCCESSFULLY?

In this chapter, I have reviewed some successful methods of preventing offending based on knowledge about individual and family causes. My optimistic conclusions may seem strange in the light of the widespread belief that arose in the 1970s, stimulated by influential reviews by Martinson (1974) in the United States and Brody (1976) in England, suggesting that existing treatment techniques had no differential effects on the recidivism of detected offenders. This conclusion was substantially endorsed by a National Academy of Sciences panel in an impressive, methodologically sophisticated review (Sechrest, White & Brown, 1979). However, for a number of reasons, it should not be concluded that "nothing works", nor even that everything works equally well.

Martinson's (1974) conclusions were based on the Lipton, Martinson & Wilks (1975) review of 231 studies of the effectiveness of correctional treatment between 1945 and 1967. However, Thornton (1987b) found that only 38 of these studies met minimum methodological standards, included matched or randomized comparison groups, and included an outcome measure of recidivism. For nearly all of these studies (34 out of 38), the treatment was "psychological" in nature, such as individual counselling, psychotherapy or casework. Of these 34 psychological studies, 16 showed that the treatment was effective in reducing recidivism, 17 found no significant difference, and only one found that the treatment was harmful. These numbers were more compatible with the hypothesis that psychological treatment had beneficial effects than with the hypothesis that psychological treatment had no effect (since that would have predicted equal numbers of positive and negative results). Other commentators (e.g. Gendreau & Ross, 1979, 1987; Ross & Gendreau, 1980) also argued that there were many examples of effective correctional treatment.

Interestingly, Martinson (1979, pp. 253–254) explicitly rejected his original conclusion before he committed suicide. This rejection was based on his investigation of 555 studies of recidivism:

> My conclusion was: "With few and isolated exceptions, the rehabilitative efforts that have been reported so far have had no appreciable effect on recidivism" . . . The very evidence presented in the article indicates that it would have been incorrect to say that treatment had *no* effect. Some studies showed an effect, others did not. But, all together, looking at this entire body of research, I drew this conclusion . . . On the basis of the evidence in our current study, I withdraw this conclusion. I have often said that treatment added to the networks of criminal justice is "impotent", and I withdraw this characterization as well. I protested at the slogan used by the media to sum up what I said – "nothing works". The press has no time for scientific quibbling and got to the heart of the matter better than I did. But for all of that, the conclusion is not correct. More precisely, treatments will be found to be "impotent" under certain conditions, beneficial under others, and detrimental under still others.

In the past decade, reviews of the effectiveness of correctional treatment have increasingly used the technique of meta-analysis (Hedges & Olkin, 1985) to summarize results from a number of studies. This technique requires the calculation of a comparable effect size (ES) in each study, usually defined as the difference between the average score of a treated group and the average score of a control group, expressed in standard deviation units. This ES measure is not very relevant to studies of correctional treatment, where the main interest is usually in the difference between the proportion of a treated group reconvicted and the proportion of a control group reconvicted. However, at least for effect sizes below 1, the difference in proportions is roughly half the ES. Thus, an ES of 0.2 corresponds to a 10% difference in recidivism rates (e.g. 40% versus 50%) between treated and control groups. An ES of 0.2 or greater has considerable practical significance.

The most important meta-analyses all focus on adjudicated juvenile delinquents. In an analysis of 111 institutional treatment studies, Garrett (1985) reported a mean ES of 0.37 for all outcomes of correctional treatment, but only 0.13 for recidivism specifically. Most of her outcome measures were of institutional or psychological adjustment or academic or vocational skills. Behavioural treatments were generally effective in reducing recidivism (mean ES = 0.18), but psychodynamic techniques were not (mean ES = −0.01). In an analysis of 90 community-based treatment studies, Gottschalk et al. (1987) reported an identical mean ES of 0.37 for overall effectiveness in treatment–control comparisons, but a higher ES for recidivism of 0.33. They considered that 56% of treatments had beneficial effects, 43% had no marked effect, and only 1% had harmful effects.

Whitehead & Lab (1989) drew more pessimistic conclusions from their meta-analysis of 50 studies of juvenile correctional treatment, largely because they set a very high criterion (a phi correlation of at least 0.2) for concluding that a treatment was effective. Only 16 of their 50 studies met this criterion for recidivism. This value of the phi correlation approximates to a 20% difference in recidivism rates (Farrington & Loeber, 1989) and to an ES of 0.4. According to Lipsey (1992), their mean ES was 0.25, which has some practical significance. Andrews et al. (1990b) criticized Whitehead and Lab's review and reanalysed their data, concluding that the mean phi correlation for "appropriate" treatments was 0.3, corresponding to a halving of recidivism rates in many cases. Overall, behavioural treatments had a high mean phi correlation of 0.29 (or a mean ES of about 0.6), whereas non-behavioural treatments had a mean phi correlation of only 0.04 (Andrews et al., 1990a).

Roberts & Camasso (1991) reviewed 46 studies of juvenile correctional treatment published between 1980 and 1990, and reported a mean ES of 0.36 for recidivism. However, the largest meta-analysis, based on 443 studies, was completed by Lipsey (1992). Overall, he considered that the treatment reduced offending in 64% of studies, increased offending in 30%, and made no difference in 6%. The mean ES for delinquency outcomes in all studies was 0.17, and behavioural and skill-oriented programmes were most effective, with mean ESs in the 0.2–0.3 range after various adjustments.

It is reasonable to conclude from the meta-analyses that psychological, and especially behavioural, treatments generally succeed in reducing the recidivism rates of adjudicated juvenile offenders. The effect sizes are not large (of the order 0.2–0.3), but they correspond to reductions of 10–15% in the proportion reconvicted, which to my mind is a decrease of some practical significance. Personally, I prefer more traditional methods of reviewing and summarizing the literature rather than meta-analysis. It seems more useful to identify the most adequate studies methodologically (e.g. randomized experiments with large samples, long follow-up periods and outcome measures of offending) and to review the best studies in detail rather than to try to summarize a large number of projects with varying degrees of methodological adequacy and relevance.

Why do treatments not cause a greater reduction in recidivism? There are many possible reasons for this, including the fact that interventions may not be sufficiently powerful [e.g. averaging only one hour per week in the review by Gottschalk et al. (1987)] especially in comparison to the overwhelming influence of environmental (e.g. family, peer, community) factors. Another problem is the persistence of offending and antisocial behaviour over time. Kazdin (1987) suggested that serious antisocial behaviour might be viewed as a chronic disease that requires continuous monitoring and intervention over the life course. It might be desirable to distinguish chronic and less seriously delinquent juveniles, and to apply different types of interventions to these two categories (LeBlanc & Frechette, 1989). If the chronics are the worst 5%, interventions applied to the next 10% may be more successful.

CONCLUSIONS

The most important individual factors in offending are high impulsivity and low intelligence. Both of these may be linked to a poor ability to manipulate abstract concepts, which may also be related to other individual factors such as egocentricity and low empathy. The most important family factors are poor parental supervision, harsh and erratic parental discipline, cold and rejecting parental attitude, separation from a parent, large family size and having a criminal parent.

Most psychological theories assume that there are consistent individual differences in an underlying construct such as criminal potential or antisocial personality. Most assume that hedonism or the pursuit of pleasure is the main energizing factor. Most assume that there is internal inhibition of offending through the conscience or some similar mechanism, and that methods of child rearing used by parents are crucial in developing this in a socialization process. However, where parents provide antisocial models, there can also be learning of antisocial behaviour. Most theories assume that the commission of offences in any situation essentially involves a rational decision in which the likely costs are weighed against the likely benefits. And most assume that impulsivity, or a poor ability to take account of and be influenced by the possible future consequences of offending, is an important factor.

The major implications of research on individual and family factors are for early prevention rather than treatment. Cognitive–behavioural interpersonal skills training, pre-school intellectual enrichment programmes and parent management training all seem to be effective methods of preventing offending. Cognitive–behavioural techniques have also proved to be effective in the treatment of identified juvenile delinquents.

This chapter argues that the roots of crime lie in individual and family factors and describes methods of reducing crime by targeting these factors. Because of the link between offending and numerous other social problems, any measure that succeeds in reducing crime will have benefits that go far beyond this. Any measure that reduces crime will probably also reduce alcohol abuse, drunk driving, drug abuse, sexual promiscuity, family violence, truancy, school failure, unemployment, marital disharmony and divorce. It is clear that problem children tend to grow up into problem adults, and that problem adults tend to produce more problem children. Major efforts to tackle the roots of crime are urgently needed.

REFERENCES

Alexander, J.F. & Parsons, B.V. (1973) Short-term behavioural intervention with delinquent families: impact on family process and recidivism. *Journal of Abnormal Psychology*, **81**, 219–225.

Alexander, J.F., Barton, C., Schiavo, R.S. & Parsons, B.V. (1976) Systems-behavioural intervention with families of delinquents: therapist characteristics, family behaviour and outcome. *Journal of Consulting and Clinical Psychology*, **44**, 656–664.

American Psychiatric Association (1994) *Diagnostic and Statistical Manual of Mental Disorders*, 4th edn, Washington, DC: APA.

Andrews, D.A., Zinger, I., Hoge, R.D., Bonta, J., Gendreau, P. & Cullen, F.T. (1990a) A human science approach or more punishment and pessimism: a rejoinder to Lab and Whitehead. *Criminology*, **28**, 419–429.

Andrews, D.A., Zinger, I., Hoge, R.D., Bonta, J., Gendreau, P. & Cullen, F.T. (1990b)

Does correctional treatment work? A clinically relevant and psychologically informed meta-analysis. *Criminology*, **28**, 369–404.

Andry, R.G. (1960) *Delinquency and Parental Pathology*. London: Methuen.

Arbuthnot, J. & Gordon, D.A. (1988) Crime and cognition: community applications of sociomoral reasoning development. *Criminal Justice and Behaviour*, **15**, 379–393.

Bachman, J.G., O'Malley, P.M. & Johnston, J. (1978) *Youth in Transition*, Vol. 6. Ann Arbor, MI: University of Michigan Institute for Social Research.

Bandura, A. (1977) *Social Learning Theory*. Englewood Cliffs, NJ: Prentice-Hall.

Barton, C., Alexander, J.F., Waldron, H., Turner, C.W. & Warburton, J. (1985) Generalizing treatment effects of functional family therapy: three replications. *American Journal of Family Therapy*, **13**, 16–26.

Berrueta-Clement, J.R., Schweinhart, L.J., Barnett, W.S., Epstein, A.S. & Weikart, D.P. (1984) *Changed Lives*. Ypsilanti, MI: High/Scope.

Blackburn, R. (1993) *The Psychology of Criminal Conduct*. Chichester: Wiley.

Blouin, A.G., Conners, C.K., Seidel, W.T. & Blouin, J. (1989) The independence of hyperactivity from conduct disorder: methodological considerations. *Canadian Journal of Psychiatry*, **34**, 279–282.

Blum, H.M., Boyle, M.H. & Offord, D.R. (1988) Single-parent families: child psychiatric disorder and school performance. *Journal of the American Academy of Child and Adolescent Psychiatry*, **27**, 214–219.

Blumstein, A., Cohen, J. & Farrington, D.P. (1988) Criminal career research: its value for criminology. *Criminology*, **26**, 1–35.

Blumstein, A., Cohen, J., Roth, J.A. & Visher, C.A. (Eds) (1986) *Criminal Careers and "Career Criminals"*. Washington, DC: National Academy Press.

Bowlby, J. (1951) *Maternal Care and Mental Health*. Geneva: World Health Organization.

Boyle, M.H. & Offord, D.R. (1986) Smoking, drinking and use of illicit drugs among adolescents in Ontario: prevalence, patterns of use and socio-demographic correlates. *Canadian Medical Association Journal*, **135**, 1113–1121.

Brody, S.R. (1976) *The Effectiveness of Sentencing*. London: HMSO.

Chandler, M.J. (1973) Egocentrism and antisocial behaviour: the assessment and training of social perspective-taking skills. *Developmental Psychology*, **9**, 326–332.

Cohen, A.K. (1955) *Delinquent Boys*. Glencoe, IL: Free Press.

Consortium for Longitudinal Studies (1983) *As the Twig is Bent . . . Lasting Effects of Pre-school Programmes*. Hillsdale, NJ: Erlbaum.

DiLalla, L.F. & Gottesman, I.I. (1991) Biological and genetic contributors to violence – Widom's untold tale. *Psychological Bulletin*, **109**, 125–129.

Dishion, T.J., Loeber, R., Stouthamer-Loeber, M. & Patterson, G.R. (1984) Skill deficits and male adolescent delinquency. *Journal of Abnormal Child Psychology*, **12**, 37–54.

Dishion, T.J., Patterson, G.R. & Kavanagh, K.A. (1992) An experimental test of the coercion model: linking theory, measurement and intervention. In J. McCord & R. Tremblay (Eds), *Preventing Antisocial Behaviour*, pp. 253–282. New York: Guilford.

Duguid, S. (1981) Moral development, justice and democracy in the prison. *Canadian Journal of Criminology*, **23**, 147–162.

Ellis, L. (1987) Relationships of criminality and psychopathy with eight other apparent behavioural manifestations of sub-optimal arousal. *Personality and Individual Differences*, **8**, 905–925.

Ensminger, M.E., Kellam, S.G. & Rubin, B.R. (1983) School and family origins of delinquency. In K.T. Van Dusen & S.A. Mednick (Eds), *Prospective Studies of Crime and Delinquency*, pp. 73–97. Boston: Kluwer–Nijhoff.

Erickson, M.F., Sroufe, L.A. & Egeland, B. (1985) The relationship between quality of attachment and behaviour problems in preschool in a high-risk sample. In I. Bretherton & E. Waters (Eds), *Growing Points of Attachment Theory and Research*, pp. 147–166. Monographs of the Society for Research in Child Development, Serial no. 209, Vol. 50.

Eysenck, H.J. (1977) *Crime and Personality*, 3rd edn. London: Routledge and Kegan Paul.

Eysenck, H.J. & Eysenck, S.B.G. (1976) *Psychoticism as a Dimension of Personality*. London: Hodder and Stoughton.

Farley, F.H. & Sewell, T. (1976) Test of an arousal theory of delinquency: stimulation-seeking in delinquent and non-delinquent black adolescents. *Criminal Justice and Behaviour*, 3, 315–320.

Farrington, D.P. (1973) Self-reports of deviant behaviour: predictive and stable? *Journal of Criminal Law and Criminology*, **64**, 99–110.

Farrington, D.P. (1978) The family backgrounds of aggressive youths. In L. Hersov, M. Berger & D. Shaffer (Eds), *Aggression and Antisocial Behaviour in Childhood and Adolescence*, pp. 73–93. Oxford: Pergamon.

Farrington, D.P. (1979a) Delinquent behaviour modification in the natural environment. *British Journal of Criminology*, **19**, 353–372.

Farrington, D.P. (1979b) Environmental stress, delinquent behaviour, and convictions. In I.G. Sarason & C.D. Spielberger (Eds), *Stress and Anxiety*, Vol. 6, pp. 93–107. Washington, DC: Hemisphere.

Farrington, D.P. (1983) Randomized experiments on crime and justice. In M. Tonry & N. Morris (Eds), *Crime and Justice*, Vol. 4, pp. 257–308. Chicago: University of Chicago Press.

Farrington, D.P. (1984a) Delinquent and criminal behaviour. In A. Gale & A.J. Chapman (Eds), *Psychology and Social Problems*, pp. 55–77. Chichester: Wiley.

Farrington, D.P. (1984b) Measuring the natural history of delinquency and crime. In R.A. Glow (Ed.), *Advances in the Behavioural Measurement of Children*, Vol. 1, pp. 217–263. Greenwich, CT: JAI Press.

Farrington, D.P. (1986a) Age and crime. In M. Tonry & N. Morris (Eds), *Crime and Justice*, Vol. 7, pp. 189–250. Chicago: University of Chicago Press.

Farrington, D.P. (1986b) Stepping stones to adult criminal careers. In D. Olweus, J. Block & M.R. Yarrow (Eds), *Development of Antisocial and Prosocial Behaviour*, pp. 359–384. New York: Academic Press.

Farrington, D.P. (1987a) Epidemiology. In H.C. Quay (Ed.), *Handbook of Juvenile Delinquency*, pp. 33–61. New York: Wiley.

Farrington, D.P. (1987b) Implications of biological findings for criminological research. In S.A. Mednick, T.E. Moffitt & S.A. Stack (Eds), *The Causes of Crime: New Biological Approaches*, pp. 42–64. Cambridge: Cambridge University Press.

Farrington, D.P. (1989a) Early predictors of adolescent aggression and adult violence. *Violence and Victims*, **4**, 79–100.

Farrington, D.P. (1989b) Self-reported and official offending from adolescence to adulthood. In M.W. Klein (Ed.) *Cross-national Research in Self-reported Crime and Delinquency*, pp. 399–423. Dordrecht: Kluwer.

Farrington, D.P. (1990a) Age, period, cohort, and offending. In D.M. Gottfredson & R.V. Clarke (Eds), *Policy and Theory in Criminal Justice: Contributions in Honour of Leslie T. Wilkins*, pp. 51–75. Aldershot: Avebury.

Farrington, D.P. (1990b) Implications of criminal career research for the prevention of offending. *Journal of Adolescence*, **13**, 93–13.

Farrington, D.P. (1991a) Antisocial personality from childhood to adulthood. *The Psychologist*, **4**, 389–394.

Farrington, D.P. (1991b) Childhood aggression and adult violence: early precursors and later life outcomes. In D.J. Pepler & K.H. Rupin (Eds), *The Development and Treatment of Childhood Aggression*, pp. 5–29. Hillsdale, NJ: Erlbaum.

Farrington, D.P. (1991c) Psychological contributions to the explanation of offending. In M. McMurran & C. McDougall (Eds), *Proceedings of the First DCLP Annual Conference*, Vol. 1, pp. 7–19. Leicester: British Psychological Society.

Farrington, D.P. (1992a) Criminal career research in the United Kingdom. *British Journal of Criminology*, **32**, 521–536.

Farrington, D.P. (1992b) Explaining the beginning, progress and ending of antisocial behaviour from birth to adulthood. In J. McCord (Ed.), *Facts, Frameworks and Forecasts: Advances in Criminological Theory*, Vol. 3, pp. 253–286. New Brunswick, NJ: Transaction.

Farrington, D.P. (1992c) Juvenile delinquency. In J.C. Coleman (Ed.), *The School Years*, 2nd edn, pp. 123–163. London: Routledge.

Farrington, D.P. (1993a) Childhood origins of teenage antisocial behaviour and adult social dysfunction. *Journal of the Royal Society of Medicine*, **86**, 13–17.

Farrington, D.P. (1993b) Have any individual, family or neighbourhood influences on offending been demonstrated conclusively? In D.P. Farrington, R.J. Sampson & P.O. Wikstrom (Eds), *Integrating Individual and Ecological Aspects of Crime*, pp. 3–37. Stockholm: National Council for Crime Prevention.

Farrington, D.P. (1993c) The psychosocial milieu of the offender. In J. Gunn & P. Taylor (Eds) *Forensic Psychiatry: Clinical, Legal and Ethical Issues*, pp. 252–285. Oxford: Butterworth-Heinemann.

Farrington, D.P. (1994) Childhood, adolescent and adult features of violent males. In L.R. Huesmann (Ed.), *Aggressive Behaviour: Current Perspectives*, pp. 215–240. New York: Plenum.

Farrington, D.P., Ohlin, L.E. & Wilson, J.Q. (1986) *Understanding and Controlling Crime*. New York: Springer–Verlag.

Farrington, D.P., Biron, L. & LeBlanc, M. (1982) Personality and delinquency in London and Montreal. In J. Gunn & D.P. Farrington (Eds), *Abnormal Offenders, Delinquency, and the Criminal Justice System*, pp. 153–201. Chichester: Wiley.

Farrington, D.P. & West, D.J. (1990) The Cambridge study in delinquent development: a long-term follow-up of 411 London males. In H.J. Kerner & G. Kaiser (Eds), *Criminality: Personality, Behaviour, Life History*, pp. 115–138. Berlin: Springer–Verlag.

Farrington, D.P., Gallagher, B, Morley, L. St Ledger, R.J. & West, D.J. (1988a) A 24-year follow-up of men from vulnerable backgrounds. In R.L. Jenkins & W.K. Brown (Eds), *The Abandonment of Delinquent Behaviour*, pp. 155–173. New York: Praeger.

Farrington, D.P., Gallagher, B., Morley, L. St Ledger, R.J. & West, D.J. (1988b) Are there any successful men from criminogenic backgrounds? *Psychiatry*, **51**, 116–130.

Farrington, D.P. & Hawkins, J.D. (1991) Predicting participation, early onset, and later persistence in officially recorded offending. *Criminal Behaviour and Mental Health*, **1**, 1–33.

Farrington, D.P. & Loeber, R. (1989) Relative improvement over chance (RIOC) and phi as measures of predictive efficiency and strength of association in 2×2 tables. *Journal of Quantitative Criminology*, **5**, 201–213.

Farrington, D.P., Loeber, R. & Van Kammen, W.B. (1990) Long-term criminal outcomes of hyperactivity-impulsivity-attention deficit and conduct problems in childhood. In L.N. Robins & M. Rutter (Eds), *Straight and Devious Pathways from Childhood to Adulthood*, pp. 62–81. Cambridge: Cambridge University Press.

Ferguson, T. (1952) *The Young Delinquent in his Social Setting*. London: Oxford University Press.

Fischer, D.G. (1984) Family size and delinquency. *Perceptual and Motor Skills*, **58**, 527–534.

Garrett, C.J. (1985) Effects of residential treatment on adjudicated delinquents: a meta-analysis. *Journal of Research in Crime and Delinquency*, **22**, 287–308.

Gendreau, P. & Ross, R.R. (1979) Effective correctional treatment: bibliotherapy for cynics. *Crime and Delinquency*, **25**, 463–489.

Gendreau, P. & Ross, R.R. (1987) Revivification of rehabilitation: evidence from the 1980s. *Justice Quarterly*, **4**, 349–407.

Gordon, D.A. & Arbuthnot, J. (1987) Individual, group and family interventions. In H.C. Quay (Ed.), *Handbook of Juvenile Delinquency*, pp. 290–324. New York: Wiley.

Gottfredson, M. & Hirschi, T. (1990) *A General Theory of Crime*. Stanford, CA: Stanford University Press.

Gottschalk, R., Davidson, W.S., Gensheimer, L.K. & Mayer, J.P. (1987) Community-based interventions. In H.C. Quay (Ed.), *Handbook of Juvenile Delinquency*, pp. 266–289. New York: Wiley.

Guerra, N. (1989) Consequential thinking and self-reported delinquency in high school youth. *Criminal Justice and Behaviour*, **16**, 440–454.

Hawkins, J.D., Von Cleve, E. & Catalano, R.F. (1991) Reducing early childhood aggression: results of a primary prevention programme. *Journal of the American Academy of Child and Adolescent Psychiatry*, **30**, 208–217.

Hawkins, J.D., Catalano, R.F., Morrison, D.M., O'Donnell, J., Abbott, R.D. & Day, L.E. (1992) The Seattle social development project: effects of the first four years on protective factors and problem behaviours. In J. McCord & R. Tremblay (Eds), *Preventing Antisocial Behaviour*, pp. 139–161. New York: Guilford.

Hedges, L.V. & Olkin, I. (1985) *Statistical Methods for Meta-analysis*. Orlando, FL: Academic Press.

Henggeler, S.W., Melton, G.B. & Smith, L.A. (1992) Family preservation using multi-systemic therapy: an effective alternative to incarcerating serious juvenile offenders. *Journal of Consulting and Clinical Psychology*, **60**, 953–961.

Henggeler, S.W., Melton, G.B., Smith, L.A., Schoenwald S.K. & Hanley, J.H. (1993) Family preservation using multi-systemic treatment: long-term follow-up to a clinical trial with serious juvenile offenders. *Journal of Child and Family Studies*, **2**, 283–293.

Hindelang, M.J., Hirschi, T. & Weis, J.G. (1981) *Measuring Delinquency*. Beverly Hills, CA: Sage.

Hirschi, T. & Hindelang, M.J. (1977) Intelligence and delinquency: a revisionist review. *American Sociological Review*, **42**, 571–587.

Hollin, C.R. (1989) *Psychology and Crime*. London: Routledge.

Hollin, C.R. (1990) Social skills training with delinquents: a look at the evidence and some recommendations for practice. *British Journal of Social Work*, **20**, 483–493.

Hollin, C.R. (1992) *Criminal Behaviour*. London: Falmer Press.

Horacek, H.J., Ramey, C.T., Campbell, F.A., Hoffmann, K.P. & Fletcher, R.H. (1987) Predicting school failure and assessing early intervention with high-risk children. *Journal of the American Academy of Child and Adolescent Psychiatry*, **26**, 758–763.

Huizinga, D. & Elliott, D.S. (1986) Reassessing the reliability and validity of self-report measures. *Journal of Quantitative Criminology*, **2**, 293–327.

Jones, M.B. & Offord, D.R. (1989) Reduction of antisocial behaviour in poor children by non-school skill-development. *Journal of Child Psychology and Psychiatry*, **30**, 737–750.

Jones, M.B., Offord, D.R. & Abrams, N. (1980) Brothers, sisters and antisocial behaviour. *British Journal of Psychiatry*, **136**, 139–145.

Kagan, J., Reznick, J.S. & Snidman, N. (1988) Biological bases of childhood shyness. *Science*, **240**, 167–171.

Kandel, E., Mednick, S.A., Kirkegaard-Sorenson, L., Hutchings, B., Knop, J., Rosenberg, R. & Schulsinger, F. (1988) IQ as a protective factor for subjects at high risk for antisocial behaviour. *Journal of Consulting and Clinical Psychology*, **56**, 224–226.

Kazdin, A.E. (1985) *Treatment of Antisocial Behaviour in Children and Adolescents*. Homewood, IL: Dorsey Press.

Kazdin, A.E. (1987) Treatment of antisocial behaviour in children: current status and future directions. *Psychological Bulletin*, **102**, 187–203.

Kazdin, A.E., Siegel, T.C. & Bass, D. (1992) Cognitive problem-solving skills training and parent management training in the treatment of antisocial behaviour in children. *Journal of Consulting and Clinical Psychology*, **60**, 733–747.

Kazdin, A.E., Esveldt-Dawson, K., French, N.H. & Unis, A.S. (1987) Effects of parent management training and problem-solving skills training combined in the treatment of antisocial child behaviour. *Journal of the American Academy of Child and Adolescent Psychiatry*, **26**, 416–424.

Kazdin, A.E., Bass, D., Siegel, T. & Thomas, C. (1989) Cognitive–behavioural therapy and relationship therapy in the treatment of children referred for antisocial behaviour. *Journal of Consulting and Clinical Psychology*, **57**, 522–535.

Klein, N.C., Alexander, J.F. & Parsons, B.V. (1977) Impact of family systems intervention on recidivism and sibling delinquency: a model of primary prevention and programme evaluation. *Journal of Consulting and Clinical Psychology*, **45**, 469–474.

Kline, P. (1987) Psychoanalysis and crime. In B.J. McGurk, D.M. Thornton & M. Williams (Eds), *Applying Psychology to Imprisonment*, pp. 59–75. London: HMSO.

Kohlberg, L. (1976) Moral stages and moralization: the cognitive–developmental approach. In T. Lickona (Ed.), *Moral Development and Behaviour*, pp. 31–53. New York: Holt, Rinehart and Winston.

Kohlberg, L. & Candee, D. (1984) The relationship of moral judgment to moral action. In L. Kohlberg (Ed.), *The Psychology of Moral Development*, pp. 52–73. San Francisco: Harper and Row.

Kolvin, I., Miller, F.J.W., Fleeting, M. & Kolvin, P.A. (1988) Social and parenting factors affecting criminal-offence rates: findings from the Newcastle Thousand Family Study (1947–1980). *British Journal of Psychiatry*, **152**, 80–90.

Kolvin, I., Miller, F.J.W., Scott, D.M., Gatzanis, S.R.M. & Fleeting, M. (1990) *Continuities of Deprivation?* Aldershot: Avebury.

Lally, J.R., Mangione, P.L. & Honig, A.S. (1988) Long-range impact of an early intervention with low-income children and their families. In D.R. Powell (Ed.), *Parent Education as Early Childhood Intervention*, pp. 79–104. Norwood, NJ: Ablex.

LeBlanc, M. & Frechette, M. (1989) *Male Criminal Activity from Childhood Through Youth*. New York: Springer-Verlag.

Lewis, C., Newson, E. & Newson, J. (1982) Father participation through childhood and its relationship with career aspirations and delinquency. In N. Beail & J. McGuire (Eds), *Fathers: Psychological Perspectives*, pp. 174–193. London: Junction.

Lipsey, M.W. (1992) Juvenile delinquency treatment: a meta-analytic inquiry into the variability of effects. In T.D. Cook, H. Cooper, D.S. Cordray et al. (Eds), *Meta-analysis for Explanation*, pp. 83–127. New York: Russell Sage.

Lipton, D., Martinson, R. & Wilks, J. (1975) *The Effectiveness of Correctional Treatment*. New York: Praeger.

Loeber, R. (1987) Behavioural precursors and accelerators of delinquency. In W. Buikhuisen & S.A. Mednick (Eds), *Explaining Criminal Behaviour*, pp. 51–67. Leiden: Brill.

Loeber, R. & Dishion, T. (1983) Early predictors of male delinquency: a review. *Psychological Bulletin*, **94**, 68–99.

Loeber, R. & Stouthamer-Loeber, M. (1986) Family factors as correlates and predictors of juvenile conduct problems and delinquency. In M. Tonry & N. Morris (Eds). *Crime and Justice*, Vol. 7, pp. 29–149. Chicago: University of Chicago Press.

Loeber, R. & Stouthamer-Loeber, M. (1987) Prediction. In H.C. Quay (Ed.), *Handbook of Juvenile Delinquency*, pp. 325–382. New York: Wiley.

Lynam, D., Moffitt, T. & Stouthamer-Loeber, M. (1993) Explaining the relation between IQ and delinquency: class, race, test motivation, school failure or self-control? *Journal of Abnormal Psychology*, **102**, 187–196.

Martinson, R.M. (1974) What works? questions and answers about prison reform. *The Public Interest*, **35**, 22–54.

Martinson, R.M. (1979) New findings, new views: a note of caution regarding sentencing reform. *Hofstra Law Review*, **7**, 243–258.

Mawson, A.R. (1987) *Transient Criminality*. New York: Praeger.

McCord, J. (1977) A comparative study of two generations of native Americans. In R.F. Meier (Ed.), *Theory in Criminology*, pp. 83–92. Beverly Hills, CA: Sage.

McCord, J. (1979) Some child-rearing antecedents of criminal behaviour in adult men. *Journal of Personality and Social Psychology*, **37**, 1477–1486.

McCord, J. (1982) A longitudinal view of the relationship between paternal absence and crime. In J. Gunn & D.P. Farrington (Eds), *Abnormal Offenders, Delinquency, and the Criminal Justice System*, pp. 113–128. Chichester: Wiley.

McCord, J. & Tremblay, R. (Eds) (1992) *Preventing Antisocial Behaviour*. New York: Guilford.

McDaniel, E., Balis, G.U. & Strahan, S. (1990) Psychodynamic antecedents of violence. In L.J. Herzberg, G.F. Ostrum & J.R. Field (Eds), *Violent Behaviour*, Vol. 1, pp. 69–84. Great Neck, NY: PMA.

Mednick, S.A., Gabrielli, W.F. & Hutchings, B. (1983) Genetic influences on criminal behaviour: evidence from an adoption cohort. In K.T. Van Dusen & S.A. Mednick (Eds), *Prospective Studies of Crime and Delinquency*, pp. 39–56. Boston: Kluwer-Nijhoff.

Michelson, L. (1987) Cognitive–behavioural strategies in the prevention and treatment of antisocial disorders in children and adolescents. In J.D. Burchard & S.N. Burchard (Eds) *Prevention of Delinquent Behaviour*, pp. 275–310. Beverly Hills, CA: Sage.

Mischel, W., Shoda, Y. & Rodriguez, M.L. (1989) Delay of gratification in children. *Science*, **244**, 933–938.

Moffitt, T.E. (1990) The neuropsychology of juvenile delinquency: a critical review. In M. Tonry & N. Morris (Eds), *Crime and Justice*, Vol. 12, pp. 99–169. Chicago: University of Chicago Press.

Moffitt, T.E. & Henry, B. (1989) Neuropsychological assessment of executive functions in self-reported delinquents. *Development and Psychopathology*, **1**, 105–118.

Moffitt, T.E. & Silva, P.A. (1988a) IQ and delinquency: a direct test of the differential detection hypothesis. *Journal of Abnormal Psychology*, **97**, 330–333.

Moffitt, T.E. & Silva, P.A. (1988b) Neuropsychological deficit and self-reported delinquency in an unselected birth cohort. *Journal of the American Academy of Child and Adolescent Psychiatry*, **27**, 233–240.

Morash, M. & Rucker, L. (1989) An exploratory study of the connection of mother's age at childbearing to her children's delinquency in four data sets. *Crime and Delinquency*, **35**, 45–93.

Newson, J. & Newson, E. (1989) *The Extent of Parental Physical Punishment in the UK*. London: Approach.

Newson, J., Newson, E. & Adams, M. (1993) The social origins of delinquency. *Criminal Behaviour and Mental Health*, **3**, 19–29.

Nietzel, M.T. (1979) *Crime and its Modification*. New York: Pergamon.

Patterson, G.R. (1982) *Coercive Family Process*. Eugene, OR: Castalia.

Patterson, G.R., Chamberlain, P. & Reid, J.B. (1982) A comparative evaluation of a parent training programme. *Behaviour Therapy*, **13**, 638–650.

Patterson, G.R., Reid, J.B. & Dishion, T.J. (1992) *Antisocial Boys*. Eugene, OR: Castalia.

Pulkkinen, L. (1986) The role of impulse control in the development of antisocial and prosocial behaviour. In D. Olweus, J. Block & M.R. Yarrow (Eds), *Development of Antisocial and Prosocial Behaviour*, pp. 149–175. New York: Academic Press.

Pulkkinen, L. (1988) Delinquent development: theoretical and empirical considerations. In M. Rutter (Ed.), *Studies of Psychosocial Risk*, pp. 184–199. Cambridge: Cambridge University Press.

Reiss, A.J. & Farrington, D.P. (1991) Advancing knowledge about co-offending: results from a prospective longitudinal survey of London males. *Journal of Criminal Law and Criminology*, **82**, 360–395.

Riley, D. & Shaw, M. (1985) *Parental Supervision and Juvenile Delinquency*. London: HMSO.

Roberts, A.R. & Camasso, M.J. (1991) The effect of juvenile offender treatment programmes on recidivism: a meta-analysis of 46 studies. *Notre Dame Journal of Law, Ethics and Public Policy*, **5**, 421–441.

Robins, L.N. (1979) Sturdy childhood predictors of adult outcomes: replications from longitudinal studies. In J.E. Barrett, R.M. Rose & G.L. Klerman (Eds), *Stress and Mental Disorder*, pp. 219–235. New York: Raven Press.

Robins, L.N. & Ratcliff, K.S. (1978) Risk factors in the continuation of childhood antisocial behaviour into adulthood. *International Journal of Mental Health*, **7**, 96–116.

Robins, L.N., West, P.J. & Herjanic B.L. (1975) Arrests and delinquency in two generations: a study of black urban families and their children. *Journal of Child Psychology and Psychiatry*, **16**, 125–140.

Ross, R.R. & Gendreau, P. (Eds) (1980) *Effective Correctional Treatment*. Toronto: Butterworths.

Ross, R.R. & Ross, B.D. (1988) Delinquency prevention through cognitive training. *New Education*, **10**, 70–75.

Ross, R.R., Fabiano, E.A. & Ewles, C.D. (1988) Reasoning and rehabilitation. *International Journal of Offender Therapy and Comparative Criminology*, **32**, 29–35.

Rutter, M. (1981) *Maternal Deprivation Reassessed*, 2nd edn. Harmondsworth: Penguin.

Rutter, M. (1989) Psychosocial risk trajectories and beneficial turning points. In S. Doxiadis (Ed.), *Early Influences Shaping the Individual*, pp. 229–239. New York: Plenum.

Sarason, I.G. (1978) A cognitive social learning approach to juvenile delinquency. In R.D. Hare & D. Schalling (Eds), *Psychopathic Behaviour*, pp. 299–374. Chichester: Wiley.

Scharf, P. & Hickey, J. (1976) The prison and the inmate's conception of legal justice: an experiment in democratic education. *Criminal Justice and Behaviour*, **3**, 107–122.

Schweinhart, L.J. & Weikart, D.P. (1980) *Young Children Grow Up*. Ypsilanti, MI: High/Scope.

Schweinhart, L.J., Barnes, H.V. & Weikart, D.P. (1993) *Significant Benefits*. Ypsilanti, MI: High/Scope.

Sechrest, L., White, S.O. & Brown E.D. (1979) *The Rehabilitation of Criminal Offenders: Problems and Prospects*. Washington, DC: National Academy of Sciences.

Shedler, J. & Block, J. (1990) Adolescent drug use and psychological health. *American Psychologist*, **45**, 612–630.

Shore, M.F. & Massimo, J.L. (1979) Fifteen years after treatment: a follow-up study of comprehensive vocationally-oriented psychotherapy. *American Journal of Orthopsychiatry*, **49**, 240–245.

Smetana, J.G. (1990) Morality and conduct disorders. In M. Lewis & S.M. Miller (Eds), *Handbook of Developmental Psychopathology*, pp. 157–179. New York: Plenum.

Snyder, J. & Patterson, G.R. (1987) Family interaction and delinquent behaviour. In H.C. Quay (Ed.), *Handbook of Juvenile Delinquency*, pp. 216–243. New York: Wiley.

Sroufe, L.A. (1986) Bowlby's contribution to psychoanalytic theory and developmental psychology. *Journal of Child Psychology and Psychiatry*, **27**, 841–849.

Stein, K.B., Sarbin, T.R. & Kulik, J.A. (1968) Future time perspective: its relation to the socialization process and the delinquent role. *Journal of Consulting and Clinical Psychology*, **32**, 257–264.

Taylor, E.A. (1986) Childhood hyperactivity. *British Journal of Psychiatry*, **149**, 562–573.

Taylor, E.A., Schachar, R., Thorley, G. & Wieselberg, M. (1986) Conduct disorder and hyperactivity. I. Separation of hyperactivity and antisocial conduct in British child psychiatric patients. *British Journal of Psychiatry*, **149**, 760–767.

Tennenbaum, D.J. (1977) Personality and criminality: a summary and implications of the literature. *Journal of Criminal Justice*, **5**, 225–235.

Thornton, D. (1987a) Moral development theory. In B.J. McGurk, D.M. Thornton & M. Williams (Eds.), *Applying Psychology to Imprisonment*, pp. 129–150. London: HMSO.

Thornton, D.M. (1987b) Treatment effects on recidivism: a reappraisal of the "Nothing Works" doctrine. In B.J. McGurk, D.M. Thornton & M. Williams (Eds.), *Applying Psychology to Imprisonment*, pp. 181–189. London: HMSO.

Tisdelle, D.A. & St Lawrence, J.S. (1986) Interpersonal problem-solving competency: review and critique of the literature. *Clinical Psychology Review*, **6**, 337–356.

Tolan, P.H., Cromwell, R.E. & Brasswell, M. (1986) Family therapy with delinquents: a review of the literature. *Family Process*, **25**, 619–649.

Trasler, G.B. (1962) *The Explanation of Criminality*. London: Routledge and Kegan Paul.

Tremblay, R.E., McCord, J., Boileau, H. Charlebois P., Gagnon, C., LeBlanc, M. & Larivee, S. (1991) Can disruptive boys be helped to become competent? *Psychiatry*, **54**, 148–161.

Tremblay, R.E., Vitaro, F., Bertrand, L., LeBlanc, M., Beauchesne, H., Boileau, H. & David, L. (1992) Parent and child training to prevent early onset of delinquency: the Montreal longitudinal experimental study. In J. McCord & R. Tremblay (Eds.), *Preventing Antisocial Behaviour*, pp. 117–138. New York: Guilford.

Utting, D., Bright, J. & Henricson, C. (1993) *Crime and the Family*. London: Family Policy Studies Centre.

Venables, P.H. & Raine, A. (1987) Biological theory. In B.J. McGurk, D.M. Thornton & M. Williams (Eds.), *Applying Psychology to Imprisonment*, pp. 3–27. London: HMSO.

Wadsworth, M. (1979) *Roots of Delinquency*. London: Martin Robertson.

Walsh, A., Petee, T.A. & Beyer, J.A. (1987) Intellectual imbalance and delinquency: comparing high verbal and high performance IQ delinquents. *Criminal Justice and Behaviour*, **14**, 370–379.

Wells, L.E. & Rankin, J.H. (1991) Families and delinquency: a meta-analysis of the impact of broken homes. *Social Problems*, **38**, 71–93.

West, D.J. (1982) *Delinquency: Its Roots, Careers and Prospects*. London: Heinemann.

West, D.J. & Farrington, D.P. (1973) *Who Becomes Delinquent?* London: Heinemann.

West, D.J. & Farrington, D.P. (1977) *The Delinquent Way of Life*. London: Heinemann.

White, H.R., Labouvie, E.W. & Bates, M.E. (1985) The relationship between sensation seeking and delinquency: a longitudinal analysis. *Journal of Research in Crime and Delinquency*, **22**, 197–211.

White, J.L., Moffitt, T.E. & Silva, P.A. (1989) A prospective replication of the protective effects of IQ in subjects at high risk for juvenile delinquency. *Journal of Consulting and Clinical Psychology*, **57**, 719–724.

Whitehead, J.T. & Lab, S.P. (1989) A meta-analysis of juvenile correctional treatment. *Journal of Research in Crime and Delinquency*, **26**, 276–295.

Widom, C.S. (1989) The cycle of violence. *Science*, **244**, 160 166.

Wikstrom, P.O. (1987) *Patterns of Crime in a Birth Cohort*. Stockholm: University of Stockholm Department of Sociology.

Wilson, H. (1980) Parental supervision: a neglected aspect of delinquency. *British Journal of Criminology*, **20**, 203–235.

Wilson, H. (1987) Parental supervision re-examined. *British Journal of Criminology*, **27**, 275–301.

Wilson, J.Q. & Herrnstein, R.J. (1985) *Crime and Human Nature*. New York: Simon and Schuster.

CHAPTER TWO

PSYCHOLOGY AND THE LAW

Gisli H. Gudjonsson

INTRODUCTION

This chapter is about the application of psychology to legal practice, which is nowadays commonly referred to as "forensic psychology". Haward (1981) defines "forensic psychology" as "that branch of applied psychology which is concerned with the collection, examination and presentation of evidence for judicial purposes" (p. 21). However, Bartol & Bartol (1987) use the term "forensic psychology" far more broadly, and view it as any "professional practice" and "research endeavour" where psychology and the law interact.

Golding (1992) argues that the structure of both civil and criminal law "is based, in part, upon a variety of theories and expectations of human behavior, perception, intentionality, and judgement. As a consequence, social scientists, in general, and psychologists, in particular, are called upon, with increasing frequency, to offer expert evidence at various stages of adjudicatory and legislative process" (p. 253).

Haney (1993) discusses the ways in which improved psychological knowledge and empirical data over the past decade have profoundly influenced the legal structures, procedures and case law in the USA. Of fundamental importance here are the impact of:

1. empirical research findings

Working with Offenders: Psychological Practice in Offender Rehabilitation.
Edited by C.R. Hollin. © 1996 John Wiley & Sons Ltd.

2. the application of psychological techniques to the examination and presentation of evidence at judicial proceedings.

In practice, these two different ways of influencing the legal system overlap. That is, theory, research and empirical findings may influence the legal system in their own right, like in the case of eyewitness testimony in the USA (Haney, 1993), but often they also stimulate the development of psychological techniques used in clinical practice, which is probably most clearly seen in the assessment of cases of retracted confession (Gudjonsson, 1992a).

The primary objective of this chapter is to provide practical advice for psychologists who have been instructed to conduct assessments in civil and criminal cases. The different roles of forensic psychologists within the context of civil and criminal jurisprudence are discussed and their unique contribution to court proceedings are highlighted. It is argued that forensic psychology has an important historical background, which differs markedly from forensic psychiatry. Their current contribution to legal proceedings is discussed both in terms of historical and legal developments.

BRIEF HISTORICAL BACKGROUND

It was about a century ago that psychologists began to enter the courtroom (Gudjonsson, 1991). Undoubtedly, the stimulus behind court work had come from the work carried out in the world's first psychological institute, which was founded by Wilhem Wundt in Leipzig in 1879 (Eysenck & Meili, 1972). Wundt was a philosopher and an experimenter who was cautious about applying psychological knowledge to specific problems until sufficient research had been carried out to demonstrate its validity. His institute soon became internationally recognized and a number of psychologists from different countries went there to study experimental psychology.

James Cattell, Schrenck-Notzing, Karl Marbe and Hugo Münsterberg were German psychologists who applied experimental methodology effectively to court-related problems. Their influence on the development of "forensic psychology" was important.

Cattell (1895) produced the first experimental study into the psychology of testimony, and showed the need to look at both the role of individual differences and the conditions which influence the accuracy of recall. Cattell's experiment stimulated further research into testimony, including that of Binet (1900) and Stern (1910), which was to mark the beginning of work into interrogative suggestibility. Parallel with this important development into the psychology of human testimony was the development of standardized intelligence tests (Matarazzo, 1990).

Schrenck-Notzing (1897) was probably the first psychologist to present experimental evidence in a criminal court. He gave evidence on laboratory research into memory and suggestibility at a murder trial in Munich in 1896 (Bartol & Bartol, 1987). In 1911, Karl Marbe, a German psychologist and a pupil of Wundt, applied experimental findings to a civil court proceeding. He demonstrated the phenomenon of "reaction time" in a civil court case concerning alleged negligence by a train driver. He argued, on the basis of experimental evidence, that the train driver could not have stopped in time to prevent a crash (McCary, 1956).

An influential early forensic psychologist, Hugo Münsterberg, introduced the phenomenon of colour vision to a German civil court before making a name for himself in the USA (Haward, 1990). Münsterberg, who wrote a highly controversial book on witness testimony (Münsterberg, 1908), is referred to by Bartol & Bartol (1987) as the father of applied psychology. Münsterberg made some important experimental contributions to the phenomena of perception, memory and auditory discrimination, and stimulated the interest of American psychologists in court work. His weakness appears to have been his willingness to apply psychological principles without sufficient empirical data.

The development of forensic psychology was stimulated by William M. Marston, the first American professor of legal psychology. Marston had been a student of Münsterberg and became well known for his work on lie detection. He carried out experimental work into the effectiveness of systolic blood pressure in detecting lies, and claimed almost 100% per accuracy (Marston, 1917). His exaggerated claims created a myth about the validity of the polygraph as a "lie detector". Similar unrealistic claims were reported for drug-aided interviews (House, 1931).

Forensic hypnosis was established in the Netherlands in the 19th century and was first used in the USA in 1905 (Haward, 1990). However, it tends to distort the memory process and its admissibility in court is often disputed (Gudjonsson, 1992a). Recently, techniques such as "cognitive interviewing" (Geiselman & Fisher, 1989) have reduced the need for hypnosis to enhance memory. Similarly, the development of "statement reality analysis" (Undeutsch, 1989) has reduced the need to rely exclusively on the polygraph for detecting deception.

Many of the early contributions of "forensic psychologists" were concerned with *evaluating* the reliability of testimony by employing various assessment procedures (e.g. suggestibility, lie detection). Experimental psychology, whose foundation was developed by Wundt, formed an important basis for court-related work. However, forensic psychology as currently practised in the USA is very much based on clinical practice rather than experimental psychology. That is, experimental techniques and procedures are hardly ever applied to individual cases, although experimental research data are sometimes used to establish general principles. An example of this is the research carried out into eyewitness testimony which has been used to demonstrate the conditions under which eyewitnesses' accounts become unreliable (Loftus, 1979).

In contrast to the practice of American forensic psychologists, in the UK there has been more emphasis on applying experimental techniques in a unique way to a variety of forensic problems concerning individual cases (Haward, 1981, 1990; Gudjonsson, 1992a). With regard to the reliability of witnesses' and suspects' accounts, expert witnesses in the UK have focused much more than their American colleagues on individual differences and psychological vulner-abilities (Schooler & Loftus, 1986; Gudjonsson, 1992a, 1993; Gudjonsson et al., 1993).

THE LEGAL FRAMEWORK

Psychologists may find themselves having to present written or oral evidence in a variety of legal settings, relating to civil, criminal, military and mental health legislation. As far as courts are concerned, these involve three different jurisdictions, referred to as courts of criminal jurisdiction, courts of civil jurisdiction and courts of special jurisdiction (Haward, 1981).

COURTS OF CRIMINAL JURISDICTION

Cases within the courts of criminal jurisdiction are those considered to be against the public interest. They are generally brought against defendants by the Crown Prosecution Service in England or the Procurator Fiscal in Scotland, who are acting on behalf of the State.

Criminal offences in England and Wales are divided into three classes, referred to as "summary", "indictable" and "either-way" offences. Summary offences are the less serious type of offences (e.g. traffic violations) and are tried in the magistrates' court either by Justices of the Peace (lay magistrates) or stipendiary magistrates. The former individuals are unpaid, work part-time and are not legally qualified. They are appointed by the Lord Chancellor and normally sit on the bench in a group of three. Stipendiary magistrates are full-time, salaried magistrates who sit alone. They are qualified and experienced legal advocates (i.e. either solicitors or barristers).

Indictable offences (i.e. those tried on indictment), on the other hand, are tried by jury in the Crown Court in contested cases. They are the most serious offences, such as murder or rape. Either-way offences, which include theft, burglary and indecent assault, are those which can be tried either within the jurisdiction of the magistrates' court or the Crown Court. The mode of trial is decided by the magistrates, but the defendant has the choice to be tried in the Crown Court if he or she so wishes. If the magistrates accept jurisdiction then the defendant, if convicted, may nevertheless be sent to the Crown Court for sentencing when the magistrates consider that they have insufficient powers to sentence the offender after having heard all the evidence. The magistrates' courts try the great majority of all criminal cases (about 97%), as well as dealing with bail applications and committal to the Crown Court in the more serious cases.

When defendants wish to appeal against the decision of magistrates, this is heard in the Crown Court. Further appeals are heard in the Court of Appeal, which is divided into civil and criminal divisions. Final appeals, which are generally on points of law and of general public importance, are heard in the House of Lords.

COURTS OF CIVIL JURISDICTION

The civil courts deal with disputes which do not pose a threat to the safety and welfare of the general public. Litigation typically involves breach of contract or tort and is heard either in the High Court (Queen's Bench Division) or in local county courts. Almost all (93%) civil litigation proceedings are settled out of court and liability is contested in only about 1% of cases (Barker et al., 1993). As far as forensic psychology is concerned, psychologists commonly prepare reports in cases of suspected head injury and compensation cases but would very rarely have to give oral evidence (Gudjonsson, 1985).

The magistrates' courts also process some civil cases, such as domestic disputes and child care proceedings. Clinical psychologists sometimes give evidence in the magistrates' court, particularly in juvenile and domestic cases (Lane, 1987; Parker, 1987). In the Crown Court psychologists tend to be instructed in the more serious cases, such as those involving sexual offences, violence and unlawful killing.

COURTS OF SPECIAL JURISDICTION

The courts of special jurisdiction exist to deal with matters which are not manifestly either public or private. These "administrative" courts include the coroner's courts (which determine the cause and circumstances of death), courts martial which deal with military personnel under military law, social security tribunals and mental health review tribunals (Barker et al., 1993).

Forensic psychologists are sometimes required to prepare reports for the courts of special jurisdiction. This includes preparing reports for mental health tribunals which may focus on assessment, treatment and prediction of dangerousness issues (Gunn & Monahan, 1993).

A recent document on the Criminal Justice Act 1991, prepared for mental health professionals (Health Service Guidelines, 1993), provides guidelines about the implications of the new Criminal Justice Act. In particular, there are important changes in the way mentally disordered persons are dealt with, which principally affect the probation service but are likely to be accompanied by increased requests for "medical reports" where persons are suspected to be suffering from mental disorder. According to the Act, a "medical report means a report about an offender's mental condition made or submitted orally or in writing by a registered medical practitioner who is approved" [as defined by Section 4(5) of the Criminal Justice Act 1991]. Such a report should include information about the defendant's condition, the treatment available, and the likely effect of a custodial sentence on the person's mental condition.

The implications of the Criminal Justice Act for forensic psychologists are indirect. That is, a medical practitioner may refer the case on to a psychologist for his or her opinion. By definition, psychologists cannot accept such reports directly from the court.

PSYCHOLOGICAL VS PSYCHIATRIC EVIDENCE

Forensic psychology and forensic psychiatry have separate historical backgrounds (Bartol & Bartol, 1987). Comprehensive accounts are available about the history of forensic psychiatry in England (Forshaw & Rollin, 1990), Europe (Barras & Bernheim, 1990) and the USA (Quen, 1990).

Faulk (1988) argues that the role of the forensic psychiatrist involves the preparation of court reports concerning the mental state of persons suspected to be suffering from mental abnormality and the provision of treatment whenever appropriate. A more medical definition is given by Gunn & Taylor (1993), who define forensic psychiatry as "the prevention, amelioration and treatment of victimization which is associated with mental disease" (p. 2). This definition is unsatisfactory in that it makes no mention of assessment of mental disorder for judicial purposes. The definitions of Faulk and Gunn & Taylor both highlight the importance of *mental disorder* as a part of forensic psychiatry practice. That is, without mental disorder there would be no forensic psychiatry. In contrast, the definition of Haward (1981), quoted earlier, implies the application of *psychological techniques* in the collection, examination and presentation of evidence. Here there is no necessary prerequisite for the existence of mental disorder. Even if mental disorder did not exist, there would still be forensic psychology. This is because forensic psychology arose historically from psychology's focus on understanding human behaviour generally, rather than specifically in relation to mental disorder which is the essence of psychiatry.

Grisso (1993) argues that both forensic psychologists and forensic psychiatrists may be losing credibility in the eyes of the America judiciary and the public, which has been partly caused by adverse publicity in relation to some recent cases. There are, according to Grisso, two factors that contribute to the problem. Firstly, both disciplines have a "fragile scientific base", even though forensic psychiatry has gathered much clinical and research data on mental disorder, and forensic psychologists "can borrow from knowledge accumulated across decades of controlled, empirical research on human behavior in the basic fields of developmental, personality, cognitive, social and abnormal psychology" (p. 135). The second problem relates to the lack of quality control concerning the practice of forensic psychiatrists and psychologists, which has resulted in inadequate and unethical practices by some experts who sell themselves as "hired guns" for whichever side is paying their fees.

In order to be able to make recommendations about how psychiatrists and psychologists can improve their credibility in legal forums, Grisso outlines the similarities and differences between the two professions. With respect to similarities, both have a rather weak scientific base, share constant threat to their credibility, work on similar cases, are subjected to the same courtroom procedures and cross-examination, face similar ethical dilemmas, and share similar theories and research findings.

Grisso discusses four important differences between psychiatrists and psychologists. First, there are differences in the *content* of their respective contributions to individual cases. Psychiatrists are specifically trained to deal with biological, medical and psychopharmacological questions, whereas psychologists, in contrast, are better trained to deal with issues that go beyond mental disorder, such as describing the person's abilities, behaviour, personality and coping strategies.

Second, the two disciplines use different *methods* in their assessment of individual cases. Whereas psychiatrists mainly use interviews and observation, psychologists more commonly use standardized and qualitative assessment methods (e.g. IQ tests, personality tests), which are based on recognized scientific principles.

Third, there is an *epistemological* difference between the research of psychologists and psychiatrists. That is, psychiatrists more commonly base their research on observations of large clinical samples, whereas psychologists are likely to conduct controlled experiments. This difference relates mainly to the fact that psychologists' training in general psychology requires them to be able to design and perform controlled experimental studies on a variety of psychological issues.

Fourth, the two professions use different *mentoring* systems. Forensic psychiatry training more often makes use of teaching hospital departments and residency training, whereas graduate programmes in psychology are based within the psychology departments of universities.

The main implication of the differences between psychologists and psychiatrists is that they have different skills, which when used jointly can be employed to their maximum effect.

Grisso argues that the potential loss of credibility can be overcome by forensic psychiatrists and psychologists collaborating in three distinct areas:

1. working jointly on cases, whenever appropriate;
2. working together to improve the quality of forensic practice, for example by conducting joint workshops and seminars;
3. improved training clinical and research programmes for psychiatrists and psychologists.

COLLABORATION BETWEEN PSYCHOLOGY AND PSYCHIATRY

It seems from Grisso's (1993) review that in the USA forensic psychologists and psychiatrists rarely work together on cases. This also seems to be the case in the UK. However, psychologists and psychiatrists clearly have complementary skills and I agree with Grisso that their individual contributions can jointly maximize the understanding of some cases. Indeed, over the years I have worked jointly on a number of cases with psychiatrists, which has proved very fruitful. I have worked particularly closely with one consultant forensic psychiatrist, Dr James MacKeith, and our joint effort on numerous cases has resulted in increased recognition of expert evidence in some landmark cases of retracted confession (Gudjonsson, 1992a). In addition, since the early 1980s we have conducted joint research into false confession (Gudjonsson & MacKeith, 1982, 1988, 1990, 1994).

To illustrate the importance of our joint psychological and psychiatric contributions I shall discuss one well-publicized case, that of the "Guildford Four". This case, like so many others, shows that sometimes both psychiatric and psychological aspects are relevant when considering the reliability of confession evidence. In my experience, the great majority of cases of retracted confession require a psychological assessment, because of the relevance of a functional assessment to the legal issues (see Gudjonsson, 1992a, for a review). In a small minority of cases, where mental illness or drug-related problems are present, a psychiatric assessment is also required. It is often useful for the psychiatrist and psychologist to interview defendants together, because they can watch each other and ensure that all the relevant questions are asked and issues are covered. This is the way that Dr MacKeith and I prefer to work.

THE CASE OF CAROLE RICHARDSON

Carole Richardson, one of the so-called "Guildford Four", was arrested by the police on 3 December 1974, suspected of being responsible for planting two bombs in public houses in Guildford, Surrey, on 5 October 1974. Five people were killed and a further 57 were injured. Miss Richardson, who was 17 years of age at the time of her arrest, was convicted in September 1975 of terrorist offences, along with three other defendants (Paul Hill, Gerry Conlan and Paddy Armstrong). On 19 October 1989, the convictions of the four persons were overturned by the Court of Appeal. They had served 15 years in prison before their release.

Dr MacKeith and I initially examined Miss Richardson in 1986 at Styal Prison at the request of the prison medical service (see Gudjonsson, 1992a, for a detailed account of the case). The reason for the assessment was to provide an independent evaluation of Miss Richardson's mental state and the likely reliability of her confession to the police in 1974. We interviewed her in great detail on three separate occasions and I administered a number of different psychological tests in order to assess her intellectual functioning, personality and mental state. She proved to be an intelligent person, but was clearly vulnerable to suggestions and interrogative pressure on repeated testing. At the time of her arrest in 1974 she was very young, addicted to drugs and had very low self-esteem. In my view, she was sufficiently psychologically vulnerable when interviewed by the police in 1974 to cast doubt on the reliability of her confession. Dr MacKeith concentrated on the medical and psychiatric aspects of the case, which included concern about Miss Richardson's mental state at the time of her police interviews in 1974 as a result of withdrawal from barbiturates, on which she was dependent at the time. We prepared detailed reports for the Home Secretary which assisted in having the case against the "Guildford Four" reopened (Gudjonsson, 1992a).

In view of Miss Richardson's drug dependency problems at the time of her arrest, it was essential to instruct an experienced psychiatrist to investigate the likely influence of drug withdrawal on the reliability of her confession. Indeed, Dr MacKeith's report proved invaluable to the case. A detailed psychological assessment of Miss Richardson was helpful in identifying psychological strengths and vulnerabilities which assisted in being able to evaluate her likely reaction to the demanding police interviews in 1974. In addition, by jointly working on the case, Dr MacKeith and I were able to discuss in detail the various aspects of the case and ensure that no important issues were left uninvestigated or unattended.

ADMISSIBILITY OF PSYCHOLOGICAL EVIDENCE

Evidence is only allowed in legal proceedings when it is considered to be *relevant* and *admissible*. Relevance is determined on the basis of the logically probative value of the evidence, whereas admissibility refers to evidence which is legally receivable irrespective of whether or not it is logically probative (Curzon, 1986). Therefore, evidence may be highly relevant but be inadmissible for legal reasons (e.g. because it was obtained unfairly).

There have been two recent reviews of the admissibility of psychological evidence (Mackay & Coleman, 1991; Gudjonsson, 1992b). Mackay & Coleman (1991) argue that the admissibility of expert evidence is more acute in relation to psychology than psychiatry, because psychology is a science concerned mainly with the study of normal behaviour whereas psychiatry deals primarily with mental disorders. This statement overlooks the fact that most psychologists who prepare court reports are clinical psychologists

(Gudjonsson, 1985, 1987a) who have specialized in the assessment and treatment of mental disorders. It is their clinical findings that they commonly testify to in court rather than general psychological matters concerning normal behaviour. When psychologists describe a specific clinical condition, then the admissibility of their evidence follows the path already established by psychiatrists (Fitzgerald, 1987).

The evidence of psychologists and psychiatrists diverges when the former begin to comment on the development and mental functioning of ordinary individuals. As discussed earlier, psychologists do devote more of their training to the understanding of normal human behaviour than their psychiatrist colleagues. They are therefore better qualified than psychiatrists to testify about how normal individuals might react to unusual predicaments or special circumstances, such as being interrogated by the police. However, this does not mean that all qualified clinical psychologists are invariably able to give a competent opinion about how suspects may react to police interrogation. The individual assessment of suspects' reactions to a stressful demand, such as an interrogation, is an area which requires specialized psychological knowledge and experience (Gudjonsson, 1992a).

Psychologists are increasingly allowed to testify in England about personality traits in the absence of psychiatric abnormality. For example, scores from tests of suggestibility or compliance are sometimes allowed in evidence even when they do not fall outside the normal range (Gudjonsson, 1992a). The scores obtained on testing can be converted into percentile scores to demonstrate how they compare with respective normative scores.

There is an important distinction between a statistical abnormality and other forms of abnormality. Statistical abnormality deals with the frequency with which a particular score (e.g. IQ, suggestibility) occurs in a given normative population. For example, an IQ of 70 falls at the bottom 2% of the general population which means that it is sufficiently low to be considered to fall outside the normal range, even when taking into account inherent errors in test scores (Gudjonsson, 1992a). In contrast, the diagnosis of a psychiatric abnormality is based on a clinical opinion of the presence of various symptoms which can be classified as constituting mental disorder.

Psychological evidence has gained increased recognition and acceptance in the UK (Gudjonsson, 1992a, b). The judgement of the Court of Appeal on 5 December 1991 in the case of *Regina v. Raghip* (Law Report, the *Independent* 6 December 1991) has had important implications for the admissibility of psychological evidence. This landmark ruling has widened the criteria for psychological evidence. First, psychological evidence is now viewed in law as important in its own right, rather than relying on medical criteria for admissibility. Second, even if defendants have an IQ above the cut-off point of 70, the psychological evidence is still admissible. Third, evidence of psychological characteristics, such as suggestibility, was accepted by the Court of Appeal as important and admissible, even in the absence of psychiatric abnormality. Fourth, psychological evidence concerning a defendant is viewed as being valuable even when the jury has good opportunity to observe defendants testifying in court. In other words, expert psychological evidence is needed when defendants have significant psychological incapacity and the jury is not expected to be in a position to judge the defendant's vulnerabilities.

The recent legal acceptance of the diagnosis of post-traumatic stress disorder (PTSD) has had an enormous impact on both civil and criminal law (Stone, 1993). The identification of PTSD symptoms can form the basis for defining psychological injury in civil (compensation) cases as well as negating culpability or mitigating sentences in criminal cases.

THE ROLES OF THE FORENSIC PSYCHOLOGIST

Forensic psychologists may fulfil numerous different roles when contributing to legal proceedings (Cooke, 1980; Haward, 1981; Blau, 1984; Weiner & Hess, 1987). The specific role they fulfil will depend upon the issue they are asked to address. Haward (1981, 1990) defines four main roles and describes the types of court where psychologists may find themselves giving evidence. These roles are classified by Haward as "experimental", "clinical", "actuarial" and "advisory" roles. I shall give a brief description of each type of role.

In the experimental role psychologists may either give evidence about general research findings (e.g. problems with eyewitness testimony) or carry out experiments that are directly relevant to the individual case. With regard to the latter, psychologists perform a unique function which is generally outside the expertise of forensic psychiatrists. In this role human behaviour is studied by experimentation rather than by a clinical interview and it requires the ability and knowledge to apply psychological principles and techniques to individual forensic problems. Sometimes it involves devising ingenious experiments, both in civil and criminal cases (Haward, 1981).

As an example of experimentation within an individual case, Gudjonsson & Sartory (1983) used an experimental procedure involving the use of a polygraph as an aid to the diagnosis of blood injury phobia. I presented the findings in court which resulted in the overturning on appeal of a defendant's conviction for failing to provide a specimen of blood in a suspected drunken driving case.

The clinical role is the most common role and almost invariably requires clinical training and experience. It overlaps with the role fulfilled by the forensic psychiatrist (Gudjonsson, 1984a,b 1985) and typically involves the psychologist interviewing a client and carrying out the required assessment, which may include extensive psychometric testing (e.g. the administration of tests of intelligence, neuropsychological functioning, personality, mental state) and behavioural data (Cooke, 1980; Haward, 1981; Blau, 1984; Gudjonsson, 1985; Martell, 1992). The nature of the assessment carried out will depend upon the instruction of the referral agent and the type of problem being assessed. Sometimes clients need to be assessed on more than one occasion and whenever possible and appropriate, informants should be consulted for providing corroboration and further information. Previous reports, including school reports and psychological and psychiatric assessments, will need to be obtained whenever they are likely to be relevant to the assessment.

The actuarial role involves the application of statistical probabilities to behavioural data. This role is not confined to psychologists and is commonly used by statisticians and other scientists when interpreting observational and behavioural data. The types of probability and observational data analysed by psychologists are discussed by Haward (1981).

The advisory role involves psychologists advising counsel about what questions to ask when cross-examining psychologists who are testifying for the other side. On occasions, the prosecution may request that a psychologist sits by counsel in court and advises him how to cross-examine the defence psychologist. Court reports are increasingly being subjected to peer review by an expert for the other side. That expert would typically have carefully studied the psychological report and, in addition, may have carried out an assessment of the defendant.

PSYCHOLOGISTS' CONTRIBUTIONS TO CRIMINAL PROCEEDINGS

Most criminal proceedings involve three distinct stages: pre-trial, trial and sentencing. Each stage addresses of different legal issues and it is essential that psychologists who are preparing court reports are familiar with the relevant legal concepts and issues relevant at each stage.

PRE-TRIAL ISSUES

The defendant's fitness to plead and fitness to stand trial may be raised by the defence at the pre-trial stage (Chiswick, 1990). This happens when the defendant's physical or mental state at the time of the trial is thought to interfere with the due process of the law (i.e. the defendant may not have a fair trial if the case proceeds). The ability of the defendant to give adequate instructions to his or her lawyers, to understand the charge against him or her, to distinguish between a plea of guilty and not guilty, and to follow the proceedings in court are the main legal issues to be decided upon at the pre-trial stage. The fitness to plead and stand trial issues are typically only generally raised in serious cases because of their legal and clinical significance (Chiswick, 1990).

The main problem for the forensic psychiatrist and psychologist, which applies equally to British and American expert witnesses, is that the legal constructs of fitness criteria are defined and described inadequately in case law, which means that the expert may find it difficult to evaluate the defendant's psychiatric and psychological vulnerabilities within the context of the legal criteria. This means that the psychiatric evaluation is often going to be peripherally related to the legal criteria (Grisso, 1986).

In the USA clinical psychologists are actively involved in this area of the criminal proceedings, where their role overlaps considerably with that of psychiatrists (Blau, 1984). Special instruments, commonly referred to as "competency tests", have been developed by American psychologists in order to assess objectively the functional deficits that are relevant to the legal issues (Blau, 1984). Recent factor analytic studies into "competency tests" have raised concern about the lack of stable factor structure across different subject samples (Bagby et al., 1992). Bagby et al. recommend that what is needed is a further development of empirical measures that better match the legal construct of competency to stand trial.

In the UK, psychiatrists are mainly involved at this stage of the proceedings. In recent years psychologists in England are more frequently being instructed by defence lawyers to carry out a psychological assessment on these cases, because it provides the court with an objective and standardized assessment of the defendant's functional deficits. This may involve an assessment of the defendant's intellectual and neuropsychological status, as well as an assessment of problems related to anxiety and depression.

TRIAL ISSUES

In English law, a criminal offence consists of a number of different elements which fall into two main categories, referred to as *actus reus* and *mens rea* (Leng, 1990). The former comprises elements relevant to the criminal act itself, whereas the latter generally focuses on the mental state of the defendant. During the *actus reus* stage the crown has to prove:

1. that a criminal offence was committed;
2. that the defendant committed it.

Mens rea issues focus on the state of mind of the accused at the time of the alleged offence and its blameworthiness (e.g. whether the offence was committed either recklessly or intentionally).

The criteria for establishing *mens rea* are dependent upon the nature of the offence, because each offence is defined separately in law and there are no standard criteria for defining *mens rea* across different offences. Certain offences do not require an element of *mens rea* for the defendant to be convicted (i.e. they are offences of "strict liability" and the Crown only has to prove *actus reus*). However, in such cases a mental condition relevant to *mens rea* can be used as mitigation at the sentencing stage.

Psychologists in England are often instructed to prepare Court Reports which are relevant to both *actus reus* and *mens rea* issues, and their involvement in such cases is expanding (Gudjonsson, 1986, 1992a; Fitzgerald, 1987).

The contribution of clinical psychologists to *mens rea* issues complements that of their psychiatrist colleagues (Gudjonsson, 1984a, 1986). This may include dealing with issues relevant to "abnormality of mind" and diminished responsibility in cases of homicide and the question of intent in cases of theft.

SENTENCING ISSUES

Sentencing takes place after the defendant has been found guilty of the offence. Various sentencing options are available, depending on the nature of the offence and the circumstances of the case. These include a financial penalty, probation, community service orders, and a prison sentence. In the case of minor offences a fine is the most common sentence. In more serious cases the defendant may be sentenced to prison or given up to 240 hours of community service (i.e. given some tasks to do in the local community under close supervision).

Psychologists are increasingly being asked to provide reports about factors which are relevant to mitigation and sentencing (Gudjonsson, 1986). This may involve offering an opinion about treatment options and prognosis. The recommendation may involve offering treatment to persons convicted of sexual offences (Clare, 1993; Lang, 1993), compulsive shoplifting (Gudjonsson, 1987b) and car theft (Brown, 1985).

THE PSYCHOLOGICAL EVIDENCE

Whether or not the psychologist is required to give oral evidence in court depends on a number of factors, including the nature of the case and how favourable the evidence is to the side instructing the psychologist. In the great majority of civil cases, including head injury and psychological trauma cases, the case will be settled out of court. In contrast, in criminal cases psychologists often have to give evidence concerning their assessment (Gudjonsson, 1992a). The defence does not normally forward a copy of the expert's report to the prosecution unless it is favourable to the defence, in which case the psychologist would not be required to give oral evidence. If the psychologist has been instructed by the prosecution then the report is forwarded to the defence, irrespective of whether or not the findings are favourable to the prosecution.

As far as the psychological report is concerned, the findings must be presented clearly, succinctly and in non-technical language whenever possible. The opinions should be substantiated and made relevant to the issues addressed. On occasions, the report may be accepted by the respective legal advocates without the psychologist having to give oral evidence. Indeed, the prosecution may withdraw the charges after considering the psychological findings, particularly in cases of learning disability and mental illness.

A number of authors have provided expert witnesses with useful information about how to present themselves and their findings when testifying in court (e.g. Haward, 1981; Carson, 1990; Cooke, 1990). Expert witnesses are well advised to concentrate on factual evidence and limit their opinions to evidence which can be substantiated by empirical testing (Carson, 1990).

Courts are formal settings where certain customs and conventions must be followed. The expert witness should be formally dressed and speak clearly and confidently. The expert first provides evidence in chief and he or she will then be cross-examined about the evidence, after which there may be re-examination of various matters raised during the cross-examination. When testifying the psychologist can be asked challenging questions by the legal advocates and the judge. He or she should always be fully prepared by knowing the basic facts of the case, being intimately familiar with the tests used in the assessment, and any relevant documents. Interview notes and test forms may be closely inspected.

CONCLUSIONS

Psychology can contribute to legal proceedings in a number of different ways. In this chapter I have discussed forensic psychology within an historical context. It is now about a century since psychologists entered the courtroom. The early psychologists used an experimental approach to solving legal problems, following the tradition of William Wundt, the founder of experimental psychology. The reliability of testimony was an area where psychologists had a unique contribution to make, following the early experimental work into suggestibility.

Since the turn of the century the contribution of psychologists to legal proceedings has widened considerably. They currently function in four different roles, referred to by Haward (1981) as experimental, clinical, actuarial and advisory, in three different court jurisdictions, criminal, civil and special jurisdictions. Their primary role at present is a clinical one rather than an experimental one. This is particularly true in the USA where there is a considerable overlap between the contribution of forensic psychologists and forensic psychiatrists. Where the experimental role exists, American psychologists generally present general research findings in legal proceedings rather than applying experimental procedures and techniques to individual cases. In contrast, some British psychologists have employed a variety of experimental procedures in a unique way for criminal and civil cases.

REFERENCES

Bagby, R.M., Nicholson, R.A., Rogers, R. & Nussbaum, D. (1992) Domains of competency to stand trial. A factor analytic study. *Law and Human Behavior*, **16**, 491–507.
Barker, A., Gunn, J., Hamilton, J. & Stanley, S. (1993) The courts and bodies

overseeing and administering the laws in the United Kingdom (and Northern Ireland). In J. Gunn & P.J. Taylor (Eds), *Forensic Psychiatry. Clinical, Legal and Ethical Issues*, pp. 167–251. Oxford: Butterworth-Heinemann.

Barras, V. & Bernheim, J. (1990) The history of law and psychiatry in Europe. In R. Bluglass and P. Bowden (Eds), *Principles and Practice of Forensic Psychiatry*, pp. 103–109. London: Churchill Livingstone.

Bartol, C.R. & Bartol, A.M. (1987) History of forensic psychology. In I.B. Weiner & A.K. Hess (Eds), *Handbook of Forensic Psychology*. New York: John Wiley.

Binet, A. (1900) *La suggestibilite*. Paris: Schleicher.

Blau, T.H. (1984) *The Psychologist as a Expert Witness*. New York: John Wiley.

Brown, B. (1985) The involvement of psychologists in sentencing. *Bulletin of the British Psychological Society*, **38**, 180–182.

Carson, D. (1990) *Professionals and the Courts. A Handbook for Expert Witnesses*. Birmingham: Venture Press.

Cattell, J.M. (1895) Measurements of the accuracy of recollection. *Science*, **2**, 761–766.

Chiswick, D. (1990) Fitness to stand trial and plead, mutism and deafness. In R. Bluglass and P. Bowden (Eds), *Principles and Practice of Forensic Psychiatry*, pp. 171–178. London: Churchill Livingstone.

Clare, I.C.H. (1993) Issues in the assessment and treatment of male sex offenders with mild learning disabilities. *Sexual and Marital Therapy*, **8**, 167–180.

Cooke, D. (1990) Being an "expert" in Court. *The Psychologist*, **3**, 216–221

Cooke, G. (Ed.) (1980) *The Role of the Forensic Psychologist*. Springfield: Charles C. Thomas.

Curzon, L.B. (1986) *A Dictionary of Law*, 2nd edn. London: Pitman Publishing.

Eysenck, H.J. & Meili, W.A.R. (Eds) (1972) *Encyclopedia of Psychology*, Vol. 3 New York: Plenum Press.

Faulk, M. (1988) *Basic Forensic Psychiatry*. London: Blackwell Scientific Publications.

Fitzgerald, E. (1987) Psychologists and the law of evidence: admissibility and confidentiality. In G. Gudjonsson & J. Drinkwater (Eds), *Psychological Evidence in Court*, pp 39–48. Issues in Criminological and Legal Psychology, No. 11. Leicester: British Psychological Society.

Forshaw, D. & Rollin, H. (1990) The history of forensic psychiatry in England. In R. Bluglass & P. Bowden (Eds, Principles and Practice of Forensic Psychiatry, pp 61–101. London: Churchill Livingstone.

Geiselman, R.E. & Fisher, R.P. (1989) The cognitive interview technique for victims and witness of crime. In D.C. Raskin (Ed.), *Psychological Methods in Criminal Investigation and Evidence*, pp 191–215. New York: Springer.

Golding, S.L. (1992) Increasing the reliability, validity, and relevance of psychological expert evidence. *Law and Human Behavior*, **16**, 253–256.

Grisso, T. (1986) *Evaluating Competencies Forensic Assessments and Instruments*. New York: Plenum Press.

Grisso, T. (1993) The differences between forensic psychiatry and forensic psychology. *Bulletin of the American Academy of Psychiatry and Law*, **21**, 133–145.

Gudjonsson, G.H. (1984a) The role of the "forensic psychologist" in England and Iceland. *Nordisk Psykologi*, **36**, 256–263.

Gudjonsson, G.H. (1984b) The current status of the psychologist as an expert witness in criminal trials. *Bulletin of the British Psychological Society*, **37**, 80–82.

Gudjonsson, G.H. (1985) Psychological evidence in court: results from the BPS survey. *Bulletin of the British Psychological Society*, **38**, 327–330.

Gudjonsson, G.H. (1986) Criminal court proceedings in England: the contribution of the psychologist as expert witness. *Medicine and Law*, **5**, 395–404.

Gudjonsson, G.H. (1987a) The BPS survey and its implications. In G. Gudjonsson & J. Drinkwater (Eds), *Psychological Evidence in Court*, pp 6–11. Issues in Criminological and Legal Psychology, No. 11. Leicester: British Psychological Society.

Gudjonsson, G.H. (1987b) The significance of depression in the mechanism of compulsive shoplifting. *Medicine, Science and the Law*, **27**, 171–176.

Gudjonsson, G.H. (1991) Forensic psychology: the first century. *Journal of Forensic Psychiatry*, **2**, 129–131.

Gudjonsson, G.H. (1992a) *The Psychology of Interrogation, Confessions and Testimony*. Chichester: John Wiley.

Gudjonsson, G.H. (1992b) The admissibility of expert psychological and psychiatric evidence in England and Wales. *Criminal Behaviour and Mental Health*, **2**, 245–252.

Gudjonsson, G.H. (1993) Confession evidence, psychological vulnerability and expert testimony. *Journal of Community and Applied Social Psychology*, **3**, 117–129.

Gudjonsson, G.H. & MacKeith, J.A.C. (1982) False confessions, psychological effects of interrogation. A discussion paper. In A. Trankell (Ed.), *Reconstructing the Past: The Role of Psychologists in Criminal Trials*, pp 253–269. Holland: Kluwer, Deventer.

Gudjonsson, G.H. & MacKeith, J.A.C. (1988) Retracted confessions: legal, psychological and psychiatric aspects. *Medicine, Science and the Law*, **28**, 187–194.

Gudjonsson, G.H. & MacKeith, J.A.C. (1990) A proven case of false confession: psychological aspects of the coerced-compliant type. *Medicine, Science and the Law*, **30**, 187–194.

Gudjonsson, G.H. & MacKeith, J.A.C. (1994) Learning disability and the Police and Criminal Evidence Act 1984. Protection during investigative interviewing: a video-recorded false confession to double murder. *Journal of Forensic Psychiatry*, **5**, 35–49.

Gudjonsson, G.H. & Sartory, G. (1983) Blood-injury phobia: a "reasonable excuse" for failing to give a specimen in a case of suspected drunken driving. *Journal of the Forensic Science Society*, **23**, 197–201.

Gudjonsson, G.H., Clare, I., Rutter, S. & Pearse, J. (1993) *Persons at Risk During Interviews in Police Custody: The Identification of Vulnerabilities*. Royal Commission on Criminal Justice. London: HMSO.

Gunn, J. & Monahan, J. (1993) Dangerousness. In J. Gunn & P.J. Taylor (Eds), *Forensic Psychiatry. Clinical, Legal and Ethical Issues*, pp. 624–645. Oxford: Butterworth-Heinemann.

Gunn, J. & Taylor, P.J. (Eds) (1993) *Forensic Psychiatry. Clinical, Legal and Ethical Issues*. Oxford: Butterworth-Heinemann.

Haney, C. (1993) Psychology and legal change. *Law and Human Behavior*, **17**, 371–398.

Haward, L.R.C. (1981) *Forensic Psychology*. London: Batsford.

Haward, L.R.C. (1990) *A Dictionary of Forensic Psychology*. Chichester: MediLaw/Barry Rose.

Health Service Guidelines (1993) Criminal Justice Act 1991: Mentally disordered offenders. NHS Management Executive. HSG (93) 49.

House, R.E. (1931) The use of scopolamine in criminology. *American Journal of Police Science*, **2**, 328–336.

Lane, D.A. (1987) Psychological evidence in the juvenile court. In G. Gudjonsson and J. Drinkwater (Eds), *Psychological Evidence in Court*, pp 20–28. Issues in Criminological and Legal Psychology, No. 11. Leicester: British Psychological Society.

Lang, R.A. (1993) Neuropsychological deficits in sexual offenders: implications for treatment. *Sexual and Marital Therapy*, **8**, 181–200.

Leng, R. (1990) Mens rea and the defences to a criminal charge. In R. Bluglass & P. Bowden (Eds), *Principles and Practice of Forensic Psychiatry*, pp 237–250. London: Churchill Livingstone.

Loftus, E. (1979) *Eyewitness Testimony*. London: Harward University Press.

Mackay, R.D. & Coleman, A.M. (1991) Excluding expert evidence: a tale of ordinary folk and common experience. *Criminal Law Review*, 800–810.

Marston, W.M. (1917) Systolic blood pressure changes in deception. *Journal of Experimental Psychology*, **2**, 117–163.

Martell, D.A. (1992) Forensic neuropsychology and the criminal law. *Law and Human Behavior*, **16**, 313–336.

Matarazzo, J.D. (1990) Psychological assessment versus psychological testing. *American Psychologist*, **45**, 999–1017.

McCary, J.L. (1956) The psychologist as an expert witness in court. *American Psychologist*, **11**, 8–13.

Münsterberg, H. (1908) *On the Witness Stand: Essays on Psychology and Crime*. New York: McClure.

Parker, H. (1987) The use of expert reports in juvenile and magistrates' courts. In G. Gudjonsson & J. Drinkwater (Eds), *Psychological Evidence in Court*, pp 15–19 Issues in Criminological and Legal Psychology, No. 11. Leicester: British Psychological Society.

Quen, J.M. (1990) The history of law and psychiatry in America. In R. Bluglass & P. Bowden (Eds), *Principles and Practice of Forensic Psychiatry*, pp 111–116. London: Churchill Livingstone.

Schooler, J.W. & Loftus, E.F. (1986) Individual differences and experimentation: complementary approaches to interrogative suggestibility. *Social Behaviour*, **1**, 105–112.

Schrenck-Notzing, A. (1897) *Uber suggestion und erinnerungsfalschung im berchthold-process*. Leipzig: Johann Ambrosius Barth.

Stern, L.W. (1910) Abstracts of lecturers on the psychology of testimony. *American Journal of Psychology*, **21**, 273–282.

Stone, A.A. (1993) Post-traumatic stress disorder and the law: critical review of the new frontier. *Bulletin of the American Academy of Psychiatry and Law*, **21**, 23–36.

Undeutsch, U. (1989) The development of statement reality analysis. In J.C. Yuille (Ed.), *Credility Assessment*. London: Kluwer Academic.

Weiner, I.B. & Hess, A.K. (1987) *Handbook of Forensic Psychology*. New York: John Wiley.

SERVICE PROVISION

CHAPTER THREE

COMMUNITY-BASED INTERVENTIONS

James McGuire

This chapter has three aims. First, the basic legal framework for community-based interventions with offenders, and the network of agencies designed to provide them, will be outlined. Second, the principal kinds of work which are currently undertaken in the community setting, and research bearing on the question of their effectiveness, will be described. Third, the sizeable gap which currently exists between the two – between the types of work that are possible and would be valuable, and the actual scale of work undertaken – will be considered, and some possible means of reducing it will be suggested.

THE RATIONALE OF IMPRISONMENT

Before embarking on these however, a prior issue will be addressed: that of the relationship between community-based interventions and the usage of imprisonment. The latter, in states which do not have the death penalty or corporal punishments, is the most severe sanction which the courts can dispense. There is a widespread belief that imprisonment is the correct, if not the only possible course of action in response to some types of crime. Yet it is simultaneously acknowledged that custodial sentences have damaging and often counter-productive effects; in that they increase rather than decrease the likelihood that the individual will offend again.

A sentence of imprisonment is imposed, in principle, to deprive the individual

Working with Offenders: Psychological Practice in Offender Rehabilitation.
Edited by C.R. Hollin. © 1996 John Wiley & Sons Ltd.

of his or her freedom; the experience of restriction of liberty in itself is intended to be punitive. Deriving from it there are assumed to be three types of outcome:

1. the immediate one of "incapacitation": so protecting the public at least for the period of the sentence;
2. the direct deterrent effect of the experience on the individual's own behaviour;
3. a general deterrent effect, by which the visible use of prison sustains the law-abiding behaviour of other citizens.

Prison stands, in a sense, as the ultimate symbol of the power of the State to enforce conformity with the law and maintenance of social order.

These three justifications however have little empirical evidence to support them. Regarding the first, it is obvious *de facto* that removal of an individual from circulation means he or she cannot be a danger to members of the public during the period of incarceration. It is less obvious, however, whether marginal increases in the prison population, removing progressively more offenders from the public arena, can have a measurable effect on the overall crime rate, unless the number so dealt with is very large (Tarling, 1993). The resultant prison population would have to increase to a level that would currently be seen as unacceptable both in ethical terms and in its monetary costs.

Concerning the second justification, imprisonment fulfils very few of the criteria known to be necessary for a punisher to be effective as a method of behaviour change (immediacy after the unwanted response; comprehensibility in relation to it, and so on: see Sundel & Sundel, 1993). Further, though most offenders are aware of the possibility of being imprisoned and do not want to be caught, studies of offence motivations or decisions show that the prospect plays little active part in their thinking in the moments immediately prior to an offence (Light, Nee & Ingham, 1993; Morrison & O'Donnell, 1994). It is not surprising therefore that evaluations of the effects of punitive sanctions show them to have a net effect of increasing recidivism (Wooldredge, 1988; Lipsey, 1992).

The third question, as to whether imprisonment acts as a general deterrent, presents a very difficult hypothesis to test. The fact that being imprisoned is universally viewed as an undesirable experience does not in itself confirm it, given the complex interrelationships of the factors which influence criminal behaviour. The most serious penalty of all, the sentence of death, has not been shown to have any clear-cut effect on rates of serious crime. When comparisons have been made between states with or without it, or in which it has been abolished or restored after a period of abstention, no strong evidence emerges of a general deterrent effect (Hood, 1989).

In any case the view, popularized by sections of the media, that most people want severe penalties to follow from criminal behaviour, is not supported by more systematic survey research. Questions concerning this issue were asked in the British Crime Survey of 1984. The sentences respondents (many of whom had been victims of crime) thought suitable were not dissimilar to the actual sentencing practices of the courts, and if anything they were marginally more lenient (Hough & Mayhew, 1985). Other studies too have shown that, while there is support for punishment, this is associated with its supposed rehabilitative effects, and not simply for retribution (Cullen Cullen & Wozniak, 1988). A strong wish of most individuals, having suffered a theft or an assault, is simply that it should not happen again either to themselves or to other people. Here the fundamental question becomes: what will achieve this aim? In searching for an answer to this, the use of community-based interventions offers a number of important advantages.

ADVANTAGES OF COMMUNITY-BASED SANCTIONS

The first is that they are closer to the actual situations, and especially the interpersonal milieux, in which the offence occurred. The realities of the individual's environment, and other problems which are causally associated with offending are present and operational. This may sound as if it would make reoffending more likely. But a larger proportion of the individual's transactions will be with non-offenders than would be the case in prison. Community-based interventions thus provide important prerequisites for programmes of behavioural or personal change. First, in familiar surroundings, the person who has been involved in crime can make more accurate, or at least better informed, estimates of the likely outcomes of selected courses of action. It is commonly observed that in institutions, the human tendency to make unrealistic predictions of behaviour becomes even more pronounced. The more distant any set of demands, such as pressures to reoffend, the less potent they are likely to appear. Second, alongside this, imprisonment has the ironic effect of allowing individuals to escape the consequences of, and responsibility for, their actions. Preoccupied with their own discomfort, prisoners can more easily avoid thoughts of the distress they have caused others. Finally, from a psychological perspective, opportunities for real learning and skills practice are much more restricted in a custodial setting. Many structured interventions offering the prospect of behaviour change are dependent on the availability of opportunities for reality testing and obtaining feedback. In the community context, this is available with virtually immediate impact.

A second advantage of community-based working is the presence or proximity of social supports, in the form of spouses, partners, relatives or friends. Again, some of them may be the sources of problems, or be obstacles to progress and change. But even if this is so, in the majority of cases temporary removal from them simply postpones rather than averts the recurrence of difficulties. Too often, imprisonment severs links with social supports and makes meaningful rehabilitation more difficult.

Third, and this factor is in many ways a pivotal one in the recent evolution of policy, community interventions cost significantly less than any work done in institutions. The cost of community supervision works out, on average, at approximately one-twentieth that of imprisonment (Home Office, 1993).

Finally, as will be discussed more fully below, large-scale integrative reviews of research on offender "treatment" (e.g. Lipsey, 1992, 1995) suggest that interventions located in the community are more likely to be effective in reducing reoffence rates than those conducted in penal institutions. Such findings do not as yet permit the drawing of firm conclusions concerning the reasons for this difference. It is a reasonable hypothesis, however, that some of the factors recited above are likely to play a part.

THE SENTENCING FRAMEWORK AND COMMUNITY PENALTIES

Most of the modes of dealing with individuals convicted of offences that are now in use in the UK have been established or revised by the Criminal Justice Act of 1991, which came into force in October 1992. The Act has since been amended and extended by the Criminal Justice Acts of 1993 and 1994, and in a Green Paper in early 1995 the government proposed a further series of adjustments to the range of community penalties available (Home Office, 1995). The 1991 Act, however, created the presently existing framework of sentencing, and replaced large sections of previous legislation affecting the placement of offenders in the community, such as the Criminal Justice Acts of 1972, 1982 and 1988, and the Powers of Criminal Courts Act 1973 (Wasik & Taylor, 1991). It also altered or augmented crucial sections of the Children and Young Persons Acts of 1933 and 1969. It furnishes, within one frame-work, a wide range of sentencing options, which, whether custodial or non-custodial, are seen mainly as forms of punishment. The principal courses of action through which an offender may remain in the community will each be briefly described.

1. Discharge. Dealing with relatively minor offences a court may deem that it is "inexpedient to inflict punishment" and may discharge the offender (absolutely, or conditionally upon no further offence being committed for a predetermined period of up to three years).
2. Suspended sentence. Where a sentence of not more than two years' imprisonment might be imposed, the court may suspend it. In other words, immediate imprisonment is not enacted but held back subject to the individual's avoidance of further law breaking within a fixed period. Prior to 1991, the sentence could be "partly suspended" and partly served; this option was abolished by the 1991 Act. A suspended sentence may be combined with financial penalties and such a course of action is recommended.
3. Fines and compensation orders. These are financial penalties and may be imposed for a wide range of offences; the former are payable to the court, the latter through the court to the victim of the offence. For all offences concerned, fines are subject to fixed maximum amounts. Prior to 1992, the amount of a fine could be varied by courts according to the seriousness of the offence, though it was also influenced by the offender's known ability to pay. In the Criminal Justice Act 1991 a new principle of unit fines was introduced. This allowed the amount of the fine to be calculated in relation to the offender's income, i.e. through a form of "means testing", as used in many other European countries. Following adverse publicity in 1993, however, this system was abandoned.

None of the above measures is likely to involve any direct work with offenders (with the exception of a very small number placed on suspended sentence supervision orders). Currently however a number of options exist for courts under the explicit heading of "community sentences", and here a range of more directly "interventionist" strategies may be adopted. These sentences include the following.

1. Supervision order. This is a form of community intervention designed for younger offenders, aged between 10 and 17. The order may run for up to three years. The present form of it stems from the Children and Young Person's Act 1969 and the Criminal Justice Act 1982. The 1991 Act incorporated a number of revisions. The order may include provision for intermediate treatment, or participation in specified activities organized by juvenile justice workers. It may also include residence requirements in local authority accommodation, compulsory education, night curfews, or medical treatment.
2. Community service order. Here the offender (from age 14 upwards) is

required to undertake, for a fixed number of hours, some form of unpaid work that will be of value to the community. Schemes of this sort are managed and supervised by staff of the probation service and the hours served may be raised by the courts up to a specified maximum.

3. Probation order. Now available for offenders aged 16 and over, probation has traditionally been, in formal terms, an alternative to a sentence, to which the offender had to give consent. In the Criminal Justice Act of 1991, though consent was still required, the usage of probation became a sentence in itself. The offender is required to report to a supervising officer, a qualified social worker, on a regular basis for a fixed period of between six months and three years.

4. Probation order with additional requirements. Since 1972 probation orders could include added stipulations, for example that the individual should attend a day centre, for a fixed period of time. In the 1982 Criminal Justice Act these "additional requirements" were extended to include attendance at "specified activities" thought to be in the offender's interests and to help him or her address problems linked to offending. These options were further formalized in the Criminal Justice Act of 1991. "Additional requirements" placed on probation clients may include a broad variety of conditions, for example that they accept psychiatric medication, attend a treatment centre for drug or alcohol dependency, or participate in a therapeutic group focused on sexual offences.

5. Combination order. Also in the 1991 Act, a new form of combined order was created, in which community service (of up to 100 hours) and probation (with a minimum one-year order), potentially including various specified activities, could be assembled together in a package thought suitable to the individual offender/client.

6. Curfew order. The 1991 Act also consolidated and extended forms of sentence in which the movements of offenders could be restricted whilst in the community. Existing legislation already allowed this in certain respects, such as night restriction orders, or prohibitions from entering certain licensed premises or football grounds. Thus individuals could be required to remain in certain locations or to avoid others, within specified times. For the new curfew order, it was initially envisaged that checks on individuals' movements could be made through technical innovations like electronic monitoring, which has been extensively used in the USA. Following pilot studies in three sites however, in which this was tested with individuals subject to bail conditions, reports proved unfavourable (Mair & Nee, 1990); courts appeared unimpressed and there were numerous technical problems. The option of using "tags" remains open for sentencing purposes but has not as yet been implemented in practice.

7. Attendance centre order. This is a requirement (introduced by the Criminal Justice Act of 1982) which may be imposed on offenders aged 10

to adult, that they regularly report to an attendance centre (run by the police or other agencies) at specified times each week. The 1991 Act raised the maximum attendance time that could be required of 16 year olds, bringing it into line with that for 17 year olds. This type of order has been principally used with juveniles, but its usage has declined slightly since 1981. In 1991, 8200 such orders were made.

The governmental impetus which created the present framework of community sentences was directly and unreservedly punitive. The guiding principle of the policy which led to the creation of the 1991 Act was that of "just deserts". In less colloquial terms this is sometimes called the principle of "proportionality", that the severity of the sentence should be matched to the seriousness of the crime. But many courses of action contain rehabilitative elements, usually based on forms of social work intervention. In some penalties, the notion of making reparation to society is still present even if only at an implicit level. Other measures are designed purely and simply to monitor or limit the individual's movements. Each of these measures is rooted in very different, sometimes conflicting, admixtures of ethical principles and basic approaches to crime, indeed to human behaviour generally. The philosophical basis of criminal justice is in little less than a profoundly confused state.

Conceptual muddles notwithstanding, many more cases are dealt with in the community than through custodial sentencing. In 1991 for example (the most recently available criminal statistics at the time of writing), 68 000 persons convicted of criminal offences were given sentences of immediate imprisonment. The corresponding number given non-custodial sentences was 1 421 600 (Home Office, 1992). The ratio of non-custodial to custodial sentences was therefore of the order of 20:1.

In that same year, 102 000 persons were given conditional discharges, 28 100 were given fully suspended sentences, 42 500 were given community service orders, and 47 500 probation orders. Of the last, a large majority (76%) carried no additional requirements. However, 4473 individuals were made subject to "specified activity" requirements, and a further 3030 were required to attend probation (day) centres. A total of 942 persons were required to reside in approved probation hostels; 801 were required to undergo non-residential, and 121 residential psychiatric treatment. In late 1990 in the USA, 2 670 234 adults were on probation orders.

PRINCIPAL SERVICES AND AGENCIES

The main agencies and associated personnel involved in community provision for those who have committed criminal offences are as follows.

1. Probation services. The origins of probation go back to the mid-nineteenth century when charitable work was undertaken to rescue offenders from the full wrath of the criminal courts, and in recognition of the personal needs and hardships which had contributed to their breaking the law. The possibility of working with individuals in this way was put on a formal footing in Massachusetts in 1878, and subsequently extended throughout and beyond the USA. Today in England and Wales, there are 55 probation services, covering (with a few exceptions such as Inner London) areas corresponding to county divisions. They vary considerably in size, from a few dozen to several hundred trained probation officers. Each provides the same services, which include: preparation of pre-sentence reports; through-care and after-care of prisoners; after-care of mentally disordered offenders discharged from hospitals (Mace, 1991); supervision of probation orders; organization of community service schemes; running probation centres, some of which offer "drop-in" facilities for homeless, rootless clients, others with structured group activities (many offering both). National standards have been established for the quality assurance of these services. Probation staff also run hostels, employment schemes, and a range of other specialized activities such as outdoor pursuits, offence-focused groups and therapeutic groupwork. While most probation work is with offenders, a proportion of civil court work is also undertaken, in providing family court welfare services.

2. Social services departments. These are financed and run by local authorities and provide a wide range of services to families, children, people with sensory or learning disabilities, the elderly and so on. They are also jointly responsible with the probation service for preparation of court reports and provision of services for juvenile offenders. The latter may take the form of statutory supervision, including programmes of intermediate treatment. This requires young people to attend for a fixed number of hours and participate in a timetable of prearranged activities. The programmes are usually located in juvenile justice centres, but these also offer a variety of services, such as links with schools, to help those whose education has been disrupted to return; home tuition schemes where this is not possible; accommodation for those estranged from families; resource centres with a range of educational and leisure facilities; individual counselling; work with families, including family therapy; and a number of other specialized interventions. Young persons aged 16 or 17 are now (since the 1991 Act) subject to the principle of "flexible jurisdiction". This means that they may be supervised either by juvenile justice agencies or by the probation service (on supervision or probation orders respectively), depending on their perceived level of maturity.

3. Addictions centres and units. These are specialized services run by National Health Service Trusts or district health authorities and are

staffed by a range of medical and allied personnel, including psychiatrists, community psychiatric nurses and occupational therapists; but also social workers and clinical psychologists. Their focus is upon problems of substance abuse, which may involve alcohol, heroin, cocaine, amphetamines, antidepressants and numerous other chemicals. This may involve direct hospitalization of clients or provision of physical medical care. A number of the units run "needle exchange" schemes for regular drug users in an attempt to control the spread of HIV infection. Apart from use of controlled drugs in itself, and acts committed in attempting to obtain them, a significant proportion of those who attend addictions centres have committed other criminal offences. There are thus close links between these agencies and courts, probation and other services.

4. Community forensic psychiatry services. These are also financed and run by NHS Trusts or district health authorities and have close links with courts, probation and related agencies. Their client group is offenders thought to be suffering from mental disorder as defined by the Mental Health Act 1983. Again, they are multi-disciplinary in professional make-up. Psychiatry could be described as the "lead profession"; other staff generally include clinical psychologists, community psychiatric nurses and social workers. Most services of this kind also operate secure wards or units in local hospitals, known as regional secure units, which were established following the recommendations of the Butler report (Home Office & DHSS, 1975). Nationally in the UK, approximately 650 beds are available in such units, though there are plans for this number to expand as a result of recommendations made by a recent joint review of services by the Department of Health and the Home Office (1992). However, the possibility that at some stage a new form of order may be introduced, for the compulsory treatment of mentally disordered offenders in the community, has also been under consideration by the Department of Health.

   The range of duties carried out by forensic psychiatry services has been described by Higgins (1991). They carry out specialized assessments and prepare reports for courts. They also provide community-based treatment, which may include medication, psychological therapies, nursing interventions and family work. A number have specialized programmes for sex offenders, in some cases also run jointly with probation services. A number of health regions also operate diversion schemes through which attempts are made to detect mental disorder or the need for psychiatric intervention at an early stage, for example, in police cells within hours of arrest. Early reports on such schemes suggest they have already proven their value in this respect (Tonak & Cawdron, 1988; Cooke, 1995).

5. Voluntary organizations. The above has described statutory services and agencies (funded through direct taxation by central or local authorities, separately or in some financial combination). However, many services are

also provided by voluntary organizations, which are supported in whole or in part by charitable contributions. These may consist simply of accommodation and catering for basic needs, but many organizations also provide employment, counselling, detoxification, alcohol education, and a variety of other services depending on the needs of specific client groups.

The organization of these various agencies differs slightly from one part of the UK to another. The above descriptions apply directly to England and Wales. In Scotland, there is at present no separate probation agency; all social work functions including offender services are performed by unitary agencies, the nine regional social work departments though these are being re-organized into smaller units from April, 1996. Juvenile justice is organized along different lines. There are no juvenile courts as such; instead, a wide range of problems involving children, including delinquency, are examined in the less formal setting of children's hearings, staffed on a voluntary basis by members of the public. In Northern Ireland, probation is run by a separate authority, the Probation Board for Northern Ireland, covering the entire province. Other services are administered conjointly by three Health and Social Services Boards covering separate parts of the province.

It is frequently acknowledged that the above agencies do not always work together as well as they might. In a system of services so complex, the intricacies of which vary between different local areas, some mistakes are probably very difficult to avoid. Proposals have recently been made by central government for better partnership strategies in community provision for offenders (Home Office, 1990). One suggestion put forward has been that the probation service might be instrumental as a core agency in a new pattern of provision, acting in a coordinating role, and serving a "brokerage" function. Thus, court reports would be prepared on a statutory footing, but subsequent services would be delivered as a form of tailor-made "package", different components of which were provided by specialized agencies or units as appropriate in each individual case.

In other countries forms of service organization vary enormously. The USA has both state and federal probation agencies, with different remits and powers depending on the nature of the criminal violation. Thus probation in Chicago, for example, is administered by four separate departments. Canada, Australia and other predominantly English-speaking countries have probation and juvenile justice services similar to British or American models. Most countries of continental Europe have similar forms of provision, though there are marked differences between northern and southern European states in this respect.

MINIMAL INTERVENTION

Before considering the nature of community interventions as such, a more fundamental issue needs to be addressed, and this is the radical one of whether or not to "intervene" at all. If it is accepted that experience of criminal justice networks has the capacity to increase offence rates, then any prolonged interference in the lives of offenders confronts us with a potentially serious dilemma.

A number of very influential criminal justice policies have originated from the application of the "labelling" perspective in sociological theory. This is not a theoretical account of the origins of crime, but rather of its maintenance and "amplification". According to this view, the formal adjudication of offenders has a number of destructive social and intrapersonal effects. It is accompanied by a process of stigmatization which in turn produces changes in attitudes and self-definition. As a result of this, so the argument runs, the individual feels farther separated from society than before, and consequently is more rather than less prone to offend (Lilly, Cullen & Ball, 1989).

Such a standpoint has some far-reaching implications for the organization of criminal justice. It has led to a range of proposals including:

1. *decriminalization* of some behaviours (such as possession of cannabis or soliciting by prostitutes) by their removal from the purview of the criminal law;
2. *non-intervention* or minimal intervention, taking action to avoid drawing young offenders into criminal justice processes (Schur, 1973).

In practical terms, these proposals have had a variety of effects. One has been a call for the extended use of police *cautioning*. Police may exercise discretion in deciding whether or not offenders should be prosecuted. The alternative is a formal warning given to the offender by a senior police officer; in the case of juveniles, in the presence of their parents. The numbers of persons cautioned increased steadily between 1981 and 1991. However, there were marked variations in its use in different police areas. Where used most extensively, cautioning has been successful in achieving the aim of reducing the harmful impact of more punitive sanctions, particularly on younger offenders.

A second development is the process of *diversion* from the criminal justice system (which as noted above is now also used with mentally disordered offenders). Diversion has been in use in the USA since it was initially proposed by the President's Commission on Law Enforcement and Administration of Justice in 1967. Its effects on a number of outcome variables including recidivism have been evaluated by meta-analyses reported by Gensheimer et al. (1986) and by Whitehead & Lab (1989). The former carried out an analysis of 44 studies of programmes formally called "diversion", but some of which focused on adjudicated youth and took place within criminal justice agencies. Overall, while there was some evidence of behavioural and attitudinal change amongst programme participants, no convincing evidence emerged of any clear effects on recidivism. It should be noted that in the majority of the programmes, there was very little contact (an average of 15 hours over four months) between offenders and service personnel; but there was a significant relationship between hours of contact and effect size. Whitehead & Lab (1989) analysed 50 studies of "correctional treatments" including 30 focused on diversion schemes. Again, there was no clear-cut effect on recidivism. Although 24 of the programmes obtained positive effects, in most this was on a fairly minor scale, though it was judged to be significant (effect size greater than 0.2) in 10 studies. Somewhat confounding the non-interventionist argument, more success was achieved among "system-based" than in "non-system-based" diversion projects. An equally important finding of this study was that of seven institutionally based programmes examined, three produced significant increases in recidivism.

Thus even within avowedly "non-interventionist" strategies, some form of offender/service contact often takes place. The relatively weak effects observed may, it is plausible to argue, be due to the limited scale of such contacts. This is not to argue for greater agency involvement, as this in itself is by no means guaranteed to help; in its stronger forms it may do more harm. What matters much more is the nature and content of any work done. Clearer guidelines as to the components of effective community interventions can only be obtained by examining a wider range of methods.

APPROACHES TO INTERVENTION

SOCIAL CASEWORK

The longest standing and most extensively practised of these is probably social casework counselling. As noted above, the majority of personnel employed in probation and juvenile justice services are professionally trained in social work.

The principle underlying such work is a sound one, in that it is assumed that individuals who commit offences are beset by numerous other problems in living. Survey work with both community and prison populations supplies abundant evidence that this is certainly the case for a large proportion of persistent offenders (McWilliams, 1975; Priestley et al., 1984). It seems a reasonable approach therefore to address such difficulties and attempt to remedy them. Thus social work provision has been directed at "welfare" issues and the delivery of both immediate and long-term help, focused on employment, family, health and other personal problems. This is both valuable in itself and may have the added by-product of reducing offence-proneness.

But apart from direct practical help in solving such problems, for example by helping clients negotiate with bureaucracies over social security payments, social casework has consisted predominantly of individual counselling processes rooted in personal change models of working. Until approximately the 1970s this was influenced and informed by psychodynamic ideas, but later these were supplanted by person-centred approaches derived from the work of Carl Rogers. A wide range of psychotherapies, from transactional analysis to personal construct counselling, have been imported into social work and have been adapted by individual workers for a range of specific purposes.

Regrettably, few systematic evaluations exist of the social casework model applied to offender populations. A number of early studies in the USA reported uniformly negative results (Gordon & Arbuthnot, 1987). One controlled experimental trial in the UK showed significant effects on recidivism when casework was tested in a prison setting (Shaw, 1974), but a later replication did not obtain similar results (Fowles, 1978). Another experimental trial which involved the matching of clients to workers in a "differential treatment" paradigm also yielded disappointing outcomes (Folkard, Smith & Smith, 1976).

Available evaluations of casework in community settings have focused mainly upon its application with mental health problems. Russell (1990) has reviewed this literature and described the evolution of casework over the past two decades. Earlier evaluations by Fischer (1973, 1978) showed casework to be a very loosely defined enterprise, focused predominantly on intrapsychic processes. This was somewhat paradoxical as its principal applications were amongst clients whose primary problems were social deprivation and associated environmental difficulties. Little evidence could be adduced, therefore, for its effectiveness, though most research reports combined cases of different types (including offenders) making clear conclusions difficult to draw.

In response to criticisms by Fischer and others, social casework gradually became more structured, incorporating for example greater use of behavioural and cognitive–behavioural methods (Rubin, 1985; Sheldon, 1987, 1994). One example of this is the task-centred casework approach of Reid & Epstein (1977). This incorporates goal analysis, planning, modelling, practice and other methods which parallel those used in social learning-based interventions. A study by Goldberg, Stanley & Kenrich (1985) evaluated this method with probation clients, and found both greater consumer satisfaction and moderately reduced levels of recidivism amongst this group compared with others subject to standard methods of supervision.

There are tentative findings then that individual casework has the capacity to bring about change, but is more likely to do so when clearly formulated, focused methods are imported into it. In general, individual counselling does not fare well when placed alongside other forms of work in meta-analytic reviews. For example, Lipsey (1992, 1995) found that while it had a positive effect in reducing recidivism, this was comparatively slight in extent and considerably less than that obtained from more structured, learning-based approaches. A partial explanation for this may be found in what Andrews et al. (1990) have called the "responsivity principle". Unstructured, non-directive approaches, the distant roots of which are in dynamic psychotherapies, may simply be inappropriate for the learning styles of individuals who are not mentally disordered, do not have intrapsychic problems but are beset by numerous everyday stressors. Neither in-depth self-analysis nor loosely formed group discussion will be seen by such individuals as relevant to their needs. More active, problem-solving strategies are required, a proposal borne out by the majority of evaluations now available.

STRUCTURED PROGRAMMES

More highly structured forms of community interventions however show a considerable diversity within themselves. They have varied according to their targets of change, selected client groups, application setting, and method of evaluation. The following are some of the principal forms such programmes have taken in practice.

Psycho-educational Programmes

A number of programmes can be described as having a primary aim of increasing individuals' knowledge where this was thought to be a factor in their difficulties, including their risk of offending. In some instances this could be described as aimed at "damage limitation" where larger scale change was thought to be unlikely. The most commonly undertaken work of this kind is alcohol education which is very widely used in both community and institutional settings (Baldwin, 1990).

In an evaluation of a drink-driving project for probationers in Greater Manchester, McGuire et al. (1995) reported positive short-term effects of such a programme on alcohol knowledge, self-esteem, self-rated control and attitudes to drinking and driving. These differences were significant for the programme participants whilst no change was observed amongst a comparison group matched on numbers of previous convictions.

Evidence of the longer term value of such work comes from a study by Jamieson & Stone (1991) of educational programmes for DWI (driving-while-intoxicated) offenders. This reported a success rate of 88.8% (no reoffence) over a two-year follow-up period after participation in such schemes. No control group comparison was made, but standard predictions for this type of offence would uniformly indicate a high expected rate of recurrence.

Skills Training Activities

Given that many offenders are known to experience multiple problems in economic, social and other respects, many intervention programmes focus on development of skills or problem-solving capacities which will ameliorate these stresses. Work of this kind has taken many forms, including programmes of social skills training, enhancement of leisure skills and opportunities, and job search workshops. Some of this work was surveyed by Hudson (1986) who noted its considerable diversity, a reliance on client feedback as a main form of evaluation, and the absence of more systematic attempts to gather other types of information on behaviour change.

Many informal reports exist on the development and running of such programmes, but they are not published in research journals and in any case rarely involve controlled research designs or external evaluations. In one larger scale evaluation, Priestley et al. (1984) showed that the establishment of such a "life skills" programme in a probation day centre significantly reduced the client absenteeism rate (from 30% to 5%) over successive intake groups. A one-year follow-up found improved employment records of participants, and a slight but non-significant drop in reoffending rates for the day centre groups as compared with Home Office prediction tables.

Offending Behaviour Programmes

Work of this variety takes the offence committed by an individual as its starting point. This is based on two interrelated arguments. First, it is this behaviour and no other which has caused the individual to come to the attention of the law. Given then that it is the primary reason for official processing and invasion of his or her life, it is (at least initially) the only issue on which workers have any entitlement to focus. Second, attempts to alter any form of behaviour are more likely to be successful if they direct their effort at that behaviour itself (McGuire & Priestley, 1985). Neither of these arguments excludes the possibility of addressing other problems if assessment shows them to be associated with offending or of concern to individuals themselves.

Offence-focused work based on these arguments has been widely practised in a number of community agencies in the UK, especially in probation and juvenile justice settings. For the most part this work is carried out with small groups of clients, and forms part of supervision in Probation Orders with additional requirements. Most groups of this kind contain individuals who have committed a variety of offences, and activities focus on general factors influencing their behaviour, and which they may be able to change.

However, many variants on this approach have been developed, in which there is a specific focus on one type of offence. Examples of this are anger-control groups for violence; programmes addressed at shop theft or burglary; projects focusing on car crime; and groups dealing with aspects of sexual offending. Numerous internal documents have been written in the respective agencies in which such work has been undertaken, most describing purposeful participation by clients, and reporting positive end-of-session feedback. However, no systematic, controlled studies have been undertaken of this work and no follow-up data concerning recidivism have been collected, although short-term effects of placement in sex offender treatment have been studied by Beckett, Beech, Fisher and Fordham (1994).

Cognitive Skills Training

In a wide-ranging review of research on highly convicted offenders, Ross & Fabiano (1985) contended that the single factor most frequently differentiating such groups from others was a failure of cognitive skills. Persistent offenders, it was argued, were more prone to act impulsively; to be rigid in their thinking; to fail to consider alternatives, or to anticipate the consequences of their actions. Similarly, a meta-analysis comparing programmes with and without cognitive components showed the former to be significantly more effective than the latter in reducing recidivism (Izzo & Ross, 1990). Based on these conclusions, the authors developed a 35-session programme of cognitive skills exercises, entitled "Reasoning and Rehabilitation", which contained work not only on problem solving but also on social skills, self-control, moral education and critical reasoning (Ross & Fabiano, 1990). This was tested in a pilot experiment in probation services in Ontario (Ross, Fabiano & Ewles, 1988), yielding nine-month follow-up data which showed that probationers given this training had significantly lower reconviction rates than comparison groups given life skills training or regular probation supervision.

This programme is now under test at a large number of sites both in North America and in Europe, principally within probation services though a number of other agencies, and especially prison establishments, are also engaged in pilot studies. Knott (1995) has described preliminary results which are highly encouraging from its application in Mid-Glamorgan probation service, where more than 150 clients were placed on the programme in an 18-month period in 1992–1993. Despite significantly higher risk of conviction scores, an index of likelihood of future reoffending, at the outset (nearly twice that of comparison groups), the trained group showed lower reoffence rates at a one-year follow-up. By late 1993, no fewer than 13 probation areas in England and Wales were undertaking pilot work with this programme (McGuire, 1995). In a few cases, preliminary data showed encouraging downward trends in reoffending in favour of the programme. Regrettably, however, in a majority of areas no systematic data gathering was being conducted, evaluation being based on client feedback only.

A number of other programmes exist which combine elements of social skills training, self-control training and moral values enhancement in an integrated multi-modal "package". They include, for example, Aggression Replacement Training, which as its name suggests has been used with violent offenders (Goldstein et al., 1986; Goldstein & Keller, 1987), and has recently yielded encouraging outcomes from work based with street gangs in New York City (Goldstein et al., 1994).

Intensive Probation and Smart Sentencing

Throughout the 1980s in both the USA and in Britain, there was a steady revival of the "neo-classical" approach to criminal justice. Based on the 18th century theory of crime as rational calculation, this view asserted that increasing the costs of law breaking to the offender was the most likely route to reducing criminal behaviour. At the same time, it was seen as important to reduce the heavy financial burden of incarceration. Attempts to solve this problem led, in due course, to the development of probation programmes involving intensive supervision; and in some instances to community-based procedures which were closely akin to institutional punishment. This so-called "justice model" was associated with a reaffirmation of punishment as a viable, desirable and effective response to crime, and led to a search for improved methods of surveillance and control. While it is well established that 80% of probation orders are completed satisfactorily, it is also recognized that a proportion of the remaining clients are responsible for a disproportionate number of reoffences or returns to court. It was for this "high-risk" group that new measures were sought, coupled with potential savings by reducing the prison inmate population.

One outcome of this was the advent of personal telemonitoring or electronic tagging which had been first piloted as early as 1964. It appeared to offer the prospect of maintaining high-risk offenders in the community by confining their movements to home. Following the dramatic expansion of such schemes in the United States in the 1980s, early enthusiasm (Gable, 1986) was dampened by fuller consideration of their relative cost–benefits, and more moderate pronouncements were called for (Baumer & Mendelsohn, 1992). As noted above, recent British studies have raised similar doubts (Mair & Nee, 1990).

In parallel with this, however, many other developments in probation were advocated and developed. Variously known as "intermediate sanctions" or "smart sentencing", these measures included short initial periods in custody, home arrest, intensive supervision, day reporting centres and reparative work projects. Cumulatively, they may be seen as products of the twin pressures of the search for financial savings in criminal justice and the ideological shift towards more punitive sanctions. Evaluative findings to date, however, have not been encouraging, and in many ways reinforce a point to be made more fully below: "The available evidence points towards a renewed awareness of the importance of offender treatment as a recidivism reduction strategy and the futility of simply increasing the level of offender surveillance and/or control" (Byrne & Pattavina, 1992, p. 300; see also McIvor, 1990). These caveats notwithstanding, there is evidence that such programmes have succeeded in diverting individuals from custody, and have managed them at significantly lower cost than imprisonment (Pearson, 1988; Brownlee & Joanes, 1993). A more systematic large-scale evaluation has however called even this into doubt. Petersilia & Turner (1993) found that the costs of these programmes were sometimes surprisingly high. Furthermore, there was no evidence that they had any impact on recidivism, and the only effects of this kind obtained were in programmes which contained a significant "treatment" component, especially drugs-related counselling services.

Physical Challenge and "Wilderness" Programmes

Despite many anecdotal reports concerning the value of outdoor pursuit and adventure-type programmes for offenders, available systematic evaluations are both sparse and unencouraging. These projects have been justified on the grounds that they promote personal growth and increase self-confidence.

Reviews, however, suggest these gains are fairly short-lived, and no changes in levels of reoffending have been reported (Winterdyk & Roesch, 1981; Palmer, 1992).

Victim–Offender Mediation and Reparation

Programmes of this kind are based on a different set of assumptions from many of the interventions considered so far. They are planned, not simply as alternatives to custody, but as alternatives to criminal law; testing the proposal that victims and offenders may be able to resolve the damage done by crime within the framework of civil law. Unfortunately, like several of the innovations already described, existing schemes have not been rigorously evaluated, and available studies have not provided much positive support (Hughes & Schneider, 1989). Doubts have been expressed concerning the possibility of extending these principles to more than a minority of offences. To the extent that work of this kind continues, it is carried out on the initiative of interested workers as no legislative framework exists for it; the possibility of extending it in the UK was excluded from the 1991 Criminal Justice Act. While many apparently promising ventures of this kind have been launched, a "credibility gap" in having them incorporated into official policy appears to block their further development in many countries (Snare, 1993).

OVERALL RESEARCH OUTCOMES

The question of whether or not it is possible to influence those who persistently offend, and reduce rates of reoffending, has been a recurrent one since reviews by Martinson (1974) and Brody (1976) questioned whether anything could "work" in this respect. Both these authors offered pessimistic conclusions on the basis of research they had reviewed. Much of it suffered from serious methodological flaws, but even so the net finding was stated to be that little or nothing proved effective. In the 20 years since these papers were published, this view has become an almost unshakeable belief in the minds of many working in criminological and penal settings.

A number of authors who have commented on these early reviews have however recorded marked disagreement with their conclusions (Palmer, 1975; Blackburn, 1980; Gendreau & Ross, 1980, 1987; McGuire & Priestley, 1985, 1992; Thornton, 1987), and one of the early reviewers later revised his own initially negative position (Martinson, 1979). In addition, since 1985, a number of meta-analyses have been conducted which have provided a more comprehensive and penetrating survey of previous research work (Garrett, 1985; Gottschalk et al., 1987; Lösel & Koferl, 1989; Whitehead & Lab, 1989;

Izzo & Ross, 1990; Andrews et al., 1990; Lipsey, 1992). These reviews suggest, in contrast to the 1970s statements, that interventions overall have a net positive effect on recidivism, by reducing it on average by 10–12% as compared with non-treatment control groups. This "effect size" can be increased if a number of other requirements of interventions programmes are met, with reductions in follow-up delinquency rates in some cases up to 50%.

Broadly speaking, programmes are more likely to be effective if they are targeted on higher risk offenders, following what Andrews et al. (1986) call the "risk principle". They are more likely to focus on "criminogenic needs" or factors which are closely associated with offence behaviour; Andrews and colleagues (1990; Gendreau & Andrews, 1991) call this the "needs principle". Activities which are more structured and more directive correspond more closely with the learning styles of most offenders than do open-ended, non-directive counselling approaches. This in turn is known as the "responsivity principle". Interventions are more likely to work if participants are helped to secure employment, or if they use a range of techniques to help individuals acquire social or cognitive skills for solving real-life problems. Of the various "treatment modalities" examined in the reviews, those utilizing cognitive–behavioural methods emerge as producing more effective outcomes. Finally, on balance, programmes located in community settings fare better than those based in penal institutions (Andrews et al., 1990; Wooldredge, 1988).

Another very important point concerning the design of intervention programmes has been made by Palmer (1992). Most offenders are faced with multiple problems which Palmer classifies into three groups. Group A comprises skill/capacity deficits, developmental or social skills difficulties in educational, vocational, or interpersonal domains. Group B consists of external pressures and disadvantages, including family or community stressors or lack of support. Group C are internal difficulties, such as aspects of self-perceptions, attitudes or personal commitments, which may hinder change. To make these points is not to adopt the medical model, nor to pathologize the individual, but simply to recognize difficulties he or she is encountering which may be conducive to crime. To the list of programme features given above, therefore, Palmer adds the "breadth principle", the view that programmes with multiple components, if properly designed, are more likely to be effective than those with a single "active ingredient" only.

Promising results in accordance with this proposal have been obtained in outcome studies of work with sex offenders. Combined cognitive–behavioural programmes, incorporating a range of ingredients and addressed towards a number of separate change "targets", have been shown to offer the best prospects of reducing reoffending amongst this group (Dwyer & Myers, 1990;

Miner et al, 1990; Marshall et al., 1991). The Miner et al. study in particular underlines the importance of community-based relapse prevention work with this group.

SPECIFIC PSYCHO-SOCIAL INTERVENTIONS

From the list given earlier, it can be seen that many apparently useful forms of work are currently being undertaken with offenders in community settings. For a proportion of them, there is independent evidence that they have an impact in helping individuals to solve problems, and in reducing their rates of reoffence. But a glance at the approaches listed also shows that to date, only a small portion of the potential of psycho-social interventions has been actively put into service by criminal justice practitioners. Many other interventions for which there is supportive evaluation evidence have scarcely been exploited at all.

There is considerable evidence, for example, that behaviour modification methods can be applied effectively to the reduction of offence-related behaviours. These have more often been used in institutions where greater control is possible over the environment (Hollin, 1993). Nevertheless a number of studies have obtained positive outcomes when these methods have been applied in community locations. Such methods include contingent reinforcement (Miller et al., 1974), covert self-punishment contingencies (Guidry, 1975), covert modelling (Hay, Hay & Nelson, 1977), self-reinforcement (Stumphauzer, 1976), contingency contracts (Welch, 1985) and covert sensitization, used in work with sexual offenders against children (Brownell, Hayes & Barlow, 1977; Harbert et al., 1974). Studies of contingency contracts in probation by Polakow & Doctor (1973, 1974) and Polakow & Peabody (1975) showed not only that this was effective in reducing offence behaviours such as illegitimate drug use and child abuse, but also that it proved more effective than intensive supervision on a number of outcome variables. In a slightly different vein, a study of youths convicted of vandalism used restitution (repair of damage done) alongside a skills training programme, and showed significant reductions in reoffending for a moderate-risk group (Hauber, 1989).

While recognizing the potential of behaviour modification methods and the receptiveness of probation staff to them, Remington & Remington (1987) have indicated limitations on their usage. One requirement is for more thorough training in such approaches if these staff groups are to implement them on a regular basis. There are clear possibilities here for collaboration between probation or other criminal justice personnel and psychologists who have prior training in the use of the methods.

Behaviour therapy techniques of relaxation and systematic desensitization have been effectively directed towards a number of offence-related behaviours such as alcohol problems (Lanyon et al., 1972; Hedberg & Campbell, 1974), sexual exhibitionism (Bond & Hutchinson, 1960; Wickramasekera, 1968), kleptomania (Marzagao, 1972) and aggression and violence (Deffenbacher, 1988; Evans & Hearn, 1973; O'Donnell & Worrall, 1973).

Social learning and cognitive–behavioural methods, such as social skills training, have also been extensively used in institutions, yielding significant reductions in recidivism at follow-up (Chandler, 1973; Sarason, 1978; Rice & Chaplin, 1979). There are good grounds for proposing that they may be more effective still when applied in community settings, and there is evidence in support of this (Hazel et al., 1982; Mulvey, Arthur & Reppucci, 1993). An alternative form of social skills training is illustrated in its usage in assertion training, and in the process of anger replacement, and this has been achieved successfully in a number of studies (Rimm et al., 1974; Foy, Eisler & Pinkston, 1975; Foy et al., 1976; Frederiksen et al., 1976; Rahaim, Lefebvre & Jenkins, 1980).

Cognitive self-instruction methods are already deployed to some extent in existing interventions, principally in the form of anger control training. This too has been widely adapted in institutions, but Novaco (1980) demonstrated the feasibility of training probation staff in the use of the method. Both the original study and a number of later reports of its effective use have been with groups located in the community (Novaco, 1975; Schrader et al., 1977; McCullough, Huntsinger & Nay, 1977; Denicola & Sandler, 1980; Moon & Eisler, 1983; Nomellini & Katz, 1983; Bistline & Freiden, 1984; Feindler, Marriott & Iwata, 1984;).

A number of other potentially valuable but relatively little used methods have been identified by Gordon & Arbuthnot (1987). They include training in socio-moral reasoning, based on the proposal that it is possible to increase individuals' levels of moral maturity through the use of guided dilemma discussions. Using the related technique of role reversal, reduction of antisocial attitudes has been achieved in relation to such problems as racial hostility (Culbertson, 1957) and football violence (McDougall, Thomas & Wilson, 1987). Moral education programmes of the kind described by Gordon & Arbuthnot have been shown to have potential for securing a wide range of changes in juvenile offenders (Gibbs et al., 1984; Arbuthnot & Gordon, 1986; Rosenkoetter, Landman & Masak, 1986).

A second area which warrants much further research is that of family-based interventions. One of the largest reductions in recidivism yet achieved was through the family systems studies of Klein, Alexander & Parsons (1977) which involved training parents and delinquent children in negotiation skills to resolve interpersonal conflicts. Over a three-year follow-up period, this study reported a 50% reduction in recidivism rates for trained groups over comparison groups and controls. Similarly impressive results are reported in a related study conducted by Gordon et al. (1988). Gordon, Graves & Arbuthnot (1995) report on a follow-up of the juveniles in this experiment three years into adulthood. At that point, there remained a significant difference in overall offence rates between the trained group and controls (9% as against 41%). Another set of studies using behaviourally based family teaching programmes also yielded significant effects in reducing stealing and aggression (Reid & Patterson, 1976; Bank, Patterson & Reid, 1987). A third set of studies, employing behavioural interventions which have been effective in reducing child abuse and neglect, has been reviewed by Morton & Ewald (1987).

THE GULF BETWEEN RESEARCH RESULTS AND PRACTICE

On the basis of the work just reviewed it can be contended, with a moderate degree of confidence, that the past 15 years of research effort have produced some reasonably promising results. There is a convergence of findings amongst major research reviews, using statistically refined methods of analysis, that interventions have an overall positive effect. Within this, some parameters have been identified which, cumulatively, may be capable of yielding still stronger effects.

These findings are not random but are conceptually and empirically inter-linked. They are congruent with a scientifically based understanding of human behaviour grounded in psychological and social research (Platt & Prout, 1987; Hollin, 1990). This does not "pathologize" individuals, as earlier psychological approaches have been accused of doing (Taylor, Walton & Young, 1973). On the contrary, its postulates encompass normal, routinized, everyday behaviour and harmful, antisocial acts within the same theoretical framework.

Despite these very encouraging findings, and associated theoretical develop-ments, an inordinate gap remains between what research has shown to be possible and what typically happens in practice (van Voorhis, 1987). This paradoxical situation arguably ought to be a central issue in criminal justice policy. Yet, in the face of recurrent widespread concern over crime, there are continuing difficulties in including the issue of effective intervention on the public policy agenda.

The contemporary debate in criminal justice continues to be shaped around the metaphor of the "swing of a pendulum" between "hard" and "soft", conservative and liberal, responses to criminal acts. The dimension of "constructive intervention" depicted here cuts across its trajectory at right angles. The core proposal emanating from it is that there should now be a policy of systematic research into methods which will reduce the harm which offenders do, by assisting them in finding ways to accomplish behavioural and personal change.

There are identifiable causes of the gulf just described. It repeatedly proves difficult for staff groups interested in developing programmes to do so unencumbered within their respective agencies. Formidable obstacles stand almost omnipresent in their path. They include:

1. Inadequate, or inappropriate staff skills and the need for new departures in basic professional training.
2. Limited vision regarding the aims and practices of agencies, which under central government pressure have had basic principles eroded, resources curtailed, and have moved steadily towards more control and less constructive intervention.
3. Some agencies have in many ways evolved into bureaucracies, and their organizational climates are often obstructive of innovation and development.
4. There is a continuing need for practice-based evaluation and research.

The latter has been recommended not just by researchers (Petersilia, 1991; Palmer, 1992) but also by governmental agencies such as the Audit Commission (1989) in its report on the probation service. Were evidence gathering and evaluation to become part of the culture of offender services, a habit as natural doing the job itself, much more evidence would be available concerning effective interventions. This in turn might strengthen arguments for improvements in resources.

ACKNOWLEDGEMENT

The author wishes to thank Andy Stelman, Assistant Chief Probation Officer, Merseyside, for valuable comments on portions of this chapter.

REFERENCES

Andrews, D.A., Kiessling, J.J., Robinson, D. & Mickus, S. (1986) The risk principle of case classification: an outcome evaluation with young adult probationers. *Canadian Journal of Criminology*, 377, 377–384.

Andrews, D.A., Zinger, I., Hoge, R.D., Bonta, J., Gendreau, P. & Cullen, F.T. (1990) Does correctional treatment work? A clinically relevant and psychologically informed meta-analysis. *Criminology*, 28, 369–404.

Arbuthnot, J. & Gordon, D.A. (1986) Behavioral and cognitive effects of a moral reasoning development intervention for high-risk behavior-disordered adolescents. *Journal of Consulting and Clinical Psychology*, 54, 208–216.

Audit Commission (1989) *The Probation Service: Promoting Value for Money*. London: HMSO.

Baldwin, S. (Ed.) (1990) *Alcohol Education and Offenders*. London: Batsford.

Bank, L., Patterson, G.R. & Reid, J.B. (1987) Delinquency prevention through training parents in family management. *Behavior Analyst*, 10, 75–82.

Baumer, T.L. & Mendelsohn, R.I. (1992) Electronically monitored home confinement: does it work? In J.M. Byrne, A.J. Lurigio & J. Petersilia (Eds), *Smart Sentencing: The Emergence of Intermediate Sanctions*. Newbury Park: Sage.

Beckett, R., Beech, A., Fisher, D. & Fordham, A.S. (1995) Community-based treatment for sex offenders: an evaluation of seven treatment programmes. London: Home Office.

Bistline, J.L. & Frieden, F.P. (1984) Anger control: a case study of a stress inoculation treatment for a chronic aggressive patient. *Cognitive Therapy and Research*, 8, 551–556.

Blackburn, R. (1980) Still not working? A look at some recent outcomes in offender rehabilitation. Paper presented to the Scottish Branch of the British Psychological Society, Conference on Deviance, University of Stirling.

Bond, I.K. & Hutchinson, H.C. (1960) Application of reciprocal inhibition therapy to exhibitionism. *Canadian Medical Association Journal*, 83, 23–25.

Brody, S. (1976) *The Effectiveness of Sentencing*. Home Office Research Study No. 35. London: HMSO.

Brownell, K.D., Hayes, S.C. & Barlow, D.H. (1977) Patterns of appropriate and deviant sexual arousal: the behavioral treatment of multiple sexual deviations. *Journal of Consulting and Clinical Psychology*, 45, 1144–1155.

Brownlee, I.D. & Joanes, D. (1993) Intensive probation for young adult offenders. *British Journal of Criminology*, 33, 216–230.

Byrne, J.M. & Pattavina, A. (1992) The effectiveness issue: assessing what works in the adult community corrections system. In J.M. Byrne, A.J. Lurigio & J. Petersilia (Eds), *Smart Sentencing: The Emergence of Intermediate Sanctions*. Newbury Park: Sage.

Chandler, M.A. (1973) Egocentrism and anti-social behaviour: the assessment and training of social perspective-taking skills. *Developmental Psychology*, 9, 326–332.

Cooke, D. (1995) Diversion from prosecution: a Scottish experience. In J. McGuire (Ed.), *What Works: Reducing Re-offending: Guidelines from Research and Practice*. Chichester: John Wiley.

Culbertson, F. (1957) Modification of an emotionally held attitude through role playing. *Journal of Abnormal and Social Psychology*, 54, 230–233.

Cullen, F.T., Cullen, J.B. & Wozniak, J.F. (1988) Is rehabilitation dead? The myth of the punitive public. *Journal of Criminal Justice*, 16, 303–317.

Deffenbacher, J.L. (1988) Cognitive-relaxation and social skills treatments of anger: a year later. *Journal of Counselling Psychology*, **35**, 234–236.

Denicola, J. & Sandler, J. (1980) Training abusive parents in child management and self-control skills. *Behavior Therapy*, **11**, 263–270.

Department of Health & the Home Office (1992) *Review of Health and Social Services for Mentally Disordered Offenders and Others Requiring Similar Services. Final Summary Report* (The Reed Report). Cm 2088. London: HMSO.

Dwyer, S.M. & Myers, S. (1990) Sex offender treatment: a six-month to ten-year follow-up study. *Annals of Sex Research*, **3**, 305–318.

Evans, D.R. & Hearn, M.T. (1973) Anger and systematic desensitization: a follow-up. *Psychological Reports*, **32**, 569–570.

Feindler, E.L., Marriott, S.A. & Iwata, M. (1984) Group anger control training for junior high school delinquents. *Cognitive Therapy and Research*, **8**, 299–311.

Fischer, J. (1973) Is casework effective? A review. *Social Work*, **18**, 5–20.

Fischer, J. (1978) Does anything work? *Journal of Social Service Research*, **3**, 213–243.

Folkard, M.S., Smith, D.E. & Smith, D.D. (1976) *IMPACT: Intensive Matched Probation and After-care Treatment. Vol. II. The Results of the Experiment.* Home Office Research Study No.36. London: HMSO.

Fowles, A.J. (1978) *Prison Welfare: An Account of an Experiment at Liverpool.* Home Office Research Study No.45. London: HMSO.

Foy, D.W., Eisler, R.M. & Pinkston, S. (1975) Modeled assertion in a case of explosive rages. *Journal of Behavior Therapy and Experimental Psychiatry*, **6**, 135–138.

Foy, D.W., Miller, P.M. Eisler, R.M. & O'Toole, D.H. (1976) Social-skills training to teach alcoholics to refuse drinks effectively. *Journal of Studies on Alcohol*, **37**, 1340–1345.

Frederiksen, L.W., Jenkins, J.O., Foy, D.W. & Eisler, R.M. (1976) Social skills training to modify abusive verbal outbursts in adults. *Journal of Applied Behavior Analysis*, **9**, 117–125.

Gable, R.K. (1986) Application of personal telemonitoring to current problems in corrections. *Journal of Criminal Justice*, **14**, 167–176.

Garrett, C.J. (1985) Effects of residential treatment on adjudicated delinquents; a meta-analysis. *Journal of Research in Crime and Delinquency*, **22**, 287–308.

Gendreau, P. & Andrews, D.A. (1991) Tertiary prevention: what the meta-analyses of the offender treatment literature tell us about "what works". *Canadian Journal of Criminology*, **32**, 173–184.

Gendreau, P. & Ross, R.R. (1980) Effective correctional treatment: bibliotherapy for cynics. In R.R. Ross & P. Gendreau (Eds) *Effective Correctional Treatment.* Toronto: Butterworths.

Gendreau, P. & Ross, R.R. (1987) Revivification of rehabilitation: evidence from the 1980s. *Justice Quarterly*, **4**, 349–407.

Gensheimer, L.K., Mayer, J.P., Gottschalk, R. & Davidson, W.S. (1986) Diverting youth from the juvenile justice system: a meta-analysis of intervention efficacy. In S.J. Apter and A.P. Goldstein (Eds), *Youth Violence: Program & Prospects.* New York: Pergamon.

Gibbs, J.C., Arnold, K.D., Ahlborn, H.H. & Cheesman, F.L. (1984) Facilitation of sociomoral reasoning in delinquents. *Journal of Consulting and Clinical Psychology*, **52**, 37–45.

Goldberg, E.M., Stanley, S.J. & Kenrich, J. (1985) Task-centred casework in a probation setting. In E.M. Goldberg, J. Gibbons & I. Sinclair (Eds), *Problems, Tasks and Outcomes: The Evaluation of Task-centred Casework in Three Settings.* London: Allen & Unwin.

Goldstein, A.P. & Keller, H. (1987) *Aggressive Behavior: Assessment and Intervention.* New York: Pergamon Press.
Goldstein, A.P., Glick, B., Reiner, S., Zimmerman, D., Coultry, T.M. & God, D. (1986) Aggression Replacement Training: a comprehensive intervention for the acting-out delinquent. *Journal of Correctional Education*, **37**, 120–126.
Goldstein, A.P., Glick, B., Carthan, W. & Blancero, D.A. (1994) *The Prosocial Gang: Implementing Aggression Replacement Training.* Thousand Oaks: Sage Publications.
Gordon, D.A. & Arbuthnot, J. (1987) Individual, group, and family interventions. In H.C. Quay (Ed.), *Handbook of Juvenile Delinquency.* New York: John Wiley.
Gordon, D.A., Arbuthnot, J., Gustafson, K. & McGreen, P. (1988) Home-based behavioral-systems family therapy with disadvantaged juvenile delinquents. *American Journal of Family Therapy*, **16**, 243–255.
Gordon, D.A., Graves, K. & Arbuthnot, J. (1995) The effect of functional family therapy for delinquents on adult criminal behavior. *Criminal Justice and Behavior*, **22**, 60–73.
Gottschalk, R., Davidson, W.S., Mayer, J.P. & Gensheimer, L.K. (1987) Behavioral approaches with juvenile offenders: a meta-analysis of long-term treatment efficacy. In E.K. Morris & C.J. Braukmann (Eds), *Behavioral Approaches to Crime and Delinquenc.* New York: Plenum Press.
Guidry, L.S. (1975) Use of a covert punishment contingency in compulsive stealing. *Journal of Behavior Therapy and Experimental Psychiatry*, **6**, 169.
Harbert, T.L., Barlow, D.H., Hersen, M. & Austin, J.B. (1974) Measurement and modification of incestuous behavior: a case study. *Psychological Reports*, **34**, 79–86.
Hauber, A.R. (1989) Influencing juvenile offenders by way of alternative sanctions in community settings. In H. Wegener, F. Lösel & J. Haisch (Eds), *Criminal Behavior and the Justice System: Psychological Perspectives.* New York: Springer-Verlag.
Hay, W.M., Hay, L.R. & Nelson, R.O. (1977) The adaptation of covert modeling procedures to the treatment of chronic alcoholism and obsessive-compulsive behavior: two case reports. *Behavior Therapy*, **8**, 70–76.
Hazel, J.S., Schumaker, J.B., Sherman, J.A. & Sheldon-Wildgen, J. (1982) Group training for social skills. *Criminal Justice and Behavior*, **9**, 35–53.
Hedberg, A.G. & Campbell, L. (1974) A comparison of four behavioral treatments of alcoholism. *Journal of Behavior Therapy and Experimental Psychiatry*, **5**, 251–256.
Higgins, J. (1991) The mentally disordered offender in the community. In K.R. Herbst & J. Gunn (Eds), *The Mentally Disordered Offender.* London: Butterworth/ Heinemann and Mental Health Foundation.
Hollin, C.R. (1990) *Cognitive–Behavioral Interventions with Young Offenders.* Elmsford, New York: Pergamon Press.
Hollin, C.R. (1993) Advances in the psychological treatment in delinquent behaviour. *Criminal Behaviour and Mental Health*, **3**, 142–57.
Home Office (1990) *Partnership in Dealing with Offenders in the Community: A Discussion Paper.* London: Home Office.
Home Office (1992) *Criminal Statistics England and Wales 1991.* Cm 2134. London: HMSO.
Home Office (1993) *Digest 2. Information on the Criminal Justice System in England and Wales.* London: Home Office Research and Statistics Department.
Home Office (1995) *Strenthening Punishment in the Community: A Consultation Document.* Cm 2780. London: HMSO.
Home Office & Department of Health and Social Security (1975) *Report of the Committee on Mentally Abnormal Offenders* (The Butler Report). Cm 6244. London: HMSO.

Hood, R. (1989) *The Death Penalty: A World-wide Perspective*. Oxford: Oxford University Press.

Hough, M. and Mayhew, P. (1985) *Taking Account of Crime: Key Findings from the 1984 British Crime Survey*. Home Office Research Study No. 85. London: HMSO.

Hudson, B. (1986) Community applications of social skills training. In C.R. Hollin & P. Trower (Eds), *Handbook of Social Skills Training*, Vol.1. Oxford: Pergamon Press.

Hughes, S.P. & Schneider, A.L. (1989) Victim–offender mediation: a survey of program characteristics and perceptions of effectiveness. *Crime and Delinquency*, **35**, 217–33.

Izzo, R.L. & Ross, R.R. (1990) Meta-analysis of rehabilitation programmes for juvenile delinquents. *Criminal Justice and Behavior*, **17**, 134–42.

Jamieson, J.D. & Stone, W.E. (1991) Predicting DWI education success. *Federal Probation*, **55**, 43–47.

Klein, N.C., Alexander, J.F. & Parsons, B.V. (1977) Impact of family systems intervention on recidivism and sibling delinquency: a model of primary prevention and program evaluation. *Journal of Consulting and Clinical Psychology*, **45**, 469–474.

Knott, C. (1995) The STOP Programme: reasoning and rehabilitation in a British setting. In: J. McGuire (Ed.), *What Works: Reducing Re-offending: Guidelines from Research and Practice*. Chichester: John Wiley.

Lanyon, R.I., Primo, R.V. Terrell, F. & Wener, A. (1972) An aversion–desensitization treatment for alcoholism. *Journal of Consulting and Clinical Psychology*, **38**, 394–98.

Light, R., Nee, C. & Ingham, H. (1993) *Car Theft: The Offender's Perspective*. Home Office Research Study 130. London: HMSO.

Lilly, J.R., Cullen, F.T. & Ball, R.A. (1989) *Criminological Theory: Causes and Consequences*. Newbury Park: Sage.

Lipsey, M.W. (1992) Juvenile delinquency treatment: a meta-analytic inquiry into the variability of effects. In T. Cook, D. Cooper, H. Corday, H. Hartman, L. Hedges, R. Light, T. Louis & F. Mosteller (Eds), *Meta-analysis for Explanation: A Casebook*. New York: Russell Sage Foundation.

Lipsey, M.W. (1995) What do we learn from 400 research studies in the outcome of treatment with juvenile delinquents? In J. McGuire (Ed.), *What Works: Reducing Re-offending: Guidelines from Research and Practice*. Chichester: John Wiley.

Lösel, F. & Koferl, P. (1989) Evaluation research on correctional treatment in West Germany: a meta-analysis. In H. Wegener, F. Loesel & J. Haisch (Eds), *Criminal Behavior and the Justice System: Psychological Perspectives*. New York: Springer.

Mace, A.E. (1991) A probation service perspective. In K.R. Herbst & J. Gunn (Eds) *The Mentally Disordered Offender*. London: Butterworth/Heinemann and Mental Health Foundation.

Mair, G. & Nee, C. (1990) *Electronic Monitoring: The Trials and their Results*. Home Office Research Study No. 120. London: HMSO.

Marshall, W.L., Jones, R., Ward, T., Johnston, P. & Barbaree, H.E. (1991) Treatment outcome with sex offenders. *Clinical Psychology Review*, **11**, 465–485.

Martinson, R. (1974) What works? Questions and answers about prison reform. *The Public Interest*, **10**, 22–54.

Martinson, R. (1979) New findings, new views: a note of caution regarding sentencing reform. *Hofstra Law Review*, **7**, 243–258.

Marzagao, L.R. (1972) Systematic desensitization treatment of kleptomania. *Journal of Behavior Therapy and Experimental Psychiatry*, **3**, 327–328.

McCullough, J.P., Huntsinger, G.M. & Nay, W.R. (1977) Self-control treatment of aggression in a 16-year-old male. *Journal of Consulting and Clinical Psychology*, **45**, 322–331.

McDougall, C., Thomas, M. & Wilson, J. (1987) Attitude change and the violent football supporter. In B.J. McGurk, D.M. Thornton & M. Williams (Eds), *Applying Psychology to Imprisonment: Theory and Practice.* London: HMSO.

McGuire, J. (1995) Community-based reasoning and rehabilitation programs in the UK. In R.R. Ross & R.D. Ross (Eds), *Thinking Straight.* Ottawa: Air Training and Publications.

McGuire, J. & Priestley, P. (1985) *Offending Behaviour: Skills and Stratagems for Going Straight.* London: Batsford.

McGuire, J. & Priestley, P. (1992) Some things do work: psychological interventions with offenders and the effectiveness debate. In F. Lösel, D. Bender & T. Bliesener (Eds), *Psychology and Law: International Perspectives.* Berlin: Springer.

McGuire, J., Broomfield, D., Robinson, C. & Rowson, B. (1994) Short-term impact of probation programs: an evaluative study. *International Journal of Offender Therapy and Comparative Criminology*, **39**, 23–42.

McIvor, G. (1990) *Sanctions for Persistent or Serious Offenders: A Review of the Literature.* Social Work Research Centre, University of Stirling.

McWilliams, W. (1975) *Some Male Offenders' Problems. I: Homeless Offenders in Liverpool.* Home Office Research Study No. 28. London: HMSO.

Miller, P.M., Hersen, M., Eisler, R.M. & Watts, J.G. (1974) Contingent reinforcement of lowered blood/alcohol levels in an outpatient chronic alcoholic. *Behaviour Research and Therapy*, **12**, 261.

Miner, M.H., Marques, J.K., Day, D.M. & Nelson, C. (1990) Impact of relapse prevention in treating sex offenders: Preliminary findings. *Annals of Sex Research*, **3**, 165–185.

Moon, J.R. & Eisler, R.M. (1983) Anger control. an experimental comparison of three behavioral treatments. *Behavior Therapy*, **14**, 493–505.

Morrison, S. & O'Donnell, I. (1994) *Armed Robbery: A Study in London.* Oxford: Centre for Criminological Research, University of Oxford.

Morton, T.L. & Ewald, L.S. (1987) Family-based interventions for crime and delinquency. In E.K. Morris & C.J. Braukmann (Eds), *Behavioral Approaches to Crime and Delinquency.* New York: Plenum.

Mulvey, E.P., Arthur, M.W. & Reppucci, N.D. (1993) The prevention and treatment of juvenile delinquency: a review of the research. *Clinical Psychology Review*, **13**, 133–167.

Nomellini, S. & Katz, R.C. (1983) Effects of anger control training on abusive parents. *Cognitive Research and Therapy*, **7**, 57–68.

Novaco, R.W. (1975) *Anger Control: The Development and Evaluation of an Experimental Treatment.* Lexington: D.C. Heath.

Novaco, R.W. (1980) Training of probation counselors for anger problems. *Journal of Counseling Psychology*, **27**, 385–390.

O'Donnell, C.R. & Worell, L. (1973) Motor and cognitive relaxation in the desensitization of anger. *Behaviour Research and Therapy*, **11**, 473–481.

Palmer, T. (1975) Martinson re-visited. *Journal of Research in Crime and Delinquency*, **12**, 133–152.

Palmer, T. (1992) *The Re-emergence of Correctional Intervention.* Newbury Park: Sage.

Pearson, F.S. (1988) Evaluation of New Jersey's intensive supervision program. *Crime and Delinquency*, **34**, 437–448.

Petersilia, J. (1991) The value of corrections research: learning what works. *Federal Probation*, **55**, 23–25.

Petersilia, J. and Turner, S. (1993) Intensive probation and parole. *Crime and Justice*, **17**, 281–335.

Platt, J.J. & Prout, M.F. (1987) Cognitive–behavioral theory and interventions for crime and delinquency. In E.K. Morris & C.J. Braukmann (Eds), *Behavioral Approaches to Crime and Delinquency*. New York: Plenum.

Polakow, R.L. & Doctor, R.M. (1973) Treatment of marijuana and barbiturate dependency by contingency contracting. *Journal of Behavior Therapy and Experimental Psychiatry*, **4**, 375–377.

Polakow, R.L. & Doctor, R.M. (1974) A behavioral modification program for adult drug offenders. *Journal of Research in Crime and Delinquency*, **11**, 63–69.

Polakow, R.L. & Peabody, D. (1975) Behavioral treatment of child abuse. *International Journal of Offender Therapy and Comparative Criminology*, **19**, 100–103.

Priestley, P., McGuire, J., Flegg, D., Hemsley, V., Welham, D. & Barnitt, R. (1984) *Social Skills in Prisons and the Community: Problem-solving for Offenders*. London: Routledge and Kegan Paul.

Rahaim, S., Lefebvre, C. & Jenkins, J.O. (1980) The effects of social skills training on behavioral and cognitive components of anger management. *Journal of Behavior Therapy and Experimental Psychiatry*, **11**, 3–8.

Reid, J.B. & Patterson, G.R. (1976) The modification of aggression and stealing behavior of boys in the home setting. In E. Ribes-Inesta & A. Bandura (Eds), *Analysis of Delinquency and Aggression*. Hillsdale: Lawrence Erlbaum.

Reid, W.J. & Epstein, L. (1977) *Task-centered Practice*. New York: Columbia University Press.

Remington, B. & Remington, M. (1987) Behavior modification in probation work: a review and evaluation. *Criminal Justice and Behavior*, **14**, 156–174.

Rice, M.E. & Chaplin, T.C. (1979) Social skills training for hospitalized male arsonists. *Journal of Behavior Therapy and Experimental Pschiatry*, **10**, 105–108.

Rimm, D.C., Hill, G.A., Brown, N.N. & Stuart, J.E. (1974) Group-assertive training in the treatment of expression of inappropriate anger. *Psychological Reports*, **34**, 791–798.

Rosenkoetter, L.I., Landman, S. & Mazak, S.G. (1986) The use of moral discussion as an intervention with delinquents. *Psychological Reports*, **16**, 81–84.

Ross, R.R. & Fabiano, E.A. (1985) *Time to Think: A Cognitive Model of Offender Rehabilitation*. Ottawa: Cognitive Centre.

Ross, R.R. & Fabiano, E.A. (1990) *Reasoning and Rehabilitation. Instructor's Manual*. Ottawa: Cognitive Station.

Ross, R.R., Fabiano, E.A. & Ewles, C.D. (1988) Reasoning and rehabilitation. *International Journal of Offender Therapy and Comparative Criminology*, **32**, 29–35.

Rubin, A. (1985) Practice effectiveness: more grounds for optimism. *Social Work*, **30**, 469–476.

Russell, M.N. (1990) *Clinical Social Work*. Newbury Park: Sage.

Sarason, I.G. (1978) A cognitive social learning approach to juvenile delinquency. In R.D. Hare & D. Schalling (Eds), *Psychopathic Behavior: Approaches to Research*. New York: John Wiley.

Schrader, C., Long, J., Panzer, C., Gillet, D. & Kornblath, R. (1977) *An Anger-control Package for Adolescent Drug Abusers*. Glen Oaks, New York: Long Island Jewish-Hillside Medical Center.

Schur, E. (1973) *Radical Non-Intervention: Rethinking the Delinquency Problem*. Englewood Cliffs, NJ: Prentice-Hall.

Shaw, M. (1974) *Social Work in Prison. An Experiment in the Use of Extended Contact with Offenders.* Home Office Research Study No.22. London: HMSO.

Sheldon, B. (1987) Implementing findings from social work effectiveness research. *British Journal of Social Work*, **57**, 573–586.

Sheldon, B. (1994) Social work effectiveness research: implications for probation and juvenile justice services. *Howard Journal of Criminal Justice*, **33**, 218–235.

Snare, A. (1993) Psychosocial interventions aimed at resolving the conflict between the perpetrator and the victim, for example within the framework of mediation and compensation programmes. Paper presented at the Twentieth Criminological Research Conference, Council of Europe, Strasbourg.

Stumphauzer, J.S. (1976) Elimination of stealing by self-reinforcement of alternative behavior and family contracting. *Journal of Behavior Therapy and Experimental Psychiatry*, **7**, 265–268.

Sundel, S.S. & Sundel, M. (1993) *Behavior Modification in the Human Services: A Systematic Introduction to Concepts and Applications.* Newbury Park: Sage.

Tarling, R. (1993) *Analysing Offending: Data, Models and Interpretations.* London: HMSO.

Taylor, I., Walton, P. & Young, J. (1973) *The New Criminology: For a Social Theory of Deviance.* London: Routledge and Kegan Paul.

Thornton, D.M. (1987) Treatment effects on recidivism: a reappraisal of the "nothing works" doctrine. In B.J. McGurk, D.M. Thornton & M. Williams (Eds), *Applying Psychology to Imprisonment: Theory and Practice.* London: HMSO.

Tonak, D. & Cawdron, G. (1988) Mentally disordered offenders and the courts: cooperation and collaboration of disciplines involved. *Justice of the Peace*, **152**, 504–507.

Van Voorhis, P. (1987) Correctional effectiveness: the high cost of ignoring success. *Federal Probation*, **51**, 56–62.

Wasik, M. & Taylor, R.D. (1991) *Blackstone's Guide to the Criminal Justice Act 1991.* London: Blackstone Press.

Welch, G.J. (1985) Contingency contracting with a delinquent and his family. *Journal of Behavior Therapy and Experimental Psychiatry*, **16**, 253–259.

Whitehead, J.T. & Lab, S.P. (1989) A meta-analysis of juvenile correctional treatment. *Journal of Research in Crime and Delinquency*, **26**, 276–295.

Wickramasckcra, I. (1968) The application of learning theory to the treatment of a case of sexual exhibitionism. *Psychotherapy: Theory, Research, and Practice*, **5**, 108–112.

Winterdyk, J. & Roesch, R. (1981) A wilderness experimental program as an alternative for probationers: an evaluation. *Canadian Journal of Criminology*, **23**, 39–49.

Wooldredge, J.D. (1988) Differentiating the effects of juvenile court sentences on eliminating recidivism. *Journal of Research in Crime and Delinquency*, **25**, 264–300.

CHAPTER FOUR

WORKING IN SECURE INSTITUTIONS

Cynthia McDougall

Some readers of this chapter may start with a feeling of resistance to the idea of working in secure institutions, either as a matter of principle or from a knowledge of the difficulties of working in an environment which at the very least may have competing priorities thought to hinder the aim of rehabilitation. This chapter will refer to the specific problems of working in secure institutions, will illustrate how these environments have become more oriented towards rehabilitation in recent years, and will discuss strategies for achieving effective rehabilitation at national, establishment and individual practitioner levels. It will also describe the many positive aspects of working in secure institutions, however those who do not enjoy a challenge need not read on!

THE CHALLENGES

Although many of the problems of working with offenders in secure institutions apply equally to community settings, it is true that problems are frequently intensified by the need for co-operation among a range of staff with different backgrounds, experience and approaches which may have competing influences on the client who has no means of withdrawing from the situation. Hollin highlights some of the problems which impact on programme integrity (Hollin, 1995) and on programme design and effectiveness (Hollin, 1993). The point is forcefully made by Burchard and Lane (1982) who state that ". . . behaviour modification advocates who do not recognise that much of their

Working with Offenders: Psychological Practice in Offender Rehabilitation.
Edited by C.R. Hollin. © 1996 John Wiley & Sons Ltd.

time will be spent trying to change behaviour of staff and policy administrators are in for a rude awakening" (p. 616). Since this was said few remedies have been found and more recently similar points were made by Hollin et al. on rehabilitation in prisons (Hollin et al., 1992):

> Too many rehabilitative or offence-related programmes are dealt with as bolt-on activities that exist at the periphery of mainstream activity. This marginalisation tends to make programmes vulnerable to the vagaries of resourcing and competing demands, suspicion and antagonism from staff and inmates not involved, and a cultural bias against success . . . To deliver a focused, holistic output, a multi-disciplinary approach is essential.

Although in prisons, specialists may see prison officers as responsible for creating some of the barriers, where prison officers themselves are involved in running rehabilitation programmes they can encounter similar problems. Officers involved in setting up an anger management programme in a young offender institution found that they had to negotiate for rooms and resources (McDougall et al., 1990). However, officers were invaluable in organizing access to inmates, in an establishment where the systems did not readily adapt to facilitating programmes.

This illustrates the point made by Hollin et al. (1992) that programmes will not succeed if they are add-ons to systems already in existence. Programmes cannot survive at the periphery, they must be in the mainstream, and rehabilitation must be what the whole organization is about.

THE ENVIRONMENT

There is agreement internationally on factors which often make correctional systems appear ineffective or counter-productive in achieving their ultimate purpose (Inkster, Johnson & Edstedt, 1991). In my view the three most significant ways in which the institutional environment can militate against a holistic rehabilitation approach are:

1. Multidisciplinary teams, now established in most secure institutions, sometimes have difficulty in practice in agreeing common aims and methods, while the management of the organization may not always give recognition to the contribution which can be made by specialists to planning at a senior management level.
2. Operational interests and security can sometimes be seen to compete with rehabilitation. In the prison system the effects of overcrowding can make containment a main preoccupation. In such situations staff involved in

treatment programmes can be required for other duties and programmes may be suspended.

3. The effectiveness of the whole rehabilitation process in secure institutions may be questioned because of its isolation from the real world. The argument can be made that clients may undertake treatment for the wrong reasons; they come to programmes because of boredom with other activities, or, of more concern, they may not be entirely volunteers, being under pressure to demonstrate co-operation for parole and early release.

Although ideally there should be an institutional approach to rehabilitation, one of the major difficulties in developing such an approach is the range of opinion and attitude held within institutions (McCord et al., 1991). Staff in institutions can vary in attitude to their role in rehabilitation and have an ambivalence to whether rehabilitation can be achieved. This range of views is reflected in society with the debate as to whether prisons should be places of rehabilitation, education and support, or primarily seen in terms of punishment and deterrent. Although these attitudes may not be so clearly focused on special hospitals and regional secure units, more punitive attitudes can be expressed within society when released patients reoffend, or notorious murderers are transferred to hospitals from prisons. As our staff are all part of society it is not surprising that a wide range of views are often present in institutions.

Knowledge of individual offenders can also create an anti-rehabilitation atmosphere where there are difficult-to-manage patients/prisoners whose behaviour is such that they may become labelled as "not worth the effort" or "not deserving of help".

Specialists can therefore find themselves in an atmosphere of hostility to what they are trying to achieve. Added to this is the tension already referred to, which can be caused by the difficulty among specialist groups in agreeing on a common theoretical base and a common approach to rehabilitation (Laws, 1974; Cullen & Seddon, 1981). These conflicts and inability to agree common aims often lead to less than effective multi-disciplinary teamwork.

NEW APPROACHES TO REHABILITATION IN SECURE INSTITUTIONS

Although institutional resistance to rehabilitation appears to have persisted over many years, more recently there have been significant changes in approach. The "nothing works" philosophy of Martinson (1974) which held sway for so long has been overtaken by the more positive search for "what works" (Gendreau & Andrews, 1990; Lipsey, 1992). Many staff in secure institutions see this as a worthwhile aim.

Although special hospitals, regional secure units and the Youth Treatment Service are recognized as having a clear aim and commitment to rehabilitation, the Prison Service, which might be considered to have a more punitive role, also includes in its Statement of Purpose a commitment to rehabilitation.

> Her Majesty's Prison Service serves the public by keeping in custody those committed by the courts. Our duty is to look after them with humanity and help them lead law-abiding and useful lives in custody and after release.

Any debate therefore is not about whether we should rehabilitate those offenders in secure institutions, but how we can achieve this aim. Much credit for the positive steps taken in the Prison Service towards effective rehabilitation must go to the report by Lord Justice Woolf (Woolf & Tumim, 1991) following the Strangeways riot, and the subsequent Government White Paper on "Custody, Care and Justice" (Home Office, 1991).

These papers recommended and resulted in a commitment towards better conditions for prisoners, more constructive regimes, and more positive approaches to rehabilitation and throughcare. This commitment was demonstrated when the Prison Service was restructured in the same year to create a Directorate of Inmate Programmes with responsibility for sentence planning, throughcare and programme development.

More importantly, the Prison Service developed a strategy for a national approach to setting up, resourcing, managing and evaluating inmate programmes, which would set a clear lead for establishments throughout the Service.

THE NATIONAL PROGRAMME MANAGEMENT STRATEGY

The strategy began by addressing the question of sex offender treatment (Directorate of Inmate Programmes, 1991), and subsequently anger management and cognitive skills programmes.

Although sentence planning and inmate programme development has always taken place at a local establishment level, there were reasons for restructuring to allow these processes to be centrally managed. Local sentence planning and inmate programmes had in many cases been effective, and indeed some locally developed programmes were the basis for national programme development. In the past, however, local difficulties meant that some interventions were not maintained. Local programmes were often developed by enthusiastic specialists in isolation from other staff; they were subject to some of the operational difficulties already described by being "added on" to or even completely independent of the regime; they were not always evaluated and numbers were often too small to make significant claims; and all too often the groups were discontinued when the originator moved from the establishment. Although in almost all other management functions there is a move away from central co-ordination with responsibility and authority being devolved to a local level, there are strong advantages to central management of rehabilitation programmes, which overcome many of the problems of working in a secure environment already described.

The rationale for a centrally managed approach to programme development was as follows (Thornton, 1991):

> A more co-ordinated and consistent approach (to management of programmes) has the following benefits:
> i)   Economy and efficiency in the use of resources. Resources can be shared, avoiding unnecessary duplication, particularly in developing specific treatment programmes.
> ii)   Resource intensive activities can be concentrated in a few specialist establishments. Inmates who are assigned more intensive treatment can then be allocated to those establishments.
> iii) Establishments with fewer resources can be assigned inmates for whom less intensive treatment is required.
>
> Co-ordination also has clear advantages in terms of standards:
> i)   The treatment designed can be based on research, and staff trained to run the preferred programme, rather than treatment being limited to whatever existing staff can do at the time.
> ii)   Common treatment standards can be defined.
> iii) Professional and managerial support structures can be created.
> iv)   Monitoring and evaluation can allow systematic improvement in the system.

The strategy developed within Inmate Programme Development was characterized by strong management commitment; a multidisciplinary approach; commitment to staff training and programme integrity; an emphasis on "what works"; and monitoring, management and evaluation.

From the outset strong top management commitment was evident. The newly appointed Director of Inmate Programmes declared (Emes, 1991, p. 39):

Reorganisation – and with it the creation of the Directorate of Inmate Programmes – has enabled us to draw together, for the first time, many of the policy threads at headquarters concerned with creating positive regimes for prisoners. One of the strengths of the new Directorate is that it brings together a mix of skills: Area Managers and Governors with operational experience; administrators and also a wide range of specialists.

It enables us to focus on regime issues and particular activities and problems in a way which has proved very difficult in the past. It provides for you in establishments a source of advice, assistance and expertise. The structure is thus geared to respond positively to the demands we can expect from the outside – from Lord Justice Woolf Enquiry and from the recent reports of HM Chief Inspector – and to the need recognised and acknowledged within the Service to develop enhanced regimes for prisoners.

Further, the Head of Inmate Programme Division (Guy, 1991, p. 9): stated:

There can be no value whatsoever in running proposed programmes for sex offenders in a half-hearted way. Inadequate resourcing or lack of management/ staff commitment would almost certainly doom them to failure. We have started from the position that all prison establishments participating in the programmes must want to do so, and have the full support of their area manager.

The strategy proposed a multi-disciplinary approach, with wide field involvement in design and implementation, backed up with support for financial bids in establishments for staff and resources. Staff were given thorough, centrally organized training. Programme integrity was given a high priority.

An example of the monitoring and management of the process is that incorporated in the sex offender treatment programme (Thornton 1991). Thornton highlighted "quality control" and "evaluation" as being critical processes for treatment programmes. Quality control was carried out at three levels: *programme delivery*, which examined, for example, whether treatment occurred as planned, whether sessions were cancelled, whether they were run without trained leaders, etc; *inmate co-operation*, based on the percentage of inmates who declined to co-operate, the percentage that dropped out of the treatment, inmate attendance, staff-rated behaviour during sessions; and *clinical impact*, assessed three months after treatment by offenders' ability to describe cycle of offending, identify high risk situations, and demonstrate ways out of situations.

Evaluation, built into the process at the outset, was planned to focus on three elements: treatment integrity, clinical impact and re-offending, and to be carried out by independent researchers to ensure impartiality.

There seems little doubt that four years into the programme the strategy has proved effective in setting up a national sex offender treatment network which is meeting its objectives (Thornton et al., 1994). More recently national anger management and cognitive skills programmes have been set up adopting similar strategies.

ADVANTAGES OF WORKING IN SECURE INSTITUTIONS

Working within an organization where a clear lead has been set, as with the National Inmate Programme Strategy, has very much assisted specialists working towards rehabilitation in establishments, as there is support through management commitment, and consequently adequate training and resources. Agreement to deliver a specified number of courses in a particular way is built into the Governor's contract or strategic plan which is submitted to the Prisons Board. Programmes are therefore less likely to be subject to the vagaries of operational pressure.

Formal recognition of the value of programmes for offending behaviour has resulted in a greater respect for specialist skills, and the demand for psychologists has grown as they are increasingly seen as necessary to support locally based programmes and in many cases to manage establishment programme provision.

In such situations there can be definite advantages to carrying out programmes in secure settings, where provision of programmes follows the planned timetable and where offenders agree and contract to regular attendance at courses and are not so prone to competing distractions. This can make groupwork more predictable and deliverable in accordance with course design, ensuring course members undertake all parts of the course, so assisting the achievement of programme integrity which is essential to effective programmes (Hollin, 1995). Although Andrews et al. (1990) stated that community programmes had a greater effect on delinquency than residential programmes, assessment of sex offender treatment programmes both in residential and community settings as part of the Sex Offender Treatment Evaluation Project indicates that residential courses can be more effective when practical aspects are more closely controlled (Beckett et al., 1994).

Andrews et al.'s (1990) findings do however suggest that more success in reducing recidivism can be achieved with offenders with medium to high risk of recidivism. Prison establishments which are likely to contain most offenders in this category have a potential for more effective targeting of programmes.

Although it has already been pointed out that different approaches within multidisciplinary groups can lead to problems, under the national strategy, where there is a wide range of staff involvement, rehabilitation is becoming not solely a concern of specialists. This gives an unrivalled opportunity for specialists to influence their establishments towards the holistic, multi-disciplinary approach described earlier as essential to effective rehabilitation, where all staff are involved and are agreed that this is what the establishment is about.

THE CONTRIBUTION OF THE SPECIALIST IN ESTABLISHMENTS

The national programme management strategy has set a lead for establish-ments in showing the value of working to a strategic plan. Psychology teams in establishments do not however work solely on inmate programmes, for example they also provide management information, and give support to staff on matters relating to prisoner management and security. There is a need therefore for a local psychology strategy which encompasses all other areas of their work.

For those who are discouraged by the concept of strategic planning, I would argue that adoption of a strategy is an essential and indeed very psychological approach. It is, at its simplest, a clear vision of what one is trying to achieve which subsequently allows for the identification of the steps necessary to achieve the vision. It also assists practical decisionmaking as, where there is doubt about which course of action is appropriate, the options can be tested against the vision of what one is trying to achieve and the preferred strategy.

An example of this might be having an agreed strategy of developing a multidisciplinary co-ordinated approach to running programmes. A treatment package becomes available which could be applied easily but can only be run by specialists. Do you accept it? Reference to the strategic plan would tell you this was counter to your main aim. Specialists need a clear vision of what they are trying to achieve in their establishment and a clear strategy of how to make their vision a reality.

If the vision is, as already suggested, to create an institution where there is a holistic, multifunctional approach to rehabilitation which is a mainstream activity, then specialists need a strategy whereby this can be achieved and maintained. It follows therefore that they must be at the centre of decision and policy making in the establishment, as well as being involved in working with the offender. This requires a specialist contribution at senior management level, where policies are formulated and plans for implementation are developed, and additionally at all other levels to give support in practice.

Although many of the following ideas are based on the experience of working as a psychologist in the Prison Service, the principles are relevant to other professional groups – such as psychologists, probation officers, social workers, teachers and chaplains – working with offenders in a range of secure settings. The management and staff titles may differ, but essentially the problems and challenges in such environments have a similarity about them, and this similarity extends to whatever position one holds in the organization, whether it be as a member of a small ward, wing or house team, as a leader of such a team, or representing the profession at a national level.

To acquire an effective strategy, specialists must first have an image of their role and purpose in the establishment. While I have suggested that the whole institution should be about working with offenders and their rehabilitation, I would argue that the elements of working *effectively* with offenders and achieving *successful* rehabilitation are those in which specialist workers in institutions make a major contribution. It is our role to ensure that developments are based on sound theories, on an understanding of the behaviour of individuals and organizations, that targets are properly defined and appropriately constructed, methods evaluated, and support given in practical implementation.

This is not to denigrate the work of other staff who bring abundant practical experience and skills to rehabilitation processes. The rationale, however, for specialists working in secure institutions is to assist the institution in meeting its objectives, using professional skills, having already assisted in defining those objectives. For example, psychologists in the Prison Service identified with management a need for a more systematic approach to assessment of lifers for release, then designed a risk assessment model and assisted in its implementation (McDougall et al., 1995). This integrates their work with the main concerns of the establishment.

Prison Service Psychology has its own Statement of Purpose which defines what the psychologist's contribution should be:

PRISON PSYCHOLOGY STATEMENT OF PURPOSE

Prison Service Psychology supports the Prison Service's Statement of Purpose and its staff by applying sound psychological principles and high professional standards to:

- The delivery of agreed organisational objectives

- The understanding of individuals and the organisation
- The design of strategies for change
- The evaluation of effectiveness.

Working in a secure environment presents very different challenges from working in the community, and requires the development of particular skills. Specialists must have an understanding of organizations, how they work and have an ability to work effectively within them. This is not an easy skill to acquire, particularly if one has been used to working semi-autonomously in the community. The opinion that specialists need to be in a strong managerial position to influence rehabilitation is not solely a personal view. The value of this was recognized by The British Psychological Society Working Party on Clinical Psychology Services for Offenders and People with Antisocial Behaviour Problems (WPSOABP, 1993) where this approach was recommended for special hospitals.

> Recommendation 20: to ensure optimal contribution of psychological resources in Special Hospitals, the Directors of Psychological Services should be directly accountable to the General Managers and should be members of the hospital management teams. We note that such an arrangement has proved beneficial to the delivery of psychological services within the prison system.

It is true that a high proportion of heads of psychology in prison establishments have achieved a position of reporting directly to the Governor and being a member of the senior management group. This has mostly been achieved by skilful marketing of psychology in line with the needs of the establishment and this forms the basis of the strategy I would recommend for attaining a managerial position. Psychology teams have adopted the aims and objectives of the establishments in which they work, demonstrating the unique contribution which can be made in helping to meet these objectives. This is illustrated in the Statement of Purpose. This has proved to be a successful strategy for becoming involved in the consultation process and psychologists who focus their work on helping governors achieve their targets, e.g. reduction of assaults and home leave failures, are much in demand. If psychologists spend time on subjects of low priority to the institution or if for example their specialist approach is not in keeping with the main direction which the Governor or General Manager wishes to take, then there is little likelihood of being consulted on the direction of the organization. There has to be a clear commitment to achieving the goals of the organization in order to become part of the management team.

This commitment in no way forces a compromise of one's own principles or approach. It is however true that a specialist unit cannot operate independently from the organization in which it works, and that it is more effective to present one's opinion within the management team than outside it. The strategy should therefore be to work with the management team to meet the needs of the organization. To achieve this one must become familiar with the main goals of the organization, as incorporated in establishment contracts, and to be aware of the areas in which targets are proving difficult to achieve. These "difficult areas" identified should be those on which we concentrate to find a psychological approach which will help solve the problem. Success in this venture leads to psychologists being consulted on other things for which they might be able to provide solutions, and consequently receiving the recognition they need to become involved in senior management discussions.

None of this can be achieved if a narrow view of rehabilitation is taken, and if psychologists see themselves either as the specialist experts who carry out the psychological treatment, or as consultants who produce solutions but do not get involved with implementation of ideas. To have a continuing influence on rehabilitation, an operational psychology approach is advocated as the most effective, with psychologists being involved with policy making and then working with other staff to put policies into practice.

To succeed, specialists must therefore take a managerial approach. As a team member, one does not gain credibility by uncompromisingly promoting one's own view without recognizing other interests, nor by suggesting impractical options. For example, systematic evaluation of programmes was for some time seen as threatening by course tutors. Sensitivity and careful timing was necessary to achieve acceptance of the principle that courses must be evaluated. In secure institutions the "pressure group" approach rarely changes views, and promoting courses of action radically different from the current approach is unlikely to succeed and likely to leave one marginalized. If one wants to promote a particular view in secure institutions, it is essential first to find a customer for the idea. This relates to earlier comments about identifying needs and suggesting a solution. If you first link your idea to a need of the Governor's then you have a customer; similarly if you identify a related need of a group of staff and a solution, this will gain their support.

This approach is not devious. It is a means of finding a way that a specialism can be of most value to an organization. The approach is quite different from, and more effective than, making one's own decision about what one wants to see in the organization and pressing for it. This can only have limited success.

It is recognized, however, that many specialists do not want to work in a management-focused way and want to follow their own interests. This is a problem in these days when skills must be marketable. Unless your professional interest coincides with what the customer is ready to pay for, then attempts to sell the idea will not succeed. Specialists therefore have to work with the organization. This is true of both secure and community settings.

Where targets and methods have not been set at a national level, those who have worked in multidisciplinary teams will know that relationships can sometimes break down because of commitment to different theoretical bases of treatments and disagreements on methods. There is a need for common aims and agreed approaches, but these can be difficult to achieve. There is also often conflict over roles where they are not clearly defined. One of the most encouraging developments in recent years has been the concept of "what works", largely driven by researchers in Canada (Gendreau & Andrews, 1990) who have led the movement away from the "nothing works" doctrine of Martinson (1974). It is encouraging that "what works" has received acclaim from many professional groups, and that there has been a development of interest in pursuing courses of action based on evidence of "what works" (see Chapter 9). This is something on which members of multidisciplinary teams can agree, and is a good starting point for a common approach. Along with the "what works" approach comes a commitment to evaluation and to programme integrity; if we define "what works", we must then ensure that this is what we deliver.

A multidisciplinary team working to the "what works" philosophy with a carefully defined programme such as the Reasoning and Rehabilitation programme of Ross & Fabiano (1985) does not present a problem. However, where programmes are in the development stage, for example being designed to meet the needs of different kinds of sex offender, there can be disagreements about methods of implementation. Evaluation should be able to overcome disagreements about method, as the range of approaches can be evaluated. The method which proves to be the most effective is that which is adopted. Although all members of the team may work with the offender, covering mental health, behavioural problems, social and throughcare processes, residential care and control, educational and spiritual perspectives, there should nevertheless be an agreed overall approach to the treatment or programme design. It is this area of determining the approach which is likely to be the most effective based on previous research, designing programmes and evaluating their success, which incorporates the psychologist's skills. Where there is disagreement on which of the proposed approaches will be most effective, an experimental design can be set up with programmes running in parallel and being evaluated. After evaluation is completed, all should be committed to following the most effective means of rehabilitation.

Smooth working among professionals from different disciplines is not easy to achieve, but flows from all being willing to adopt the aims of the organization rather than setting their own.

Examples of the way in which operational constraints impact on rehabilitation have already been described, but such situations mainly apply where a traditional view of rehabilitation is taken. Where there is a holistic view, then security and operational needs are part of rehabilitation. How the offender is treated in his or her residential base, how visits are organized, and his or her security category, are all part of the rehabilitation plan. "What works" in terms of security is often determined by good staff–prisoner/client relationships, so in a whole institution approach, good sentence planning for inmates would include staged down-grading of levels of security, based on individual progress, as assessed by agreed methods of behavioural monitoring (McDougall, Clark & Woodward, 1995).

Essential to the effectiveness of rehabilitation within secure institutions are good quality assessment and sentence planning methods. There needs to be a clear focus on what is to be achieved, agreement in the team about how this can be achieved, and the part members of the multidisciplinary team play. Monitoring and evaluation of the change process is essential to further development of sentence plans throughout sentence stages.

Evaluation of programmes in secure institutions does not allow for the traditional measure of reconviction rates, as release may be a long way off. However, useful indicators can be obtained through psychometric, physiological and behavioural measures of targeted behaviour, as part of the planned holistic staged evaluation up to and beyond release. This process establishes "what works" for each offender and consequently the treatment approach to be adopted.

STAFF TRAINING

Most staff come to rehabilitation teams with some prior professional training in the delivery of rehabilitation programmes, and bring with them methods most widely adopted by their professional group, such as psychiatry, social work and teaching. The exceptions are special hospital nurses/prison officers, who receive initial basic training, but which is not necessarily focused on rehabilitation programmes, and prison psychologists, who receive MSc training as an integral part of their first two years' employment. Clinical psychologists in the forensic field will have previously had generic clinical psychology training. Additionally, opportunities exist for non-psychologists to train on diploma courses in behavioural sciences.

Some of the problems within multidisciplinary teams are exacerbated by the diversity of background training, which is contrary to the aim of an agreed approach to programme design, and makes a case for joint training for all members of teams. This generic training does not negate the professional background training of the staff involved, for instance nurses will still provide care in the residential function in line with their training, and probation officers/social workers can still apply their skills in the social and throughcare elements of their work. However, where rehabilitation programmes are included, a team approach must be adopted with programme integrity being maintained.

For these reasons the Prison Service has adopted multidisciplinary training for its national treatment programmes for sex offenders, anger management and cognitive skills. All staff involved in delivery of programmes undergo the same training and follow identical programmes which are currently being nationally evaluated. These programmes have been based on research findings as to which programmes have proved to be most effective (Andrews et al., 1990; Lipsey, 1992; McDougall et al., 1987; Thornton et al., 1994).

Multidisciplinary training was the preferred option for the Prison Service. However, in situations where the increasing demands for specialist staff outstrip supply and where there is a shortage of specialist staff, there is no alternative other than to operate in this way (WPSOABP, 1993).

Although in the past there was scepticism about prison officers carrying out a welfare role, now in the Prison Service there is almost universal acceptance of "the personal officer". This entails the allocation of officers to take care of front-line welfare needs and report writing for a specified group of inmates. Training for this role is now part of initial officer training but has not been systematic for more experienced officers. However, many local courses do exist, often supported by attachment to prison probation service units.

As prison officers are expected to deal with welfare matters, the Service now selects officers with this as part of their job description, however this does not necessarily mean all officers are suitable for running rehabilitation courses. In such situations they need to be more carefully selected for appropriate attitudes and skills. A prerequisite is a genuine willingness to be involved in the treatment programme, appropriate attitudes to the subject focus of the programme and to offenders, personal integrity, and ability and confidence to manage and tutor the programme. In the case of sex offender programmes, attitudes are particularly important and the need for support of tutors on such programmes is recognized.

An important issue relates to the ability of staff without prior treatment experience to carry out treatment programmes. Evidence suggests that they can do so successfully providing they are motivated, properly trained, and programme integrity is maintained through clearly defined session objectives and monitoring (McDougall et al., 1987).

Officers were trained to run anger management courses at a young offender institution, by undergoing first a short course in group work practice and presentation skills and then in the principles and practice of anger management training. They were next tutored with a trained psychologist and then, when both the tutor and officer were confident that appropriate levels of skill were achieved, two officers tutored courses unsupervised. Courses were monitored by video and important elements of the course were later viewed and discussed by the psychologist tutor. Course evaluations indicated that officer tutors were as effective in achieving significant reduction in governors' disciplinary reports as psychologist tutors (McDougall et al., 1987).

National anger management training courses are now being run in the Prison Service for multidisciplinary teams. The course is largely practical, with course members acting as both tutors and anger management course attenders, and undergoing training by running a whole programme. Early anger management courses run in establishments are supported by qualified tutors. The success of anger management courses is being evaluated on a national basis.

Officers trained in methods of risk assessment based on patterns of behaviour associated with offending demonstrated that, having received appropriate training in carrying out the procedure, they were able to identify similar risk factors as psychologists when assessed by independent raters (Clark, 1993). Officers who have been trained in sex offender treatment programmes have similarly shown themselves able to succeed in training along with other specialists. This is assessed by evidence that results of courses run by officers demonstrate they are as effective as those run by specialists (Thornton et al., 1994).

RESEARCH AND DEVELOPMENT

For a system of rehabilitation to be based on "what works" there must be a strong and effective research and development programme. The importance of applied research and development is never questioned in the business world. As reported in *Management Today* (Foster, 1993);

> For almost any ambitious manufacturer (and for many service organisations too) research and development is not a fashion, nor is it an option; it is an essential business activity. It is also, obviously, a pre-requisite for membership of the first division: the company that does not keep up with the technology loses its ability to compete.

Although much prison-based and generic research to provide a knowledge base has been carried out in universities and by some notable researchers, some of whom are featured in this book, evaluation of rehabilitation programmes has been intermittent, numbers of subjects have been small, with different methodologies to such an extent that much of our knowledge of what is effective is based on meta-analyses (Lipsey, 1992). The need for more operational research has been recognized with the creation of multidisciplinary research units at Ashworth and Rampton Special Hospitals, and a Research and Development Group in the Prison Service. Interest in research is being promoted by the introduction of a *Special Hospitals Research Bulletin* (Editor R. Blackburn). The means of facilitating research has been described (McMurran, 1992) as requiring provision of research guidelines, quality standards, research support meetings, conferences and seminars, publications, planning of major projects, involvement of students and trainees, teaching and supervision of staff from other disciplines, representation on ethics committees, formation of outside links and encouragement by carrying out one's own research.

Psychologists in the Prison Service have for many years carried out research, but the information has not always been well enough co-ordinated or widely disseminated. In recent years, since the inception of the MSc in Applied Criminological Psychology, supervised and university-approved research projects have begun to produce a wealth of research information on subjects of operational relevance to the Service.

Also, more recently, the national inmate treatment programmes have given the opportunity for large-scale evaluation, with programme integrity over a range of establishments. This co-ordination has already provided psychometric and behavioural data on effectiveness not previously available (Thornton et al., 1994), but reconviction data will not be available until an adequate time period has elapsed.

In line with earlier views that specialists need to be at the heart of management, research and development should be also at the heart of management decision-making. The new Research and Development function within the Planning Group in the Prison Service has the purpose of providing a research and development service to the Executive Committee, Prisons Board, HQ Divisions and prison establishments.

Research has traditionally been seen as independent of the operation, taking an objective, impartial view. This is often necessary to ensure the validity of results, however there is also a need for quick, though good quality research which informs the developmental process and interacts with the operation. This operational/action research approach is increasingly of value in a changing organization.

The Planning Group will commission and manage two kinds of research, which might be described as strategic and tactical. Strategic research is fundamental research which provides the knowledge base to inform long-term strategic planning and to review existing strategy. Tactical research is operational/action research to inform policy and to identify and assess tactical approaches designed to achieve strategic aims.

Within this framework the Research and Development Group has the potential to fulfil the following functions.

Strategic research functions:

- Provide information to all Prison Service managers and administrators from a bank of research knowledge.
- Identify fundamental questions which need to be answered through research to augment the knowledge base for strategic planning.
- Advise the Prisons Board on long-term strategy based on existing research knowledge and research targeted to provide a comprehensive knowledge base.
- Commission and supervise internal/external research contracts.
- Liaise with Research and Statistics Department on criminal justice research topics.
- Foster links with outside and international agencies to seek new approaches, increase creativity and validate research.

Tactical research functions:

- Provide information to all Prison Service managers and administrators from a bank of research knowledge.
- Respond quickly to the need for research on operational matters.
- Advise on policy development through quick operational research

evaluation, action research and reference to background research and statistical information.

- Identify areas of research which could be carried out to answer tactical questions.
- Provide information to Prisons Board and HQ Divisions on field-initiated research.
- Support and encourage field research on relevant topics.
- Co-ordinate field-initiated research across establishments where appropriate.
- Develop practical approaches to the assimilation of research findings into routines.
- Disseminate research findings in easily understood style.

This approach has the value of focusing research on subjects of main importance in Prison Service planning, in addition to improving and encouraging research at establishment level, and making links with other establishments, so that similar methodologies can be adopted and results co-ordinated. The most important feature is that it is linked to policy development and will influence direction and future operation of the Prison Service.

HOW TO SURVIVE SECURE INSTITUTIONS – A PERSONAL STRATEGY

At the beginning of this chapter I advised readers not to consider working in secure institutions if they did not relish a challenge. This is meant very much from a personal as well as a professional point of view. Institutions can be testing and confrontational, you will have to earn your credibility, and your professional viewpoint will be frequently questioned. From regular discussions with groups of psychologists in their early weeks of working in secure institutions, I have an up-to-date view of some of the problems they face, which serves to remind me of how it felt being a new psychologist working in an institution. Mostly these new psychologists want to know how to handle situations at a personal level; they are conscious of their lack of experience; most have already heard the psychology profession being attacked; the women have sometimes heard sexist remarks. Occasionally someone has got off to a bad start, by having made a complaint about an officer to his/her superior, and although this has not helped relationships, felt justified in doing so. These can be difficult times for new psychologists, but a strategy can help.

It is important to recognize that all psychologists, no matter how experienced and knowledgeable, will at times be faced with these problems. They are not reserved for newly appointed psychologists, although it sometimes appears so.

The difference is that more experienced psychologists have developed a means of coping with, or deflecting, such situations.

I would like to say that most staff are helpful and supportive and it is usually a minority who may present problems. Often comments made are light-hearted and are merely irritating, however occasionally they can be seen as hostile. One of the things which sometimes does surprise me however is that, in dealing with situations which are personally threatening, our psychological knowledge and expertise sometimes deserts us, and I will try, in developing this survival strategy, to identify how psychology can help.

Firstly, you will remember from Novaco's (1975) principles of anger man-agement, that angry aggression often occurs when people feel insecure or threatened in some way, and they use aggression to try to take control of the situation. Bear in mind therefore that the presence of specialists with qualifications and skills can be threatening to establishment staff. It is up to you therefore to demonstrate that you are not a threat, rather than reinforcing this impression. Unfortunately, under such circumstances, because of our own insecurity, there is a tendency to try to demonstrate that we have superior skills, and this can be counter-productive.

We also know from Novaco (1975) that how we react is based on our cognitive appraisal of a situation. If we consider comments made against our profession as a personal attack we are likely to react angrily. This is usually a function of seeing ourselves as individuals working within an organization rather than as a member of a professional group with a respected role within the institution and a planned strategy for coping with the problems which arise. If we take the view that institutions are imperfect, as are the teams working within them, and that our role is to help change the culture, we perceive the situation very differently, and our behaviour of necessity must be different. As psychologists running a programme for a group of offenders, we would not contemplate becoming angry or reporting a member of a group for an inappropriate comment. We would make it clear we did not approve, but work towards improvement, encouraging appropriate behaviour, and ignoring inappropriate behaviour. Why then do we not take the same approach to staff in the establishment? If we revert to being an individual and taking things personally, then we will not succeed in our aim as part of the professional group to work towards changing the culture of the establishment. If you regard the provocative behaviours as something on your list of things to change, it is much less painful and potentially a very creative approach.

In discussion with new psychologists about the strategy for survival, they have often wanted to know what tactics can be adopted, and I have described the things that I think have been important for me in working successfully within establishments and reaching my current position.

It is important to aim for high professional standards, both in personal behaviour and in quality of work. The psychology profession will be judged by how you and others in your team perform. Therefore be dependable, trustworthy, and always do what you say you will do. This will be the basis for your credibility.

Do the job which needs doing rather than what you want to do. As mentioned earlier, you will be appreciated if you meet the needs of the organization rather than your own. Often there is scope for both.

Be prepared to learn and listen. A psychology degree does not answer all questions. Practical experience counts for a lot so recognize how your skills and the practical skills of others can and do complement each other.

Respect the skills of other groups of staff and involve them in your work where possible. You will find it pays off, and the more you co-operate with others, the more in demand you will become. National treatment programme strategies which involve prison officers as tutors, far from decreasing job opportunities, have led to a greater demand for psychologists.

Finally, enjoy what you do. We have an extremely varied and valuable range of skills of which we can be confident. These are in demand and, providing we fulfil expectations through our professionalism, that progress will continue.

Specialists have a great deal to offer secure institutions, and that is increasingly being recognized and welcomed.

REFERENCES

Andrews, D.A., Zinger, I., Hoge, R.D., Bonta, J., Gendreau, P. & Cullen, F.T. (1990) Does correctional treatment work? A clinically relevant and psychologically informed meta-analysis. *Criminology* **28**, 369–404.
Beckett, R., Beech, A., Fisher, D. & Scott-Fordham, A. (1994) *Community Based Treatment for Sex Offenders; An Evaluation of Seven Treatment Programmes.* London: Home Office Publications Unit.
Burchard, J.D. & Lane, T.W. (1982) Crime and delinquency. In: A.S. Bellack, M. Hersen & A.E. Kazdin (Eds), *International Handbook of Behavior Modification and Therapy*, pp. 613–652. New York: Plenum.
Clark, D. (1993) Risk assessment: pilot study evaluation. *Inside Psychology: The Journal of Prison Service Psychology*, **1**, No.2.

Cullen, J.E. & Seddon, J.W. (1981) The application of a behavioural regime to disturbed young offenders. *Personal and Individual Differences*, **2**, 285–292.

Home Office (1991) Custody, Care and Justice – The Way Ahead for the Prison Service in England and Wales. Government White Paper. London: HMSO.

Directorate of Inmate Programmes (1991) Treatment Programmes for Sex Offenders in Custody: A Strategy (1991) Internal HM Prison Service publication by Directorate of Inmate Programmes.

Emes, B.A. (1991) Opening address. In: *Treatment Programmes for Sex Offenders in Custody: A Strategy*. Internal HM Prison Service publication by Directorate of Inmate Programmes.

Foster, G. (1993) The innovation imperative. *Management Today, April edition*, 60–63.

Gendreau, P. & Andrews, D.A. (1990) Tertiary prevention: what the meta-analysis of the offender treatment literature tells us about "what works". *Canadian Journal of Criminology*, **32**, 173–184.

Guy, E. (1991) Management summary. In: *Treatment Programmes for Sex Offenders in Custody: A Strategy*. Internal HM Prison Service publication by Directorate of Inmate Programmes.

Hollin, C.R. (1993) Advances in the psychological treatment of delinquent behaviour. *Criminal Behaviour and Mental Health*, **3**, 142–157.

Hollin, C.R. (1995) The meaning and implications of "programme integrity". In J. McGuire (Ed.), *What Works: Effective Methods to Reduce Reoffending*. Chichester: Wiley.

Hollin, C.R., Howells, K., Powls, J. & McDougall, C. (1992) Controlling violent behaviour; theory, practice, training and management, Unpublished paper.

Inkster, N.D., Johnson, P. & Ekstedt, J. (1991) The reality of corrections: impediments and opportunities for realizing the purposes of Corrections. In *Proceedings from the International Symposium on the Future of Corrections*. Ottawa: Correctional Service of Canada.

Laws, D.R. (1974) The failure of a token economy. *Federal Probation*, **38**, 33–38.

Lipsey, M. (1992) Juvenile delinquency treatment: a meta-analytic inquiry into the viability of effects. In T. Cook, H. Cooper, D. Corday, H. Hartman, L. Hedges, R. Light, T. Louis & F. Mosteller (Eds), *Meta-Analysis for Explanation: A Casebook*. New York: Russell Sage Foundation.

Martinson, R. (1974) "What Works"? Questions and answers about prison reform. *The Public Interest*, **35**, 22–54.

McCord, D., Morris, N., Peters, T. & Stern, V. (1991) The identification of the core values. In *Proceedings from the International Symposium on the Future of Corrections*. Ottawa: Correctional Service of Canada.

McDougall, C., Barnett, R.M., Ashurst, B & Willis, B. (1987) Cognitive control of anger. In B.J. McGurk, D.M. Thornton & M. Williams (Eds), *Applying Psychology to Imprisonment: Theory and Practice*. London: HMSO.

McDougall, C., Boddis, S., Dawson, K. & Hayes, R. (1990) Developments in anger control training. In M. McMurran (Ed.), *Applying Psychology to Imprisonment: Young Offenders*. Issues in Criminological and Legal Psychology, No. 15. Leicester: The British Psychological Society for the Division of Criminological and Legal Psychology.

McDougall, C., Clark, D. & Woodward, R. (1995) Application of operational psychology to assessment of inmates. *Psychology, Crime and Law*, **2**, 85–99.

McMurran, M. (1992) Facilitating research. *Special Hospitals Research Bulletin*, **1**, No.2.

Novaco, R.W. (1975) *Anger Control*. Lexington MA: Lexington Books.

Ross, R.R. & Fabiano, E.A. (1985) *Time to Think: A Cognitive Model of Delinquency Prevention and Offender Rehabilitation.* Johnson City, TN: Institute of Social Sciences and Arts.

Thornton, D. (1991) Treatment of sexual offenders in prison: a strategy. In *Treatment Programmes for Sex Offenders in Custody: A Strategy.* Internal HM Prison Services publication by Directorate of Inmate Programmes.

Thornton, D., Nooney, K., Travers, R. & Francis, C. (1994) Programmes for imprisoned sex offenders: case management; treatment strategy; short term effects. Paper presented at The Sex Offender Treatment Conference, Coventry, convened by HM Prison Service.

Woolf, Right Hon. Lord Justice & Tumim, Judge Stephen (1991) *Prison Disturbances April 1990. Report of an Inquiry by the Right Hon. Lord Justice Woolf (Parts I & II) and His Honour Judge Stephen Tumim (Part II).* London: HMSO.

WPSOABP (1993) Psychology and antisocial behaviour. *A report prepared for the Professional Affairs Board by the Working Party on Clinical Psychology Services for Offenders and People with Antisocial Behaviour Problems.* Leicester: The British Psychological Society.

WORKING WITH OFFENDERS

CHAPTER FIVE

MENTALLY DISORDERED OFFENDERS

Ronald Blackburn

INTRODUCTION

Offenders dealt with under the Mental Health Act in Britain become the responsibility of the psychiatric services. While treatment facilities have traditionally centred on secure psychiatric hospitals catering for patients presumed to be dangerous, the need for gradations of secure provision has been increasingly recognized, and secure hospitals now form part of a wider network of custodial and community services. Mentally disordered offenders are therefore likely to be encountered in all settings dealing with offenders.

Most countries make special provision for this group, but their recognition is the outcome of social policy rather than the identification of a specific kind of psychological or criminological problem. Legal and administrative factors consequently determine how mentally disordered offenders are defined and where services are provided. Before examining the relationship of mental disorder to crime and service provision for mentally disordered offenders, the distinctive features of this group need to be considered.

WHO IS THE MENTALLY DISORDERED OFFENDER?

The term "mentally disordered offender" is sometimes taken literally to denote an offender known to suffer from a recognized psychiatric disorder. However,

Working with Offenders: Psychological Practice in Offender Rehabilitation.
Edited by C.R. Hollin. © 1996 John Wiley & Sons Ltd.

it is more commonly a formal designation reflecting legal recognition of a disorder of sufficient severity to justify interventions beyond those of the usual criminal justice process (Halleck, 1987). These may include diversion to health care facilities, or treatment in special units in the prison system.

Halleck (1987) identifies five points in the criminal justice process at which evidence of mental disorder influences legal action. First, most jurisdictions allow the police discretion in charging someone causing a public nuisance or suspected of a crime who may be mentally disordered, and provide for admission to hospital without prosecution. Section 136 of the Mental Health Act for England and Wales, for example, empowers the police to remove "to a place of safety" any person thought to be suffering from mental disorder and in immediate need of care and control. Second, a defendant may be found incompetent or "unfit to plead" at the time of trial, and detained in a mental hospital without a conviction being recorded. Third, insanity may be pleaded as a defence to a criminal charge, resulting, if successful, in the "special verdict" of "not guilty by reason of insanity". A more widely used alternative in British murder trials is the plea of "diminished responsibility", which may lead to a manslaughter verdict. Fourth, a defendant may be found guilty, but evidence of mental disorder may mitigate the severity of sentence, or the court may order "treatment" rather than "punishment". Finally, convicted prisoners who become mentally disordered may be transferred to the mental health system.

Populations of mentally disordered offenders therefore comprise a diverse group which includes some who have not been tried or found guilty of an offence, and who are not therefore technically "offenders". In Britain, most mentally disordered offenders are dealt with by hospital orders following a conviction, and few of those compulsorily detained have been judged incompetent or not guilty by reason of insanity. However, defendants are more likely to be found incompetent in Scotland than in England.

The 1983 Mental Health Act for England and Wales defines mental disorder as "mental illness, arrested or incomplete development of mind, psychopathic disorder and any other disorder or disability of mind". *Mental illness* is not defined, but generally covers the most serious mental disorders, such as schizophrenia or affective psychosis, and the majority of patients in secure hospitals fall in this category. *Mental impairment* refers to "a state of arrested or incomplete development of mind (not amounting to severe mental impairment) which includes significant impairment of intelligence and social functioning and is associated with abnormally aggressive or seriously irresponsible conduct on the part of the person concerned". Patients in this category will usually show a combination of learning disability or mental handicap and personality disorder. *Severe mental impairment* is defined similarly, except that impairment is "severe" rather than "significant". *Psychopathic disorder* is "a persistent disorder or disability of mind, whether or not including significant impairment of intelligence, which results in abnormally aggressive or seriously irresponsible conduct on the part of the person concerned".

These are legal categories, not clinical diagnostic terms. Psychopathic disorder has given rise to particular problems, partly because of the circularity of the definition, and partly because of doubts about the amenability of "psychopaths" to treatment. In practice, legally identified "psychopaths" are clinically heterogeneous, and include more serious violent and sexual offenders who additionally show personality disorder. However, personality disorders, as defined in DSM-III-R (American Psychiatric Association, 1987), are also common among those in the mental illness and mental impairment categories.

Jurisdictions vary, however, in what is legally recognized as mental disorder. The Mental Health Act for Scotland, for example, does not explicitly recognize mental impairment or psychopathic disorder. In fact, not all psychiatric disorders constitute mental disorder in law, and it is unusual for neurotic disorders to be accepted as "mental illness". In particular, personality disorder and alcohol or drug abuse, which are common among prisoners, are not usually sufficient to identify an offender as mentally disordered, although the former has sometimes been successfully used in insanity or diminished responsibility pleas.

Clinically, then, formally designated mentally disordered offenders are an arbitrarily defined group, which excludes many psychologically disabled offenders. It is frequently argued that offenders should have greater access to health care facilities. Gunn, Maden & Swinton (1991), for example, estimated that out of an adult prison population of some 50 000 in England and Wales, some 2% exhibited serious mental disorders which would be more appropriately dealt with in the mental health system. The view that it is more humane to treat those who are "ill" than to subject them to imprisonment underlies recent moves to divert more mentally disordered offenders to community facilities (Department of Health/Home Office, 1992). However, legal recognition of mental disorder is not predicated solely on what is humane, and the reasons why mental disorder in an offender should constitute a case for special legal disposal continue to be debated (Radden, 1985).

Mentally disordered offenders make up only a small minority of either psychiatric patients on the one hand, or convicted criminals on the other. For example, of the 16 830 patients compulsorily admitted to hospital in England and Wales during 1989–1990, 2578 (15%) came via the courts, prisons or police (Department of Health, 1992a). During the same period, over a million offenders were convicted by the courts of crimes other than motoring offences.

Most mentally disordered offenders are dealt with as patients of the NHS, in open psychiatric hospitals or as out-patients on probation orders, although during the past decade, services in England have centred increasingly on regional secure units (RSUs) offering medium levels of secure confinement. Some 200 a year are admitted to the special hospitals, which are maximum security hospitals for patients who "require treatment under conditions of special security on account of their dangerous, violent or criminal propensities". There are four such hospitals in Britain, these being Broadmoor, Rampton, Ashworth and the State Hospital at Carstairs in Scotland. Together, they house some 2000 patients, four-fifths of them male. About 70% have committed serious crimes such as murder, arson or sexual assault, but the hospitals also admit mentally disordered prisoners, and psychiatric patients who exhibit serious violence in other hospitals.

MENTAL DISORDER, CRIME AND VIOLENCE

Serious mental disorders occur sufficiently frequently among offenders to justify provision of services, and it is sometimes apparent that mental disorder has contributed to an offence in the individual case. However, this does not imply any more general relationship between mental disorder and crime. Since some 40% of males and 14% of females are likely to be convicted of a crime during their lifetime (Farrington, 1981), and mental disorders afflict over 10% of the population, the two may well be found together with some regularity even in the absence of any causal relationship. Detention under the Mental Health Act does not, in fact, require evidence of a causal association between the disorder and a crime, except in the case of psychopathic disorder and mental impairment.

Attempts to establish whether there is any systematic relationship have generated an extensive literature (Monahan & Steadman, 1983; Wessely & Taylor, 1991; Hodgins, 1993), but research has been hampered by both conceptual and methodological problems. Menzies & Webster (1989) noted that mental disorder and crime are not readily defined independently of each other, since both are socially constructed terms influenced by similar social processes. For example, psychiatry has increasingly included antisocial behaviour among the criteria for mental disorder.

Systems for dealing with offenders and the mentally disordered are also interdependent, and deinstitutionalization of mental hospital patients is widely believed to have led to more of them being processed by the criminal justice system. This "criminalization" hypothesis is not new. Penrose (1939) found an inverse relation between psychiatric bed provision and prison populations in European countries, and proposed that changes in the population of one institutional system force an inverse change in the other. Consistent with this hypothesis, Weller & Weller (1988) found a strong correlation between the falling numbers in psychiatric hospitals in England since 1950 and the increasing numbers in prison.

Research has also suffered from the lack of an agreed and reliable diagnostic framework for identifying mental disorders, making comparisons between studies problematic. Moreover, studies have frequently relied on samples whose representativeness of the wider population of either offenders or the mentally disordered is unknown. Monahan & Steadman (1983) note the utility of the epidemiological distinction between "true" and "treated" prevalence. Those identified as patients by the receipt of health services represent only "treated" rates of mental disorder, which substantially underestimate the "true" prevalence in the community at large. Convicted offenders similarly represent the "treated" minority of those committing criminal offences, as indicated by the "dark figure" of crimes not leading to an arrest. Ideally, true prevalence rates of both should be determined from random community samples, preferably using non-official criteria of crime or disorder. Few studies approximate to this ideal.

CRIMINAL BEHAVIOUR IN THE MENTALLY DISORDERED

The only study which comes close to ascertaining true crime prevalence among the "untreated" mentally disordered appears to be that of Teplin (1984). She describes observations of 1382 American police–citizen encounters, in which presence of severe mental illness was assessed by a brief symptom checklist. Of 506 persons suspected of a crime, 30 showed signs of mental illness, and significantly more of these were arrested than other suspects (47% vs 28%). However, contact between the police and the mentally ill was not determined primarily by suspicion of a crime, and the mentally ill were more often the objects of concern or assistance. Also, crimes for which they were suspected did not differ from those of other suspects. These findings therefore suggest a bias towards arrest of the mentally ill, but not their greater proneness to criminal behaviour.

Research concerned with the violent behaviour of psychiatric patients prior to and during hospitalization is not directly germane to the issue of criminality, and is considered below. More pertinent are American studies examining subsequent arrest rates of patients following discharge from state hospitals, which were reviewed by Rabkin (1979). She found that studies prior to 1965 consistently showed former patients to be *less* likely to be arrested after release than members of the general population. Studies reported after 1965 indicated that patients were *more* likely to be arrested, and for more serious crimes. However, the best predictor of later arrest was previous arrest, and comparisons between earlier and later research suggested that the difference was largely due to the hospitalization of increased numbers of patients with previous arrest histories, these accounting for most of the post-discharge offending. The later data are therefore attributed to changes in mental health policies, with hospital admission being increasingly restricted to the more socially disruptive or dangerous. Consistent with the interpretation that serious mental disorder does not increase the risk of crime are findings from a recent 15-year follow-up of all schizophrenic patients discharged from hospital in Stockholm in 1971 (Lindqvist & Allebeck, 1990). Offence rates for males were only marginally higher than the general population rate. Female patients, on the other hand, offended at twice the expected rate.

Much of this research makes untested assumptions about psychiatric status at discharge, the demographic comparability of patients with the general population, and absence of bias in liability to arrest. Both Rabkin (1979) and Monahan & Steadman (1983) concluded that when demographic differences are taken into account, offending among psychiatric patients is associated more with the same factors of age, gender, social class and ethnicity which predict crime in general than with psychiatric disorder itself. Recent findings, however, question this conclusion, at least as it applies to violent crime (Monahan, 1993). For example, Lindqvist & Allebeck (1990) found that violent offending in discharged schizophrenic patients was four times more frequent than expected, although this was confined to only 7% of the sample. An American survey by Link, Cullen & Andrews (1992), which compared patients in the community with a random community sample, also found evidence of higher levels of violence in patients. Patients were divided into former patients, those with a first psychiatric contact, and those with repeated contacts, and on official measures of arrest and self-reported violence, all groups showed higher levels than those with no psychiatric history. However, differences in official arrests reflected mainly violent crimes, and there was little difference between groups in arrests for other crimes. Moreover, the major contributory variable was the presence of active psychotic symptoms, not patient status itself.

Hodgins (1992, 1993) presents evidence that serious mental disorders not only increase the risk of violence, but also increase the risk of criminal behaviour more generally. She reports a longitudinal study of a birth cohort of 15 000 individuals born in Stockholm county in 1953, who were followed up for 30 years. Those developing mental disorders, as determined from hospital admission records, were divided into those showing major disorders (schizophrenia, major depression, bipolar disorders), substance abuse, and other mental disorders, while intellectual deficiency was defined by admission to special schools. Males and females with major mental disorders and substance abuse, and males showing intellectual handicap were more likely to have a criminal record than those who were not disordered, while all groups were more likely to have a record of at least one violent crime. Hodgins cautions against generalizing the results to societies with different levels of crime.

There is little support from these studies for the notion that psychiatric disorder *in general* increases the risk of criminal behaviour, and some disorders may actually lessen the risk. While one recent study suggests that more serious mental disorders are associated with greater criminality, this has not been consistently indicated. Recent research, however, consistently points to an association of psychotic disorder with violence.

MENTAL DISORDER IN CRIMINALS

An alternative approach is to ascertain the presence of mental disorder among known criminals. There are no recent studies of court samples, who would be most representative of apprehended offenders, but a few studies have examined pre-trial detainees in British remand prisons or American jails. Most studies have concerned sentenced prisoners, who are unlikely to be representative of active criminals more generally, and the prevalence of mental disorder may well be underestimated by the filtering out of many disordered offenders at an early stage in criminal justice processing.

Brodsky (1972) summarized American studies of court or prison samples from 1918 to 1970 which suggested rates of psychiatric disorder ranging from 16% to 95%. Rates of psychosis ranged from 1% to 4%, while highest rates were for personality disorder or "behaviour disorders". Vague criteria for these latter disorders account for much of the variation. Guze (1976) used more reliable research diagnostic criteria in interviewing male and female prisoners in Missouri prior to release. All females and 90% of the males received a psychiatric diagnosis. Rates of psychosis and mental retardation were low, but 78% of males and 65% of females received a diagnosis of sociopathy. However, the criteria for sociopathy were mainly a history of social deviance, such as delinquency or prostitution, and the significance of this category is questionable. Similar criticisms apply to the DSM-III category of antisocial personality disorder, which has been diagnosed in about a half of prisoners in recent American studies.

Lower rates of disorder have been estimated in British prison surveys. Gunn, Maden & Swinton (1991) assessed a random sample of 1365 adult males and 404 young males from 16 English prisons, deriving ICD diagnoses by means of a semi-structured interview and file information. Overall, 37% received a primary diagnosis. Main diagnoses were substance abuse (23%), personality disorder (10%), neurosis (6%), psychosis (2%), mental handicap (0.9%) and organic disorders (0.8%). However, reliability of diagnosis was not assessed, and it is noted that personality disorders may be underestimated. While the findings suggest that psychosis is infrequent among prisoners, data from a remand sample point to a much higher rate (Taylor & Gunn, 1984). Recent research on pre-trial detainees in American jails has also identified between 4% and 12% as schizophrenic or psychotic (Teplin, McLelland & Abram, 1993).

Conclusions from these studies are limited by varying diagnostic criteria and the absence of comparable data from non-prisoners, but recent North American research has employed uniform (DSM-III) diagnostic criteria and standardized instruments which permit comparisons with general population surveys (Hodgins, 1993). These typically indicate higher rates of severe mental disorders and substance abuse among prisoners. For example, Hodgins & Côté (1990) found schizophrenia to be seven times higher among penitentiary inmates in Quebec than in the general population, and bipolar disorder four times higher. Minor disorders, such as generalized anxiety or phobias, were also common, and only 5% of inmates were free of a history of any disorder.

Overall, then, the evidence suggests that prison populations contain more mentally disordered individuals than would be expected by chance. Substance abuse and personality disorders are the most common disorders, but recent research indicates that more severe disorders are also overrepresented. However, comparisons between prevalence of disorder among prisoners and general population estimates may be misleading in the absence of controls for socioeconomic status (Monahan & Steadman, 1983), and while studies of mental disorder among prisoners are important to health care planning, they do not permit any firm generalizations about the relationship of mental disorder to crime.

VIOLENCE AND MENTAL DISORDER

Evidence relating psychiatric disorders to specific offence categories is fragmentary. Shoplifting is not associated with mental disorder to a significant extent, although among the disordered minority, depression is overrepresented (Gibbens, 1981). Property destruction, on the other hand, may be correlated with disorder. For example, in their study of London remand prisoners, Taylor & Gunn (1984) found signs of disorder in 60% of those charged with or convicted of arson or criminal damage. Half of these showed psychotic symptoms.

There is a more extensive literature on mental disorder and violence. While the mentally disordered are commonly perceived as dangerous, social scientists have argued that any observed relationship reflects methodological artefacts or criminalization. However, as noted earlier, recent research suggests that more serious disorders increase the risk of violent crime.

Several studies have examined the prevalence of violent incidents among psychiatric patients. Some of these focus on violent acts committed in the weeks preceding admission to hospital, and apparently high rates of between 10% and 40% have been reported (Wessely & Taylor, 1991; Monahan, 1993). However, psychiatric admissions are a biased sample, and violence itself is often the main reason for hospitalization.

Evidence from several countries suggests an increase in violence in psychiatric hospitals since the 1970s, apparently as a result of changing admission policies (Haller & Deluty, 1988; Davis, 1991). However, violent incidents in hospitals are typically minor, and few lead to serious injuries. There may well be qualitative differences between violent crimes and the minor incidents observed in hospitals. Quinsey & Maguire (1986), for example, found that assaultive behaviour in a maximum security hospital did not predict subsequent violent crime in the community, and some studies find females more likely to be the perpetrators. Violence is also perpetrated by a small minority, and Harris & Varney (1986) found that less than 5% of residents in a maximum security hospital were responsible for 74% of incidents. While some studies suggest a greater involvement of schizophrenic patients, findings are not entirely consistent, and violence in hospital may be as much a product of institutional factors such as overcrowding, staff expectations, staff experience and management practices, as of patient pathology (Davis, 1991).

While this research is relevant to the management of disruptive behaviour, selection biases in admission preclude any general conclusions about propensities for violence among the mentally disordered. Monahan (1993) emphasizes the need for prevalence data from community samples not selected for treatment, and these are provided by an epidemiological study involving 10 000 residents of three American cities (Swanson et al., 1990). An index of violence was derived from self-reports of assaultive acts committed during the previous year, and DSM-III diagnoses were derived from a standardized interview. Personality disorders were not assessed, but all other psychiatric disorders were associated with higher rates of violence. For example, while 2.1% of the non-disordered reported at least one violent act, this applied to 5.0% of those considered phobic, 11.7% of those with major depression, 12.7% of schizophrenics, 24.6% of alcohol abusers and 34.7% of substance abusers. Apart from the latter two, the absolute rates are not high, but these findings suggest that most disorders increase the risk of violence for a significant minority.

Some research has attempted to determine whether mental disorder is more prevalent among those who exhibit violence. Homicide has attracted particular attention, and high police clearance rates for this crime ensure relatively unbiased samples. However, data are confounded by national variations in the recording of homicide and by the possible contaminating effect of violence on diagnosis. Also, homicide is not necessarily representative of violent behaviour more generally.

Häfner & Böker (1982) surveyed all 533 cases of serious violence (murder, attempted murder and manslaughter) in the Federal Republic of Germany between 1955 and 1964, who were excused legal responsibility because of serious mental disorder (schizophrenic or affective psychosis, organic brain disorder, mental retardation). Although unable to derive strictly comparable official crime data, the authors estimated that the mentally disordered accounted for only 2.9% of convictions for serious violence, and for 5.6% of murder victims. However, a greater involvement of mental disorder is suggested by recent studies from Scandinavia, where those charged with homicide routinely undergo psychiatric examination (Hodgins, 1993). Lindqvist (1986), for example, found that over half of those charged with homicide in northern Sweden were suffering from a serious mental disorder. Almost 40% of these were also substance abusers, most of whom were intoxicated at the time of the crime.

In Britain, mental disorder has been recognized in 30–40% of homicides for much of this century, and about a fifth of those charged with murder in recent years have been convicted of manslaughter on the grounds of diminished responsibility. Among 107 remand prisoners in London charged with or convicted of homicide, Taylor & Gunn (1984) found that more than a third showed symptoms of disorder (schizophrenia, 9.3%; affective psychosis, 1.9%; mixed disorders, 26%).

While there is therefore evidence of high rates of abnormality among homicides, the use of proportions may be misleading, given variations in national homicide rates. In a cross-cultural comparison, Coid (1983) found the rate of mentally disordered homicides per head of population to be relatively constant across countries and over time, at about 0.10 per 100 000. Fluctuations in homicide rates are therefore likely to reflect social factors which influence "non-pathological" murder. This would account for the proportionate decline of abnormal homicides in Britain as the overall murder rate has risen.

VIOLENCE AND SPECIFIC PSYCHIATRIC DISORDERS

In several respects, the question of whether mental disorder increases the risk of crime or violence is not particularly meaningful. Both mental disorders and crimes are heterogeneous phenomena, and global measures of either may obscure relationships between some forms of disorder and some forms of crime (Wessely & Taylor, 1991).

Evidence from several sources suggests that some disorders increase the risk of violence more than others. Häfner & Böker (1982) found that compared with non-offender patients, schizophrenia was overrepresented, and affective psychosis underrepresented in their violent mentally disordered group, although there were sex differences. They estimated that the risk of serious violence in schizophrenia was 0.05% (i.e. five of every 10 000 schizophrenics are likely to commit a serious violent crime), while in affective disorders and mental retardation, it was 0.006%. While emphasizing the low rates of violence in these disorders, this suggests that schizophrenia carries the greater risk. Swanson et al. (1990) also found that schizophrenia was associated with greater risk of violence than absence of disorder or neurotic disorder, although with a much lower risk than alcohol or drug abuse. However, in their study, the rate of violence reported by those with affective disorder did not differ from that of the schizophrenic subjects. Other findings on the contribution of affective disorders to violence are inconclusive. Depression has been associated with serious violence, but primarily among females, and in the context of "extended suicide", in which the killing of associates is linked to the killing of oneself (Häfner & Böker, 1982). Häfner & Böker suggest that in males, depression may actually decrease the risk of violence. Collins & Bailey (1990), on the other hand, found that depressive symptoms were associated with a history of adult fighting among prisoners.

Psychotic patients, however, are not homogeneous, and violent behaviour seems more likely in the presence of particular symptoms. As Krakowski, Volavka & Brizer (1986) note, planned, successful violence assumes a degree of intact functioning not compatible with severe impairment or disorganization, and violent acts by schizophrenic patients are more likely during the acute, active phase of disorder (Planasky & Johnson, 1977; Häfner & Böker, 1982; Link et al., 1992). The presence of delusions is the most frequent correlate of violence. Planasky & Johnson (1977) found that of 59 schizophrenics who made threats or assaults, nine complained of urges to kill, seven claimed hallucinatory instructions, and six catatonic patients attacked suddenly and in a frenzy, but 39% of incidents involved delusional misperceptions. Persecutory delusions are not necessarily the most prominent symptom, and some clinical studies have found that delusions of infidelity (morbid jealousy) and misidentification (the transformation of others) may be equally associated with serious violence.

Whether psychotic symptoms are sufficient to explain violence is debatable, since not all violent acts by patients can be attributed to their disorder. Violent incidents in hospital, for example, more often relate to provocations or disputes over personal space than to psychotic symptoms. Taylor (1985) estimated that 20% of the offences of schizophrenic prisoners were definitely motivated by delusional or hallucinatory symptoms, and a further 26% probably so. However, while abnormal beliefs or perceptions may be necessary to explain the violence in such cases, they are rarely, if ever, sufficient, and an understanding of violence in the context of those beliefs requires reference to the personal, social and situational factors associated with violence in the population generally (Davis, 1991).

Aggression is the most common form of "challenging behaviour" among the learning disabled (Murphy, 1993), and recent data suggest that intellectual handicap increases the risk of violent crime (Hodgins, 1992). However, sexual and arson offences are more prominent than crimes of violence among detained mentally handicapped offenders (Day, 1993). In a study of sexual offending among special hospital patients, Murrey, Briggs & Davis (1992) found that the offences of mentally impaired patients were less likely to be associated with violence than those of patients in the mental illness or psychopathic disorder categories. Use of violence was also correlated positively with IQ in all categories. The causal role of low intelligence in antisocial behaviour remains unclear. There is now consistent evidence of a moderate correlation of low IQ with crime, even after controlling for socio-economic factors, but while this is generally assumed to be mediated by effects on the acquisition of self-regulatory or problem-solving skills, there is also evidence for an interaction with deviant temperament or familial factors (Blackburn, 1993a).

The category most often associated with violence in clinical lore is personality disorder. However, the relationship is often confounded by the use of social deviance as a criterion of personality disorder (Blackburn, 1988), and the tendency to make global diagnoses of personality disorder, ignoring heterogeneity. While evidence is lacking on the relative risk of violence among different categories of personality disorder as defined in DSM-III, aggression or anger appear among the criteria for antisocial, borderline, narcissistic and passive–aggressive disorders. Coid (1992) found high rates of these disorders in a special unit for difficult to manage prisoners.

Several studies have examined reoffending in mentally disordered offenders (Murray, 1989). Since these samples have already been identified as violent, this research only indirectly addresses the question of differential susceptibility to violence of particular psychiatric disorders. However, some findings suggest that personality disorders carry a greater risk of violence than does psychosis. Quinsey et al. (1975), for example, found higher rates of violent recidivism in released maximum security patients with a diagnosis of personality disorder than in those with a diagnosis of psychosis, although this was not replicated in a later study of the same institution (Quinsey & Maguire, 1986). Patients admitted to English special hospitals in the legal category of psychopathic disorder also tend to commit more violent offences following release than those categorized as mentally ill (Murray, 1989; Bailey & MacCulloch, 1992).

Studies based on stricter criteria of psychopathy support an association with violence, both in prisoners and mentally disordered offenders. Recent research has employed the Psychopathy Checklist (PCL; Hare & Hart, 1993). Prisoners identified as psychopaths by the PCL have more extensive criminal records, are more involved in rule violations in prison, and are more likely than nonpsychopaths to reoffend following release. These differences hold particularly for violence, and while the offending of psychopaths appears to decline with age, this is not so for violence (Hare, McPherson & Forth, 1988). Since personality disorders and psychosis are not mutually exclusive, the PCL may also predict violence in other forms of mental disorder.

In summary, with the notable exception of substance abuse disorders, and some forms of personality disorder, none of the major categories of mental disorder seems strongly associated with a propensity for violence. Although there appears to be an increased risk in schizophrenia, only a small minority of patients in this category become violent, and recent work suggests that it is the presence of active psychotic symptoms, particularly delusions, rather than diagnostic category which increases the risk. As yet, however, our understanding of the factors which distinguish mentally disordered offenders from the mentally disordered more generally remains meagre.

INTERVENTIONS WITH MENTALLY DISORDERED OFFENDERS

Health care facilities for disordered offenders are identified as the domain of forensic psychiatry, but the implication that this is a specialized area of clinical *intervention* is misleading. The adjective "forensic" applies to argument in a legal setting, and forensic experts, whatever their discipline, are those who examine and present evidence to a court in a particular case (Haward, 1981). It does not therefore denote an area of specialized clinical knowledge or skill, but rather the application of such knowledge in a judicial context. The forensic role is also exercised on behalf of legal officials who are most likely to be concerned with preventing reoffending, and traditional allegiance to the patient as client is hence compromised. Work with mentally disordered offenders therefore raises a number of questions about professional goals and obligations.

Although mentally disordered offenders do not encompass all dysfunctional offenders, there are no psychological disorders which are unique to this group. They therefore pose broadly the same *clinical* problems as other mental health clients. Since it is the mental disorder of mentally disordered offenders which determines their placement in the mental health system, not their offending behaviour, the goals of clinical intervention would appear to be to reduce the likelihood of further antisocial acts by ameliorating the mental disorder of which these are a function. This, however, risks oversimplification, since apart from the absence of any general causal relationship between psychiatric disorder and crime, the relationship is often obscure in the individual case. For example, a persecutory delusion may obviously have contributed to an assault, but arson by a mentally handicapped person is not explained by intellectual deficit.

There is disagreement about what should be targeted and how successful outcome should be evaluated. Behaviourists often see criminal behaviour as the appropriate target of intervention. Crawford (1984), for example, argues that concepts of "mental abnormality" have no utility for a deterministic behavioural science, and that a behavioural analysis calls for examination of the development of the offending behaviour. Some psychiatrists similarly argue that reduced recidivism is the primary goal of interventions with disordered offenders (MacCulloch & Bailey, 1991).

While there are merits in a *functional analysis*, which focuses on the immediate antecedents and consequences of the offence, it would be foolish to ignore "mental states" in such an analysis. The association of psychotic beliefs with violence is well supported (Link, Collen & Andrews, 1992), and antisocial attitudes are significant mediators of criminal behaviour (Andrews, Bonta &

Hoge, 1990). A comprehensive analysis must also be concerned with the tendency to *repeat* deviant acts, and cannot avoid reference to the more general dispositions a person brings to a situation. These represent the products of prior learning and development which mediate new experiences. For example, intervention with a murderer must be concerned less with the prior criminal act than with the persisting personal and social factors which may support violence in the future. It is these mediators which need to be identified and targeted.

Crawford's view also raises ethical problems, since the criteria for judging which offenders should be subject to psychological intervention become political rather than clinical. Crime is defined by the state, not by behavioural or medical science, and the implication that all offenders are potential subjects for psychological intervention reduces the role of the psychologist to that of agent of social control. Programmes defined by offence category rather than psychological problem may also deny patients treatment. Patients should not have to commit a sexual *offence* to get treatment for a sexual *problem*.

Robertson (1989), in contrast, argues that reduced recidivism is not an appropriate criterion for judging the success of programmes for detained mentally disordered offenders. He suggests that treatment in the form of hospitalization contributes only a small part of the variance in reoffending, which has more to do with events following discharge. However, this assumes a medical conception of treatment as symptom removal, rather than a psychological conception of intervention as the provision of skills for avoiding further difficulties.

The primary justification for any rehabilitation programme for offenders cannot be simply the prevention of reoffending, since this can be accomplished by cheaper though more drastic measures, such as execution or surgical incapacitation. Rather, the rehabilitation "ideal" is aimed at increasing personal effectiveness, of which avoiding further offending is only one component (Blackburn, 1993a). In the case of mentally disordered offenders, this implies that the targets of intervention are those cognitive, emotional and interpersonal disabilities which impede social reintegration. Reduced recidivism is therefore a necessary but not sufficient criterion of the effectiveness of intervention.

ASSESSMENT STRATEGIES

Legal recognition of mental disorder in an offender requires a psychiatric diagnosis, but diagnostic labels are of limited utility in treatment planning.

Mental Health Act categories are an even cruder guide to treatment needs. Blackburn et al. (1990), for example, found little difference in the prevalence of personality disorders between patients in the mental illness and psychopathic disorder categories, two-thirds of each group showing evidence of one or more disorders. Violent offending is also associated with a variety of psychological problems, such as neuropsychological deficits, dysfunctional cognitive processing and deviant interpersonal beliefs (Blackburn, 1993a; also Chapter 7). Since mentally disordered offenders commonly have multiple disabilities, assessment needs to examine not only cognitive and affective symptoms of dysfunction, but also lifestyle factors conducive to deviant behaviour, such as attitudes to self and others, interpersonal style, recreations and substance use.

Clinical assessment is the process of gathering information necessary for making informed decisions about a client, and involves the testing of hypotheses leading to the formation of a model of the client's problems. The critical starting point is usually an analysis of the offence or current antisocial behaviour, but as has been emphasized, this must be seen in the broader context of personal and social characteristics. Assessment therefore relies on a combination of interviews, psychometric measures and file information recording social, psychiatric and criminal history and the observations of significant others. While concerns about the "tester" role, and muddled thinking about dispositional concepts have led to a decline in the use of standardized tests of intellectual functioning, personality and psychopathology, these have a significant contribution to make to assessment as a hypothesis generating and testing process, as well as in evaluating treatment change. Evidence from the offender rehabilitation literature, for example, indicates that treatment planning requires assessment of individual characteristics which influence response to treatment, such as interpersonal maturity, cognitive skills, psychopathy and motivation for change (Andrews, Bonta & Hoge, 1990). Psychometric principles of reliability and validity also remain crucial to any psychological assessment, and in the absence of sound assessment skills and objective procedures for identifying problems and evaluating outcomes, psychologists risk losing their claims to unique professional competencies.

Comprehensive individualized assessments are often neglected by psychologists on the grounds that they are uneconomic. However, it is even less economic to set up treatment groups which are offered indiscriminately without regard for their relevance to the individual patient. In the context of multidisciplinary treatment, psychological assessment is also often critical to the planning and monitoring of interventions undertaken by others.

The following short case history of a young, "mentally ill" patient in a maximum security hospital illustrates not only how comprehensive assessment can facilitate treatment progress, but also how inadequate assessment can be detrimental to patient care.

Peter was compulsorily detained in hospital following an attack on two youths with a knife. For some months prior to the assault, he had been unemployed, isolated, withdrawn and unkempt in appearance, and the examining clinicians could elicit no motive for the assault. Largely on the evidence of the marked decline in his social functioning, and reports by his victims that verbal abuse during the assault included reference to divine retribution, schizophrenia was diagnosed, and neuroleptic medication prescribed. While several psychiatrists subsequently commented on the lack of clear psychotic symptoms, the label persisted, and his continued withdrawn and uncommunicative behaviour was attributed to persisting psychosis. Peter therefore joined the ranks of patients who "disappear into the furniture", and was given little priority by the team psychologist who came to work on the ward. Eventually, however, the psychologist was asked to examine Peter with a view to improving his social interactional skills. He found Peter initially anxious and unforthcoming, but gradually learned that Peter was unwilling to co-operate with staff or to participate in hospital activities because he saw hospitalization as punishment for justified self-defence. Further exploration revealed that prior to the offence, he had become depressed and left his job because of the death of a workmate for which he blamed himself. During one of his occasional walks, he was taunted for his unkempt appearance by the two youths, and after they threatened him on another occasion, he bought a knife for protection. The offence followed further taunting and fears that he was about to be assaulted. Psychological testing revealed no evidence of psychotic symptoms or cognitive impairment, but signs of depression, anxiety and hostility. It also indicated avoidant, dependent and passive–aggressive personality traits. While some of the team remained convinced that Peter was concealing psychotic thinking and remained dangerous, the psychologist suggested that on balance, Peter's account was plausible, and that his reaction following the death of his workmate and the behaviour culminating in the offence could be accounted for in terms of his interpersonal style and limited coping skills. His withdrawn and uncooperative behaviour in hospital were also understandable in this light. Peter agreed to participate in cognitive therapy directed towards his depression, resentment, and coping style, and after a few months became more relaxed and co-operative. The team subsequently accepted the psychological formulation, and instituted his transfer to less secure facilities.

ASSESSING DANGEROUSNESS AND TREATABILITY

Assessment of mentally disordered offenders draws on the range of procedures used in mental health settings. The more distinctive features arise from the fact that it is behaviour which is a problem to others which determines both entry into and exit from the system. Not only are mentally disordered offenders often reluctant clients, their potential for future harmful behaviour has to be addressed in treatment planning and monitoring. Clinicians therefore need to be familiar with procedures developed for the assessment of proneness to violence and deviant sexual behaviour (see Chapters 6 and 7).

Dangerousness has traditionally been the central consideration in the admission of mentally disordered offenders to secure psychiatric hospitals and in their release. Much has been written about the defects of clinicians' assessments of dangerousness (Monahan, 1981), and earlier conclusions were that clinical predictions were little better than chance. More recent appraisals, however, acknowledge deficiencies in the evidence, and suggest that clinicians may be relatively accurate under some conditions (Mulvey & Lidz, 1984; Monahan, 1988). One problem is the ambiguity of the prediction task, and the failure to distinguish the identification of a violent tendency or *disposition* from the forecasting of a future violent *act*. Clinicians may well be competent in assessing the former, but their success is judged in terms of the latter. However, since dispositions are only realized as acts in the presence of particular situations, whose occurrence cannot readily be predicted, it would seem unrealistic to expect high degrees of accuracy in forecasting future dangerous behaviour. It is now recognized that risk assessments are made in a variety of clinical settings, and that clinical decision making can be improved by attention to common judgmental biases (Kleinmuntz, 1990). The view that statistical or actuarial prediction is superior to clinical judgment also continues to have its proponents. However, as Pollock, McBain & Webster (1989) have argued, it is probably more appropriate to focus on theoretically based decision-making procedures for arriving at defensible clinical decisions about dangerousness.

While the prediction of dangerousness remains a central consideration in the discharge of mentally disordered offenders, *treatability* has become a more important criterion for their admission to psychiatric facilities. The English Mental Health Act, for example, requires that in the case of psychopathic disorder and mental impairment, a hospital order will only be made if admission is "likely to alleviate or prevent a deterioration of his condition". The available evidence, however, suggests that clinical judgments about treatability are even less reliable than those of dangerousness (Quinsey, 1988).

A study at one special hospital, for example, found that a purpose of admission had been stated for only 43% of patients deemed treatable, and a comparison of demographic, psychiatric and criminological variables revealed virtually no differences between those admitted as treatable and those rejected as untreatable (Collins, 1991).

Treatability in a forensic context is an ambiguous concept, given the variety of possible goals (Rogers & Webster, 1989), which in the case of the Mental Health Act criteria include "not getting worse". Uncertainty about treatment goals and outcome criteria inevitably limit the accuracy of treatability decisions. To affirm that treatment will alleviate a person's disorder, clinicians need to specify the nature of the disorder to be treated, the targets of therapeutic change, and the kinds of interventions which will achieve those changes. Dell & Robertson (1988) argue that these requirements are not met in the case of psychopathic disorder, since forensic psychiatry lacks a relevant *medical* formulation of psychopathy. However, forensic psychiatry embraces psychological as well as biological models of disorder.

A more serious problem is that like dangerousness evaluations, treatability decisions blur the distinction between assessment and prediction. If a disorder is to be alleviated, the first requirement is the assessment of *amenability to treatment* as a constellation of personal and situational characteristics. These include factors such as the individual's motivation, likely compliance with treatment, and the availability of treatment and environmental resources. However, these are not necessarily stable factors, and predictions of treatment *outcome* inevitably involve "unspoken conditional clauses" about unchanging conditions (Rogers & Webster, 1989). Treatability decisions in the individual case therefore require more than simply empirical evidence on the efficacy of treatment for the particular kind of disorder.

COMMUNITY TREATMENT OF MENTALLY DISORDERED OFFENDERS

Most disordered people coming to the attention of the criminal justice system are minor offenders whose needs overlap with those of persistently aggressive or "socially inadequate" non-offender patients, and the Royal College of Psychiatrists (1980) argued for an integrated system which took account of the needs of mentally disordered offenders who may be a social nuisance but who are not dangerous. Progress towards such a system has been slow, but recent policies have affirmed the need for diversion of mentally disordered offenders to community-based programmes (Department of Health/Home Office, 1992). Services available, however, remain poorly documented.

Psychological treatment involving stress management and social problem-solving skills is now seen to be central to community-based rehabilitation programmes for mentally disordered offenders, but this has to be set in the context of inter-agency communication. Tonak & Cawton (1988) found widespread dissatisfaction among probation officers with the services provided to the courts by the psychiatric services, particularly over the adequacy of assessments and reports, contacts with psychologists and sharing of responsibility. They describe a scheme developed in Hertfordshire aimed at improving multidisciplinary collaboration. More effective planning and advice to the courts was achieved by having offenders seen by a multidisciplinary panel and regular links of the probation service with a psychologist and community nurse. The scheme was apparently cost-effective and reduced recidivism and relapse. Cooke (1991) also reports successful out-patient psychological treatment of minor offenders with problems of depression, anxiety and alcohol abuse who were referred to a multidisciplinary clinic through a Scottish court diversion scheme.

While the courts are more willing to order community treatments for minor offenders, Bloom, Williams & Bigelow (1991) note that conditional and monitored release to community programmes based on psychosocial rehabilitation may also be a feasible and cheaper option to prolonged detention for many chronically mentally ill offenders. One example is a multidisciplinary out-patient clinic in Chicago for patients with major psychiatric disorders and a history of serious violence described by Rogers & Cavanaugh (1981). Patients with primary diagnoses of antisocial personality disorder or substance abuse were excluded, and treatment entailed an eclectic problem-oriented approach combining biological and psycho-social interventions aimed at reduced violence, symptom remission and improved interpersonal functioning. During the first 20 months of the programme, half of the patients improved "substantially", and there was no violent recidivism. Close co-operation with the courts, continued support and follow-up, and facilities for rehospitalization were essential features.

TREATMENT IN SECURITY HOSPITALS

For many, if not most mentally disordered offenders, skilled supervision in small special units in open hospitals or hostels is often the primary need. However, the major issues surrounding the treatment of mentally disordered offenders continue to centre on those detained in maximum security hospitals. The majority suffer from major mental disorders, typically paranoid schizophrenia, and for many, "cure" is an unrealistic expectation. Mentally ill and learning disabled offenders present problems of motivational and social deficits typical of long-stay patients, and often exhibit socially unacceptable behaviour which impedes their return to less restricted environments. Rehabilitative goals are therefore most commonly symptom remission or stabilization, and the provision of coping and interpersonal skills to enable them to survive in their optimal environment, whether an open hospital, hostel or their own home.

Barriers to achieving these pragmatic goals arise from the system itself as much as the clinical challenges posed by this group (Royal College of Psychiatrists, 1980; Webster, Hucker & Grossman, 1993). Since questions of public safety dictate both admission to and release from secure facilities, the balance between security and treatment is often tipped in favour of the former. The expectation that treatment will not only ameliorate disorder but also reduce the likelihood of future offending creates ambiguities for treatment staff, and hospitalization may hence become a form of incapacitation or preventive detention in which containment rather than rehabilitation is the overriding goal. This problem is exacerbated by the lack of control of clinical staff over release decisions. In England, for example, when the court has imposed a "restriction order" in addition to a hospital order, the patient can only be discharged by the Home Secretary or a mental health review tribunal, and decisions are strongly influenced by the nature of a patient's offence, particularly in the case of psychopathic disorder (Dell & Robertson, 1988).

Attempts to transfer patients to less secure settings are also frequently delayed or obstructed by limited facilities or the unpopularity of offender patients with the psychiatric services. Brown, Shubsachs & Larkin (1992) investigated the outcome of referrals of mentally ill patients from one special hospital for transfer to local services. Successful outcome was unrelated to clinical or criminal variables, but patients requiring long-term care and those with a history of in-patient assaultiveness were more likely to be rejected. Many patients are therefore detained in secure hospitals long after clinical staff consider them "safe".

Maximum security hospitals therefore deal with a long-term population. Since many patients do not need to be there, and are simply marking time, patient management is often not clearly linked to individualized rehabilitation programmes aimed at reintegration, and sometimes amounts to "benign warehousing". While the press (and sometimes staff associations) are apt to stress that these institutions contain the "most dangerous" offenders, it has to be noted that for many, their dangerousness is limited to contexts in the community from which they have been removed, and the immediate management task may be primarily to counter institutionalization by providing occupation and recreational activity.

However, tensions created by enforced living in a closed community as well as mental disorder itself give rise to disruptive behaviour in a minority, whose management falls primarily on nursing staff. This may take the form of violent incidents which have traditionally been dealt with coercively by, for example, the use of seclusion or a "chemical straitjacket". Criticisms of these approaches have led to increased attention to the social and psychological factors in violence (Alty & Mason, 1994), and to staff training in negotiation and prevention. Similarly, responses to self-harming behaviour, which is prevalent among incarcerated women, are primarily the use of medication, restraint clothing or seclusion, but the need to consider factors in the social environment, such as peer group support and authoritarian staff–patient relations, is now being recognized (Burrow, 1992). The urgent need for more constructive institutional practices has been highlighted by continued evidence that hospital staff are not immune to prejudices and punitive attitudes towards patients. A recent enquiry investigating allegations of abuse at one special hospital described ". . . a brutalising, stagnant, closed institution" (Department of Health, 1992b).

Such reports present a depressing picture of maximum security hospital environments, but the majority of staff are committed to patient care, and the treatment services developed match those of most psychiatric hospitals. Nevertheless, as Quinsey (1988) notes, treatment programmes have frequently been noteworthy by their absence, poor implementation, unevaluated status, lack of conceptual sophistication and incomplete description. Most psychological interventions developed in the psychiatric services have been applied with institutionalized mentally disordered offenders. These include group and individual psychotherapy, token economies, therapeutic communities, social skills training, desensitization, anger management, problem-solving training and behavioural procedures for dealing with deviant sexual behaviour. However, while within programme changes are sometimes documented (e.g. Crawford & Allen, 1979), the literature consists mainly of descriptive reports or illustrative case studies.

Two factors limit generalizations about the utility of psychological interventions with seriously disordered offenders. First, they are applied with only a minority of patients, and for limited periods. In a survey of American forensic psychiatric facilities, for example, Kerr & Roth (1986) found that pharmacological treatment was used in 98% of all units, and received by 61% of patients, but only a third received weekly individual therapy. Similarly, Dell & Robertson (1988) noted that 89% of mentally ill patients at Broadmoor received medication, but only 31% had ever received psychological treatment. Even among legal psychopaths, for whom medication was rare, less than half had received behavioural treatment or individual psychotherapy.

Second, long-term outcome evaluations are rare, and given the variety of influences to which patients in security hospitals are exposed during their stay, rigorous evaluations of the efficacy of specific treatment modalities may not be feasible. Follow-ups have focused mainly on reoffending (Murray, 1989). These generally reveal lower reconviction rates for mentally disordered offenders than for released prisoners, but strict comparisons are questionable. They also indicate that "psychopathic" patients reoffend at higher rates than the mentally ill, and that conditionally released patients fare better than those given absolute discharge (Bailey & MacCulloch, 1992). However, these studies address primarily the decision to release, and do not permit conclusions about the effects of treatment programmes. The most systematic evaluations of specific interventions come from Oak Ridge at Penetanguishene in Ontario. For example, a five-year follow-up of a token economy revealed that about half the patients reoffended, but that outcome was not related to performance in the programme itself (Rice, Quinsey & Houghton, 1990). However, a long-term outcome study of a therapeutic community in the same institution found that while psychopaths were more likely to be violent recidivists than untreated psychopaths, non-psychopaths, many of whom were psychotic, appeared to benefit from the programme (Rice, Harris & Cormier, 1992).

TREATMENT OF OFFENDERS WITH LEARNING DISABILITIES

Facilities for offenders with learning disabilities are currently agreed to be inadequate (Day, 1993). The use of hospital orders for mentally impaired offenders has declined substantially in the last two decades, and this is reflected in a fall in the numbers of special hospital places. This is particularly so for the "severely impaired", most of whom present problems of institutional management rather than dangerous offending. Corresponding services offering medium security or community care have been slow to develop.

One problem is that the special needs of this group have not been clearly specified. It is commonly observed that handicapped people may have difficulty surviving in residences for the non-handicapped because of social rejection and exploitation, and it is generally assumed that cognitive deficits render many conventional psychological treatments inapplicable. However, the problems of learning disabled offenders are largely those shared with other mentally disordered offenders, and indeed offenders generally. They include undersocialization (i.e. failure to internalize social rules and values), deficient self-control, and limited educational and occupational skills. They also include deficient sexual and interpersonal skills, often in the context of neglectful or abusive family relationships. It is perhaps worth noting in this context that the wording of the Mental Health Act category of psychopathic disorder makes the category of mental impairment redundant.

Institutional programmes have traditionally emphasized occupational and educational training and a structured, disciplined environment, and outcome studies indicate comparable effects to those of programmes for mentally disordered offenders more generally (Tong & Mackay, 1959). Justification for a structured environment is provided by Craft, Stephenson & Granger (1964), who found that mildly handicapped "psychopaths" managed in a secure, authoritarian ward responded better in terms of cognitive and social development and reduced offending than those in a therapeutic community. Craft (1984) also observed similar effects in an open hospital, finding that a disciplined regime produced a more favourable outcome than one focusing on education and counselling. He also notes that successful rehabilitation depends on continuing support following discharge.

Psychological treatment developed for the learning disabled has included behavioural interventions for institutional conduct problems, and the applied behaviour analysis literature contains a number of reports on short-term modification of aggression, stealing and self-injury. Early applications focused on the reduction of undesired behaviours through operant procedures such as time out from reinforcement, but these have been criticized for inadequate functional analysis and overemphasis on aversive methods (Murphy, 1993). Current approaches emphasize a constructional strategy in which attention is paid to the development of alternative repertoires, and not simply the elimination of antisocial behaviour (Murphy, 1993; Cullen, 1993).

Skills training methods for improving social and occupational adjustment are likely to be prominent parts of comprehensive programmes for this group, which may also offer token economies, education, counselling and supportive psychotherapy, and drug treatment (Day, 1993). However, there have been few psychological interventions for this group devoted specifically to problems associated with low frequency offending behaviour, and empirically based guidance for treatment planning is currently lacking. Nevertheless, some attention is being given to the use of behavioural self-control procedures, particularly adaptations of Novaco's anger management package (Murphy, 1993; Cullen, 1993). Results have so far been inconclusive, and Cullen notes that the different skills required for self-control have not as yet been adequately delineated. Similarly, the skill deficits of this group need further examination. For example, conventional cognitive–behavioural methods may not be effective with the learning disabled because of difficulties in acquiring rule-governed behaviour.

TREATMENT OF PSYCHOPATHS AND THE PERSONALITY DISORDERED

Uncertainties about treatability and the prediction of dangerousness centre particularly on "psychopaths". Not only does the stereotypic psychopath embody the most intractable psychological problems, there continues to be debate about whether such people are "mad or bad", and whether they should be dealt with by the health care system. Mental health professionals frequently feel uncomfortable with this group because of the moral and professional dilemmas of trying to understand offensive crimes in terms of "sickness", and many psychiatrists claim that psychopaths are untreatable.

At least some of the difficulties arise from conceptual confusion between the terms psychopathic personality, psychopathic disorder and personality disorder, which do not identify the same group of people (Blackburn, 1988). Older conceptions of psychopathic personality denoted several kinds of abnormal personality who were not necessarily criminal. These are broadly equivalent to the current classes of personality disorder in DSM-III. Over time, however, the term psychopath has been narrowed to identify a specific kind of antisocial person. For some clinicians, recalcitrant social deviance has been a sufficient criterion. Others, however, have specified personality characteristics such as egocentricity, callousness and impulsivity (Cleckley, 1976). This "classical" conception has empirical support (Blackburn, 1975; Hare, 1986), but only a minority of those who are socially deviant can be described as "psychopaths" in these terms. The legal category of psychopathic disorder bears little resemblance to this classical concept, and Coid (1992) found that only 23% of male patients in this category, and 31% of females were identified as "psychopaths" by Hare's PCL. The confusion has been compounded by the tendency to equate psychopathic disorder with personality disorder. However, many people legally categorized as mentally ill also exhibit personality disorders (Blackburn et al., 1990).

Legal psychopaths, then, are heterogeneous, and most offenders who attract this label are not "psychopathic" in any strict sense. Most have some form of personality disorder, but many also have symptoms of illness. Some are depressed or anxious, some are sexually deviant, many have abused drugs or alcohol, and some have post-traumatic stress disorders arising from early physical or sexual abuse or from their own violent crimes (Kruppa, Hickey & Hubbard, 1995). This "co-morbidity" means that any treatment planning must take account of the relationships between criminal *acts*, dysfunctional *traits* of personality disorder and *symptoms* of emotional disorder.

In practice, clinical programmes for this group do not assume a single focal problem, and treatment is typically multifaceted. Grounds et al. (1987), for example, describe an eclectic programme for legal psychopaths in Broadmoor, which combines group and individual dynamic psychotherapy with social skills training, anger management, sex education and cognitive therapy for depression and sexual problems. Case histories of special hospital patients treated both successfully and unsuccessfully by multimodal methods are also described in previous reviews (Blackburn, 1989, 1993b). However, few patients have as yet received the intensive and extensive treatment which seems necessary to deal with their multiple problems, and there is little basis for determining which treatment modalities might be effective for particular problems.

The voluminous literature on the treatment of "psychopaths" provides little clinical guidance, since for the most part it is concerned with vaguely defined samples exposed to poorly described programmes with uncertain goals. Where outcomes are evaluated, it is usually in terms of reoffending. Recent reviews suggest that methodological deficiencies preclude any clear conclusions about whether or not psychopaths are treatable (Blackburn, 1993b; Dolan & Coid, 1993). Outcome evaluations have been reported of group psychotherapy, therapeutic communities, token economies, cognitive–behavioural procedures and cognitive therapy, but while a few successes can be identified, none of these approaches can claim to be consistently successful. A common problem is not simply the absence of untreated controls, but also the absence of criteria for distinguishing psychopaths from non-psychopaths. The study cited earlier by Rice, Harris & Cormier (1992) is one of the few to use such criteria, but contrary to expectation, it found that a therapeutic community was primarily beneficial to *non*psychopaths

The preoccupation with treatment for "psychopathy" may be misguided. The term has no precise meaning outside the classical concept of psychopathic personality, but as has been emphasized, only a minority of those in the psychopathic disorder category are psychopathic in this sense. It may therefore be fruitful to focus clinical attention more broadly on the personality disorders manifest in this group, and to identify and target those dysfunctional interpersonal traits related to socially deviant behaviour. Psychologists have neglected personality disorders, but the evidence that the presence of a personality disorder reduces the efficacy of most interventions for psychological problems indicates that effective programmes must take them into account (Beck & Freeman, 1990; Reich & Green, 1991). Theoretically coherent procedures for dealing with personality disorders have recently been described (Kiesler, 1986; Beck & Freeman, 1990; Benjamin, 1993), but their utility with mentally disordered offenders awaits exploration.

REFERENCES

American Psychiatric Association (1987) *Diagnostic and Statistical Manual of Mental Disorders*, 3rd edn, revised. Washington, DC: APA.

Alty, A. & Mason, T. (1994) *Seclusion and Mental Health: A Break with the Past.* London: Chapman and Hall.

Andrews, D.A., Bonta, J. & Hoge, R.D. (1990) Classification for effective rehabilitation: rediscovering psychology. *Criminal Justice and Behavior*, **17**, 19–52.

Bailey, J. & MacCulloch, M. (1992) Patterns of reconviction in patients discharged directly to the community from a special hospital: Implications for aftercare. *Journal of Forensic Psychiatry*, **3**, 445–461.

Beck, A.T. & Freeman, A. (1990) *Cognitive Therapy of Personality Disorders.* New York: Guilford Press.

Benjamin, L.S. (1993) *Interpersonal Diagnosis and Treatment of Personality Disorders*, New York: Guilford Press.

Blackburn, R. (1975) An empirical classification of psychopathic personality. *British Journal of Psychiatry*, **127**, 456–460.

Blackburn, R. (1988) On moral judgements and personality disorders: the myth of the psychopathic personality revisited. *British Journal of Psychiatry*, **153**, 505–512.

Blackburn, R. (1989) Psychopathy and personality disorder in relation to violence. In K. Howells & C.R. Hollin (Eds), *Clinical Approaches to Violence*. Chichester: Wiley.

Blackburn, R. (1993a) *Psychology and Criminal Conduct: Theory, Research and Practice.* Chichester: Wiley.

Blackburn, R. (1993b) Clinical programmes with psychopaths. In K. Howells & C.R. Hollin (Eds), *Clinical Approaches to the Mentally Disordered Offender*. Chichester: Wiley

Blackburn, R., Crellin, M.C., Morgan, E.M. & Tulloch, R.M.B. (1990) Prevalence of personality disorders in a special hospital population. *Journal of Forensic Psychiatry*, **1**, 43–52.

Bloom, J.D., Williams, M.H. & Bigelow, D.A. (1991) Monitored conditional release of persons found not guilty by reason of insanity. *American Journal of Psychiatry*, **148**, 444–448.

Brodsky, S.L. (1972) *Psychologists in the Criminal Justice System.* Carbondale, IL: American Association of Correctional Psychologists.

Brown, S., Shubsachs, A. & Larkin, E. (1992) Outcome of referrals from Rampton Hospital to local mental health services, 1988–1990. *Journal of Forensic Psychiatry*, **3**, 463–475.

Burrow, S. (1992) The deliberate self-harming behaviour of patients within a British special hospital. *Journal of Advanced Nursing*, **17**, 138–148.

Cleckley, H. (1976) *The Mask of Sanity*, 6th edn. St Louis: Mosby.

Coid, J. (1983) The epidemiology of abnormal homicide and murder followed by suicide. *Psychological Medicine*, **13**, 855–860.

Coid, J.W. (1992) DSM-III diagnosis in criminal psychopaths: a way forward. *Criminal Behaviour and Mental Health*, **2**, 78–94.

Collins, J.J. & Bailey, S.L. (1990) Relationship of mood disorders to violence. *Journal of Nervous and Mental Disease*, **178**, 44–47.

Collins, P. (1991) The treatability of psychopaths. *Journal of Forensic Psychiatry*, **2**, 103–110.

Cooke, D. (1991) Treatment as an alternative to prosecution: offenders diverted for treatment. *British Journal of Psychiatry*, **158**, 785–791.

Craft, M. (1984) The results of treatment. In M. Craft & A. Craft (Eds), *Mentally Abnormal Offenders*. London: Bailliere Tindall.

Craft, M., Stephenson, G. & Granger, C. (1964) A controlled trial of authoritarian and self-governing regimes with adolescent psychopaths. *American Journal of Orthopsychiatry*, **64**, 543–554.

Crawford, D.A. (1984) Behaviour therapy. In M. Craft & A. Craft (Eds), *Mentally Abnormal Offenders*. London: Bailliere Tindall.

Crawford, D.A. & Allen, J.V. (1979) A social skills training program with sex offenders. In M. Cook & G. Wilson (Eds), *Love and Attraction*. Oxford: Pergamon.

Cullen, C. (1993) The treatment of people with learning disabilities who offend. In K. Howells & C.R. Hollin (Eds), *Clinical Approaches to the Mentally Disordered Offender*. Chichester: Wiley.

Davis, S. (1991) Violence by psychiatric inpatients: a review. *Hospital and Community Psychiatry*, **42**, 585–590.

Day, K. (1993) Crime and mental retardation: a review. In K. Howells & C.R. Hollin (Eds), *Clinical Approaches to the Mentally Disordered Offender*. Chichester: Wiley.

Dell, S. & Robertson, G. (1988) *Sentenced to Hospital: Offenders in Broadmoor*. Maudsley Monographs No. 32. Oxford: Oxford University Press.

Department of Health (1992a) In-patients formally detained in hospitals under the Mental Health Act 1983 and other legislation. *Statistical Bulletin*, 2(7) 92. London: Department of Health.

Department of Health (1992b) *Report of the Committee of Inquiry into Complaints about Ashworth Hospital*. Cm 2028. London: HMSO.

Department of Health/Home Office (1992) *Review of Health and Social Services for Mentally Disordered Offenders and Others Requiring Similar Services*. Cm 2088. London: HMSO.

Dolan, B. & Coid, J. (1993) *Psychopathic and Antisocial Personality Disorders: Treatment and Research Issues*. Gaskell: Royal College of Psychiatrists.

Farrington, D.P. (1981) The prevalence of convictions. *British Journal of Criminology*, **21**, 173–175.

Gibbens, T.C.N. (1981) Shoplifting. *British Journal of Psychiatry*, **138**, 346–347.

Grounds, A.T., Quayle, M.T., France, J., Brett, T., Cox, M. & Hamilton, J.R. (1987) A unit for "psychopathic disorder" patients in Broadmoor hospital. *Medicine, Science and the Law*, **27**, 21–31.

Gunn, J., Maden, A. & Swinton, M. (1991) Treatment needs of prisoners with psychiatric disorders. *British Medical Journal*, **303**, 338–341.

Guze, S.B. (1976) *Criminality and Psychiatric Disorders*. New York: Oxford University Press.

Häfner, H. & Böker, W. (1982) *Crimes of Violence by Mentally Abnormal Offenders*. Cambridge: Cambridge University Press.

Halleck, S.L. (1987) *The Mentally Disordered Offender*. Washington, DC: American Psychiatric Press.

Haller, R.M. & Deluty, R.H. (1988) Assaults on staff by psychiatric inpatients. *British Journal of Psychiatry*, **152**, 174–179.

Hare, R.D. (1986) Twenty years of experience with the Cleckley psychopath. In W.H.

Reid, D. Dorr, J. Walker & J.W. Bonner (Eds), *Unmasking the Psychopath: Antisocial Personality and Related Syndromes.* New York: Norton.

Hare, R.D. & Hart, S.D. (1993) Psychopathy, mental disorder, and crime. In S. Hodgins (Ed.), *Mental Disorder and Crime.* Newbury Park, CA: Sage.

Hare, R.D., McPherson, L.M. & Forth, A.E. (1988) Male psychopaths and their criminal careers. *Journal of Consulting and Clinical Psychology*, **56**, 710–714.

Harris, G.T. & Varney, G.W. (1986) A ten-year study of assaults and assaulters on a maximum security psychiatric unit. *Journal of Interpersonal Violence*, **1**, 173–191.

Haward, L.R.C. (1981) *Forensic Psychology.* London: Batsford.

Hodgins, S. (1992) Mental disorder, intellectual deficiency, and crime. *Archives of General Psychiatry*, **49**, 476–483.

Hodgins, S. (1993) The criminality of mentally disordered persons. In S. Hodgins (Ed.), *Mental Disorder and Crime.* Newbury Park, CA: Sage.

Hodgins, S. & Côté, G. (1990) Prevalence of mental disorders among penitentiary inmates in Quebec. *Canada's Mental Health*, **38**, 1–4.

Kerr, C.A. & Roth, J.A. (1986) Populations, practices, and problems in forensic psychiatric facilities. *Annals of the American Academy of Political and Social Science*, **484**, 127–143.

Kiesler, D.J. (1986) The 1982 interpersonal circle: an analysis of DSM-III personality disorders. In T. Millon & G. Klerman (Eds), *Contemporary Directions in Psychopathology: Towards DSM-IV.* New York: Guilford.

Kleinmuntz, B. (1990) Why we still use our heads instead of formulas: toward an integrative approach. *Psychological Bulletin*, **107**, 296–310.

Krakowski, M., Volavka, J. & Brizer, D. (1986) Psychopathology and violence: a review of the literature. *Comprehensive Psychiatry*, **27**, 131–148.

Kruppa, I., Hickey, N. & Hubbard, C. (1995) The prevalence of PTSD in a special hospital population of psychopaths. *Psychology, Crime, and Law*, **2**, 131–141.

Lindqvist, P. (1986) Criminal homicide in Northern Sweden 1970–1981: alcohol intoxication, alcohol abuse and mental disease. *International Journal of Law and Psychiatry*, **8**, 19–37.

Lindqvist, P. & Allebeck, P. (1990) Schizophrenia and crime: a longitudinal follow-up of 644 schizophrenics in Stockholm. *British Journal of Psychiatry*, **157**, 345–350.

Link, B., Cullen, F. & Andrews, H. (1992) The violent and illegal behavior of current and former mental patients compared to community controls. *American Sociological Review*, **57**, 275–292.

MacCulloch, M.J. & Bailey, J. (1991) Issues in the provision and evaluation of forensic services. *Journal of Forensic Psychiatry*, **2**, 247–265.

Menzies, R.J. & Webster, C.D. (1989) Mental disorder and violent crime. In N.A. Weiner & M.E. Wolfgang (Eds), *Pathways to Criminal Violence.* Newbury Park, CA: Sage.

Monahan, J. (1981) *Predicting Violent Behavior: An Assessment of Clinical Techniques.* Beverly Hills, CA: Sage.

Monahan, J. (1988) Risk assessment of violence among the mentally disordered: generating useful knowledge. *International Journal of Law and Psychiatry*, **11**, 249–257.

Monahan, J. (1993) Mental disorder and violence: another look. In S. Hodgins (Ed.), *Mental Disorder and Crime.* Newbury Park, CA: Sage.

Monahan, J. & Steadman, H.J. (1983) Crime and mental disorder: an epidemiological approach. In N. Morris & M. Tonry (Eds), *Crime and Justice: An Annual Review of Research*, Vol.3. Chicago: University of Chicago Press.

Mulvey, E.P. & Lidz, C.W. (1984) Clinical considerations in the prediction of dangerousness in mental patients. *Clinical Psychology Review*, **4**, 379–401.

Murphy, G. (1993) The treatment of challenging behaviour in people with learning difficulties. In C. Thompson & P. Cowen (Eds), *Violence: Basic and Clinical Science*. Oxford: Butterworth-Heinemann.

Murray, D.J. (1989) *Review of Research on Re-offending of Mentally Disordered Offenders*. Research and Planning Unit Paper 55. London: Home Office.

Murrey, G.J., Briggs, D. & Davis, C. (1992) Psychopathic disordered, mentally ill, and mentally handicapped sex offenders: a comparative study. *Medicine, Science and the Law*, **32**, 331:336.

Penrose, L.S. (1939) Mental disease and crime: Outline of a comparative study of European statistics. *British Journal of Medical Psychology*, **18**, 1–15.

Planasky, K. & Johnson, R. (1977) Homicidal aggression in schizophrenic men. *Acta Psychiatrica Scandinavica*, **55**, 65–73.

Pollock, N., McBain, I. & Webster, C.D. (1989) Clinical decision making and the assessment of dangerousness. In K. Howells & C.R. Hollin (eds.). *Clinical Approaches to Violence*. Chichester: Wiley.

Quinsey, V.L. (1988) Assessment of the treatability of forensic patients. *Behavioral Sciences and the Law*, **6**, 443–452.

Quinsey, V.L. & Maguire, A. (1986) Maximum security psychiatric patients: Actuarial and clinical prediction of dangerousness. *Journal of Interpersonal Violence*, **1**, 143–171.

Quinsey, V.L., Warneford, A., Pruesse, M. & Link, N. (1975) Released Oak Ridge patients: a follow-up study of review board discharges. *British Journal of Criminology*, **15**, 264–270.

Rabkin, J.G. (1979) Criminal behavior of discharged mental patients: a critical appraisal of the literature. *Psychological Bulletin*, **86**, 1–29.

Radden, J. (1985) *Madness and Reason*. London: Allen and Unwin.

Reich, J. & Green, A.I. (1991) Effect of personality disorders on outcome of treatment. *Journal of Nervous and Mental Disease*, **179**, 74–82.

Rice, M.E., Harris, G.T. & Cormier, C.A. (1992) An evaluation of a maximum security therapeutic community for psychopaths and other mentally disordered offenders. *Law and Human Behavior*, **16**, 399–412.

Rice, M.E., Quinsey, V.L. & Houghton, R. (1990) Predicting treatment outcome and recidivism among patients in a maximum security token economy. *Behavioral Sciences and the Law*, **8**, 313–326.

Robertson, G. (1989) Treatment for offender patients: how should success be measured? *Medicine, Science and the Law*, **29**, 303–307.

Rogers, R. & Cavanaugh, J.L. (1981) A treatment program for potentially violent offender patients. *International Journal of Offender Therapy and Comparative Criminology*, **25**, 53–59.

Rogers, R. & Webster, C.D. (1989) Assessing treatability in mentally disordered offenders. *Law and Human Behavior*, **13**, 19–27.

Royal College of Psychiatrists (1980) *Secure Facilities for Psychiatric Patients: A Comprehensive Policy*. London: Royal College of Psychiatrists.

Swanson, J., Holzer, C., Ganju, V. & Jono, R. (1990) Violence and psychiatric disorder in the community: evidence from the Epidemiologic Catchment Area surveys. *Hospital and Community Psychiatry*, **41**, 761–770.

Taylor, P. (1985) Motives for offending among violent and psychotic men. *British Journal of Psychiatry*, **147**, 491–498.

Taylor, P & Gunn, J. (1984). Risk of violence among psychotic men. *British Medical Journal*, **288**, 1945–1949.

Teplin, L.A. (1984) Criminalising mental disorder: the comparative arrest rate of the mentally ill. *American Psychologist*, **39**, 794–803.

Teplin, L.A., McLelland, G.M. & Abram, K. (1993) The role of mental disorder and substance abuse in predicting violence among released offenders. In S. Hodgins (Ed.), *Mental Disorder and Crime*. Newbury Park, CA: Sage.

Tonak, D. & Cawdron, G. (1988) Mentally disordered offenders and the courts: cooperation and collaboration of disciplines involved. *Justice of the Peace*, **August**, 504–507.

Tong, J.E. & Mackay, G.W. (1959) A statistical follow-up of mental defectives of dangerous or violent propensities. *British Journal of Delinquency*, **9**, 276–284.

Webster, C.D., Hucker, S.J. & Grossman, M.G. (1993) Clinical programmes for mentally ill offenders. In K. Howells & C.R. Hollin (Eds), *Clinical Approaches to the Mentally Disordered Offender*. Chichester: Wiley.

Weller, M.P.I. & Weller, B.G.A. (1988) Crime and mental illness. *Medicine, Science and the Law*, **28**, 38–46.

Wessely, S. & Taylor, P.J. (1991) Madness and crime: criminology versus psychiatry. *Criminal Behaviour and Mental Health*, **1**, 193–228.

CHAPTER SIX

SEX OFFENDERS

Kevin Epps

The sexual difficulties of clients presenting to psychologists working in applied settings can be divided into three broad categories: sexual dysfunction, sexual deviance, and sexual offending. Whilst there is considerable overlap between each of these areas, many psychologists find themselves working predominantly with one or two groups. Unfortunately, there is not space in this chapter to do justice to all three areas. Rather, the aim here is to focus on the management and treatment of individuals, most of whom are men, who sexually offend. The sexual behaviour of many of these men will also be considered psychiatrically abnormal (i.e. deviant). It is therefore necessary to begin with a brief look at sexual deviation.

SEXUAL DEVIATION

The extent to which any sexual behaviour is considered to be deviant or abnormal depends on changing societal standards. Thus, homosexual behaviour was once considered to be deviant and deserving of treatment until it was decriminalised in the 1960s. The existing classifications of sexual deviance are often slow in reflecting changes in social attitudes. Further, they rarely contribute to a greater understanding of the origins of sexual deviance and fail to provide treatment guidelines. Generally speaking, sexual deviation is construed as any departure from the norm of genital intercourse between mature, opposite sex partners. DSM-III-R (American Psychiatric Association, 1987), adopts the term "paraphilia" to refer to sexual deviation, to emphasize that the deviation (para) lies in that to which the person is attracted (philia).

Working with Offenders: Psychological Practice in Offender Rehabilitation.
Edited by C.R. Hollin. © 1996 John Wiley & Sons Ltd.

Table 6.1 Paraphilias

Type	Characteristics
Exhibitionism	Exposure of one's genitals to a stranger, sometimes while masturbating; further sexual involvement is not attempted
Fetishism	Use of non-living objects, such as female underwear or boots, frequently involving masturbation while holding, rubbing or smelling the object, or sometimes the wearing of the object by a sexual partner
Frotteurism	Touching and rubbing against a non-consenting person, usually in a crowded place, excitement being derived from the contact
Paedophilia	Sexual activity with a prepubertal child by a person of 16 years or older, and at least 5 years older than the child: activity may be limited to touching or fondling, but may involve fellatio, cunnilingus and vaginal or anal penetration
Sexual masochism	The act of being humiliated, beaten, bound, or otherwise made to suffer by a partner, or the self-infliction of pain for sexual excitement
Sexual sadism	Acts in which psychological or physical suffering of the victim is sexually exciting, including domination or torture
Transvestic fetishism	Cross-dressing in female clothes, often entirely as a woman, although basic preferences are heterosexual; distinguished from *trans-sexualism*, in which the person wishes to acquire opposite sex characteristics, and is not sexually excited by the cross-dressing
Voyeurism	Observing unsuspecting people who are naked, disrobing, or engaged in sexual activity

Source: Adapted from DSM-III-R, American Psychiatric Association; 1987.

Paraphilias are construed as recurrent intense sexual urges and arousing fantasies involving non-human objects, or the suffering or humiliation of oneself or one's partner, or children or other non-consenting persons. To be diagnosed as exhibiting a paraphilia the individual must have experienced the fantasies or urges for at least six months and acted upon them, or at least be experiencing considerable distress. A vast number of paraphilias have been defined, some of which are summarized in Table 6.1.

It is noteworthy that rape is not included in this list, although Abel & Rouleau (1990) have suggested that it should be, given that many convicted rapists report cycles of compulsive urges and rape fantasies. According to DSM-III-R most sexually deviant men have on average three to four different paraphilias. Further, some individuals are said to require triggering factors, such as stress, while for others the behaviour is more or less continuous, such that situational factors may not be involved.

Table 6.2 Notifiable sexual offences recorded by police (England and Wales)

Offence classification	No. of offences recorded	
	1986	1988
Indecent assault on a female	11 839	14 112
Unlawful sexual intercourse with a girl under 16	2 555	2 552
Attempted buggery etc.	2308	2512
Rape	2288	2855
Indecency between males	990	1306
Buggery	794	951
Gross indecency with a child	666	871
Incest	444	516
Unlawful sexual intercourse with a girl under 13	362	283
Abduction	192	277
Procuration	170	201
Bigamy	76	93
Total	22 684	26 529

Source: Adapted from *Criminal Statistics England and Wales 1988* (Home Office, 1989).

Individuals suffering from paraphilias that are classed as criminal offences are more likely to be referred for treatment than those that are not. For example, 95% of sex offenders presenting at clinics are exhibitionists (Marshall, Hudson & Ward, 1992), whilst fetishists are unlikely to refer themselves unless under considerable pressure from their spouse or partner.

SEXUAL OFFENDING

In English law, sexual offending is described in the Sexual Offences Act 1957. Sexual offences constitute only a small proportion of officially recorded crimes. In 1988, they represented 0.7% of notifiable offences in England and Wales, and fewer than 2% of offenders convicted (Home Office, 1989). Recent statistics from the Home Office of notifiable recorded sexual offences are shown in Table 6.2.

It is important to note that some sexual offences are absent from this list. Indecent exposure (i.e. exhibitionism), for example, is dealt with under the Public Order Act 1936, whilst property offences that involve theft of clothing are included in the Theft Act 1968. Whilst there has been a slight increase in reported sex offences over the past few decades, the rate of increase has been less than that of crime in general. However, there is increasing evidence of under-reporting in many categories of sexual offence, including rape and child sexual abuse. For example, a general population survey in the USA found that 19% of female students and 9% of male students reported having some sexual experience with an adult during childhood (Finkelhor, 1979). Generally speaking, the victims of sexual offences appear less likely to report the assault than victims of other crimes, even when the assault was of a serious nature. Sometimes the victim is too young (as in the case of child victims), or is a relative of the offender (as in the case of incest). Alternatively, the victim may be intimidated by the offender or feel unable to bear the stress and anxiety of appearing in court to give evidence.

The majority of convicted sex offenders are dealt with by non-custodial disposals, such as fines and conditional discharges. A minority, however, especially those convicted of violent offences, receive custodial sentences. Most of these offenders will be incarcerated within the prison system, with those below the age of 21 years being detained in young offender institutions or secure therapeutic establishments, such as offered by the Youth Treatment Service. A few may require psychiatric hospitalization. However, most sex offenders are not mentally disordered under the terms of the Mental Health Act 1983. That is, they are not considered to be suffering from a mental illness, psychopathic disorder, or to be mentally impaired. Those mentally disordered sexual offenders who are regarded as presenting a "grave and immediate danger" to the public (Mental Health Act 1983) may be detained in one of the three special hospitals in England and Wales (Ashworth, Broadmoor and Rampton) or the Scottish equivalent, the State Hospital Carstairs. Less dangerous mentally disordered offenders may be dealt with either as in-patients or out-patients in regional secure units.

Historically, there has been little opportunity for sex offenders to receive treatment within the British prison system. However, a recent initiative (Thornton, 1991) has introduced a system-wide programme for the treatment of sex offenders. Treatment is split into two tiers. The *core programme* consists of a group-based treatment programme using a cognitive–behavioural approach focused mainly on changing offence-related cognitions and developing a relapse-prevention strategy for release (to be discussed later in this chapter). The *extended programme* includes a variety of individual and group interventions aimed at modifying a range of problems, such as deviant sexual arousal and poor anger control.

Before examining in more detail the content and operation of treatment programmes for sexual offenders, it is necessary to look briefly at what is known about the characteristics of men who perpetrate sexual offences and the kinds of offences they commit. Emphasis here will be given to offenders who commit "hands-on" offences, such as child molestation and rape, as opposed to offences involving no physical contact, such as exhibitionism.

Consideration will also be given to adolescent offenders, who seem to be responsible for one-third of child sexual abuse (Davis & Leitenberg, 1987) and who have recently attracted considerable attention (Ryan & Lane, 1991).

ADULT OFFENDERS

OFFENCES AGAINST CHILDREN

Incidence and Prevalence

Peters, Wyatt & Finkelhor (1986) reviewed studies investigating the prevalence of child sexual abuse. They found considerable variation across studies, ranging from estimates of 6% to 62% for girls, and 3% to 31% for boys. Part of the difficulty with these studies is under-reporting, such that most knowledge comes from victimization surveys and small clinical studies. Further difficulties arise from the adoption of differing definitions of child sexual abuse and different survey methodologies. In a review of surveys using stringent criteria, Mullen (1990) estimates that 10% to 15% of females experience sexual abuse in childhood.

It has been suggested that girls are abused in a ratio to boys of 9:1 (Cupoli & Sewell, 1988). However, other studies indicate that the sexual abuse of boys has been vastly underestimated and that rates of abuse in girls are only slightly higher than in boys (Finkelhor, 1984; Baker & Duncan, 1985). It is probable that boys are even less likely than girls to report sexual assaults or have such assaults reported on their behalf. It also appears that extrafamilial abuse in boys is more common than incest (Finkelhor, 1984). A partial explanation for the greater extrafamilial incidence of abuse is the fact that older boys are less often supervised in the community (Budin & Johnson, 1989) and are therefore more vulnerable. Frequently, boys are considered to need less protection as they are judged in terms of "toughness", in contrast to the "vulnerability" of girls (Pierce & Pierce, 1985).

Typologies of Child Molesters

Several researchers have attempted to construct typologies of child molesters. Whilst this often involves an over-simplification of existing data, typologies can be useful at the clinical practitioner level in helping to choose between various forms of disposal or treatment options. In an early typology, Cohen, Seghorn & Calmas (1969) divided child molesters into three groups: *fixated*, *regressed* and *aggressive*. They proposed that the fixated offender prefers the company of children, and seeks out those that are known to them. The regressed offender has some adult heterosexual interest, but also has feelings of inadequacy, and may react to a child following a threat to his masculinity. Finally, the aggressive type engages in sadistic acts, usually with boys.

Groth & Burgess (1977) adopted a different approach, based on clinical observations. They emphasized the role of non-sexual motives, dividing child molesters into two broad groups on the basis of the degree of force used in the offence. The first group, the *sex-force* offender, uses coercion or physical force, and is either *exploitive*, using the child for sexual relief without any further relationship, or *sadistic*, obtaining pleasure from hurting and humiliating the child. The second group, the *sex-pressure* offender, is characterized by an absence of physical force. This kind of offender feels safer with children and desires the child as a "love object". Offenders in this group are subdivided into those who use enticement or persuasion, and those who use entrapment in the form of bribes.

More recently, Knight & Prentky (1990) have developed a sophisticated empirical classification typology, building on the work of Cohen, Seghorn & Calmas (1969). This typology, called MTC:CM3, consists of two axes. The first axis involves a dichotomous rating on two dimensions, degree of fixation and social competence, giving rise to four subgroups. The second axis refers to the amount of contact with children, and involves further sequential decisions according to the context, the amount of physical injury, and the meaning of aggression to the offender. Knight & Prentky (1990) view their typology as defining stable subtypes among child molesters; as yet, however, it has not been validated. Nevertheless, it may be the first step in improving research which, until now, has either relied on simple dichotomies or treated child molesters as a homogeneous group.

Characteristics of Child Molesters

A number of researchers and practitioners have described the characteristics of child molesters (Howells, 1981; Quinsey, 1986; Finkelhor, 1986). The work of Finkelhor (1984, 1986) has undoubtedly had the biggest impact on the field. He proposed a four-factor psychological/sociological model for understanding child molestation. The strength of the model lies in its ability to account for existing empirical research findings. The model proposes that four pre-conditions needs to be met in order for sexual abuse to take place. First, the offender needs appropriate motivation, of which there are three components:

1. the sexual abuse satisfies some important emotional need in the abuser;
2. the child is a source of sexual arousal and gratification;

3. alternative sources of sexual gratification are blocked or inhibited in some way.

Second, internal inhibitions against acting on these motivations need to be overcome. These inhibitions may be specific to the abuser, such as alcohol or drug abuse, or they may be socio-cultural, such as social toleration of sexual interest in children. Third, there is a need to overcome external inhibiting influences, such as the protection usually offered by parents. Fourth, the abuser must overcome the child's resistance. This may involve the use of physical force; alternatively, the abuser may "groom" the victim, establishing a position of trust and authority over the child. Finkelhor's model provides a useful framework for identifying and describing some of the characteristics of men who sexually abuse children.

MOTIVATIONAL FACTORS

Emotional Congruence

Several hypotheses have been advanced to explain why child molesters find sexual relations with a child emotionally satisfying. Psycho-dynamic theorists have suggested that the "fixation" of many child molesters implies developmental immaturity and feelings of inadequacy (Groth, Hobson & Gary, 1982). The offenders' primary motivation is considered not to be sexual, but the expression of non-sexual needs and unresolved life issues. Thus, child sexual relations are perceived by the offender as less threatening than those with adults, and make the molester feel more powerful and in control. However, Groth, Hobson & Gary (1982) excluded child molesters who use actual or threatened physical force, preferring to call them "child rapists" rather than child molesters.

In a comparison of the repertory grid profiles of heterosexual paedophiles and non-sex offenders, Howells (1979) provided some evidence to support the proposition that child molesters find children less threatening than adults. He found that paedophiles construed adult relationships more strongly in terms of dominance–submission: adults were more likely to be seen as imposing, while children were seen as non-dominant.

Sexual Arousal

It is not clear why some men show sexual arousal to children. Learning theory proposes that sexual preferences are learnt through the process of conditioning, with early sexual experiences being reinforced through masturbatory fantasies (McGuire, Carlisle & Young, 1965). However, direct evidence for this is lacking in the case of child molesters, many of whom appear to show a mixed pattern of arousal. In a review of the literature on the penile plethysmograph (PPG) responses of child molesters, Barbaree & Marshall (1989) concluded that while child molesters as a group were more aroused by sexual stimuli depicting children than adults, substantial proportions of them were more aroused by adult stimuli than by child stimuli.

Some research suggests that a significant proportion of child molesters have themselves been victims of childhood sexual abuse and as a consequence go on to abuse children themselves. For example, in one study 57% of child molesters reported sexual abuse in childhood, compared with 23% of rapists (Carter et al., 1987). In contrast, however, Williams & Finkelhor (1990) found low rates of childhood sexual abuse in their review of research on incestuous fathers.

Other researchers have suggested that biological variables may contribute to the learning of sexual preferences. Support for this view comes from the findings of Flor-Henry and colleagues, who reported EEG anomalies in the dominant hemispheres of paedophiles and exhibitionists, suggesting that neurological mechanisms for learning sexual preferences may be impaired in sexual deviants (Flor-Henry et al., 1991). In another study, child molesters were compared with non-sex offenders on two neuropsychological test batteries and computer tomography (CT) scans (Hucker et al., 1986). The results showed more neuropsychological impairment in child molesters than non-sex offenders, although there was some overlap between the two groups. The overall pattern of results suggested greatest abnormalities in the left parieto-temporal lobe. It is unclear, however, to what extent such brain abnormalities contribute to the development of deviant patterns of sexual arousal.

Blockage

Whilst sexual attraction to children can be seen to "pull" child molesters towards children, the blockage or inhibition of alternative sources of sexual gratification suggests that they are also "pushed". There is research evidence to support the view that many child molesters lack heterosexual and hetero-social skills. In a study by Segal & Marshall (1985), for example, child molesters were rated as more inept in interactions with females; they also rated themselves as less assertive and more anxious. Similarly, Overholser & Beck (1986) found that, whilst rapists and child molesters both had social skill deficits, the latter described themselves as less assertive and had greater fears of negative evaluation. More recently it has been found that child molesters, as well as rapists and exhibitionists, are socially lonely and lack intimacy in their lives (Garlick, 1991).

Overcoming Internal Inhibitions

A range of factors may be responsible for the absence or loss of conventional inhibitions against sex with children. Physiological disinhibition may occur in response to alcohol or drugs. However, there is no evidence that child molesters are more frequent or heavier users of disinhibiting substances than other offenders. More significant are the cognitive distortions used by child molesters to excuse their behaviour and give themselves "permission" to abuse. Most child molesters are aware that child abuse is legally and morally wrong, and thus seek ways to excuse and justify their behaviour. This not only permits them to carry out abusive acts, but also alleviates feelings of guilt or remorse. Abel, Becker & Cunningham-Rathner (1984) identified several cognitive distortions commonly found in child molesters. These include the belief that lack of resistance by a child implies willingness; that children do not perceive genital fondling as assault; that the experience teaches the child about sex; and that society will one day come to accept adult–child sexual relations.

OFFENCES AGAINST ADULTS

Incidence and Prevalence

Excluding exhibitionism, the most common sexual offences against adults, usually women, are indecent assault and rape. Estimates of the prevalence of rape vary enormously across both time and culture. Proportions of American adult females reporting experience of rape or attempted rape range from 9% (Kilpatrick et al., 1985) to 44% (Russell, 1984), while 28% of a national sample of American female students reported such experiences (Koss, Gidycz & Wisniewski, 1987). Self-report data also suggest higher rates of victimization than suggested by official data. In 1988 the British Crime Survey estimated that less than one-fifth of rapes and indecent assaults were recorded by the police (Mayhew, Elliott & Dowds, 1989). Similarly, only 10% of sexual offences known to the police actually result in a conviction (Lloyd & Walmsley, 1989).

In a study by Koss, Gidycz & Wisniewski (1987), looking at the prevalence of sexual aggression and victimization in a sample of higher education students, 8% of males admitted to rape or attempted rape. Similarly, Abel & Rouleau (1990) found that a volunteer clinic sample of sexual deviants admitted to a total of 291 737 paraphilic acts involving 195 407 victims. Although the majority of these involved exhibitionism, frottage or voyeurism, 126 rapists reported a total of 907 rapes.

In addition to under-reporting, it is difficult to know to what extent it is possible to generalize from one sample to another. There is much evidence to suggest that the prevalence of rape and other sexual assaults on women varies across cultures (Sanday, 1979). Several authors (Edwards, 1987; Koss & Leonard, 1984) are critical of the way research has approached the measurement of sexual aggression towards women, viewing it as a continuum rather than as a set of discrete behaviour categories.

Typologies of Male Sexual Assaulters

A number of researchers and clinical practitioners have attempted to identify homogeneous subgroups of rapists. Cohen, Seghorn & Calmas (1969) identified four groups: *displaced aggression*, in which the rapist is hostile to women, the rape constituting a hostile act instigated by an altercation with a female, with minimal sexual excitation; *compensatory rape*, in which aggression is minimal, sexual gratification being sought in the context of feelings of sexual inadequacy; *sex-aggression diffusion*, in which aggression is eroticized, resulting in sexual sadism; and the *impulsive rapist*, in which the rape is an opportunistic act, with minimal aggression or sexual intent, often committed during the course of another predatory crime, such as burglary. Prentky, Cohen & Seghorn (1985) and Knight & Prentky (1990) have subjected this typology to empirical analysis. They identified four superordinate types: opportunistic; pervasively angry; sexual (sadistic and non-sadistic); and vindictive. Each of these subgroups was also divided according to social competence, giving a total of nine subgroups.

An alternative approach, which has been influential among clinical practitioners working with sexual offenders, is that proposed by Groth and his colleagues (Groth & Burgess, 1977; Groth, Burgess & Holstrom, 1977). In this scheme, rape motivation is believed to be a "pseudo-sexual act" dominated by either power needs or anger needs. The *power rapist* seeks to control and dominate, either to express virility and dominance (power-assertive) or to resolve doubts about his own sexual adequacy and masculinity (power-reassurance). In *anger rape*, the offender seeks to express rape, contempt and hate for women, perhaps to retaliate for perceived wrongdoings or rejections he has suffered at the hands of women. Sex is viewed as a weapon and, not surprisingly, anger rapists not only use excessive force whilst perpetrating rape but are often physically assaultive towards women in other contexts. Groth proposed two subtypes: anger-retaliation, in which the rape is motivated by perceived wrongs; and anger-excitation, in which the rapist experiences sadistic pleasure and excitement as a result of his victim's suffering.

Although the psychodynamic scheme proposed by Groth and his colleagues has intuitive appeal and has had a considerable impact on clinical practice, it does not appear to have resulted in significant advances in treatment and is, as yet, unsupported by research findings.

Characteristics of Male Sexual Assaulters

Unlike child molestation, rape and indecent assault are not considered to be paraphilias, except in instances where the attacker is sexually excited by the physical or psychological suffering of the victim (sadism). Historically, there have been two sometimes conflicting approaches to understanding rape and other sexual assaults on women: the medical model and feminist theories.

Medical Model

Within the medical or disease framework, rape is considered to be the result of individual psychopathology. Psychiatrists in particular have dominated the literature on rape over the last half century. Through pathologizing rape the medical profession has acquired the power to recommend and control the treatment of rapists. Within this model, rape has often been construed as an "excess" of normal sexual drives and impulses. For example, the sexual psychopath laws adopted in parts of the USA generally define a rapist in terms of "a person unable to control his sexual impulse or having to commit sex crimes" (Bowman & Engle, 1965). At the core of the disease model are two main assumptions: that rape is the result of organic impairment, and that it often includes an uncontrollable sexual impulse. The assertion is that men who rape lack the ability to control themselves and that they are "sick," disordered individuals (Scully & Marolla, 1985).

The medical model has given rise to extensive research in an attempt to identify the personal, sexual or social factors that distinguish rapists from other offenders and from "normal" men. An association with psychosis is rare; only about 5% of men are psychotic at the time of their crimes (Abel, Becker & Skinner, 1980). Similarly, controlled studies do not show rapists to be distinguished by intellectual characteristics (Quinsey, 1984) and comparisons of rapists with other offenders on personality tests have shown no consistent differences, suggesting that rapists may be characterized by criminality, but not by more specific personality abilities (Koss & Leonard, 1984). However, studies on incarcerated rapists using the Minnesota Multiphasic Personality

Inventory do suggest that many are poorly socialized and among the more personally deviant criminals (Rader, 1977).

Research studies into testosterone levels have produced mixed results. Langevin, Paitich & Russon (1985) found no difference between rapists and non-violent sex offenders. However, Rada, Laws & Kellner (1976) found a small subgroup of highly aggressive rapists with abnormally high levels of testosterone. Research into patterns of deviant sexual arousal among rapists has also produced mixed results. Whilst some studies suggest that rapists are sexually deviant (Abel et al., 1977; Quinsey, Chaplin & Upfold, 1984; Lalumiere & Quinsey, 1994), other researchers have found few significant differences between rapists and non-rapists in their penile plethysmograph responses to consenting and forced sex (Baxter, Barbaree & Marshall, 1986).

A number of studies have also examined the social competence of rape offenders, especially in terms of their assertiveness and heterosocial skills (Overholser & Beck, 1986; Segal & Marshall, 1986; Stermac & Quinsey, 1986). Whilst some studies suggest that rapists view themselves as less assertive (Stermac & Quinsey, 1986), there appear to be few overall differences between rapists and other groups of offenders.

Finally, several studies have examined the attitudes of rapists towards women and rape (Burt, 1980; Scott & Tetreault, 1986; Scully, 1990). Scott & Tetreault (1986) found support for the hypothesis that rapists have more traditional and conservative attitudes towards women when compared to violent offenders committed of non-sexual offences, suggesting that male sexual assaulters can be seen as acting out cultural attitudes of male dominance. There is, however, a growing body of research that contradicts the assumption that sex offenders have different attitudes towards women (Overholser & Beck, 1986; Stermac & Quinsey, 1986; Epps, Haworth & Swaffer, 1993). Indeed, Segal & Stermac (1984) reported that their study "failed to demonstrate that rapists as a group are exclusively conservative or negative in their attitudes towards women" (p. 440). These research findings support the view that negative and stereotypical attitudes towards women are commonplace amongst men in general and are not specific to sex offenders.

Feminist Theories

In feminist theory rape is viewed as an act of violence and social control that functions "to keep women in their place", encouraged by prevailing norms and attitudes in which women are seen as inferior male property and sex as an exchange of goods (Brownmiller, 1975; Russell, 1975). Feminist theorists argue that rape is a social problem rather than the result of individual psychopathology, pointing to the failure of research to identify consistently factors that distinguish rapists from other groups of offenders and the failure of medicine to develop effective interventions. Feminists also argue that by pathologizing rape, the offender is absolved of responsibility (Scully, 1990). When rape is viewed as a disease or a symptom of some underlying disorder it casts the offender in the "sick role". It then becomes easy for the offender to attribute the rape to factors beyond his control. Further, feminists point out that pathological explanations make the assumption that male aggressive sexual behaviour is unusual or strange. Consequently, sexually violent men can be viewed as being different to "normal" men and portrayed as "perverts" or "sex monsters". Such explanations also create the tendency to look for the cause of, and solution to, complex social problems within the individual and to ignore the cultural and structural context in which it occurs. Thus, the psychopathological model of rape removes the necessity of investigating or changing those elements within a society that may precipitate sexual violence against women.

ADOLESCENT OFFENDERS

Whilst it has been recognized for some time that adolescents sexually offend (Markley, 1950), it is really only in the last decade that the issue has received serious attention. Historically, many sex offences committed by children or adolescents have been regarded as experimentation or the result of normal curiosity. Often the "boys will be boys" attitude has prevailed in the juvenile justice system and the problem has been ignored or minimized (Ryan & Lane, 1991).

Several factors may help to account for the change in attitude towards this group of young people. First, work with adult sex offenders has revealed that many of these men began offending in their adolescence (Freeman-Longo & Groth, 1983), suggesting that sex offending in adolescence is a problem that should not be ignored. Second, research in the USA revealed that 20% of all rapes, and between 30% and 50% of child molestations were perpetrated by adolescent offenders (Brown, Flanagan & McLeod, 1984). Third, there is some evidence that adolescents who commit relatively minor offences may go on to commit more serious offences in adulthood (Stenson & Anderson, 1987). It appears that many adolescents engage in a wide spectrum of sexually aggressive and abusive behaviours, the vast majority of which go unreported, and some of which are seen as socially acceptable in some cultures (Ageton, 1983).

Several samples of juvenile sex offenders have been studied. However, much of the research suffers from methodological inadequacies (Debelle et al., 1993), one of which is the failure of most studies to distinguish those who have offended against women (sexual assaulters) from those who have offended against children (child molesters) (Awad & Saunders, 1991). Generally speaking, sexual assaulters present with all the well-known difficulties in dealing with juvenile delinquents (Rutter & Giller, 1983), in addition to their sexual aggressiveness (Awad & Saunders, 1991; Epps, 1991). Most of the research to date has focused on adolescents who abuse children.

Drawing from existing research, Ryan (1991) has described the typical characteristics of juvenile sex offenders. Sexual offences are perpetrated by juveniles of all racial, ethnic, religious and geographic groups. The vast majority are male (91–93%), and the modal age is about 14. He is likely to be white and living with both parents at the time of the offence. It is unlikely that he has any previous conviction for sexual assault, but quite likely that this conviction does not represent his first offence or victim. Some, but not all, will have been victims of sexual abuse. About 30% will also have been convicted of non-sexual delinquent behaviour prior to the current offence. In terms of victims, most offences involve 7- or 8-year-old children, usually girls, who are not related to the offender. The assault usually includes genital touching and often penetration (over 60%).

Most of the pioneering work in developing treatment programmes specifically aimed at adolescents has been carried out in the USA. In the first book devoted to the subject, Knopp (1982) described nine different treatment programmes. Within two years, the number of programmes had multiplied 10-fold. By 1988, 645 specialized programmes were available nationwide in the USA for the adolescent or pre-adolescent sexual offender (Knopp & Stevenson, 1989). Developments in Great Britain have lagged behind those of the USA but are gathering strength, stimulated by the work of the National Association for the Development of Work with Sex Offenders (NOTA). Several treatment programmes have been described, in both community (Print, 1992) and residential settings (Epps, 1991).

TREATMENT

Most treatment programmes for sex offenders, both for adults and adolescents, have a cognitive–behavioural emphasis. One of the basic theoretical assumptions underlying this approach is that sexual offending reflects at least some degree of sexual attraction to inappropriate partners or acts, often associated with a relative lack of appropriate sexual arousal. The distorted thinking and belief systems of sexual offenders are seen as a consequence of deviant sexual arousal and behaviour, serving to justify and rationalize their antisocial acts. The cognitive–behavioural model also recognizes that some sexual offenders display deficits in social competence and daily living skills, thereby restricting access to appropriate partners, which may increase the probability that sexually deviant or offending behaviour will occur. The main aims of cognitive–behavioural intervention programmes, therefore, are to normalize sexual preferences, eliminate cognitive distortions, enhance social functioning and improve life management skills. The goal of treatment is to reduce the probability of future offending. Most programmes can be divided into three overlapping parts: assessment, intervention and relapse prevention. It is important to distinguish between the *content* and *process* of treatment programmes. Process issues are particularly relevant when dealing with sexual offenders. Persistent sexual offenders tend to deny that their offending was planned and repetitive, or even that they committed any offence at all. Further, they frequently distort or in other ways minimize their responsibility for their offending, its nature and its consequences.

The way in which the treatment process is managed, especially the assessment phase, will help determine the amount and quality of information that is obtained from the offender. One of the consequences of a badly managed assessment can be an offender who is even more uncooperative, withdrawn and poorly motivated, thereby reducing the likelihood of successful inter-vention. The technique of motivational interviewing has increasingly been applied to work with sex offenders. Originally developed by practitioners working with alcohol-dependent adults (Miller, 1983), it aims to assess, in an ongoing manner, the individual's perception of their sexual offending, as well as their preparedness to change their behaviour. Based on this assessment, the practitioner works with the client to increase his awareness of the conse-quences of sexual offending, both for himself and his victims; and to enhance motivation for changing problematic behaviour.

ASSESSMENT

The distinction between assessment and treatment is always an academic one, and never more so than in the case of sexual offenders. New information may be disclosed many months or even years into treatment, sometimes altering the original formulation. Continuous assessment is also necessary to monitor and evaluate response to treatment. Nevertheless, it is still useful to begin with a period of assessment during which factual information about a number of different functional areas and from a variety of sources is pulled together. The information obtained through assessment is used to address three main issues:

the extent to which the offender is considered to be dangerous and a risk to others, suitability for treatment, and the extent to which the behaviour and attitudes of the offender have changed in response to treatment.

A thorough assessment is one which combines information from a diversity of sources using a variety of methods, referred to as *multimodal assessment*. It is essential that the assessment does not rely on self-report alone. Whenever possible it is important to obtain copies of relevant documentation about the offender, including victim statements, police interview transcripts, witness statements, court transcripts, forensic medical reports on the victim, and previous psychiatric, psychological, social work, and educational reports. If the offender has previously been in a treatment programme or in custody it is also useful to obtain information about his behaviour and attitude. Where possible it is also desirable to interview the offender's family and relatives. In addition to this information, there are three other main sources of data: offender self-report, through interview or questionnaire; behavioural observation; and phallometric assessment (penile plethysmography). Before looking at these it is important to emphasize that *no assessment or test has the power to determine with complete accuracy whether or not an individual has, in fact, committed a sexual offence.* Similarly, there is no research evidence that mental health professionals can accurately differentiate sex offenders from non-sex offenders on the basis of psychological assessment (Sinclair, 1991).

Self Report

As with most other clinical assessments, *interviewing* is by far the most frequently used method for information collection. For a variety of reasons, sexual offenders often present the interviewer with difficulties necessitating skilled and thoughtful interviewing. Many have a tendency to minimize or distort accounts of their offending behaviour; indeed, those in custodial settings may feel they have good reason to do this. A variety of interviewing strategies have been described, aimed at engaging sexual offenders in a therapeutic alliance (Perkins, 1991).

Broadly speaking, the interviewer should adopt a style that is rewarding and helpful to the offender rather than one that is too confrontational. It is important to pick the right time to challenge distorted thinking. Perkins (1991) identifies contingency management strategies that can also be helpful. Their purpose is to help the offender to assess the consequences of various courses of action. For example, the offender might be asked to draw up a list of advantages and disadvantages of treatment or of stopping offending. Table 6.3 summarizes the kinds of information that should be obtained through interview.

Table 6.3   Information obtained through interview

Psycho-sexual
Sexual history and experience; attitudes to sex; sexual knowledge; sexual
orientation and preferences; sexual dysfunction; sexual deviations; sexual drive;
puberty (age of onset, adjustment to); current masturbatory and sexual fantasies;
sexual and intimate relationships (age, gender, duration); history of sexual
victimisation; use of pornography

Sexual offending
History of sexual offending (age of onset, frequency, age and sex of victims, sexual
behaviours); attitude to victims; attitude to offences (acceptance of responsibility);
use of force and physical aggression; willingness to engage in treatment; ability to
specify treatment goals

Psychological and social problems
Substance use and abuse; emotional difficulties and emotional control (anger,
depression); history of non-sexual offending and antisocial behaviour

Family
Family composition and structure; significant life events; family relationships

Lifestyle
Employment; hobbies and interests

A range of *questionnaire measures* of varying reliability and validity are also
available to facilitate self-report. Some of those that have been developed
specifically for the assessment of sexual deviancy and offending are shown in
Table 6.4. Additional measures can also be used to assess other areas of
psychological and social functioning that may be related to sexual offending in
any one case, such as anger management, assertiveness skills, depression, locus
of control, loneliness, psychosocial intimacy, self-esteem, and social skills.

Behavioural Observation

Direct behavioural observation is especially useful as a source of information
within custodial (Clark, 1991) and residential (Epps, 1991) settings. Clark,
Fisher & McDougall (1993) describe a project at Wakefield Prison, England in
which specific behavioural targets are identified for observation and recording
by prison officers. Information obtained this way is compared with offender
self-report and inconsistencies identified. For example, it may be discovered
that a child molester who claims to no longer have any sexual feelings towards
children is ordering mail order catalogues for children's clothes. Similarly, an
offender convicted of rape who maintains in interview that his attitudes to
women have changed may be observed to frequently refer to women as
"slags" in casual conversation.

Table 6.4 Questionnaire measures

Sexual deviancy & knowledge
Abel & Becker Sexual Interest Card Sort (Salter, 1988)
Clarke Sexual History Questionnaire (Langevin et al, 1983)
Multiphasic Sex Inventory (Nichols & Molinder, 1984)
Wilson Fantasy Questionnaire (Wilson, 1978)

Cognitive distortions and beliefs
Abel & Becker Cognitions Scale (Abel, Mittleman & Becker, 1985)
Attitudes Toward Women Scale (Spence & Helmreich, 1972)
Burt Rape Myth Acceptance Scale (Burt, 1980)

Phallometric Assessment

The penile plethysmograph (PPG) is an instrument designed to assess male sexual arousal. The apparatus consists of a transducer that senses changes in penile erection and an electronic recorder which provides a permanent record of these changes. There are two types of transducer: volumetric transducers, rarely used in clinical practice, measure changes in the volume of the whole penis (Freund, Sedlacek & Knob, 1965); and circumferential transducers which measure changes in penis circumference (Bancroft, Jones & Pullen, 1966; Barlow et al., 1970). Two forms of circumferential transducers are commercially available: the Barlow gauge (Barlow et al., 1970), which is a flexible light-weight stainless steel metallic clip and the mercury strain gauge (Bancroft, Jones & Pullen, 1966) which consists of a thin rubber tube filled with mercury. Both types produce very similar results (Laws, 1977). The introduction of computers (Farrall & Card, 1988) has greatly facilitated the operation of the PPG, helping to control the presentation of stimuli and producing an immediate analysis of the assessment. The design and operation of PPG laboratories has been extensively described in recent publications (Coleman & Dwyer, 1990; Farrall, 1992). Several other authors have also highlighted some of the ethical and legal issues involved in its use (Greenland, 1988; Travin, Cullen & Melella, 1988), whilst others have drawn attention to issues surrounding reliability and validity (Hall, Proctor & Nelson, 1988; Earls, 1992; Hall, Shondrick & Hirschman, 1993). Adherence to good practice guidelines (Launay, 1994) can help to minimize some of these difficulties.

In the USA over one-third of all sex offender assessment centres use PPG as an integral part of their assessment (Knopp & Stevenson, 1989). In Britain, however, the technique remains controversial, with a large number of practitioners doubting its usefulness or harbouring ethical reservations. A recent survey of forensic psychologists in England and Wales (Houston, Thomson &

Wragg, 1993) revealed that only 99 offenders had been seen for PPG assessment, with only 19 psychologists (13.7 %) having used the technique over the course of a year. This is a somewhat surprising finding and suggests that the majority of practitioners rely on self-report from sex offenders, in the form of interview or questionnaire, despite the tendency of many sexual offenders to deny, distort or minimize accounts of their offending behaviour. Launay (1994) recognizes the need for widespread training in both the operation of the PPG and the interpretation of its results. Frequently, the only training available is that provided by the apparatus manufacturers, who often have little experience in its clinical applications. Similarly, there is a need for standardized procedures and stimuli and more vigorous research into its validity and reliability as an assessment tool.

CASE FORMULATION

Assessment results need to be interpreted to inform three management and clinical decisions. First, to what extent does the offender currently present a risk to others, and how can this risk best be minimized in the short term? Second, how amenable is the offender to treatment? Third, what interventions are indicated by the assessment and to what extent are these likely to reduce risk of reoffending?

Cognitive–behavioural assessments of the kind described earlier provide information of a variety of kinds, shown in Table 6.5. This information helps to create a greater understanding of the factors that cause and maintain sexual offending behaviour. They also have the advantage of identifying discrete areas of psychological and social functioning that may be amenable to intervention, with the aim of reducing risk.

The technique of functional analysis is especially useful for understanding offending behaviour (Owens & Ashcroft, 1982; Gresswell & Hollin, 1992). One of the main concerns of functional analysis is to identify the contingencies that help to maintain a particular behaviour. Thus, sexual offending behaviour (B) can be analyzed in terms of its antecedents (A) and its consequences (C). One advantage of this A:B:C approach lies in the ability to combine historical information that contributed to the development of sexual offending behaviour with more recent information. Functional analysis may show some problems to be long-standing (e.g. social isolation, loneliness), with other more recent problems serving to trigger the offence behaviour (e.g. marital breakdown). A case example encountered in clinical practice can be used to illustrate the use of functional analysis.

Table 6.5   Functional areas contributing to sexual offending behaviour

- Physical condition (e.g. tiredness, alcohol and drug use)
- Behavioural (e.g. deviant sexual arousal)
- Situational (e.g. left alone to babysit child)
- Attitudinal beliefs (e.g. it is really okay to have sex with children, even though it is illegal)
- Cognitive (e.g. "I can tell by the way that she is looking at me that she would really like to touch my penis")
- Emotional (e.g. feeling sorry for self: "nobody loves me")
- Opportunity (e.g. child asks to be taken to toilet)

CASE EXAMPLE

"Mark", a 16-year-old adolescent, was admitted to Glenthorne Centre having been convicted of attempted rape and indecent assault. He had previously received a conditional discharge for indecent assault on a teenage girl, and later received a 10-month youth custody sentence for robbery and indecent assault. He had a long history of social and behavioural problems, having spent time in residential schools and children's homes. However, he remained close to his mother and siblings, his father having died in suspicious circumstances when he was 11 years old, having been divorced from his mother several year earlier. Whilst at school, Mark was bullied due to his poor self-hygiene, and as a result often truanted. He performed poorly at school, gaining no formal qualifications. At the age of 16 his performance on the Wechsler Adult Intelligence Scale (Revised) (Wechsler, 1981) placed his IQ in the "borderline" range, and he had a reading age equivalent to 8 years on the Neale Analysis of Reading Ability (Neale, 1966). Upon admission to Glenthorne Centre he presented as a stocky, well-built boy, dishevelled in appearance, with long lank hair and numerous self-inflicted tattoos and scars over his neck, arms, hands and legs. He appeared shy and socially unskilled, tending to avoid conversation and mixing little with his peer group.

Whilst at Glenthorne he reported having committed several other, less serious sexual offences in addition to those on record. Usually these consisted of him making obscene remarks to women and sometimes attempting to put his hand up their skirt. His index offence occurred when he chased after a girl whom he claimed was his girlfriend. He caught hold of her, pulled her to the ground and threatened her with a knife. He managed to pull off her skirt and underwear but let go after she fought back and screamed.

Assessment and subsequent functional analysis indicated a variety of problems which required intervention. From this analysis several areas

Table 6.6   Key functional areas targeted for intervention

Area	Aim of intervention
Alcohol and substance use	To help Mark reduce his use of alcohol and other substances; increase his awareness of the dangers of substance abuse and their relationships to his offending behaviour
Social competence	To help Mark become more assertive; initiate and engage in appropriate conversation with peers and adults; improve self-care skills and personal hygiene
Victim empathy	To help Mark understand the effects of sexual offences on women
Deviant sexual fantasies	To help Mark reduce his frequency of masturbation to rape fantasies and increase masturbation to sexual fantasies involving consensual sex
Work skills	To explore vocational opportunities and equip Mark with basic vocational requirements; find a suitable work scheme if necessary.
Anger management	To help Mark explore the causes of his anger and enable him to gain greater control over his anger

were identified which appeared to play a central role in Mark's offending behaviour and which were also amenable to intervention. These are summarized in Table 6.6. It was hypothesized that improvements in each of these six areas would help to reduce the risk of reoffending. His use of alcohol and other substances was given priority; all of his offences occurred after he had been drinking or inhaling gas, usually a combination of both. Engaging Mark in a work scheme was also considered important; he was an opportunistic offender who made little constructive use of his time and lacked structure in his daily life.

INTERVENTION

Recent years have seen an explosion in the number of treatment programmes available for men and boys who sexually offend. The treatment of sex offenders has evolved since the "medical model" approach, described earlier in this chapter, in which the offender is viewed as sick, to the currently popular cognitive–behavioural approach. More recently, the concept of relapse prevention, referred to earlier, has also been added. In many programmes relapse prevention is used as a "bolt-on" addition, aimed at maintaining and enhancing the changes produced by the rest of the programme and ensuring that the client continues to utilize the skills he has learned once formal treatment is over. Laws (1989), however, has argued convincingly that the relapse prevention model provides a useful umbrella under which cognitive–

behavioural interventions can be organized. Thus, it makes sense to see the whole of the treatment process, and follow-up work, as an endeavour in relapse prevention.

RELAPSE PREVENTION

The strength of the relapse prevention approach lies in its emphasis on helping the offender to recognize and understand, in an on-going manner, the psychological and situational variables that put him at risk of reoffending. The precise sequence of the relapse process will be different for each offender. In some cases exposure to a particular situation may trigger the sequence of events leading to an offence; in others, it may be a negative emotional state or a specific life event, such as being reprimanded at work for poor performance. For each offender the trigger event will lead to a sequence of cognitive, affective and behavioural events that progressively takes him closer to engaging in offence behaviour. The offender can be helped to identify those "seemingly unimportant decisions" (SUDS) (Laws, 1989) that helped to take him closer to offending.

In addition to helping the offender to recognize and monitor the response chain and seemingly unimportant decisions, the offender must also be reminded throughout treatment of the skills he has learned to more effectively deal with the cognitive, affective and behavioural elements of the response chain so that he can avoid relapsing. The recurrence of deviant fantasies should be seen as inevitable and used as opportunities to practice the procedures learned in treatment. Similarly, behaviours that in the past have started the relapse process must be identified, and the offender reminded to use his acquired skills both to reduce the probability of these behaviours occurring and to deal appropriately with them when they do occur.

The process of helping the offender to recognize the processes and situations that put him at risk has been described by Pithers (1990) as the *internal management* aspect of relapse prevention training. *External management*, on the other hand, refers to the provision of supervisory control and monitoring after discharge. This entails efforts from both the offender and those responsible for supervision. Towards the end of formal treatment the offender can be helped to prepare a list of the factors, processes and situations that put him at risk; ways he can avoid the occurrence of risks; and techniques to deal with them in an effective manner when they cannot be avoided. He should carry this list around with him and refer to it frequently. Those responsible for supervision should have a copy of the list, and should monitor the offender's progress. If they recognize emerging problems (e.g. the offender entering high risk situations), they can confront the offender and take whatever action is possible to minimize risk. Abel (1987), referring to the programme he runs in the USA, describes an alternative strategy called a "surveillance group". Four to five people, who are in regular contact with the offender (e.g. friends, family), meet initially with the programme therapists to construct a list of risky and provocative situations for the offender. They subsequently monitor the offender's behaviour and provide regular reports to the therapists.

COGNITIVE–BEHAVIOURAL INTERVENTIONS

One of the advantages of treatment programmes with a cognitive–behavioural orientation is that practitioners have at their disposal a range of intervention methods, many of them with proven efficacy, and each aimed at specific functional problems. This enables practitioners to construct programmes for particular groups of offenders and to tailor programmes, where resources allow, to the needs of the individual offender. Recent reviews of treatment effectiveness with sexual offenders (Marshal et al., 1991; Marshall, Hudson & Ward, 1992) also suggest that cognitive–behavioural programmes are most effective in reducing rates of reoffending. Interventions with the families of sex offenders can also be used in conjunction with other treatment modalities (Frude, 1991; Thomas, 1991).

Most cognitive–behavioural programmes for sexual offenders have at their core a range of interventions aimed at modifying three main sets of problems common to most sexual offenders: deviant sexuality, social incompetence and attitudinal and cognitive distortions.

Deviant Sexuality

A substantial proportion of sexual offenders exhibit sexually deviant fantasies and behaviours. Where assessment has shown an offender to be aroused by deviant acts, such as sadism or sexual contact with children, two separate, although not independent, treatment targets can be identified: first, to reduce sexual arousal to the deviant act or partner; second, to enhance or establish arousal to appropriate partners or acts. As detailed below, a variety of techniques can be used, often in combination, to achieve these targets.

Masturbatory Conditioning

This technique, also referred to as orgasmic reconditioning (Marquis, 1970), was successfully introduced by Davison (1968). It involves a positive reinforcement procedure in which the offender replaces deviant with non-deviant fantasies. There are several variations to the technique. Usually it requires offenders to keep a fantasy diary in which they record typical deviant masturbatory fantasies. With the help of the therapist they are asked to create a non-deviant fantasy. A masturbatory schedule is then devised, with the offender switching from deviant to non-deviant fantasy as he approaches orgasm. As soon as orgasm occurs to the appropriate image and a refractory state onsets, the offender is instructed to abstain from masturbating and to immediately verbalize every variation he can think of on his deviant fantasies and acts. Over time the deviant fantasy is withdrawn, such that orgasm becomes contingent upon non-deviant fantasies. Relapse prevention principles can be incorporated to ensure that the offender does not construe a lapse into deviant fantasy as a failure; rather, they revert to an earlier stage in the programme and continue as before. This technique therefore gives the offender some degree of control over deviant sexual fantasies, even if they do not permanently disappear. The advantages of this technique are that it allows frequent practice in a natural setting and employs the use of masturbation, which appears to play an important role in the development of sexual deviance (McGuire, Carlisle & Young, 1965). Successful results with this technique have been reported by Abel, Barlow & Blanchard (1973) with a patient with sadistic fantasies; by Marshall (1973), using a combination of orgasmic reconditioning and aversion therapy with a group of child molesters; and by Marshall, Williams & Christie (1977) with a mixed group of incarcerated sex offenders.

Covert Sensitization

In this procedure, developed by Cautela (1967), the offender is helped to imagine a scene of relevance to his offending, following which he imagines some unpleasant consequence, such as being arrested. Essentially it is similar to masturbatory conditioning, with the addition of an aversive element. Salter (1988) reported a variant of this technique, using an imagined positive consequence of non-offending rather than a negative consequence.

Aversion Therapy

This can take a variety of forms (Marshall, 1985), but basically involves the pairing of the presently attractive but unacceptable stimuli or behaviours with a physically unpleasant experience. In the behavioural programme described by Marshall & Barbaree (1989) a moderately unpleasant electric shock is delivered to the calf muscle of the offender. However, this technique is now less widely used, partly because of the lack of evidence involving its efficacy (Quinsey & Marshall, 1983), and partly because of the ethical difficulties involved in its use. In other programmes (Laws, Meyer & Holmen, 1978) foul odours, such as ammonia, have been used in place of electric shocks. This technique has the advantage of being easily incorporated into relapse prevention programmes; offenders can carry a small bottle of smelling salts which they inhale whenever they recognize the commencement of a deviant fantasy (Hunt, 1985). Typically, offenders attend two sessions of aversive therapy per week for three weeks and then two additional sessions over a subsequent two weeks. Within each one-hour session aversion therapy lasts about 25 minutes, involving approximately 30 pairings of deviant stimuli and shocks. Marshall & Barbaree (1989) recommend the use of additional techniques, such as masturbatory conditioning, to facilitate generalization of behavioural change.

Serber (1970) described a variation of aversion therapy, shame aversion therapy. The technique involved the offender acting out his deviant behaviour, in this case exhibitionism, in front of therapist aides who were instructed to behave with ridicule or disapproval towards him. Clearly, such controversial techniques should be used only when indicated as potentially useful by the assessment findings.

Antilibidinal Medication

In some cases, especially those involving excessive sexual drive (hyper-sexuality), antilibidinal medication is used in addition to cognitive–behav-ioural techniques to control deviant sexual behaviour and fantasies. The two most commonly used forms of medication are the anti-androgen cyproterone acetate and the tranquillizer benperidol (Bancroft, 1983). Cyproterone acetate has been found to reduce the intensity both of sexual drive (Torpy & Tomison, 1986) and sexual aggression (Matthews, 1979). It can also enhance the benefits some offenders obtain from psychological intervention (Clarke, 1989). Long-term research on prolonged use of such medication, however, is not yet available. Medication should not be used in isolation from other forms of intervention. Many sex offenders commit their offences for reasons other than sexual gratification. Therefore, reducing their libido will not necessarily be sufficient to stop or reduce the risk of reoffending (Perkins, 1991). Indeed, Raboch, Cerna & Zemek (1987) report two cases of sexually motivated murderers with low levels of testosterone.

Social Competence

Social competence refers to two broad sets of skills and processes: those concerned with interpersonal behaviour, such as empathy, assertiveness, anger and anxiety management and conversational skills; and those concerned with the development and maintenance of intimate relationships involving communication, conflict resolution and intimacy skills. A range of interventions are available that have been shown to reduce deficits in these areas, including anxiety management through cue-controlled relaxation (McGlyn, 1985), assertiveness training (Gambrill, 1985), training in problem solving (Marchione, 1985) and social skills training (Burgess et al., 1980). Most sex offender programmes conduct these interventions in a group format, using modelling, role play and feedback, with the emphasis on experiential learning rather than didactic instruction. Occasionally, these interventions are used on an individual basis, such as when the offender refuses to, or is too shy, to participate in a group setting. Sex education has also been addressed in some programmes in response to the noted lack of sexual knowledge of many sex offenders in prison (Woodward, 1980) and other residential settings (Wyre, 1989). Some programmes also incorporate life skills training (Marshall & Turner, 1987). This aims to provide offenders with a variety of skills, including budgeting skills, personal hygiene, effective use of leisure time and seeking and selecting appropriate accommodation. Where possible, those offenders with complex difficulties requiring more intense therapeutic help, such as severe marital problems or addiction to alcohol or drugs, should be referred to specialized programmes.

Attitudinal and Cognitive Distortions

Group work can also be used to challenge the dysfunctional attitudes, beliefs and cognitions frequently exhibited by sexual offenders. Negative and hostile attitudes towards women, for example, can be challenged by other offenders and therapists in much the same way that cognitive therapies deal with these issues (Beck, 1976). Mixed offender groups, combining child molesters and rapists, can be advantageous in this respect, generating a wider range of views and opinions. One technique is to ask each offender to describe his offences in detail, recording the account on video. During this process other group members are not permitted to say anything. Once the offender has finished, however, he can be questioned about his offence behaviour, attitudes and beliefs. Negative attitudes and cognitive distortions can be challenged, and alternative views put forward for discussion. Frequently, offenders are more astute than therapists at detecting other offenders' attempts to minimize, deny, rationalize, justify or excuse their behaviour. They may begin to see elements of their own thinking and behaviour reflected in other offenders, which hitherto they had been able to deny or avoid. Reporting on a group for young men, many with a history of sexual offending, run at an English secure hospital, Quayle (1989) noted that it is often through the offenders' identification with the victims of other offenders' offences that they gain most insight into their own offences and the effects these are likely to have had on their victims.

The group format also enables discussion of past and present relationship difficulties, including selection of appropriate partners, effective communication, and conflict resolution. Jacobson & Dallas (1981) have shown that these behaviours are required for the full enjoyment of relationships, and that they are best trained in this type of group setting.

CASE EXAMPLE

Having reviewed some of the most commonly used methods of intervention it may prove useful to return to the case of Mark, whose assessment and formulation were outlined earlier in this chapter. The reader is referred to the functional areas targeted for intervention, shown in Table 6.6.

When Mark first entered the treatment programme at Glenthorne Centre, staff were seriously concerned about his risk to others. He was, initially, difficult to engage in conversation and steered clear of social interaction. Staff found it difficult to build up a rapport with him and therefore felt uncomfortable in his presence which, in turn, did little to improve his social competence. The treatment planning team came to the conclusion that improvement in any area of Mark's functioning would be difficult to achieve unless his social competence improved. A package of interventions was implemented, combining individual social skills training and a unit-based reinforcement programme, in which target behaviours were verbally reinforced by staff. After two months Mark entered a 12-week group programme run at the Centre aimed at improving assertiveness and social problem solving. In addition, Mark was on a unit-based level programme (Ostapiuk & Westwood, 1986) in which access to privileges are contingent upon meeting expected standards of performance on target areas, including personal hygiene and verbal behaviour. Seven months after admission (two months on assessment, five months on intervention), Mark was engaged in individual work aimed at helping him change his deviant sexual fantasies. It was discovered that he was very poor at generating new fantasy material and tended to rely on concrete, visual imagery obtained from hard-core pornography and his offence behaviour. Consequently, he was helped to generate new material which was recorded on audiotape. Mark was encouraged to listen to the tape before and during masturbation. Although PPG equipment was unavailable, Mark was able to keep a simple written record of the proportion of time spent fantasizing to deviant material, using a 1–7 analogue scale. He responded well to this technique; he was motivated and compliant, responding positively to individual attention and praise. Concurrent to this intervention, Mark also attended a 10-session group aimed at helping residents to manage and control anger and aggressive behaviour, following the approach described by Feindler & Ecton (1986). Around this time Mark also transferred from the educational programme to the work programme, aimed at developing vocational skills. This continued until Mark left Glenthorne, after a period of two and a half years. Throughout his time in security, an observational record was also kept of two behavioural targets, in addition to records of his general daily behaviour: physical proximity and touching of female staff; and initiation of appropriate conversation. These behaviours had been targeted for observation during his assessment and were considered to be indicators of his response to treatment and his risk to others.

After one and a half years, Mark was due for transfer to the open unit on the same campus. One month before this, he began individual work with two staff members (one male, one female) looking at victim empathy. This work combined role play with discussion of relevant material obtained from newspaper articles, television, films and books about the effects on victims of sexual assault. Mark also attended an educational programme run by the local health authority on the effects of alcohol and drugs. Following his graded transfer to the open unit, Mark continued to receive individual sessional work looking at his use of alcohol and drugs. The treatment planning team thought that this work was best left until his transfer to the open unit, given that the use of alcohol and drugs is prohibited in security. The work was particularly aimed at helping Mark to control his use of alcohol, using a programme for young offenders developed by Baldwin et al. (1988).

Mark spent just under one year on the open unit; staff encountered no significant behavioural or management difficulties. A risk evaluation carried out during this time suggested that his risk of reoffending had been substantially reduced. Behavioural observation indicated that his touching of female staff had ceased. He was also more relaxed, conversant and socially skilled. Indeed, staff reported enjoying his company, in contrast to when he was first admitted. At his own request Mark was also referred to a dermatologist with a view to having some of his tattoos removed, especially those on his neck and hands. Finally, in the time leading up to his return to the community, where he was to live in a hostel, Mark was involved in developing relapse-prevention strategies, to be monitored and reviewed by his probation officer.

Since leaving Glenthorne just over two years ago, Mark has not reoffended. He has recently married, has been in stable employment for the past 18 months, and no longer abuses drugs or other substances. Although this is a relatively short follow-up period, we are pleased with the outcome. Experience at Glenthorne suggests that the sexual offenders who do reoffend tend to do so within the first few months after discharge.

This case illustrates the need for multimodal intervention programmes spread, in some cases, over a considerable period of time, in this instance two and a half years. Of course, other sexual offenders with fewer and less serious problems will require less time and resources for an equally successful outcome.

TREATMENT OUTCOME

The treatment of sexual offenders can be a lengthy and costly exercise, as illustrated by the case described above. In the current economic climate programme managers are under increasing pressure to justify such high levels of expenditure on a client group who often are seen as unworthy of treatment (Kosky, 1989). Two questions need to be addressed. Is there any evidence that treatment programmes for sexual offenders are effective in reducing rates of reoffending? If so, which programmes, or elements of programmes, are most effective with which particular types of offender?

Historically, reviews of treatment effectiveness have produced mixed results (Marshall et al., 1991). The different findings can largely be explained as the consequence of methodological problems, noted below, that make comparisons between studies difficult.

Variations in Selection Criteria for Treatment Programmes

Some programmes attract only the most dangerous offenders who are in need of treatment (such as those in secure institutions), whereas others employ restrictive selection criteria, sometimes encouraging those least at risk of reoffending, thereby reducing the risk of programme failure (Furby, Weinrott & Blackshaw, 1989). Several studies (Pacht & Roberts, 1968; Soothill & Gibbens, 1978) have shown that the likelihood of reoffending among released offenders who have more than one prior conviction is far greater than among first time offenders. This is obviously an important consideration in evaluating the effects of treatment. Similarly, programmes differ in the types of offence they are willing to treat. For example, some focus on child molesters, some on rapists and others on mixed groups. In their review of treatment outcomes, Marshall et al. (1991) conclude that rapists and exhibitionists appear to profit less from treatment than do child molesters.

Length of Follow-up

Studies vary tremendously in follow-up time (i.e. time at risk for reoffending). Several researchers (Soothill & Gibbens, 1978; Marshall & Barbaree, 1988) have shown that recidivism rates continue to increase for as long as these offenders are followed, sometimes up to 22 years. Marshall, Hudson & Ward (1992) suggest that follow-up periods of less than four to five years are particularly unsatisfactory.

Adequacy of Official Records

Most follow-up studies have used official records for determining the incidence of reoffending, which often provide an underestimate of the true figure (Furby, Weinrott & Blackshaw, 1989; Marshall & Barbaree, 1988).

Treatment Emphasis and Orientation

Historically, there has been a shift in the theoretical orientation of treatment programmes for sexual offenders. Early programmes often had a medical emphasis, sometimes employing physical techniques such as castration, neuro-surgery and antilibidinal medication. The 1970s saw an increase in the number of programmes using behavioural methods; however, many of these were narrow in emphasis, focusing primarily on sexual deviation and often using aversive techniques. In the 1980s many behavioural programmes expanded to incorporate cognitive and relapse-prevention techniques. However, this was usually a gradual transition, making it difficult to evaluate the effects of these changes on treatment outcome.

Absence of Controlled Studies

The most common criticism of treatment studies is their failure to provide a controlled comparison with untreated offenders. However, as Marshall et al. (1991) point out, it is ethically unacceptable to withhold a potentially useful treatment for a group of dangerous men.

Bearing in mind the methodological difficulties outlined earlier, Marshall et al. (1991) undertook a comprehensive review of the literature on treatment effectiveness with sexual offenders. They came to the conclusion that some sex offenders can be effectively treated so as to reduce subsequent recidivism. Cognitive–behavioural programmes and those programmes that utilize antilibidinal medication in conjunction with psychological treatments appeared to maximize the chances of successful outcome. In addition, those programmes that include relapse-prevention components are generally more effective than those that do not. The treatment of sex offenders also appears to be remark-ably cost-effective (Prentky & Burgess, 1990; Marshall, Eccles & Barbaree, 1993).

However, child molesters and exhibitionists appear to respond better to treatment than rapists. For example, Pithers & Cumming (1989) report that of the 147 child molesters who completed their programme, only 3% subsequently committed a sexual offence during a six-year follow-up period. In contrast, 15% of the 20 treated rapists reoffended during the same period of time. Marshall et al. (1991) suggest that further research is needed to examine why rapists respond less well to treatment with a view to altering treatment approaches accordingly, and Marshall (1992) has gone on to suggest how this might be achieved. He recommends that more emphasis should be placed upon the following problem areas: lack of empathy; low self-esteem; motivation for treatment; inappropriate attitudes toward women and sex; a lack of intimacy and the associated experience of emotional loneliness; alcohol and drug abuse; and issues concerning power, aggression, and the intent to humiliate. Marshall (1992) also suggests that the current practice of integrating child molesters and rapists in treatment groups may be inappropriate.

Not everyone, however, is in agreement with the conclusions of Marshall and his colleagues (Quinsey et al. 1993). Quinsey et al. argue that the effectiveness of treatment in reducing sex offender recidivism has yet to be satisfactorily demonstrated, criticizing the methodology adopted by Marshall et al. (1991) in their review of the literature. Quinsey et al. suggest that to demonstrate the effectiveness of sex offender treatment, more well-controlled outcome research is required that can be evaluated with meta-analytic techniques.

REFERENCES

Abel, G.G. (1987) Surveillance groups. Paper presented at the annual meeting of the Association for the Behavioural Treatment of Sexual Abusers, Newport, OR, USA.

Abel, G.G., Barlow, D.H. & Blanchard, E.B. (1973) Developing heterosexual arousal by altering masturbatory fantasies: a controlled study. Paper presented at the Association for Advancement of Behaviour Therapy, Miami, FL, USA.

Abel, G.G., Barlow, D.H. Blanchard, E.B. & Guild, D. (1977) The components of rapists' sexual arousal. *Archives of General Psychiatry*, 895–903.

Abel, G.G., Becker, J.V. & Cunningham-Rathner, J. (1984) Complications, consent and cognitions in sex between children and adults. *International Journal of Law and Psychiatry*, 7, 89–103.

Abel, G.G., Becker, J.V. & Skinner, L.J. (1980) Aggressive behaviour and sex. *Psychiatric Clinics of North America*, 3, 133–151.

Abel, G.G., Mittleman, M.S. & Becker, J.V. (1985) Sexual offenders: results of assessment and recommendations for treatment. In M.H. Ben-Aron, S.J. Huckle & C.D. Webster (Eds), *Clinical Criminology: The Assessment and Treatment of Criminal Behaviour*. Toronto: M & M Graphic.

Abel, G.G. & Rouleau, J.L. (1990) The nature and extent of sexual assault. In W.L. Marshall, D.R. Laws & H.E. Barbaree (Eds), *Handbook of Sexual Assault: Issues, Theories, and Treatment of the Offender*. New York: Plenum.

Ageton, S.S. (1983) *Sexual Assault Among Adolescents*. Lexington, MA: Lexington Books.

American Psychiatric Association (1987) *Diagnostic and Statistical Manual of Mental Disorders*, 3rd edn, revised. Washington, DC: APA.

Awad, G.A. & Saunders, E.B. (1991) Male adolescent sexual assaulters: Clinical observations. *Journal of Interpersonal Violence*, 446–460.

Baker, A.W. & Duncan, S.P. (1985) Child sexual abuse: a study of prevalence in Great Britain. *Child Abuse and Neglect*, **9**, 457–467.

Baldwin, S., Wilson, M., Lancaster, A. & Allsop, D. (1988) Ending offending: an alcohol training resource pack for people working with young offenders. Glasgow: Scottish Council on Alcohol.

Bancroft, J. (1983) *Human Sexuality and its Problems*. Edinburgh: Churchill-Livingstone.

Bancroft, J., Jones, H.G. & Pullen, B.R. (1966) A simple transducer for measuring penile erection, with comments on its use in the treatment of sexual disorders. *Behaviour Research and Therapy*, **4**, 239–241.

Barbaree, H.E. & Marshall, W.L. (1989) The Warkworth Sexual Behaviour Clinic. Report to Correctional Series of Canada, Kingston, Ontario.

Barlow, D.H., Becker, R., Leitenberg, H. & Agras, W.S. (1970) A mechanical strain gauge for recording penile circumference change. *Journal of Applied Behaviour Analysis*, **3**, 73–76.

Baxter, D.J., Barbaree, H.E. & Marshall, W.L. (1986) Sexual responses to consenting and forced sex in a large sample of rapists and non-rapists. *Behaviour Research and Therapy*, **24**, 513–520.

Beck, A.T. (1976) *Cognitive Therapy and the Emotional Disorders*. New York: University of Pennsylvania Press.

Bowman, K. & Engle, B. (1965) Sexual psychopath laws. In R. Slovenko (Ed.), *Sexual Behaviour and the Law*. Springfield, IL: Charles C. Thomas.

Brown, E.J., Flanagan, T.J. & McLeod, M. (Eds) (1984) *Sourcebook of Criminal Justice Statistics – 1983*. Washington, DC: Bureau of Justice Statistics.

Brownmiller, S. (1975) *Against Our Will: Men, Women and Rape*. New York: Simon & Schuster.

Budin, L.E. & Johnson, C.F. (1989) Sex abuse prevention programmes: offenders' attitudes about their efficacy. *Child Abuse and Neglect*, **13**, 77–87.

Burgess, R., Jewitt, R., Sandham, J. & Hudson, B.L. (1980) Working with sex offenders: a social skills training group. *British Journal of Social Work*, **10**, 133–142.

Burt, M.R. (1980) Cultural myths and supports for rape. *Journal of Personality and Social Psychology*, **38**, 217–230.

Carter, D.L., Prentky, R.A., Knight, R.A., Vanderveer, P.L. & Boucher, R.J. (1987) Use of pornography in the criminal and developmental histories of sex offenders. *Journal of Interpersonal Violence*, **2**, 196–211.

Cautela, J. (1967) Covert sensitization. *Psychological Reports*, **20**, 459–468.

Clark, D. (1991) Identifying behavioural indicators for sex offenders: risk factors. Paper presented at the Prison Service Psychology Conference, Scarborough, England.

Clark, D.A., Fisher, M.J. & McDougall, C. (1993) A new methodology for assessing the level of risk in incarcerated offenders. *British Journal of Criminology*, **33**, 436–448.

Clarke, D.J. (1989) Antilibidinal drugs and mental retardation: a review. *Medicine, Science and the Law*, **29**, 136–146.

Cohen, M., Seghorn, T. & Calmas, W. (1969) Sociometric study of the sex offender. *Journal of Abnormal Psychology*, **74**, 249–255.

Coleman, E. & Dwyer, M. (1990) Proposed standards of care for the treatment of adult sex offenders. *Journal of Offender Rehabilitation*, **16**, 93–106.

Cupoli, J.M. & Sewell, P.N. (1988) 1059 Children with a chief complaint of sexual abuse. *Child Abuse and Neglect*, **12**, 151–162.

Davis, G.E. & Leitenberg, H. (1987) Adolescent sex offenders. *Psychological Bulletin*, **101**, 417–427.

Davison, G. (1968) Elimination of a sadistic fantasy by a client-controlled counter-conditioning technique: a case study. *Journal of Abnormal Psychology*, **73**, 84–90.

Debelle, G.D., Ward, M.R., Burnham, J.B., Jamieson, R. & Ginty, M. (1993) Evaluation of intervention programmes for juvenile sex offenders: questions and dilemmas. *Child Abuse Review*, **2**, 75–85.

Earls, C.M. (1992) Clinical issues in the psychological assessment of child molesters. In W. O'Donohue & J.H. Greer (Eds), *The Sexual Abuse of Children: Clinical Issues*, Vol.2. Hillsdale, NJ: Lawrence Erlbaum.

Edwards, A. (1987) Male violence in feminist theory: an analysis of the changing conceptions of sex/gender violence and male domination. In J. Hanmer & M. Maynard (Eds), *Women, Violence and Social Control*. Atlantic Highlands, NJ: Humanities Press International.

Epps, K. (1991) The residential treatment of adolescent sex offenders. In M. McMurran & C. McDougall (Eds), *Proceedings of the First DCLP Annual Conference*. Issues in Criminological and Legal Psychology, No. 17. Leicester: British Psychological Society.

Epps, K.J., Haworth, R. & Swaffer, T. (1993) Attitudes toward women and rape among male adolescents convicted of sexual versus nonsexual crimes. *Journal of Psychology*, **127**, 501–506.

Farrall, W. (1992) Instrumental and methodological issues in the assessment of sexual arousal. In W. O'Donohue & J.H. Greer (Eds), *The Sexual Abuse of Children: Clinical Issues*, Vol.2. Hillsdale, NJ: Lawrence Erlbaum.

Farrall, W.R. & Card, D.R. (1988) Advancements in physiological evaluation of assessment and treatment of the sexual aggressor. *Annals of the New York Academy of Sciences*, **528**, 261–273.

Feindler, E.L. & Ecton, R.B. (1986) *Adolescent Anger Control: Cognitive–Behavioural Techniques*. Oxford: Pergamon.

Finkelhor, D. (1979) *Sexually victimized Children*. New York: Free Press.

Finkelhor, D. (1984) Four preconditions: a model. In D. Finkelhor (Ed.), *Child Sexual Abuse: New theory and research*. New York: Free Press.

Finkelhor, D. (1986) *A Sourcebook on Child Sex Abuse*. Newbury Park, CA: Sage.

Flor-Henry, P., Lang, R.A., Koles, Z.J. & Frenzel, R.R. (1991) Quantitative EEG studies of paedophilia. *International Journal of Psychophysiology*, **10**, 253–258.

Freeman-Longo, R.E. & Groth, A.N. (1983) Juvenile sexual offences in the histories of adult rapists and child molesters. *International Journal of Offender Therapy and Comparative Criminology*, **27**, 150–155.

Freund, K., Sedlacek, F. & Knob, K. (1965) A simple transducer for mechanical plethysmography of the male genital. *Journal of Experimental Analysis of Behaviour*, **8**, 169–170.

Frude, N. (1991) *Understanding Family Problems: A Psychological Approach*. Chichester: John Wiley.

Furby, L., Weinrott, M.R. & Blackshaw, L. (1989) Sex offender recidivism: a review. *Psychological Bulletin*, **105**, 3–30.

Gambrill, E. (1985) Assertiveness training. In A.S. Bellack & M. Hersen (Eds), *Dictionary of Behaviour Therapy Techniques*. New York: Pergamon.

Garlick, Y. (1991) Intimacy failure, loneliness, and the attribution of blame in sexual offending. In *HM Prison Service Psychology Conference Proceedings*. London: Home Office.

Greenland, C. (1988) The treatment and maltreatment of sexual offenders: ethical issues. *Annals of the New York Academy of Sciences*, **528**, 373–378.

Gresswell, D.M. & Hollin, C.R. (1992) Towards a new methodology for making sense of case material: an illustrative case involving attempted multiple murder. *Criminal Behaviour and Mental Health*, **2**, 329–341.

Groth, A.N. & Burgess, A.W. (1977) Motivational intent in the sexual assault of children. *Criminal Justice and Behaviour*, **4**, 253–271.

Groth, A.N., Burgess, A.W. & Holstrom, L.L. (1977) Rape: power, anger and sexuality. *American Journal of Psychiatry*, **134**, 1239–1243.

Groth, A.N., Hobson, W.F. & Gary, T.S. (1982) The child molester: clinical observations. In J. Conte & D.A. Shore (Eds), *Social Work and Child Sexual Abuse*. New York: Haworth.

Hall, G.C.N., Proctor, W.C. & Nelson, G.M. (1988) The validity of physiological measures of paedophiliac sexual arousal in a sexual offender population. *Journal of Consulting and Clinical Psychology*, **56**, 118–122.

Hall, G.C.N., Shondrick, D.D. & Hirschman, R. (1993) The role of sexual arousal in sexually aggressive behaviour: a meta-analysis. *Journal of Consulting and Clinical Psychology*, **61**, 1091–1095.

Home Office (1989) *Criminal Statistics in England and Wales 1988*. London: HMSO.

Houston, J., Thomson, P. & Wragg, J. (1993) Working with sex offenders: the role of forensic psychologists. *British Psychological Society Division of Criminological and Legal Psychology Newsletter*, **35**, 16–18.

Howells, K. (1979) Some meanings of children for pedophiles. In M. Cook & G. Wilson (Eds), *Love and Attraction*. Oxford: Pergamon.

Howells, K. (1981) Adult sexual interest in children: considerations relevant to theories of etiology. In M. Cook & K. Howells (Eds), *Adult Sexual Interest in Children*. London: Academic Press.

Hucker, S.J., Langevin, R., Wortzman, G., Bain, J., Handy, L., Chambers, J. & Wright, S. (1986) Neuropsychological impairment in pedophiles. *Canadian Journal of Behavioural Science*, **18**, 440–448.

Hunt, F.M. (1985). Contingent aromatic aversion. In A.S. Bellack & M. Hersen (Eds), *Dictionary of Behaviour Therapy Techniques*. New York: Pergamon.

Jacobsen, N.S. & Dallas, M. (1981) Helping married couples improve their relationships. In W.E. Craighead, A.E. Kazdin & M.J. Mahoney (Eds), *Behaviour Modification: Principles, Issues and Applications*. Boston, MA: Houghton Mifflin.

Kilpatrick, D.G., Best, C.L., Veronen, L.J., Amick, A.E., Villeponteaux, L.A. & Ruff, G.A. (1985) Mental health correlates of criminal victimisation: a random community survey. *Journal of Consulting and Clinical Psychology*, **53**, 866–873.

Knight, R.A. & Prentky, R.A. (1990) Classifying sexual offenders: the development and corroboration of taxonomic models. In W.L. Marshall, D.R. Laws & H.E. Barbaree (Eds), *Handbook of Sexual Assault: Issues, Theories, and Treatment of the Offender*. New York: Plenum.

Knopp, F.H. (1982) *Remedial Intervention in Adolescent Sex offenses: Nine Program Descriptions*. Orwell, Vermont: Safer Society Press.

Knopp, F.H. & Stevenson, W. (1989) *Nationwide Survey of Juvenile and Adult Sex Offender Treatment programs and Models: 1988*. Orwell, VT: Safer Society Press.

Kosky, R.J. (1989). Should sex offenders be treated? *Australian and New Zealand Journal of Psychiatry*, **23**, 176–180.

Koss, M.P. & Leonard, K.E. (1984) Sexually aggressive men: Empirical findings and theoretical implications. In N. Malamuth & E. Donnerstein (Eds), *Pornography and Sexual Aggression*. New York: Academic Press.

Koss, M.P., Gidycz, C.A. & Wisniewski, N. (1987) The scope of rape: incidence and prevalence of sexual aggression and victimisation in a national sample of higher education students. *Journal of Consulting and Clinical Psychology*, **55**, 162–170.

Lalumiere, M.L. & Quinsey, V.L. (1994) The discriminability of rapists from non-sex offenders using phallometric measures: a meta-analysis. *Criminal Justice and Behaviour*, **21**, 150–175.

Langevin, R., Handy, L., Paitich, D. & Russon, A. (1983) A new version of the Clarke Sex History Questionnaire for Males. In R. Langevin (Ed.), *Erotic Preference, Gender Identity and Aggression*. Hillsdale, NJ: Lawrence Erlbaum.

Langevin, R., Paitich, D. & Russon, A.E. (1985) Are rapists sexually anomalous, aggressive, or both. In R. Langevin (Ed.), *Erotic Preference, Gender Identity and Aggression*. Hillsdale, NJ: Lawrence Erlbaum.

Launay, G. (1994) Guidelines for PPG usage. In G. Towl & M. Lloyd (Eds), *Forensic Update: A Newsletter for Forensic Psychologists*. No.3. Leicester: British Psychological Society.

Laws, D.R. (1977) A comparison of the measurement characteristics of two circumferential penile transducers. *Archives of Sexual Behaviour*, **6**, 45–51.

Laws, D.R. (Ed.) (1989) *Relapse Prevention with Sex Offenders*. New York: Guilford Press.

Laws, D.R., Meyer, J. & Holmen, M.L. (1978) Reduction of sadistic sexual arousal by olfactory aversion: a case study. *Behaviour Research and Therapy*, **16**, 281–285.

Lloyd, C. & Walmsley, R. (1989) *Changes in Rape Offences and Sentencing*. Home Office Research Study, No. 105. London: HMSO.

Marchione, K. (1985) Problem solving training. In A.S. Bellack & M. Hersen (Eds), *Dictionary of Behaviour Therapy Techniques*. New York: Pergamon.

Markley, O.B. (1950) A study of aggressive sex misbehaviour in adolescents brought to juvenile court. *American Journal of Orthopsychiatry*, **20**, 719–731.

Marquis, J.N. (1970) Orgasmic reconditioning: changing sexual choice through controlling masturbatory fantasies. *Journal of Behaviour Therapy and Experimental Psychiatry*, **1**, 263–271.

Marshall, W.L. (1973) The modification of sexual fantasies: a combined treatment approach to the reduction of deviant sexual behaviour. *Behaviour Research and Therapy*, **11**, 557–564.

Marshall, W.L. (1985) Aversive conditioning. In A.S. Bellack & M. Hersen (Eds), *Dictionary of Behaviour Therapy Techniques*. New York: Pergamon.

Marshall, W.L. (1992) A revised approach to the treatment of men who sexually assault adult females. In G.C. Nagayama Hall & R. Hirschman (Eds), *Sexual Aggression: Issues in Etiology and Assessment, Treatment and Policy*. New York: Hemishphere/Harper & Row.

Marshall, W.L. & Barbaree, H.E. (1988) The long-term evaluation of a behavioural treatment programme for child molesters. *Behaviour Research and Therapy*, **26**, 499–511.

Marshall, W.L. & Barbaree, H.E. (1989) Sexual violence. In K. Howells & C.R. Hollin (Eds), *Clinical Approaches to Violence*. Chichester: John Wiley.

Marshall, W.L., & Turner, B. (1987) *An Evaluation of Life Skills Training for Penitentiary Inmates*. Report to the Solicitor General of Canada, Ottawa.

Marshall, W.L., Eccles, A. & Barbaree, H.E. (1993) A three-tiered approach to the rehabilitation of incarcerated sex offenders. *Behavioural Sciences and the Law*, **11**, 441–455.

Marshall, W.L., Hudson, S.M. & Ward T. (1992) Sexual deviance. In P.H. Wilson (Ed.), *Principles and Practice of Relapse Prevention*. London: Guilford.

Marshall, W.L., Williams, S.M. & Christie, M.M. (1977) The treatment of rapists. In C.B. Qualls (Ed.), *Perspectives on Rape*. New York: Pergamon.

Marshall, W.L., Jones, R., Ward, T., Johnston, P. & Barbaree, H.E. (1991) Treatment outcome with sex offenders. *Clinical Psychology Review*, **11**, 465–485.

Matthews, R. (1979) Testosterone levels in aggressive offenders. In M. Sandler (Ed.), *Psychopharmacology of Aggression*. New York: Raven Press.

Mayhew, P., Elliott, D. & Dowds, L. (1989) *The 1988 British Crime Survey*. London: HMSO.

McGlyn, F.D. (1985) Cue-controlled relaxation. In A.S. Bellack & M. Hersen (Eds), *Dictionary of Behaviour Therapy Techniques*. New York: Pergamon.

McGuire, R.J., Carlisle, J.M. & Young, B.G. (1965) Sexual deviations as conditioned behaviour: a hypothesis. *Behaviour Research and Therapy*, **2**, 185–190.

Miller, W.R. (1983) Motivational interviewing with problem drinkers. *Behavioural Psychotherapy*, **11**, 147–172.

Mullen, P.E. (1990) The long-term influence of sexual assault on the mental health of victims. *Journal of Forensic Psychiatry*, **1**, 13–34.

Neale, M.D. (1966) *Neale Analysis of Reading Ability*. Basingstoke: McMillan Education.

Nichols, H.R. & Molinder, I. (1984) *Multiphasic Sex Inventory*. Tacoma, WA: Authors.

Ostapiuk, E. & Westwood, S. (1986) Glenthorne Youth Treatment Centre: working with adolescents in gradations of security. In C. Hollin & K. Howells (Eds), *Clinical Approaches to Criminal Behaviour*. Issues in Criminological and Legal Psychology, No.9. Leicester: British Psychological Society.

Overholser, J.C. & Beck, S. (1986) Multimethod assessment of rapists and child molesters and three control groups on behavioural and psychological measures. *Journal of Consulting and Clinical Psychology*, **54**, 682–687.

Owens, R.G. & Ashcroft, J.E. (1982) Functional analysis in applied psychology. *British Journal of Clinical Psychology*, **21**, 181–189.

Pacht, A.R. & Roberts, L.M. (1968) Factors related to parole experience of sexual offenders: a nine year study. *Journal of Correctional Psychology*, **3**, 8–9.

Perkins, D. (1991) Clinical work with sex offenders in secure settings. In C.R. Hollin & K. Howells (Eds), *Clinical Approaches to Sex Offenders and Their Victims*. Chichester: John Wiley.

Peters, S.D., Wyatt, G.E. & Finkelhor, D. (1986) Prevalence. In D. Finkelhor (Ed.), *A Source-book on Child Sexual Abuse*. Beverly Hills, CA: Sage.

Pierce, R. & Pierce, L.H. (1985) The sexually abused child: the comparison of male and female victims. *Child Abuse and Neglect*, **9**, 191–199.

Pithers, W.D. (1990) Relapse prevention with sexual aggressors: a method for maintaining therapeutic gain and enhancing external supervision. In W.L. Marshall, D.R. Laws & H.E. Barbaree (Eds), *Handbook of Sexual Assault: Issues, Theories, and Treatment of the Offender*. New York: Plenum.

Pithers, W.D. & Cumming, G.F. (1989) Can relapses be prevented? Initial outcome data from the Vermont Treatment Program for sexual aggressors. In D.R. Laws (Ed.), *Relapse Prevention with Sex Offenders*. New York: Guilford.

Prentky, R. & Burgess, A.W. (1990) Rehabilitation of child molesters: a cost-benefit analysis. *American Journal of Orthopsychiatry*, **60**, 108–117.

Prentky, R.A., Cohen, M.L. & Seghorn, T.K. (1985) Development of a rational taxonomy for the classification of sexual offenders: rapists. *Bulletin of the American Academy of Psychiatry and the Law*, **13**, 39–70.

Print, B. (1992) The Greater Manchester adolescent sex offender programme. *The National Association for the Development of Work with Sex Offenders Newsletter*, **2**, 17–20.

Quayle, M.T. (1989) Group therapy for personality disordered offenders. Paper presented at the Annual Conference of Special Hospital Psychologists, Scarborough, England.

Quinsey, V.L. (1984) Sexual aggression: studies of offenders against women. In D. Weisstub (Ed.), *Law and Mental Health: International Perspectives*, Vol.1. New York: Pergamon.

Quinsey, V.L. (1986) Men who have sex with children. In D. Weisstub (Ed.), *Law and Mental Health: International perspectives*, Vol.2. New York: Pergamon.

Quinsey, V.L. & Marshall, W.L. (1983) Procedures for reducing inappropriate sexual arousal: an evaluative review. In J.G. Greer & I.R. Stuart (Eds), *The Sexual Aggressor*. New York: Van Nostrand Reinhold.

Quinsey, V.L., Chaplin, T.C. & Upfold, D. (1984) Sexual arousal to non-sexual violence and sadomasochistic themes among rapists and non-sex offenders. *Journal of Consulting and Clinical Psychology*, **52**, 651–657.

Quinsey, V.L., Harris, G.T., Rice, M.E. & Lalumiere, M.L. (1993) Assessing treatment efficacy in outcome studies of sex offenders. *Journal of Interpersonal Violence*, 512–523.

Raboch, J., Cerna, H. & Zemek, P. (1987) Sexual aggressivity and androgens. *British Journal of Psychiatry*, **151**, 398–400.

Rada, R.T., Laws, D.R. & Kellner, R. (1976) Plasma testosterone levels in the rapist. *Psychosomatic Medicine*, **38**, 257–268.

Rader, C.M. (1977) MMPI profile types of exposers, rapists and assaulters in a court service population. *Journal of Consulting and Clinical Psychology*, **45**, 61–69.

Russell, D.E.H. (1975) *The Politics of Rape*. New York: Stein & Day.

Russell, D.E.H. (1984) *Sexual Exploitation: Rape, Child Sexual Abuse, and Workplace Harassment*. Beverly Hills, CA: Sage.

Rutter, M. & Giller, H. (1983) *Juvenile Delinquency: Trends and Perspectives*. Harmondsworth: Penguin.

Ryan, G. (1991) Juvenile sex offenders: defining the population. In G.D. Ryan & S.L. Lane (Eds), *Juvenile Sexual Offending: Causes, Consequences and Correction*. Lexington, MA: Lexington Books.

Ryan, G.D. & Lane, S.L. (1991) *Juvenile Sexual Offending: Causes, Consequences, and Correction*. Lexington MA: Lexington Books.

Salter, A.C. (1988) *Treating Child Sexual Offenders and Victims: A Practical Guide*. Beverly Hills, CA: Sage.

Sanday, P.R. (1979) *The Socio-cultural Context of Rape*. Washington, DC: US Department of Commerce, National Technical Information Services.

Scott, R.L. & Tetreault, L.A. (1986) Attitudes of rapists and other violent offenders towards women. *Journal of Social Psychology*, **127**, 375–380.

Scully, D. (1990) *Understanding Sexual Violence: A Study of Convicted Rapists*. London: Unwin Hyman.

Scully, D. & Marolla, J. (1985) Riding the bull at Gilley's: convicted rapists describe the rewards of rape. *Social Problems*, **32**, 233–251.

Segal, Z.V. & Marshall, W.L. (1985) Heterosexual social skills in a population of rapists and child molesters. *Journal of Consulting and Clinical Psychology*, **53**, 55–63.

Segal, Z.V. & Marshall, W.L. (1986) Discrepancies between self-efficacy predictions and actual performance in a population of rapists and child molesters. *Cognitive Therapy and Research*, **10**, 363–376.

Segal, Z.V. & Stermac, L. (1984) A measure of rapists' attitudes towards women. *International Journal of Law and Psychiatry*, **7**, 437–440.

Serber, M. (1970) Shame aversion therapy. *Journal of Behaviour Therapy and Experimental Psychiatry*, **1**, 213–215.

Sinclair, L. (1991) Assessing risk, effective interviewing, dealing with denial. Paper presented at the Regional Offender Treatment Association Second National Conference, Liverpool University, England.

Soothill, K.L. & Gibbens, T.C.N. (1978) Recidivism of sexual offenders: a re-appraisal. *British Journal of Criminology*, **18**, 267–276.

Spence, J.T. & Helmreich, R.L. (1972) The Attitudes Toward Women Scale: an objective instrument to measure attitudes towards the rights and roles of women in contemporary society. *Psychological Documents*, **2**, 153.

Stenson, P. & Anderson, C. (1987) Treating juvenile sex offenders and preventing the cycle of abuse. *Journal of Child Care*, **3**, 91–102.

Stermac, L.E. & Quinsey, V.L. (1986) Social competence among rapists. *Behavioural Assessment*, **8**, 171–185.

Thomas, J. (1991) The adolescent sex offender's family in treatment. In G.D. Ryan & S.L. Lane (Eds), *Juvenile Sexual Offending: Causes, Consequences, and Correction*. Lexington, MA: Lexington Books.

Thornton, D. (1991) Treatment of sexual offenders in prison: a strategy. In Directorate of Inmate Programmes (Ed.), *Treatment Programmes for Sex Offenders in Custody: A Strategy*. London: HM Prison Service.

Torpy, D. & Tomison, A. (1986) Sex offenders and cyproterone acetate: a review of clinical care. *Medicine, Science and the Law*, **26**, 279–282.

Travin, S. Cullen, K. & Melella, J.T. (1988) The use and abuse of erection measurement: a forensic perspective. *Bulletin of the American Academy of Psychiatry and the Law*, **16**, 235–250.

Wechsler, D. (1981) *Wechsler Adult Intelligence Scale–revised*. San Antonio, TX: The Psychological Corporation/Harcourt Brace Jovanovich.

Williams, L.M. & Finkelhor, D. (1990) The characteristics of incestuous fathers: a review of recent studies. In W.L. Marshall, D.R. Laws & H.E. Barbaree (Eds), *Handbook of Sexual Assault: Issues, Theories and Treatment of the Offender*. New York: Plenum.

Wilson, G. (1978) *The Secrets of Sexual Fantasy*. London: J.M. Dent.

Woodward, R. (1980) *Brief report on the effects of a sex education course on borstal trainees*. Home Office Prison Department Psychological Services DPS Reports, Series II, No. 78.

Wyre, R. (1989) Protecting children: treatments for offenders. Paper presented at NACRO conference: Preventing Child Sexual Abuse – Problems and Prospects in Dealing with Offenders, London, England.

CHAPTER SEVEN

VIOLENT OFFENDERS

Kevin Browne and Kevin Howells

Prior to any discussion of factors important to working with violent offenders, it is important to attempt to define and understand violence. There are numerous contributory factors to violent offending, both internal and external to the individual. Archer & Browne (1989) argue that aggression and violence are best understood in relation to the social context in which they occur. They claim that the study of violent relationships and social interactions has the potential to integrate psychological and sociological approaches that emphasize causes of violence at an individual and societal level, respectively.

Therefore, this chapter overviews physical violence against individuals in non-domestic and domestic environments. Evidence is presented for the causes of violence in people and how such predispositions can be assessed. A number of treatment strategies are then discussed.

DEFINITIONS

Three terms are often used, sometimes interchangeably, in relation to acts of a violent nature: "aggression", "violence" and "criminal violence". A number of writers, for example Megargee (1982) and Siann (1985), have offered helpful distinctions: aggression can be taken to refer to the intention to hurt or gain advantage over others, without necessarily involving physical attack; violence, at times impelled by aggressive motivation, involves the use of physical force against another individual; criminal violence is directly injurious behaviour specifically forbidden by law. Despite the usefulness of such definitions

Working with Offenders: Psychological Practice in Offender Rehabilitation.
Edited by C.R. Hollin. © 1996 John Wiley & Sons Ltd.

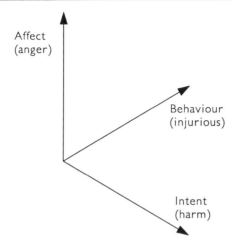

Figure 7.1   Three components characterizing violent behaviour. (Adapted from Archer & Browne, 1989, with permission.)

Blackburn (1993) illustrates the value laden nature of such concepts and warns of the "dependence of the identification of aggression or violence on the attributions and values of the observer" (p. 211). For example, Archer & Browne (1989) identify three features – intent, injurious behaviour and emotion – which if all are present, produce a prototypical case of aggression or violence. If one or more of these is absent, or present to a lesser degree, there is more disagreement about whether the category "aggression" or "violence" applies.

These three features are, of course, the ones which in more general terms characterize any behavioural output: affect, intent and behaviour (Figure 7.1). They are best regarded as related but dissociable components characteristic of a particular motivational state.

Campbell, Muncer & Bibel (1985) used a multidimensional scaling technique to investigate commonsense distinctions between descriptions of aggressive incidents. This technique involves sorting out the degree to which items are similar or different from one another. They found that the subjects' classification reflected aspects of motivation, two aspects of the form of aggression (whether it was direct or indirect), and also the motive, whether hostile, instrumental, normative or status related.

THE EXTENT OF VIOLENCE

The homicide rate in Britain is 1.3 for every 100 000 citizens; this compares to a rate of 1.1 in Japan, 2.3 in Australia and 10 individuals per 100 000 in the USA. Despite these discrepancies the amount of domestic homicides is approximately 40% of each country's total number of homicides.

The widespread nature of extreme forms of violence within the family was determined in the 1970s and has been substantiated ever since (e.g. Ammerman & Hersen, 1990; Browne & Herbert, 1996; Straus, Gelles & Steinmetz, 1988; Van Hasselt et al., 1987). This has dispelled the myth that the family home is a peaceful, non-violent environment. In fact, "people are more likely to be killed, physically assaulted, hit, beaten up, slapped or spanked in their own homes by other family members than anywhere else, or by anyone else in our society" (Gelles & Cornell, 1990, p. 11). Indeed, newspaper reports based on police records in Britain show that 42% of murder or manslaughter cases involve a domestic dispute and a third of the domestic victims are children. During 1991, newspaper reports identified that 99 children under 16 years of age died of non-accidental injury in England, Scotland and Wales (*Independent on Sunday*, 12 January 1992). However, this is likely to be an underestimate as the NSPCC claims that three children die each week at the hands of their parents (NSPCC, 1985).

The most recent British Crime Survey (Mayhew, Maung & Mirrlees-Black, 1993) estimated that 530 000 domestic assaults occurred in 1991, approximately half of which were to women.

As Figure 7.2 shows street assaults and violence in pubs and clubs were nearly as common as domestic violence. However, over 80% of the victims were men. Muggings had a similar number of male and female victims with men more likely to be robbed and women to suffer snatch thefts.

Overall, with the exception of domestic violence, men are more at risk of being a victim of violence than women, with those aged 16–29 most at risk. Similar findings have been reported for the USA (Weiner & Wolfgang, 1989).

UNDERSTANDING VIOLENCE

Accounts of aggression and violence have been advanced from a number of perspectives including biology (Mednick et al., 1982; Archer, 1988), neurology (Merikangas, 1981) and anthropology (Riches, 1986); as well as from a number of positions within psychology such as instinct theory (Lorenz, 1966; Storr,

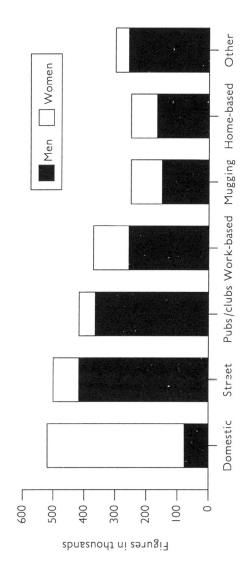

Figure 7.2 Types of violence, 1991. (From the 1992 British Crime Survey, reproduced with HMSO permission from Mayhew, Maung & Mirrlees-Black, 1993.)

1970), drive theory (Berkowitz, 1965, 1993), social psychology (Marsh, Rosser & Harre, 1978) and behavioural theory (Bornstein, Hamilton & McFall, 1981).

In relation to violence in the home, Lystad (1975) has grouped "theories of violence" into three categories: those involving psychological explanations, those involving social structural explanations and those explaining the causes within contemporary society's cultural values. Psychological explanations can be subdivided into ones which focus on the individual level and those which are more social and interactive in approach.

Individually focused explanations of violence often concentrate on personality characteristics of a psychopathological or deviant nature. This tradition is characterized by the use of rating scales to measure aggressiveness and hostility (e.g. Buss & Durkee, 1957; Edmunds & Kendrick, 1980; Spielberger et al., 1983). Some individually oriented theorists have claimed that biological variables underlie a tendency to be violent. Perhaps the most extreme version of these was the work of Mark & Ervin (1970), who advocated widespread psychosurgery as a solution to violent behaviour.

Other researchers adopting a psychobiological approach have attempted to establish a causal connection between gonadal hormone levels and violent crime (e.g. Persky, Smith & Basu, 1971; Rada, Laws & Rellner, 1976) and the identification of specific pathological conditions, such as alcoholism, which are likely to be predisposing or determining factors in violent behaviour (e.g. Byles, 1978; Gerson, 1978; Potter-Efron & Potter-Efron, 1990).

Social learning provides an alternative form of within-individual explanation to biological determinism. Schultz (1960), for example, was one of the first to claim that the source of violence in a marital context is unfulfilled childhood experiences; his work was followed by Gayford (1975), who attempted to show the learned character of domestic violence within the family of origin.

A more interactive approach includes the social relationships of the partici-pants, and their environmental setting, rather than seeking to isolate the person or situation. This entails a move from the individual psychological level to a social interactive approach. Toch (1969) looked at the characteristics of violent men in the context of their violence and the victims chosen. He concluded that aggressive behaviour was associated with "machismo" and the maintenance of a particular personal identity in relation to others.

Such findings are in apparent conflict with studies showing developmental consistency in aggressive reactions (Olweus, 1984). However, Olweus adopted a broad approach to assessing aggressiveness, rather than relying on measures applying to a limited number of settings. It seems, therefore, that there is evidence for developmental consistency in an overall trait which can be labelled "aggressiveness" yet inconsistency is found across situations for measures of aggression taken at one particular time (Kaplan, 1984).

Theories which emphasize social factors are more sociological in approach and are generally concerned with explanations of violence as a social problem rather than an individual one. Nevertheless, this distinction is not always clear-cut. Turner et al. (1984), for example, sought to explain the link between the economic recession and criminal violence in young adults in terms of perceived relative deprivation. This may be dependent on other factors, such as aspiration level, alternative resources, specific environmental cues for aggression and social learning in a criminal subculture. In relation to domestic violence, factors such as low wages, poor housing, overcrowding, isolation and alienating work conditions are seen by Gelles (1987) and Gelles & Cornell (1990) as causing frustration and stress at the individual level, which in turn may lead to violence. Gelles concluded from his research that "violence is an adaptation or response to structural stress".

Other attempts to explain domestic violence in wider social terms include the exchange theory of Goode (1971) and the general systems approach of Straus, Gelles & Steinmetz (1988). Goode argued that the family, like all social institutions, rests to some degree on force or threat to maintain order. He postulated that the more alternatives (or "resources") an individual can command, or perceive to command, the less he or she will use force (itself a "resource") in an overt manner. Goode assumed that middle-class families have more "resources", arising, for example, from their greater prestige and better economic position, and consequently will be less likely to resort to violence or threat.

Violence is seen as an option used in remedying a low-status position, and hence increasing self-esteem. Straus, Gelles & Steinmetz (1988) explained the occurrence of domestic violence in terms of "deviant family structures". They referred to deviant authority structures and claimed that the level of violence is likely to be greatest when the wife is dominant in decision making.

These two explanations view violence within the family in terms of wider societal or structural variables. A complementary approach, also couched in terms of the social position of the people involved, can be referred to as the micropolitical view. This holds that individual violence is a microcosm of the power relations in the wider society. For example, a common feminist explanation of violence towards women is to view it as a function of women's generally oppressed position in society. Within this framework the purpose of male violence is seen as to control women (Dobash & Dobash, 1987; Hanmer, 1978).

Gil (1978) argues that structural violence and personal violence should not be viewed as discrete phenomena: they are both symptoms of the same values and institutions that interact to reinforce each other. Personal violence is reactive and rooted in structural violence, since experiences which inhibit a person's development will often result in stress and frustration, and the urge to retaliate by inflicting violence on others. Domestic violence is reactive violence which often originates outside the family. It can be discharged within the family because the family is more informal with fewer punitive sanctions than for violence in other social situations.

Explanations for criminal violence have offered mainly behavioural accounts, concerned with three areas: the *acquisition* of violent behaviour; the *instigation* of violence; and the *maintenance* of violent behaviour.

In accord with operant and social learning theories, acquisition of violent behaviour may be through direct reinforcement or via observational learning (Bandura, 1973). In this respect violent behaviour is not accorded any special status, or given its high frequency, necessarily seen as pathological: it follows, as Blackburn (1993) notes, that the labelling of some violent behaviour as illegal and/or suitable for intervention is a selective process.

Instigation to violent behaviour can be understood by recourse to two areas of research:

1. situational analysis which gives some indication of the antecedents to a violent episode;
2. analysis of the individual's behaviour in response to the cue in the social environment.

Situational analysis is firmly established as a means by which to understand the environmental conditions associated with violence (Monahan & Klassen, 1982). Working within this tradition, a study by Henderson (1986) is of particular relevance.

Henderson analysed the types of violent incident – coded for example for victim age and sex, place of incident, time of day, and so on – reported by a sample of male violent offenders. The analysis revealed four broad categories of violent situation: violence in conjunction with another crime (sometimes intentionally, sometimes in panic at discovery); family violence towards women and children; violence in public places such as clubs and bars, sometimes involving gangs; and violence in institutions towards both fellow inmates and staff. Henderson's findings illustrate the difference between "premeditated" violence, typical of crimes of acquisition such as robbery, and "spontaneous" violence which arises in certain situations. This distinction is in keeping with the dichotomy traditionally drawn between "instrumental" and "hostile" aggression (Archer & Browne, 1989; Bandura, 1973; Buss, 1961; Zillman, 1979).

It is "hostile" or "angry" aggression which has attracted the most attention in clinical research. Here, situational analysis has shown that social factors such as verbal and physical provocation can instigate angry violence (Dengerink, Schnedler & Covey, 1978). This social dimension is even seen in the most extreme form of violence – murder. A number of surveys (e.g. Wolfgang, 1958) have shown that murder often begins with a seemingly trivial event, such as an insult or an argument, involving two people who, when not related, are likely at least to know each other. Luckenbill (1977) has offered an analysis of the sequence of interactions between offender and victim which culminates in murder. This view of violence as the product of a social transaction, escalating from verbal insult to physical attack, suggests an event in which the victim has some role to play, perhaps even a causative role, in their fate. This is a position of some controversy. Dobash & Dobash (1984, 1987), in a study of battered wives, suggest that this particular violent act frequently stems from the man's perceived challenge to his authority. While the victim, the woman, may attempt to negotiate a way out or to escape physically, the man is not be diverted from his chosen violent path. Thus, rather than depicting violence, particularly violence towards women, as the product of a social exchange, Dobash & Dobash suggest that violence should be seen both in a cultural context and as an intentional act by the aggressor.

It is reasonable to conclude that for "hostile" (or angry) violence in particular, instigation to violence is to be found in the aggressor's social environment. However, as Luckenbill (1977) suggests, it is the aggressor's *perception* of events which is important – the way in which the violent person has learned to view and understand the actions of others. Further, to acknowledge the point made by Dobash & Dobash (1984, 1987), such learning is influenced by the preferred rewards, punishments and modelled behaviour within a given culture. Therefore in order to begin to understand violent behaviour a model is needed which includes environmental, social and individual factors. Novaco (1976, 1978) has offered such a model (Figure 7.3) which seeks to incorporate both external and internal events in explaining hostile violence.

The determinants of anger are seen by Novaco as a combination of physio-logical arousal and a cognitive labelling of that arousal. These cognitions are

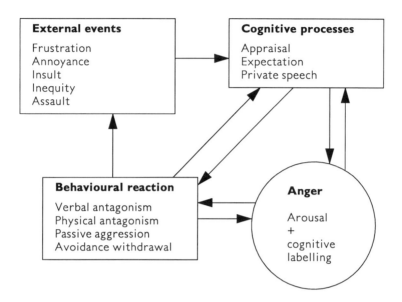

Figure 7.3 Determinants of anger arousal. (Adapted from Novaco, 1978. with permission.)

themselves influenced by internal and external factors and the behavioural responses to the situation. Hence, it is suggested that cognitive restructuring of a violent person's perceptions of social events, and their relationships with others, can help in reducing aggressive behaviour and hostility (Hollin & Howells, 1989).

Finally, with regard to the maintenance of violent behaviour, there are a number of possibilities. The products of a violent act may be rewarding in themselves – financial gain is an obvious example – but violence may have other payoffs such as improved peer group status or seeing the suffering of victims (Bandura, 1973). In such cases violence is being maintained, in an operant sense, through positive reinforcement. A number of writers have described how in some subcultures violence is a means to gain excitement or express dissatisfaction with social and economic conditions (Wolfgang & Ferracuti, 1967; Carroll & Jackson, 1983). Thus, in the sense expressed by social learning theorists, there is the possibility of self-reinforcement for violent acts.

Given this complex theoretical picture, together with the potent reinforcers, the modification of violent behaviour faces obvious difficulties. Nonetheless, recent years have seen considerable advances in behavioural intervention with violent individuals in terms of both assessment and treatment (Goldstein & Keller, 1987; Howells & Hollin, 1989).

ASSESSMENT

From a behavioural perspective, Goldstein & Keller (1987) give a comprehensive list of rating scales to assess the following components of an aggressive behaviour sequence:

- interpretation of external stimuli (arousal heightening)
- heightened affective arousal
- malcommunication
- mismanagement of contingencies
- prosocial skill deficiencies
- prosocial value deficiencies.

The chances of an individual being assessed as "dangerous" by the above criteria will depend on background factors and previous experiences. Other researchers have emphasized the following risk factors for violent behaviour (e.g. Browne & Herbert, 1996; Saunders, 1995):

- history of violence, threatening behaviour and the use of weapons;
- exposure to violence as a child;
- feelings of low self-esteem and helplessness;
- feelings of social withdrawal, isolation and lack of social support;
- feelings of jealousy;
- presence of a provocative victim who escalates arguments and shows reciprocal aggression;
- presence of an overdependent victim, possibly due to poor health or sexual problems;
- previous history of alcohol or drug abuse;
- history of psychological disorders such as anxiety and depression;
- antisocial behaviour problem;
- socio-economic problems such as unemployment and financial difficulties;
- stress at work and job dissatisfaction;
- recent aversive life event such as separation from spouse or death of a parent or child.

TREATMENT

Cognitive–behavioural approaches to treatment can be divided into those that change cognitions of the violent individual and those that change behaviour

(Hollin, 1993). This is exemplified respectively, by "anger management" techniques (Feindler & Ecton, 1986; Howells, 1989) and social skills training (Henderson & Hollin, 1983; Howells, 1986). Both these methods of treatment have met with moderate success.

A systematic evaluation of such techniques has been provided by Glick & Goldstein (1987) in their Aggression Replacement Training (ART) programme, which uses three main approaches to violent American men:

- anger control training;
- structured learning training, including social problem solving and social skills training;
- moral education.

They report the programme results in greater self-control, lower rates of violence and improved skills.

CASE EXAMPLE[1]

The following case outline gives a detailed sketch of anger assessment and anger management training in the UK.

Jim is 30 years old and was referred to an anger management group. He had a long history of scrapes with other people and with social institutions. He had frequently appeared in court and had been admitted to penal and psychiatric facilities on a number of occasions. The offending behaviour leading to court appearances was mainly acquisitive (minor theft) and violent in nature. His violent offences were the main reason for admission to prison and psychiatric clinics. He had been in a number of fights since his childhood. For the vast majority of these the outcome was non-serious, Jim and his adversary suffering minor bruises and lacerations. Occasionally, however, he has lost control entirely in a confrontation and caused serious damage to the other person.

Jim admitted to frequently being very angry and violent, the two normally being interrelated. In an interview he reported a history of confrontations with his family, teachers, the police, prison officers and hospital nurses. He admitted to being particularly sensitive to criticism and that this was often the start of a violent episode. He described himself as being easily carried away by his anger. Provocations make him physically tense and he sweats. He expressed considerable dissatisfaction with his tendency to

---

[1] A more detailed outline of Jim's case appears in Howells (1989).

"blow his top". He felt he did not understand how or why this occurred and he wished he had more control over his temper. He clearly identified his temper as a major reason for his general difficulties.

Jim's family and social background is viewed by professionals as "disturbed". In childhood he was admitted to a series of children's homes because of family disturbance. He hated, and still hates, his father, who frequently beat him. He has a strong sense of always having been "picked on" and criticized by his father. When beaten he was frightened, but later in childhood had fought back successfully.

ASSESSMENT

A number of methods were used to identify the triggers for Jim's episodes of angry violence.

He completed a modified form of the Novaco Anger Inventory, a 90-item inventory of hypothetical anger-inducing situations. Anger intensity was rated on a five-point Likert scale (Novaco, 1975). Some items were modified from Novaco's original list in order to cover provoking situations commonly experienced in psychiatric and prison settings. Amongst items given a maximum rating of 5 for anger intensity were:

1. being called a liar;
2. being called a "stupid idiot" in an argument;
3. being criticized in front of others;
4. being teased or joked about;
5. being called names;
6. being the subject of personal remarks,

High-scoring items related to the general theme of criticism and personal derogatory comments.

Jim also completed an anger diary over a two-week period. For the diary he was asked to recall experience of anger during the day and to provide written answers to the following questions:

1. What was the situation that made you angry? What happened?
2. When and where did this happen?
3. How exactly did you feel?
4. What thoughts were going through your mind?
5. What irritated you most?
6. What did you actually do?
   i. Did not show any anger at all;
   ii. showed any anger in words only;

   iii.   became aggressive (e.g. hitting, punching);

   iv.   left the situation.

The diary also involved ratings of anger intensity and of whom/what anger was directed at. Finally the diary asked whether and how Jim had tried to control his angry feelings in the situation.

Jim reported between three and five angry experiences on most days. The triggers he identified were predominantly comments of a critical, disparaging nature from other patients, particularly in a group context. A typical incident was one in which Jim was "slagged off" by another patient in a ward meeting. Jim perceived the patient as "making him look an idiot". He described his feelings as "seething" angry and his cognitions at the time were of the sort "He's a bastard . . . he's trying to turn everyone against me . . . he's always showing me up". On this particular occasion he expressed his anger mainly in verbal abuse but acknowledges "pushing" the other patient when the argument continued after the meeting. On other occasions Jim reacted with physical aggression (mainly punching) to similar triggers. He generally rated his anger as "very strong" and as directed against "other people" or "things in general" rather than himself. His diaries indicated that he was typically highly aroused physically in angry situations. He reported wanting to maintain control for many incidents but not knowing how to do it.

During the two weeks that Jim completed his diary he was also rated on a parallel observation schedule by nursing staff. A typical incident recorded by nurses involved Jim being provoked to anger by being laughed at and joked about by another patient in an occupational therapy setting. He was observed to get "tense and fidgety" in the situation, to have "furrowed eyebrows", and eventually to swear, call names and threaten the patient involved. Anger intensity was again rated as "very strong" and as manifest-ing itself verbally (e.g. shouting abuse), non-verbally (facial expression, tone of voice), and behaviourally (punching, hitting, slapping).

In addition to these measures, Jim completed the trait scale Spielberger State–Trait Anger Inventory, on which he obtained virtually the maximum score possible (Spielberger et al., 1983).

In summary then, information from case records, interviews, diaries and staff observations suggested with some consistency that particular triggers existed for anger. Critical comments, particularly in a group setting, and if made in what Jim perceived as a "joking or humiliating" way, were particularly likely to elicit a reaction.

Analysis of the cognitive component of Jim's anger was based in part on his self-reported thoughts which preceded angry incidents, as revealed by his diary. The major themes from recorded thoughts were that critical remarks from others were perceived as malevolent. A critical comment, for example, tended to be seen as part of a general attempt to humiliate him and show him up in front of others. A second theme revealed in the diaries was the tendency to construe some aversive social behaviours as deliberate social exclusions. On one occasion, for example, a member of the nursing staff baked a cake for patients on the ward, as part of a birthday celebration. In the course of distributing slices of cake to patients Jim was inadvertently omitted. He did not speak up and his exclusion was not perceived. Jim's interpretation was that he had been deliberately excluded and victimized and this left him hurt and angry.

Similar cognitive themes were elicited when previous anger-inducing situations were re-enacted in role plays or in imagination and Jim was asked to "speak aloud" his thoughts. Role plays also revealed that the thought sequence following a provocation also involved cognitive rehearsal of the consequences of not responding aggressively. Typically the sequence included self-statements of the sort "If I don't do something now . . . I will look weak, be picked on in future; never be respected by others", and so on.

The arousal component of the anger response was highly salient for Jim. In his diaries he reported that physical arousal was strong, even for minor provocations. The most frequently reported sensations were of physical tension, sweating and of legs trembling. He found this physical state to be aversive and typically labelled himself as "angry and upset" when he was in this state. His main concern was that the arousal state would sometimes persist for the rest of the day, or even longer, leaving him irritable and likely to respond to other minor provocations, and also creating sleep problems. Apparently high physiological reactions were also reported in staff ratings. It was not possible to monitor physiological activation directly, but there were good reasons to believe that heightened physiological arousal contributed to the inappropriateness of Jim's behaviour in angry situations.

Observational, self-report, role play and case record data suggested that Jim had a limited repertoire of behavioural reactions to provocation. Some angry incidents resulted in Jim becoming violent. The violent act itself rarely occurred immediately but followed an escalating sequence of angry social exchanges. The assessment task was to identify the verbal, non-verbal and paralinguistic features of Jim's social behaviour that produced the escalation effect. In essence the need was to define the difference between Jim's aggressive social style and appropriate assertion in such situations (Hollandsworth, 1977; Hollandsworth & Cooley, 1978; Hull & Schroeder, 1979; Kirchner, Kennedy & Draguns, 1979; Hedlund & Lindquist, 1984).

The task of microanalysis of aggressive social behaviour is akin to that undertaken in the context of social skills training (Howells, 1976; Trower,

Bryant & Arggle, 1978; Hollin & Trower, 1986), though the focus is on identifying aggression-inducing behaviours rather than those leading to social failure or inadequacy. In Jim's case, the following verbal behaviours were identified as escalating the situation:

1. Jim's tendency to respond to mild criticism with counter-criticism of an aggressive sort: "aggressive" counter-criticism comprised of statements which were generally disparaging and abusive;
2. Jim's tendency to swear in disagreements ("You ignorant bastard, what do you know about . . .");
3. Jim's tendency, later in the interaction, to issue a threat ("Say that again and I will down you").

In the paralinguistic channel the following behaviours were identified:

1. very high voice volume early in the interaction: Jim was perceived as shouting angrily in disputes even when his subjective sense of anger was low;
2. threatening voice tone.

In the non-verbal channel the following were identified:

1. "angry" facial expression early on in the sequence;
2. excessive proximity (standing too close) in the course of the dispute;
3. if the other person was seated, Jim "stood over" the person in a way that was threatening;
4. aggressive gesticulation (hand waving, likely to be perceived as in incipient punch);
5. excessive eye contact (staring).

Jim was unaware of any of these behaviours and of his role in escalating the interaction towards violence.

TREATMENT

An essential feature of anger management therapy with violent people is the attempt to convey to the client an understandable model of anger and its relationship to triggering events, thoughts and violent behaviour itself. Novaco (1975, 1978, 1985) labels this the "cognitive preparation phase". In

Jim's case this would involve enabling him to understand that his anger experiences do have particular accompanying triggers (for example, criticism), cognitive appraisals, and physiological changes, and also that anger can be distinguished from its behavioural expression in the form of violence.

The identification of triggering events can suggest therapeutic strategies. In Jim's case the fact that his anger occurred only in response to particular forms of criticism raises the possibility of removing triggering events themselves as a strategy for violence reduction. This was unlikely to be productive in Jim's case as criticism was likely to be an endemic social response to his behaviour and one that could not, realistically, be modified. On the other hand, much of the criticism he encountered was "normal" social reaction to his unacceptable behaviour. In particular, his propensity for stealing and his general unreliability at work provoked criticism from acquaintances and colleagues. Although Jim amplified criticism, through his appraisal of it as, for example, an attempt to humiliate him, it was objectively true that others did indeed criticize him at a high frequency. In this sense, producing general change in the area of stealing and behaviour at work might be a relevant, though indirect, component of anger management training in this case (for other examples of "stimulus control" methods see Howells, 1987).

Jim's hostile cognitive appraisals, expectations and self-talk also suggest therapeutic interventions. Producing affective and behavioural change by means of changing cognitions is the central task of "cognitive therapy" methods, which have been widely used in relation to problems of anxiety and depression (Beck et al., 1979; Clark, 1980).

Novaco's cognitive methods (1975, 1978, 1985) focus mainly on the modification of anger-inducing appraisals and on constructive use of self-instructions (private speech) so as to deal with provoking situations successfully. Jim underwent a cognitively oriented group anger management training of this sort, with particular attention being paid to demonstrating the habitual "automatic" nature of his appraisals of other people as malevolent and intent on doing him deliberate harm. The details of a programme of this sort, with descriptions of a range of practical exercises, can be found in Feindler & Ecton (1986). There was a strong element of attributional retraining in Jim's therapy (Forsterling, 1984, 1985) involving attempts to encourage him to generate and test alternative hypotheses as to why people responded to him as they did.

In Jim's therapy his increasing appreciation that his thoughts and self-statements played a role in producing and maintaining his anger, and that he had an element of choice in deciding which thoughts were helpful and which were harmful (and hence needed change), proved to be major steps in changing his violent behaviour.

The physiological arousal component of Jim's anger suggested that relaxation training might also be useful. In a group setting, deep muscle relaxation was taught and used in a variety of ways, particurly:

1. to use as a self-control technique when he found his arsoual to be escalating;
2. to teach him to monitor internal physiological changes and use these changes as a cue for taking preventative action;
3. to use as an antagonistic response in desensitization to visualized anger-inducing scenes (Evans & Hearn, 1973; Hearn & Evans, 1972).

Finally, an attempt was made to produce change in his overt behaviour itself in angry situations. Social skills training methods (Hollin & Trower, 1986) were used, including instruction, modelling, video feedback and role play rehearsal, to change his social repertoire in response to provocation and to reduce the frequency of the escalating verbal, non-verbal and paralinguistic behaviours identified above. Social skills methods were used as part of a problem-solving orientation (D'Zurilla & Goldfried, 1971; Platt, Pout & Metzger, 1986), with an emphasis on generating alternative strategies for achieving goals and on evaluating the short- and long-term advantages and disadvantages of particular ways of behaving. In practice, maintaining low voice volume and eliminating verbal threats proved to have the most obvious impact on actual angry encounters, in terms of reducing the probability of a violent outcome.

GROUP TREATMENT PROGRAMMES FOR MEN

These have mainly concentrated on cessation of violence and the restructuring of attitudes towards the use of violence (e.g. Hall & Ryan, 1984). In the family, it is generally agreed that a husband's unwillingness to admit to or work on the problem of his aggression is a major stumbling block in preventing further abuse. However, there has been emphasis on increasing group treatment programmes available for abusive men (e.g. Getzel, 1988) to challenge their belief that they "don't have a problem".

An example of a group programme aimed at teaching abusive men to observe themselves and change their violent behaviour has been described by Edleson & Tolman (1992), who used the following techniques in combination.

1. Self-observation. For many men the events leading up to a violent incident are unclear. They cannot connect prior events with the violent

act. While aggression may have satisfying effects for the man in the short term he may fail to see the long-term effects on the relationship. Self-observation helps abusive men to clarify the behavioural chains of events and identify precursors of violence in the future.

2. Cognitive restructuring. This is a process in which individuals are helped to analyse thought patterns and then change the assumptions and attitudes on which they are based. An abusive man often has a rigid set of beliefs relating to how his partner should behave. This justifies confrontation over his wife's behaviour and allows him to put blame on her for causing him to lose his temper.

3. Interpersonal skills training. As we have already seen, abusive men and abused women are often deficient in coping skills, and so have difficulty in defusing stressful situations before they lead to violence. This type of training is therefore very beneficial to both men and women. It may begin by identifying a specific situation in which a person has experienced difficulties. It is then analysed to find the "critical moment", that is, the point during the interaction when a different behaviour might have produced a more positive outcome. With the help of others the appropriate type of behaviour is decided upon, and the situation acted out as a role play so that the person can practise.

4. Relaxation training. A major link in the chain of events leading to a violent outburst is increased tension. If this tension can be recognized and dissipated, another link in the chain has been broken.

5. Small group format. Although many men who batter women express regret about what they have done, they continue to blame their partners for the abuse (Bernard & Bernard, 1984) and sometimes receive mixed messages from male peers condoning their actions (e.g. "Sometimes you've got to keep them in line"). The small group format provides counter-conditioning for such men, as they are surrounded by others who want to change their aggressive behaviour. However, there is a need for systematic evaluation of the effectiveness of most of these approaches applied to abusive husbands (Gondolf, 1987).

CONCLUSIONS

Anger management methods form part of what might be called the therapeutic approach to violence prevention. What evidence is available suggests that anger is important for many forms of violent behaviour. Thus anger management requires a multifaceted analysis of hostile aggression and violence in terms of the environmental, cognitive, physiological and behavioural components. Controlled outcome studies to date are encouraging but few studies have been conducted in which serious violence itself has been the outcome measure. However, anger management is not a panacea for the prevention of all forms of violence. These methods have undeniable potential in the field of violence prevention but research is at an early stage in assessing their actual therapeutic impact.

REFERENCES

Ammerman, R.T. & Hersen, M. (Eds) (1990) *Treatment of Family Violence*, New York: Wiley.
Archer, J. (1988) *The Behavioural Biology of Aggression.* Cambridge: Cambridge University Press.
Archer, J. & Browne, K.D. (1989) Concepts and approaches to the study of aggression. In J. Archer & K.D. Browne (Eds) *Human Aggression: Naturalistic Approaches*, pp 3–24. London: Routledge.
Bandura, A. (1973) *Aggression: A Social Learning Analysis.* New York: Prentice Hall.
Beck, A.T., Rush, A.J., Shaw, B.F. & Emery, G. (1979) *Cognitive Therapy of Depression.* New York: Guildford Press.
Berkowitz, L. (1965) The concept of aggressive drive: some additional considerations. In L. Berlowitz (Ed.), *Advances in Experimental Social Psychology*, Vol.2. New York: Academic Press.
Berkowitz (1993) *Aggression: Its Causes, Consequences and Control.* New York: McGraw-Hill.
Bernard & Bernard (1984) The abusive male seeking treatment: Jekyll and Hyde. *Family Relations*, **33**, 543–547.
Blackburn, R. (1993) *The Psychology of Criminal Conduct: Theory, Research and Practice.* Chichester: Wiley.
Bornstein, P.H., Hamilton, S.B. & McFall, M.E. (1981) Modification of adult aggression: a critical review of theory, research and practice. In M. Hersen, R.M. Eisler, & P.M. Miller (Eds), *Progress in Behavior Modification*, Vol. 12. London: Academic Press.
Browne, K.D. & Herbert, M. (1996) *Preventing Family Violence.* Chichester: Wiley.
Buss, A.H. (1961) *The Psychology of Aggression.* New York: Wiley.
Buss, A.H. & Durkee, A. (1957) An inventory for assessing different types of hostility *Journal of Consulting Psychology*, **21**, 343–349.
Byles, J.E. (1978) Violence, alcohol problems and other problems in disintegrating families. *Journal of Studies on Alcohol*, **39**, 551–553.
Campbell, A., Muncer, S. & Bibel, D. (1985a) Taxonomies of aggressive behavior: a preliminary report. *Aggressive Behavior*, **11**, 217–222.
Carroll, L. & Jackson, P.I. (1983) Inequality, opportunity and crime rates in central cities. *Criminology*, **21**, 178–93.
Clarke, R.V.G. (1980) Situational crime prevention: theory and practice. *British Journal of Criminology*, **20**, 136–47.
Dengerink, H.A., Schnedler, R.W. & Covey, M.V. (1978) The role of avoidance in aggressive responses to attack and no attack. *Journal of Personality and Social Psychology*, **36**, 1044–1053.
Dobash, R.E. & Dobash, R.P. (1984) The nature and antecedents of violent events. *British Journal of Criminology*, **24**, 269–288.
Dobash, R.E. & Dobash, R.P. (1987) Violence towards wives. In J. Orford (Ed.), *Coping with Disorders in the Family*, pp. 169–193. Surrey: Guildford Press.

D'Zurilla, T. & Goldfried, M. (1971) Problem solving and behavior modification. *Journal of Abnormal Psychology*, **8**, 107–126.

Edleson, J.L. & Tolman, R.M. (1992) *Intervention for Men Who Batter: An Ecological Approach*. Newbury Park, CA: Sage.

Edmunds, G. & Kendrick, D.C. (1980) *The Measurement of Human Aggressiveness*. Chichester: Ellis Horwood.

Evans, D.R. & Hearn, M.T. (1973) Anger and systematic desensitization: a follow-up. *Psychological Reports*, **32**, 569–570.

Feindler, E.L. & Ecton, R.B. (1986) *Adolescent Anger Control: Cognitive Behavioural Techniques*. New York: Pergamon.

Forsterling, R. (1984) Importance, attributions and the emotion of anger. *Zeitschrift fur Psychologie*, **192**, 425–432.

Forsterling, R. (1985) Attributional training: a review. *Psychological Bulletin*, **98**, 495–512.

Gayford, J.J. (1975) Wife battering: a preliminary survey of 100 cases. *British Medical Journal*, **1**, 94–97.

Gelles, R.J. (1987) *The Violent Home*, 2nd edn, Beverly Hills, CA: Sage.

Gelles, R.J. & Cornell, C.P. (1990) *Intimate Violence in Families*, 2nd edn. Beverly Hills, CA: Sage.

Gerson, L.W. (1978) Alcohol-related acts of violence. *Journal of Studies on Alcohol*, **39**, 1294–1296.

Getzel, G.S. (Ed.) (1988) *Violence: Prevention and Treatment in Groups*. London: Haworth.

Gil, D. (1978) Societal violence in families. In J. Eckelaar & S. Katz (Eds), *Family Violence*, pp. 14–33. Toronto: Butterworth.

Glick, B. & Goldstein, H.P. (1987) Aggression replacement training. *Journal of Counselling and Development*, **65**, 356–367.

Goldstein, A.C. & Keller, H. (1987) *Aggressive Behaviour: Assessment and Intervention*. New York: Pergamon Press.

Gondolf, E.W. (1987) Evaluating programs for men who batter: problems and prospects. *Journal of Family Violence*, **2**, 95–108.

Goode, W.J. (1971) Force and violence in the family. *Journal of Marriage and the Family*, **33**, 624–636.

Hall, R. & Ryan, L. (1984) Therapy with men who are violent to their spouses. *Australian Journal of Family Therapy*, **4**, 281–282.

Hanmer, J. (1978) Violence and the social control of women. In G. Littlejohn (Ed), *Power and State*. London: Croom Helm.

Hearn, M. & Evans, D. (1972) Anger and reciprocal inhibition therapy. *Psychological Reports*, **30**, 943–948.

Hedlund, B.L. and Lindquist, C.V. (1984) The development of an inventory for distinguishing among passive, aggressive and assertive behavior. *Behavioral Assessment*, **6**, 379–390.

Henderson, M. (1986) An empirical typology of violent incidents reported by prison inmates with convictions for violence. *Aggressive Behavior*, **12**, 21–32.

Henderson, M. & Hollin, C.R. (1983) A critical review of social skills training with young offenders. *Criminal Justice and Behaviour*, **10**, 316–341.

Hollandsworth, J.G. (1977) Differentiating assertion and aggression: some behavioral guidelines. *Behavior Therapy*, **8**, 347–352.

Hollandsworth, S.G. & Cooley, M.L. (1978) Provoking anger and gaining compliance with assertive versus aggressive responses. *Behavior Therapy*, **9**, 640–646.

Hollin, C.R. (1993) Contemporary psychological research into violence: an overview.

In P.J. Taylor (Ed), *Violence in Society*, pp. 55–67. London: Royal College of Physicians.

Hollin, C.R. & Howells, K. (1989) An introduction to concepts, models and techniques. In K. Howells and C.R. Hollin (Eds), *Clinical Approaches to Violence*, pp. 3–24. Chichester: Wiley.

Hollin, C.R. & Trower, P.T. (Eds) (1986) *Handbook of Social Skills Training, Vols I and II*. Oxford: Pergamon.

Howells, K. (1976) Interpersonal aggression. *International Journal of Criminology and Penology*, **4**, 319–330.

Howells, K. (1986) Social skill training and criminal and antisocial behaviour in adults. In C.R. Hollin & P. Trower (Eds), *Handbook of Social Skills Training, Vol. 1: Applications Across the Life Span*. Oxford: Pergamon.

Howells, K. (1987) The management of angry violence: a cognitive-behavioural approach. In W. Dryden & P. Trower (Eds), *Developments in Cognitive Psychotherapy*. London: Erlbaum.

Howells, K. (1989) Anger management methods in relation to the prevention of violent behaviour. In J. Archer & K.D. Browne (Eds), *Human Aggression Naturalistic Approaches*, pp. 182–216. London: Routledge.

Howells, K. & Hollin, C.R. (1989) The future of clinical approaches to violence: grounds for optimism? In K. Howell & C.R. Hollin (Eds), *Clinical Approaches to Violence*, pp. 329–330. Chichester: Wiley.

Hull, D.B. & Schroeder, H.E. (1979) Some interpersonal effects of assertion, non-assertion and aggression. *Behavior Therapy*, **10**, 20–28.

Kaplan, R.M. (1984) The measurement of human aggression. In R.M. Kaplan, V.J. Konecni & R.W. Novaco (Eds), *Aggression in Children and Youth*. The Hague: Nijihoff.

Kirchner, E.P., Kennedy, R.E. & Draguns, J.G. (1979) Assertion and aggression in adult offenders. *Behavior Therapy*, **10**, 452–471.

Lorenz, K. (1966) *On Aggression*, New York: Harcourt, Brace and World.

Luckenbill, D.F. (1977) Criminal homicide as a situated transaction. *Social Problems*, **25**, 176–186.

Lystad, M.H. (1975) Violence at home: a review of the literature. *American Journal of Orthopsychiatry*, **45**, 328–345.

Mark, V.H. & Ervin, F.R. (1970) *Violence and the Brain*. New York: Harper and Row.

Marsh, P., Rosser, E. & Harre, R. (1978) *The Rules of Disorder*. London: Routledge & Kegan Paul.

Mayhew, P., Maung, N.A. & Mirrlees-Black, C. (1993) *The 1992 British Crime Survey*. A Home Office Research and Planning Unit Report. London: HMSO.

Mednick, S.A., Pollock, V., Volavka, J. & Gabrielli, W.F. (1982) Biology and violence. In M.E. Wolfgang & N.A. Weiner (Eds), *Criminal Violence*. Beverly Hills, CA: Sage.

Megargee, E.I. (1982) Psychological determinants and correlates of criminal violence. In M.E. Wolfgang & N.A. Weiner (Eds), *Criminal Violence*. Beverly Hills, CA: Sage.

Merikangas, J.R. (1981) The neurology of violence. In J.R. Merikangas (Ed.), *Brain–Behavior Relationships*. Lexington, MA: Lexington Books.

Monahan, J. & Klassen, D. (1982) Situational approaches to understanding and predicting individual violent behavior. In M.E. Wolfgang & N.A. Weiner (Eds), *Criminal Violence*. Beverly Hills, CA: Sage.

NSPCC (National Society for the Prevention of Cruelty to Children) (1985) *Child Abuse Deaths*. Information Briefing No 5. London: NSPCC.

Novaco, R.W. (1975) *Anger Control: The Development and Evaluation of an Experimental Treatment*. Lexington, MA: DC Heath and Co.

Novaco, R.W. (1976) The functions and regulation of the arousal of anger. *American Journal of Psychiatry*, **133**, 1124–1128.

Novaco, R.W. (1978) Anger and coping with stress. In J.P. Foreyt & D.P. Rathjen (Eds), *Cognitive Behavior Therapy*. New York: Penguin.

Novaco, R.W. (1985) Anger and its therapeutic regulation. In M.A. Chesney & R.H. Rosenman (Eds), *Anger and Hostility in Cardiovascular and Behavioral Disorders*. New York: Hemisphere.

Olweus, D. (1984) Development of stable aggressive reaction patterns in males. In R.J. & D.C. Blanchard (Eds), *Advances in the Study of Aggression*. Vol.1. New York: Academic Press.

Persky, H., Smith, K.D. & Basu, G.K. (1971) Relation of psychological measures of aggression and hostility to testosterone production in man. *Psychosomatic Medicine*, **38**, 257–268.

Platt, J.J., Pout, M.F. & Metzger, D.S. (1986) Interpersonal cognitive problem-solving therapy (ICPS). In W. Dryden & W. Golden (Eds), *Cognitive-Behavioural Approaches to Psychotherapy*. London: Harper and Row.

Potter-Efron R.T. & Potter-Efron P.S., Eds (1990) *Aggression, Family Violence and Chemical Dependency*. New York: Haworth Press.

Rada, R.T., Laws, D.R. & Kellner, R. (1976) Plasma testosterone levels in the rapist. *Psychosomatic Medicine*, **38**, 257–268.

Riches, D. (Ed.) (1986) *The Anthropology of Violence*. Oxford: Blackwell.

Saunders, D.G. (1995) "Production of wife assalt". In J.C. Campbell (Ed.), *Assessing Danperoness: Vident by Sexual Offenders*, Batterers and Child Abusers. Newbury Park, CA: Sage.

Schultz, L.G. (1960) The wife assaulter. *Journal of Social Therapy*, **6**, 103–12.

Siann, G. (1985) *Accounting for Aggression: Perspectives on Aggression and Violence*, London: Allen & Unwın.

Spielberger, C.D., Jacobs, G.A., Russell, S. & Crane, R.S. (1983) Assessment of anger: the state-trait anger scale. In J. Butcher & C.D. Spielberger (Eds), *Advances in Personality Assessment, Vol. 2*, 159–187.Hillsdale, NJ Erlbaum. pp.

Straus, M.A., Gelles, R.J. & Steinmetz, S.K. (1988) *Behind Closed Doors: Violence in the American Family*. Beverley Hills, CA: Sage.

Storr, A. (1970) *Human Aggression*. Harmondsworth, Middlesex: Penguin.

Toch, H. (1969) *Violent Men*. Chicago: Aldine.

Trower, P., Bryant, B. & Argyle, M. (1978) *Social Skills and Mental Health*. London: Methuen.

Turner, C.W., Cole, A.M. & Cerro, B.S. (1984) Contributions of aversive experiences to robbery and homicide: a demographic analysis. In R. Kaplan, V. Konecki & R. Novaco (Eds), *Aggression in Children and Youths*. The Hague: Sythe.

Van Hasselt, V.B., Morrison, R.L., Bellack, A.S. & Hersen, M. (1987) *Handbook of Family Violence*. New York: Plenum.

Weiner, N.A. & Wolfgang, M.E. (Eds) (1989) *Violent Crime: Violent Criminals*. London: Sage.

Wolfgang, M.E. (1958) *Patterns in Criminal Homicide.* Philadelphia, PA: University of Pennsylvania Press.
Wolfgang, M.E. & Ferracuti, F. (1967) *The Subculture of Violence: Towards an Integrated Theory in Criminology.* London: Tavistock.
Zillman, D. (1979) *Hostility and Aggression.* Hillsdale, NJ: Erlbaum.

CHAPTER EIGHT

ALCOHOL, DRUGS AND CRIMINAL BEHAVIOUR

Mary McMurran

The existence of an association between substance use and crime is by now well established, and an understanding of the nature of that link is necessary in designing appropriate and effective interventions for offenders. In cases where offenders drink or use drugs, an assumption is often made that substance use is invariably the *cause* of criminal behaviour and these offenders are consequently directed into intervention programmes aimed at reducing their drinking and drug use. Whilst stopping or moderating substance use may be of some general benefit in improving health, wealth and happiness, it is not necessarily true that a reduction in the likelihood of offending will follow. Models of substance use and crime which propose a direct causal relationship are over-simplistic and therefore inadequate in explaining the association between these two complex behaviours. The relationship between substance use and crime will be addressed first in this chapter, and then, taking this information into account, appropriate assessment and intervention methods will be described.

THE RELATIONSHIP BETWEEN SUBSTANCE USE AND CRIME

In most societies there is legislation pertaining to the manufacture, possession and supply of drugs, including alcohol. Substance use *ipso facto* can be a violation of the criminal law. Drug legislation and its implementation are

Working with Offenders: Psychological Practice in Offender Rehabilitation.
Edited by C.R. Hollin. © 1996 John Wiley & Sons Ltd.

issues of some relevance to the clinician in that they produce the social climate which can spawn drug-specific crimes (e.g. trafficking, possession), dangerous methods of drug consumption and reluctance to seek treatment for drug-related problems. These socio-legal issues are not, however, the main topic of this chapter. Here, the interest lies primarily in the relationship between substance use and crime in individuals.

Much of the evidence for a relationship between substance use and crime comes from individual coincidence estimates, which measure substance use in groups of offenders, or criminal activity in groups of substance users. Such studies reveal that offenders are, in general, heavy substance users, and that heavy substance users are disproportionately likely to be engaged in criminal activities.

High rates of alcoholism and problem drinking have been recorded in prison populations. Using the Michigan Alcoholism Screening Test (MAST; Selzer, 1971), McLean (1988) identified 70% of males and 65% of females to be problem drinkers in a sample of New Zealand prisoners; White & Boyer (1985) found 44% of the Tasmanian prison population to be alcoholics; and Indermaur & Upton (1988) found 49% to be alcoholics in an Australian prison sample. Other researchers have measured alcohol consumption levels, often alongside self-reported alcohol-related problems. Lightfoot & Hodgins (1988) studied Canadian prisoners, finding that they reported drinking on average 14 standard drinks per day, and that 79% reported at least one alcohol-related problem, compared to 12% of a non-offender male sample. McMurran & Hollin (1989a) found that a sample of English male young offenders reported drinking on average 58 units of alcohol per week, compared with 21 units per week for a comparable normative sample, and that 38% admitted at least one alcohol-related problem.

Studies of the use of illicit drugs amongst prisoners show a similar picture. Using the Drug Abuse Screening Test (DAST; Skinner, 1982), Lightfoot & Hodgins (1988) found that 38% of their Canadian prison sample could be classified as severe or substantial drug abusers, these two classifications being typical of drug users in in-patient treatment programmes. Data from the US Bureau of Justice Statistics show that 78% of prison inmates have a history of drug use, which is about twice the rate for the general population (Peters, 1993). Maden, Swinton & Gunn (1992) found 43% illicit drug users in a sample of British prisoners, with 11% meeting criteria for drug dependence. Dembo et al. (1987), in a sample of youths in an American detention centre, found 19% to be established (as opposed to experimental) drug users. In Britain, Thornton, Cookson & Clark (1990) found that around two-thirds of young offenders had used drugs at some time or other, compared with 21% of a sample of school pupils in London (Swadi, 1988).

The conclusion that offenders are heavy drinkers and drug users seems warranted, judging by the studies reported above, however, there are two major issues to be taken into consideration. First, data are typically collected through client self-report, and there is much scepticism about the validity of self-report in the addictions field. Where offenders are concerned, validity may be affected by their understanding of what the information will be used for, particularly if they believe that their reports of substance use will influence important decisions relating to further charges, sentencing, privileges or parole. It is also important to remember that data about substance use among offenders come from studies of convicted offenders, and typically incarcerated offenders, who form an accessible pool of subjects. There is, therefore, a bias towards the study of offenders who have committed crimes of sufficient seriousness to lead to charges, conviction and sentencing.

Turning now to criminality amongst drinkers, West & Farrington (1977) found, amongst young men, that those judged to be heavy drinkers committed a high proportion of delinquent acts in comparison to lighter drinkers, and Werch, Gorman & Marty (1987) found that young heavy drinkers were more likely to run into trouble with the police. McCord (1981), as part of a longitudinal study of males, examined 70 alcoholics, finding that 40 were criminals and 30 were not criminals. Collins (1986), in his review of the relationship between problem drinking and offending, concludes that "problem drinking is associated with criminal behaviour, especially violent criminal behaviour in the young adult years" (p. 111).

With regard to illicit drug users, Hammersley & Morrison (1988) studied 149 prisoners and clients of drug treatment centres in Scotland, finding that heavier drug users commit more crimes. Dembo et al. (1990), studying juveniles in an American detention centre, found that rates of offending amongst drug users were significantly higher than for non-users. Higher rates of criminality have been found in heroin users during phases of addiction, and markedly lower rates during periods of non-addiction (Ball et al., 1981; Nurco et al., 1985).

Where arrestees are tested for recent alcohol and drug use, around 50–60% test positive (Greenberg, 1982; Peters, 1993). This gives some indication of the incidence of substance use at the time of the offence. When asked, many offenders admit to a relationship between substance use and crime (Hodgins & Lightfoot, 1988; McMurran & Hollin, 1989a). Differences in the way this question is posed across studies, and differences among users of various types of drug, lead to a wide range in the proportions who report a relationship, which can lie anywhere between 40% and 80%. Of course, when offenders are asked if they were using substances at the time of the offence and whether this was related to their offending, it may be more comfortable for the offender to blame alcohol or drugs for an antisocial act rather than accept responsibility for the behaviour.

Despite various methodological problems, there is nevertheless strong evidence to suggest that substance use and crime co-vary. First, offenders are likely to be heavy drinkers and drug users, and people who use alcohol and drugs heavily are more likely to be involved in criminal activities. Second, substance use at the time of the offence occurs in a high percentage of cases. Third, many substance-using offenders report a relationship between substance use and crime. However, these findings may be viewed from a different angle; it is also true to say that many offenders are not substance users, are not under the influence of alcohol or drugs at the time of their offence, and do not claim a relationship between their substance use and offending, and that many crimes are committed without the help of alcohol or drugs. It is quite obvious, then, that substance use is neither a necessary nor a sufficient condition for crime to occur.

Adherence to a simplistic direct-cause model postulating that substance use leads to crime is likely to yield poor results in both research and practice. It is interesting to note here that longitudinal studies of the emergence of delinquency and substance use show that delinquency precedes drinking and drug taking. For example, Temple & Ladouceur (1986) collected data on 301 delinquents from age 16 years until they reached 31 years of age. Drinking was shown to rise from age 16 to a peak at age 23, continue at a steady level until age 28 years, then begin gradually to decline. Offending was highest between ages 16 and 20, peaking at 18, and thereafter declined until by the age of 31 most had stopped offending. Three important conclusions may be drawn from these results. First, that early alcohol use is not strongly predictive of later life alcohol use; that is, most young drinkers will grow out of heavy drinking. Second, most young delinquents will grow out of crime, although serious delinquency is predictive of adult criminal involvement. Third, whilst drinking and crime appear to co-occur in adolescence, there is no evidence that drinking causes crime; delinquency peaks before drinking, and drinking increases as the level of criminality drops. A similar order of events has been shown in longitudinal studies of illicit drug use and crime; prior delinquency and involvement with delinquent peer groups predict both delinquency and drug use (Elliott, Huizinga & Ageton, 1985). Looking at the sequence of drug use, alcohol functions as the drug of initiation for those who proceed to cannabis use, and problem drinking represents a level of involvement intermediate between cannabis use and hard drug use (Donovan & Jessor, 1983).

A direct causal relationship between substance use and crime is, therefore, most unlikely, or at least very rare. The search for an answer to the question "Does substance use cause crime?" must be called off. The complex question that must be asked instead is "For whom and under what circumstances will what kind of substance use lead to which kinds of criminal behaviour?" That is, any explanation of substance use and crime must take into account *substance variables*, *situation variables* and *person variables*, all of which interact with each other to produce a variety of types of criminal behaviour.

SUBSTANCE VARIABLES

We have already seen that drinking and illicit drug use are each associated with crime, however, there is some evidence that alcohol is most strongly associated with crimes of violence (e.g. Cookson, 1992), whereas illicit drug use is associated mainly with crimes of economic necessity (e.g. Inciardi, 1979; Maden, Swinton & Gunn, 1992). In a study of offence types committed by 14 341 imprisoned offenders, Miller & Welte (1986) looked at four groups: those who reported both alcohol and drug use prior to the offence; those who reported alcohol use only; those who reported drug use only; and those who reported neither alcohol nor drug use prior to the offence. Those in the alcohol and drug group were most likely to have committed a violent crime, followed by those who used only alcohol. Offenders who used only drugs were more likely to have committed a property offence. Those who used neither alcohol nor drugs prior to the offence were more likely to have committed a drug offence.

Information from the above study supports the links between alcohol and violence, and drugs and acquisitive offences. In addition, there is evidence that multiple drug use, that is alcohol plus illicit drugs, deserves particular attention, and this is supported by other research. Hodgins & Lightfoot (1988) found higher criminality in prisoners who used both alcohol and drugs, compared with those who used only alcohol or only drugs, and more of the multiple drug users reported a relationship between their substance use and offending. In a sample of people in a drug treatment programme, Hammersley & Morrison (1987) found the highest criminality in those who used both heroin and alcohol.

There is also evidence to suggest that the two broad categories of "alcohol" and "drugs" require some refinement in the study of substance use and crime.

For example, the type of beverage is important in that consumers of beer and spirits are more likely to experience alcohol-related problems, especially legal problems (Werch, Gorman & Marty, 1987), and crimes of violence are strongly associated with spirit drinking (Cookson, 1992). With illicit drugs, users of opiates and cocaine are more likely to be convicted of crimes against the person than are users of other types of drug (McBride, 1981).

Where alcohol is concerned, it is important to take patterns of drinking into account. In their study of adult offenders, Collins & Schlenger (1988) found that offences of violence were related to intoxication, but not chronic heavy drinking, suggesting that the characteristics which dispose a person to "alcoholism" are not associated with an increased likelihood of violence.

Although in general alcohol may be more strongly associated with violent crimes, many drinkers commit acquisitive crimes from economic necessity. For example, the heavy drinker without a regular income will obviously need to find means to support the habit. The use of illicit drugs may be more strongly associated with acquisitive crimes, yet violence is not uncommon. For example, attempts to control and protect drug use, particularly in the context of drug dealing, can easily result in violence. The caveat here is that findings from aggregated data will not necessarily apply in individual cases; situational and personal factors also need to be taken into account.

SITUATION VARIABLES

The importance of situation variables can be clearly illustrated by conjuring up a rather fanciful hypothetical situation. A person isolated on a desert island with unlimited access to alcohol and drugs could indulge to extraordinary degrees of excess without crime ensuing. There is no one to fight with, sexually assault or defraud, and nothing to steal. Even if this stranded person did damage or set fire to something, there would be no one around to call the behaviour a crime and no police to make an arrest. By contrast, real life presents many opportunities for the commission of offences, and the law is enforced in some situations more than others.

Violent crimes, for example, usually occur in contexts where drinking is likely, and the probability of aggression would be elevated regardless of the occurrence of substance use (Lang & Sibrel, 1989). Violence and disorder typically occur in and around city centre licensed premises on Friday and Saturday nights (Hope, 1985; Ramsay, 1982). Tuck (1989) suggests that a group of predominantly young people, crushed together in a hot smoky atmosphere, or displaced onto the streets at closing time looking for further excitement are "tinder ready for any spark which may cause quarrels or violence" (p. 66). Murdoch, Pihl & Ross (1990) note that in crimes of violence it is not only the assailant who is likely to be under the influence of alcohol, but also the victim. They interpret this as suggesting that "the relationship between alcohol and aggression may be artifactual describing only when and where the aggression takes place" (p. 1070). Of course, it is also true that social drinking contexts are the focus of police attention, and therefore the likelihood of arrest is increased in and around such venues.

With reference to acquisitive crimes, although alcohol use has been associated with burglary, most of the offenders studied are regular drinkers, which means that almost all of their activities are related to drinking. Drinking environments may simply serve as meeting places where plans to offend are hatched (Bennett & Wright, 1984).

McBride (1981), in his review of illicit drugs and violence, suggests that it is within the context of the drug deal that most violence occurs. The dealer aims at selling the lowest quality drugs at the highest price, whereas the buyer is attempting to obtain the best quality at the lowest price, creating a situation of mutual suspicion. This situation generates an atmosphere in which violence is likely. Furthermore, the police are usually well aware of where drug dealing goes on and where drug users congregate, therefore there is a relatively high chance of being apprehended for crimes committed in these localities.

PERSON VARIABLES

In the condition where a person has been drinking or using drugs and the opportunity to commit crime is also present, only some people will actually go on to commit an offence. That is, individual differences must be taken into account in explaining the relationship between substance use and crime. These may be construed as individual risk factors, and the question, then, is "What individual characteristics increase the likelihood of a substance user committing a criminal offence?"

Substance users, like offenders in general, are more likely to offend if they are young and male. Miller & Welte (1986) found that the group in their prison sample who used both alcohol and drugs, and which was over-represented in the violent crime category, was disproportionately young and male. Offenders with high psychopathy scores are more likely to show alcohol and drug disorders (Smith & Newman, 1990), and alcohol abusers who carry a psychiatric diagnosis are likely to be more severely aggressive when under the influence of alcohol than are non-abusers (Hillbrand, Foster & Hirt, 1991).

Age, gender and psychopathology are three important person variables which need to be taken into consideration in explaining substance use and crime, particularly violent crime.

The role of cognition is one other important factor. Studies of the cognitive styles of offenders have shown this group to have poorer social problem-solving skills than non-offenders (e.g. Slaby & Guerra, 1988). The effects of alcohol and drugs may impair problem-solving skills even further, both through the acute effects of intoxication and as a consequence of chronic substance use. Social problem-solving abilities, therefore, form one personal risk factor.

Studies in the alcohol field have demonstrated the importance of psychological factors in determining behavioural outcomes, highlighting the role expectancies play in explaining behaviour which occurs after substance use. Outcome expectancies are the effects a drinker expects to experience after drinking and are predictive of the actual effects that follow. Evidence for the influence of alcohol expectancies has been gathered from balanced placebo design experiments, where half the subjects are given a drink containing alcohol and half are given a drink without alcohol, and half the subjects in each group are led to believe that their drink contains alcohol and half are led to believe that they are not drinking alcohol. These studies show that those who think they are drinking alcohol but are not, report feeling cravings for more alcohol, drink more alcohol in subsequent "taste tests", behave more aggressively and show more sexual arousal than those who are drinking alcohol but think they are not (see review by Goldman, Brown & Christiansen, 1987).

Information about alcohol-related outcome expectancies has been gathered in laboratory studies. In experiments, aggression is usually measured by the intensity and duration of electric shock that subjects are prepared to give to a "partner" in the experiment, this ostensible "partner" being in another room. Lang & Sibrel (1989), in their review of experimental studies of alcohol-related expectancies on aggression, show that the expectancy that alcohol has been consumed facilitates aggression regardless of the actual alcohol content of the drink. Those who believe they have imbibed a higher dose of alcohol behave more aggressively than those who believe they have been given a low dose. Outcome expectancies may, therefore, be seen as risk factors for aggression (e.g. "alcohol makes me violent").

A similar situation may pertain in sexual offending. In a study of rapists, McMurran & Bellfield (1993) found that those whose offences were alcohol-related believed that they were more likely to do something sexually risky after drinking, compared with rapists whose offences were not alcohol related.

This finding may be interpreted in the light of the offenders' past experience, yet because expectancies predict behaviour this belief is a risk factor for future crime.

McMurran, Hollin & Williams (1995) have examined alcohol-related expectancies in male young offenders, finding that those whose offences are alcohol related expect more global positive change from drinking, and that those who offend against the person (as opposed to property) expect more positive social change. The positive social change factor contains items relating to feelings of friendliness, joining in and having fun, and it seems logical to conclude that people who wish to be gregarious will drink in social settings such as bars and clubs. These situations, in turn, provide the opportunities for violent conflict. This demonstrates that factors relating to drinking, the situation and the person interact to raise the likelihood of crime.

RESPONSES TO ALCOHOL- AND DRUG-RELATED CRIME

Criminal sanctions may be seen as an essential response to alcohol- and drug-related crime in that they signal what constitutes reasonable behaviour and they protect society from the worst consequences of abuse. However, punishment needs to be augmented by intervention programmes which help offenders modify their behaviour.

Andrews and his colleagues, in their meta-analysis of correctional programmes, have shown that effective interventions are those which address criminogenic needs, and they identify substance use as one possible need (Andrews et al., 1990). By now it is clear that substance use may be connected to offending, but that this is not necessarily true in every case. In any attempt to reduce the likelihood of reoffending, it is important, therefore, first to assess the nature of the relationship between substance use and crime. It is logical to measure reoffending in the evaluation of interventions to reduce substance use only where there is a connection between substance use and crime. The importance of this point cannot be overemphasized; where reoffending is used inappropriately as an outcome measure, then interventions will appear to be ineffective and this contributes to the argument that, in offender rehabilitation, "nothing works". Of course, this is not to say that interventions to reduce substance use may not be provided for offenders for purposes other than to reduce the likelihood of reoffending; offenders, like others, may benefit from moderating their substance use in terms of improved health, better interpersonal relationships and fewer financial problems.

Information about the types of intervention that work best is also presented in Andrews' meta-analysis of correctional programmes; in general, structured cognitive–behavioural interventions are seen to be more effective than non-directive counselling and psychodynamic therapies. The same holds true for interventions in the addictions field (Hodgson, 1991; Miller & Hester, 1986). It is not surprising, then, that cognitive–behavioural interventions show most promise for substance users within the criminal justice system (Peters, 1993; Stitzer & McCaul, 1987). These interventions include behavioural self-control training, skills training, relapse prevention and lifestyle modification.

Before going on to describe methods of assessment and intervention, it is worth pausing to consider the relative effectiveness of voluntary versus compulsory intervention. Many offenders do not enter programmes voluntarily, but because of pressure from the criminal justice system. Professionals often believe that the motivation of coerced clients is less than that of volunteers and that outcomes will necessarily be less successful. One comparison of voluntary and criminal justice system referrals to an out-patient substance abuse programme found that the two groups did differ in levels of motivation to change; the criminal justice system referrals were less motivated (Farabee, Nelson & Spence, 1993). However, there is also evidence to suggest that compulsory programmes do work with offenders. Referrals from courts and probation officers to community-based alcohol programmes are actually more likely to complete the programme than self-referrals, and both groups show similar reductions in consumption (Hoffman et al., 1987; Stitzer & McCaul, 1987). Legal contingencies may be viewed as important motivating factors, through deferring or reducing sanctions as a consequence of participation in programmes. In their review of compulsory interventions for both alcohol and drug abusers in the criminal justice system, Stitzer & McCaul (1987) conclude that interactions between legal sanctions and intervention programmes require further investigation to determine what is most effective.

SCREENING

The first task is to identify those who may have problems with substance use and for whom further interviewing and assessment is required. Screening for substance use can be quite simply carried out by the aid of a problem checklist, asking the following questions.

- Do you drink/use drugs?
- Do you think your drinking/drug use and offending are related?

- Does drinking/drug use cause you any problems other than offending (e.g. relationship problems, violence, financial problems, health problems, work problems)?

A checklist such as this may be augmented by the use of questionnaires designed to assess the degree of involvement with alcohol or drugs. The Short Alcohol Dependence Questionnaire (SADD; Raistrick, Dunbar & Davidson, 1983; Davidson & Raistrick, 1986) is a 15-item questionnaire which has been revised and psychometrically developed with an English young offender population (McMurran & Hollin, 1989b; McMurran, Hollin & Bowen, 1990). The Drug Abuse Screening Test (DAST; Skinner, 1982) is a 20-item questionnaire designed to measure the degree of problematic drug use.

Assessment of the offender's motivation to change is also important and it is worthwhile asking questions such as:

- Do you want to reduce your drinking/drug use?
- Do you want to reduce drink/drug-related crime?
- Do you want help to make these changes?

Prochaska, DiClemente & Norcross (1992) describe a model of change in addictive behaviours, identifying five well-defined stages of change which form a predictable route from the position of not recognizing a problem, through recognition, preparing for change, and effecting change, to the point where the problem no longer exists. The five stages are:

1. pre-contemplation, where there is lack of awareness or concern about the behaviour and its consequences and no intention to change in the immediate future;
2. contemplation, where there is recognition that a problem exists but no commitment to take action at present;
3. preparation, where there is an intention to take action in the near future;
4. action, where there is ongoing modification of the target behaviour;
5. maintenance, where there is consolidation of change over time.

Change does not usually occur by steady progression through the stages; most people relapse and recycle through the stages quite frequently. Each stage is associated with a number of specific change processes, with cognitive interventions (e.g. consciousness raising) being more useful during the early stages, and behavioural techniques (e.g. behavioural self-control training) being more useful during action and maintenance.

The value of the stages of change model is that it suggests interventions which may be appropriate for those in the each stage. Pre-contemplators are most resistant to change, and indeed these are likely to be sifted out through screening and given advice about their drinking or drug use along with information about where to find help in future. Contemplators, who are thinking about change but not yet taking action, may benefit from *motivational interviewing*. After further *assessment and goal-setting*, those who are ready for action are candidates for *behavioural self-control training* and *skills training*. Those who are attempting to avoid relapse and maintain change are suitable for *relapse prevention* and *lifestyle modification*. Each of these components will be described briefly, citing key references for further reading.

MOTIVATIONAL INTERVIEWING

Given the finding that clients in the criminal justice system may be less likely to want to change their drinking or drug use than voluntary clients, motivational issues may be seen as important needs to address (Farabee, Nelson & Spence, 1993). Miller (1985) defines motivation to change as the probability that a person will enter into, continue and adhere to a specific change strategy. It is the professional's task to enhance the probability of these outcomes. Miller & Rollnick (1991) suggest that one way of doing this is through motivational interviewing, and they describe the strategies involved in their book on the subject.

The overall aim of motivational interviewing is to elicit self-motivational statements from the client. These statements relate to *problem recognition*, e.g. "I suppose my drinking does cause problems"; *expression of concern*, e.g. "I'm afraid of getting into trouble"; *intention to change*, e.g. "I think I should cut down"; and *optimism about change*, e.g. "Change won't be easy, but I can do it". Through self-motivational statements, the client is placed in the position of describing the negative effects of substance use and crime and arguing for change. The principle behind this is captured in the statement "I learn what I believe as I hear myself talk". That is, the client is the most persuasive change agent, through the mechanism of arguing his or her personal case for change. By contrast, confrontational approaches are not effective, since the client is placed in the position of defending his or her behaviour by arguing the positive side.

The key features of a motivational style are to adopt an affirmative client-centred approach to raise the client's self-esteem; to raise the client's awareness of problems by providing personal feedback and advice; and to allow the

Table 8.1   Motivational interviewing techniques

- *Avoid labelling.* Do not label the client an "alcoholic" or "addict". If the client does not agree, this will elicit denial of problems and lead to confrontation
- *Ask evocative questions.* Assume that the client recognizes that there are problems and that change is desirable, e.g. "What concerns you about your drinking?", as opposed to "Are you concerned about your drinking?"
- *Decisional balance.* Ask the client to list the advantages and disadvantages of the behaviour, both in the short term and long term
- *Acknowledge the positives.* Acknowledging the positive consequences of substance use in the client's life will enable the client to express the problematic consequences
- *Elaboration.* When a client makes a self-motivational statement, ask for elaboration to elicit further self-motivational statements
- *Voicing doubts.* Voice the client's doubts about change, e.g. "If all your friends use drugs, you may find it difficult to be different"
- *Role reversal.* The client is asked to take the role of counsellor and persuade the counsellor, who acts as client, of the need for change
- *Summarize.* Summarize at intervals, emphasizing self-motivational statements and reframing self-defeating statements (e.g. "I've tried before and can't stop" becomes "You're motivated to change but have not yet discovered the best way to go about it")

client to choose from a range of goal options and methods of achieving them. The specific strategies of motivational interviewing are listed in Table 8.1.

One particularly interesting strategy included in motivational interviewing is the "decisional balance", a cost-benefit analysis where clients are asked to list the pros and cons of their substance use. Although a simple technique, this appears to be highly effective in eliciting commitment to change. McDougall & Boddis (1991) used it as a key component in their brief intervention for aggression control with young offenders, and McMurran & Thomas (1991) reported that offenders in an alcohol programme rated it the most useful component. The decisional balance may take effect through changing the client's outcome expectancies.

Miller & Sovereign (1989) describe a "drinkers check-up", comprising two visits to a clinic for assessment and feedback, where interviews conducted using motivational interviewing proved superior in reducing alcohol consumption over a directive, confrontational style. Saunders & Wilkinson (1990) compared motivational interviewing with education for heroin addicts. Those in the motivational interviewing group made more robust decisions to abstain, viewed stopping as more valuable, and reported fewer drug-related problems, although both groups reported similar reductions in drug use. The approach has also been used in the treatment of sex offenders (Garland & Dougher, 1991).

ASSESSMENT

After addressing motivational issues, further assessment may be necessary to identify appropriate goals of intervention. In this chapter, emphasis will be placed on assessment of the relationship between substance use and crime. Detailed information about assessment in relation to substance use can be found in Donovan & Marlatt's (1988) book, *Assessment of Addictive Behaviours*.

Information is required about the development of substance use; the current status of the behaviour, including type of substances used, and quantity and frequency of use; the antecedents and consequences of the substance use; and the relationship with criminal events. Interviews with the offender are the obvious means of collecting this information. Structured formats for assessment are presented by Ghodse (1989) and McMurran & Hollin (1993). In addition, the use of self-monitoring diaries can provide useful information about the circumstances of substance use and crime, by asking the client to keep a daily record of what substances were used, in what quantities, when, where, with whom and with what consequences.

Analysis of specific criminal events will provide information about the relationship between substance use and crime. There are several possible types of relationship, as outlined in Table 8.2. These possibilities are not mutually exclusive; it is possible for several conditions to apply at the same time. It is, however, important to identify the nature of the relationship in that where relationships 1 to 5 apply, reducing substance use or changing patterns of substance use may be expected to reduce the likelihood of crime; where relationships 6 to 10 apply, although changes in substance use may be beneficial, a reduction in crime cannot be expected and in some cases the likelihood of crime may even be increased.

Information collected during interview should be integrated in a behavioural analysis identifying the *antecedents*, both historical and current, which explain the onset of the behaviours of interest (i.e. substance use and crime); specific aspects of the *behaviours*, such as quantity and frequency of substance use and types of crime; and the *consequences*, which explain the maintenance of the behaviours in terms of rewards and punishments.

Table 8.2 Possible types of relationship between substance use and crime

---

1. Substance use is the crime, for example, drunk and disorderly, under-age drinking, possession or sale of illicit drugs
2. Substance use changes behaviour, for example, through impairment of judgement, giving Dutch courage
3. Crime supports substance use, for example stealing alcohol or drugs, stealing goods or money to finance drinking or drug use
4. Substance use causes problems which lead to crime, for example over-spending, losing jobs, arguments
5. The context of substance use precipitates crime, for example planning crime with other substance users, being with others who are likely to become violent
6. Crime and substance use are connected through underlying problems, for example need for excitement, wanting to fit in with peers
7. Substance use occurs after crime, for example to cope with guilt or anxiety, to celebrate
8. Substance use increases the chance of arrest, for example by taking risks when intoxicated
9. Substance use is an excuse for crime, for example giving the authorities a reason for offending
10. Substance use decreases the chance of crime, for example because of incapacitation

---

A specific example may be instructive here in illustrating the kind of information typically collected and how this may be integrated in a behavioural analysis.

CASE EXAMPLE

William, now aged 22 years, began drinking with friends at around the age of 14 years. Being too young to drink in public houses, he and his friends would buy cider and cans of lager to drink in the local park during evenings and weekends. Along with drinking, the group often engaged in delinquent acts, such as damaging property and shoplifting. William reports that belonging to this delinquent group was fun and that both drinking and delinquency were means of alleviating boredom.

At the age of 16, William found employment as an apprentice carpenter and began to drink in pubs and clubs. Since he had more spending money and experienced no trouble in being served alcohol, his drinking increased. William says that having money to buy drink in pubs and clubs made him feel adult. He frequently got into fights with other youths in pubs and clubs, as did most of his friends. He says that he experienced pressure from his peers to act "hard" and not back down from aggressive challenges.

William had acquired three convictions of assault by the age of 18 years, for which the penalties had been a fine and two probation orders. At age 19 years, William was involved in a serious assault in a pub. He claims that he had consumed eight pints of lager at the time. A youth, whom he knew and disliked, was verbally abusive towards him, whereupon William lashed out, punching, kicking and injuring him with a broken glass. William spent 8 months in prison after this offence.

Owing to his imprisonment, William lost his job and found himself with time on his hands. He began to drink heavily, using alcohol to help him cope with boredom. He reported most days consuming around three pints in the pub over lunchtime, then, after a siesta in the afternoon, he would consume a further five or six pints of lager in the evening. Occasionally, he would stay at home and drink about half a bottle of vodka. William was, therefore, consuming approximately 100–120 units of alcohol per week. The recommended "safe" limit for men is no more than 21 units of alcohol per week. His score of 32 on the SADD indicated a high degree of dependence on alcohol. He began to shoplift and burgle houses so that he could support his drinking. He was convicted of theft, for which he received a probation order.

His social circumstances changed around this time. He left the family home because of his parents nagging him about frequently coming home late and drunk, and now lived alone in a rented room. Most of his old friends had begun to settle down with jobs and girlfriends, and he saw less of them. He described his friends in the pub as "drinking buddies" rather than close friends. William claimed to have had many short-term relationships with young women. None of these had lasted for long because "girls are not interested in you if you don't have money, and if you get the money from nicking they're not interested in you because you're in trouble with the law".

His most recent violent offence happened during a burglary. William drank four shots of vodka before the burglary to give him courage, but he claims not to have been drunk. He entered a house through the kitchen window, using a metal bar to break the frame. In the house, he was unexpectedly confronted by the resident, an elderly man. He says he panicked and hit the man several times with the metal bar, then escaped.

Afterwards, he felt very guilty about hitting the old man and spent the next few days drinking constantly. He says he was desperate to drink to forget, needed alcohol immediately, and therefore stole alcohol from supermarkets. He was apprehended by a store detective and later confessed the aggravated burglary to the police.

Table 8.3 Behavioural analysis of the case example

Stage 1. Early adolescence	
Antecedents	Associates with delinquent peers
Behaviour	1. Drinking outdoors; 1–2 days per week; 2–3 units per occasion; cider and lager
	2. Delinquency: criminal damage; shoplifting
Consequences	Group acceptance and fun
Key learning	Drinking and delinquency help you fit in with peers and alleviate boredom
Stage 2. Late adolescence	
Antecedents	Sequence in stage 1, plus income from job
Behaviour	1. Drinking in pubs and clubs; 2–3 days per week; 8–10 units per occasion; lager
	2. Violence
Consequences	Feels adult; proves himself "hard"; trouble with the law
Key learning	Drinking associated with violence
Stage 3. Early adulthood	
Antecedents	Sequence in stage 2, plus loss of job after imprisonment
Behaviour	1. Daily drinking; in pubs and at home; 15–18 units per occasion; lager and spirits
	2. Stealing to support drinking; serious assault during burglary
Consequences	Alleviation of boredom; social deterioration; guilt; trouble with the law
Key learning	Not yet consolidated

A behavioural analysis of this case can be described in developmental sequences, as suggested by Gresswell & Hollin (1992), as shown in Table 8.3 Of particular interest here is the development of alcohol-related offending. In early adolescence, drinking and delinquency were correlated, both being activities of the peer group with which William associated. In late adolescence, drinking and violent crime appear to have been determined largely by the context in which drinking took place and the belief that it is necessary for young men to act "hard". Still later, theft and burglary were means of supporting drinking. Where the index offence of aggravated burglary is concerned, a number of types of relationship between the drinking and offending are apparent. Referring back to Table 8.2 drinking was used prior to the offence to give courage (item 2); the crime was committed to support drinking (item 3); drinking had previously caused problems (loss of job) which led to crime (item 4); and drinking occurred after the crime to assuage guilt (item 7). The obvious goal choice for this client, given positive scores on items 2, 3 and 4, is to reduce his alcohol consumption, by which we can expect a reduction in crime. The amount of that reduction is something to be negotiated with the client.

GOAL SETTING

Goals for change need to be tailored to fit the offender's requirements. Lightfoot & Hodgins (1993) make suggestions based upon the results of a survey in which they identied different profiles of alcohol and drug users within the prison system in North America.

1. Drug abusers, whose drug use is associated with heavy involvement in a criminal lifestyle and who show low levels of social stability. This group needs to address broad lifestyle issues.
2. Alcohol abusers, who are heavy drinkers and whose alcohol use plays a significant role in the commission of crimes. These might aim at moderating their alcohol consumption.
3. Emotionally distressed polysubstance users, who use both drink and drugs heavily, are socially unstable, and show high levels of associated problems. Their emotional problems need to be stabilized before alcohol or drug interventions can usefully commence.
4. Organically impaired alcohol and drug abusers, who show high levels of dependence on both drink and drugs, view alcohol and drugs as playing an important role in the commission of crimes, and show signs of cognitive impairment. This group may need the clarity of an abstinence goal.

Where a reduction in consumption is concerned, a choice must be made between moderation and abstinence goals. Research in the alcohol field suggests that moderation is achievable by younger people, with lower dependence on alcohol, fewer alcohol-related problems and greater social stability (Rosenberg, 1993). Many offenders fit this profile and moderation is likely to be an appropriate goal. Offenders who are older, chronic drinkers and socially less stable may fare better in pursuing the goal of abstinence. There is, however, evidence that goal choice by the client is a predictor of successful outcome in alcohol interventions (Orford & Keddie, 1986), and negotiating a goal which suits the client is important with offenders, as with other groups.

Level of alcohol consumption is not always the most relevant goal in reducing the likelihood of crime. Changing patterns of drinking may be a valid option for some. Recommendations to avoid drinking with people who are associated with crime, to avoid drinking in known trouble spots, and to leave pubs and clubs slightly before closing time to avoid crowds are criminological harm reduction strategies.

The situation with regard to drug use is more difficult in that, being an offence by definition, abstinence may be seen as the only possible goal of intervention. However, harm reduction is a key issue in drug programmes, particularly in relation to HIV transmission. Moderation of drug use or goals to modify patterns of drug use may also be introduced from a criminological harm reduction perspective.

BEHAVIOURAL SELF-CONTROL TRAINING

Behavioural self-control training (BSCT) can be described as teaching the client to become a "personal scientist", collecting and analysing personal data, testing techniques for change, and monitoring outcome (Mahoney & Thoresen, 1974). This includes self-monitoring, using diaries; setting goals for change; changing the antecedents to the behaviour by setting personal rules (stimulus control); changing the behaviour, for example by using strategies for controlling the rate of alcohol or drug consumption; and changing the consequences by rewarding oneself for achieving one's goals (contingency management). The rule-setting component of BSCT may include strategies aimed at reducing the likelihood of crime as well as reducing substance use. For example, rules may be set to avoid certain places where crime typically occurs, or specific people with whom offending commonly occurs. BSCT procedures are described more fully by Hester Miller (1987) and McMurran & Hollin (1993).

The effectiveness of BSCT in reducing alcohol consumption is now well established. Miller (1978) found BSCT superior to aversive conditioning in reducing alcohol consumption. He and his colleagues then went on to examine BSCT more closely, finding that BSCT effected change in both group interventions and individually administered interventions (Miller, Pechachek & Hamburg, 1981; Miller & Taylor, 1980), and that self-administered BSCT using a self-help manual worked as well as therapist-directed BSCT (Miller & Baca, 1983; Miller, Gribskov & Mortell, 1981; Miller & Taylor, 1980).

Administering BSCT in the form of a self-help manual has been investigated further in the UK, using the commercially available book *Let's Drink to your Health!* (Robertson & Heather, 1986). This has proved effective in reducing alcohol consumption in media-recruited problem drinkers (Heather et al., 1987; Heather Kissoon–Singh & Fenton, 1990; Heather, Whitton & Robertson, 1986; Savage, Hollin & Hayward, 1990). Self-help manuals may offer treatment advantages for imprisoned offenders in that they may be made available in prisons where no interventions are available, and to those whose period of imprisonment is too short for intervention to take place. Manuals can also provide the prisoner with strategies for use after release when alcohol once again becomes available.

BSCT has not been widely evaluated with illicit drug users, but contingency management is strongly supported in the drug field, therefore it may be of value (Tucker, Vuchinich & Downey, 1992).

SKILLS TRAINING

There are a number of skills which may need to be addressed with substance users, including assertiveness and refusal skills, communication skills, stress management, anger management and problem solving. Such interventions are well described in the literature and a useful guidebook for counsellors is that by Monti et al. (1989). Rather than review specific skills training programmes, emphasis here will be placed on cognitive skills training.

As stated earlier, the meta-analysis of correctional programmes by Andrews et al. (1990) identified cognitive-behavioural approaches as most effective. Izzo & Ross (1990), in their meta-analysis of rehabilitation programmes for juvenile delinquents, found that those including a cognitive component were twice as effective as those without. An association between substance use disorders and psychopathy has been identified (Smith & Newman, 1990). One characteristic of those labelled "psychopathic" is that of impulsivity; that is they react to problem situations without first stopping to think. In their review of cognitive skills components in substance abuse treatments in correctional settings, Husband & Platt (1993) point out that problem-solving deficits are common amongst substance users in general and that interventions which include problem-solving training are effective in reducing substance use. The importance of including a cognitive component in substance use interventions with offenders seems, therefore, doubly important.

Problem-solving skills training helps people to identify and analyse their problems, look at a range of possible solutions, and implement an action plan. One useful approach is that deriving from the work of D'Zurilla & Goldfried (1971). They define problem solving as a process which "(a) makes available a variety of potentially effective response alternatives for dealing with the problematic situation and (b) increases the probability of selecting the most effective response from among these various alternatives" (p. 108). D'Zurilla & Nezu (1982) describe effective problem solving in five stages.

1. Orientation, where there is recognition of a problem, acceptance that

problems are part of life, the expectation that problems can be solved, and the ability to stop and think instead of acting impulsively.
2. Problem definition and goal setting, which is to define the problem clearly and set realistic goals.
3. Generation of alternatives, where a range of options is produced by brainstorming.
4. Decision making and action, where the value of each option is assessed, and the best are selected to form an action plan.
5. Evaluation, where progress is reviewed and the problem-solving process is terminated if goals have been successfully achieved or repeated if they have not. Training in specific skills may form part of the action plan where the effective execution of a selected response is limited by deficits in assertiveness, communication or management of emotions.

Chaney, O'Leary & Marlatt (1978) compared problem solving with discussion groups and no intervention controls for men in an in-patient alcoholism treatment programme, finding the problem-solving group to be drinking significantly less at one-year follow-up. Ross, Fabiano & Ross (1986) included a problem-solving component in their offender rehabilitation programme and found, in comparison with a no intervention control group, that these offenders scored lower on an impulsivity scale and had been readmitted to prison with new convictions at a lower rate.

RELAPSE PREVENTION

Maintenance of change over time is the ultimate goal, and strategies aimed at preventing relapse to addictive behaviours are crucial. Marlatt & Gordon (1985) have developed an intervention, known as relapse prevention, to address potential problems in maintenance, and helpful guidebooks for counsellors based on their work have been published (Wanigaratne et al., 1990; Chiauzzi, 1991).

Relapse prevention prepares the client to recognize and cope with situations which are high risk for relapse to the problem behaviour, for example strong emotions (pleasant or unpleasant), physical discomfort and social pressure. A personal profile of high risk situations may be drawn up by studying past relapses, day-to-day diaries and relapse fantasies (i.e. the client's dreams or fears of when he or she will indulge). Relapse prevention aims to enhance client self-efficacy so that skills are more likely to be applied effectively at times when there is a risk of relapse. Relapse prevention strategies are described more fully in Table 8.4.

Table 8.4   Relapse prevention strategies

1.	Coping with temptation. The client is led to expect to experience a desire to drink or use drugs. This can be met with.

     (i)   positive self-statements (e.g. "I won't let the feeling beat me");

     (ii)   decision review, i.e. reminding oneself of why change was instigated;

     (iii) distraction, i.e. engaging in an interesting activity, but being cautious about "seemingly irrelevant decisions" (SIDs) which may put the client in the way of further temptation. An example of an SID is where a drinker chooses to go shopping, and the supermarket has a drinks section

2.   Covert modelling. The client is asked to "practise" coping strategies in an imaginal role play. That is, the counsellor describes a high risk situation in which the client copes successfully, whilst the client imagines him or herself acting out the counsellor's script

3.   Coping with lapses. The aim is to avoid the "goal violation effect", where a small lapse leads to a full-blown relapse. This can be avoided by:

     (i)   reframing lapses as learning experiences;

     (ii)   emergency procedures, to apply when a lapse has occurred and so prevent a lapse becoming a relapse;

     (iii) relapse rehearsal, which is covert modelling applied to an imaginal situation where a lapse has occurred.

4.   Graded practice. A hierarchy of high risk situations is drawn up and the client is supported in practising new skills as progressively more difficult situations are encountered in real-life settings

One specific intervention which may be included within a relapse prevention approach is cue exposure and response prevention. This involves exposure to the cues linked with substance abuse, for example the sight of a glass of alcohol or the paraphernalia associated with illicit drug use, without allowing substance use to follow. This procedure attenuates the link between being in the presence of the substance and feeling the urge to use it. The mechanism by which this procedure takes effect is not clear; extinction may account for the attenuation of craving, but proof that consumption is not inevitable may impact on efficacy expectations (Hodgson, 1991). Where the latter is the case, it may be important to expose drinkers to a priming dose of alcohol without allowing further consumption to alter loss of control expectations.

One additional aspect to consider in reducing the likelihood of relapse to substance-related crime is that of outcome expectancies. The outcomes a person expects after drinking or taking drugs are risk factors for further offending and expectancies need to be identified and challenged. This has been tackled by giving clients drinks which they believe to contain alcohol, but may or may not do so, and then asking them to perform a task (e.g. a debate). Subsequent discussions about the effects alcohol has had on task performance can highlight the role of outcome expectancies (Baer et al., 1991; Darkes & Goldman, 1993).

Relapse prevention has been applied effectively with men in alcohol treatment (Allsop & Saunders, 1989). Those receiving relapse prevention showed improved self-efficacy ratings and fewer had relapsed to heavy drinking at six-month follow-up compared with those in a relapse discussion group and no intervention controls. Although programmes for illicit drug users have been described (Peters & Dolente, 1990; Stallard & Heather, 1989), there are as yet no outcome data. Relapse prevention has also been used with sexual offenders to address their offending behaviour *per se* (Laws, 1989; Marques & Nelson, 1989; McMurran, 1991; Pithers et al., 1983).

LIFESTYLE MODIFICATION

Lifestyle modification addresses the broader issues of developing work, leisure pursuits and social networks which will enable the client to enjoy life without needing to resort to problematic substance use. Included in this stage of intervention are life skills training (for example, managing finances, cooking, health and hygiene), educational and vocational training, leisure counselling, and family or marriage counselling. In addition, psychiatric problems may need attention.

Lifestyle modification is addressed in some relapse prevention programmes (Marlatt & Gordon, 1985), but the most comprehensive approach is described by Sisson & Azrin (1989). Their community reinforcement approach for alcoholics includes Antabuse treatment, marriage counselling, employment counselling, social skills training, recreational advice and relaxation training. In comparison with clients in a standard hospital treatment programme, their group drank on fewer days and were employed on more days.

Hall et al. (1981) compared a behavioural job seekers' workshop with job search information for heroin users on probation or parole, showing at 12-week follow-up that 86% of the workshop group had found employment compared with 54% of the information group. A more comprehensive programme for drug users in a juvenile detention centre is described by Haggerty et al. (1989). The programme aimed to reduce both drug use and criminal behaviour and included cognitive–behavioural skills training and aftercare, the latter phase addressing needs relating to home, school or work, relationships and activities. No outcome data are available as yet.

Whilst many of these components can be addressed in intervention pro-grammes, the issue of throughcare is clearly important. The risks for relapse will not disappear at the conclusion of an intervention programme, particularly for imprisoned offenders who are to be released into the community. It is important, therefore, to facilitate contact between the offender and various community agencies who can provide support in the longer term.

INTENSITY OF INTERVENTION

The broad areas of intervention described above clearly contain a whole range of components. Not all of these will be necessary for each client; a behavioural assessment will identify what is appropriate for whom. It is important to match clients with relevant components to form an optimal intervention programme for each person. Another consideration is the length of time that the offender is available for intervention, for example the period of probation, imprisonment or licence. Clearly, the programme must be designed to fit the time available and, where time is short, a brief intervention will be necessary. Indeed, in some cases contact with the criminal justice system may allow only for the identification of alcohol and drug users, the provision of information about the range of services available, and referral to community treatment agencies (Peters & Kearns, 1992). Finally, it is neither cost-effective nor good practice to engage the client in a maximally intensive intervention where this is unnecessary. Brief interventions ranging from simple advice, through assessment and feedback alone, to self-help material have been shown effective in reducing drinking, particularly for those with less severe problems (Bien, Miller & Tonigan, 1993; Heather, 1989).

McMurran & Hollin (1993) describe a modular intervention programme which comprises the interventions described in this chapter (see Figure 8.1). Of course, modules may be further divided, for example "skills training" may include problem solving, assertiveness training, communication training, stress management and anger management. The advantages of this modular approach are that:

1. clients may be matched to appropriate modules (or subdivisions of modules);
2. clients may "graduate" from one module to the next, thus enhancing motivation;
3. clients may repeat a module thus facilitating assimilation;
4. it is practical in that breaks can occur between modules to accommodate temporary staff or client absences, and different people can take responsibility for different modules thus sharing the workload.

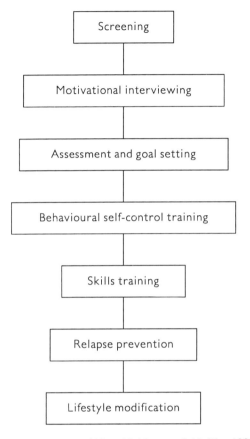

Figure 8.1   Modular programme. (After McMurran & Hollin, 1993, with permission.)

STYLE OF INTERVENTION

With regard to the style of intervention most appropriate to offenders, there is some evidence that working in groups can be problematic. Annis & Chan (1983) compared recidivism rates one year after release from prison between substance-using prisoners who had participated in confrontational group therapy and those who had not. Of those who had received group therapy, prisoners with a positive self-image showed lower rates of recidivism than the control group, whereas prisoners with a negative self-image showed increased rates of recidivism. Those with low self-esteem appear to be damaged by challenging groups. Rice, Harris & Cormier (1992), in evaluating a general therapeutic community programme, found that offenders with high psychopathy scores had higher rates of violent offending after discharge, whereas those with low psychopathy scores showed lower rates of violent recidivism. "Psychopathic" offenders may not be appropriate for some styles of group work. Clearly, close attention needs to be paid to appropriate selection for group programmes.

Where substance use is concerned, peer pressure to conform to the group norm is taken to be an important factor. Group work may provide offenders with the opportunity to promote the advantages of substance use, and so be counter-productive. It has been suggested that peer pressure could be used positively by training clients to become counsellors for their peers (Swadi & Zeitlin, 1988).

The main issue in relation to skills training is that it should be conducted in naturalistic conditions to enhance generalization to real-life settings. McMurran & Hollin (1993) recommend the use of simulated bars and also the use of real alcohol in interventions. The rationale behind this latter point is that many of the skills being taught (e.g. refusing another drink) need to be used after alcohol consumption, therefore these skills may best be taught after the client has had a drink. An additional advantage of active and naturalistic skills training is that it holds greater appeal for offenders who are typically non-academic and resistant to didactic, classroom-based teaching styles.

CONCLUSION

The principles for effective substance use interventions with offenders outlined in this chapter may be summarized as follows:

1. offenders should be assessed to identify individual criminogenic needs;
2. motivation to change is one important need;
3. structured cognitive behavioural approaches are most effective with offenders;
4. cognitive components are particularly important;
5. interventions may vary in intensity and style, according to clients needs.

The specific requirements of each offender will differ and programmes should be designed to meet individual needs.

REFERENCES

Allsop, B. & Saunders, S. (1989) Relapse and alcohol problems. In M. Gossop (Ed.), *Relapse and Addictive Behaviour*. London: Tavistock/Routledge.

Andrews, D.A., Zinger, I., Hoge, R.D., Bonta, J., Gendreau, P. & Cullen, F.T. (1990) Does correctional treatment work? A clinically relevant and psychologically informed meta-analysis. *Criminology*, **28**, 369–404.

Annis, H.M. & Chan, D. (1983) The differential treatment model: empirical evidence from a personality typology of adult offenders. *Criminal Justice and Behavior*, **10**, 159–173.

Baer, J.S., Kivlahan, D.R., Fromme, K. & Marlatt, G.A. (1991) Secondary prevention of alcohol abuse with college student populations. In N. Heather, W.R. Miller & J. Greeley (Eds), *Self Control and the Addictive Behaviours*. Botany, Australia: Maxwell MacMillan.

Ball, J.C., Rosen, L., Flueck, J.A. & Nurco, D.N. (1981) The criminality of heroin addicts when addicted and when off opiates. In J.A. Inciardi (Ed.), *The Drugs-Crime Connection*. Beverly Hills, CA: Sage.

Bennett, T.H. & Wright, R. (1984) The relationship between alcohol use and burglary. *British Journal of Addiction*, **79**, 431–437.

Bien, T.H., Miller, W.R. & Tonigan, J.S. (1993) Brief interventions for alcohol problems: a review. *Addiction*, **88**, 315–336.

Chaney, E.F., O'Leary, M.R. & Marlatt, G.A. (1978) Skill Training with alcoholics. *Journal of Consulting and Clinical Psychology*, **46**, 1092–1104.

Chiauzzi, E.J. (1991) *Preventing Relapse in the Addictions*. New York: Pergamon Press.

Collins, J.J. (1986) The relationship of problem drinking to individual offending sequences. In A. Blumstein, J. Cohen, J.A. Roth & C.A. Visher (Eds), *Criminal Careers and Career Criminals*, Vol.2. Washington, DC: National Academy Press.

Collins, J.J. & Schlenger, W.E. (1988) Acute and chronic effects of alcohol use on violence. *Journal of Studies on Alcohol*, **49**, 532–537.

Cookson, H. (1992) Alcohol use and offence type in young offenders. *British Journal of Criminology*, **32**, 352–360.

Darkes, J. & Goldman, M.S. (1993) Expectancy challenge and drinking reduction: experimental evidence for a mediational process. *Journal of Consulting and Clinical Psychology*, **61**, 344–353.

Davidson, R.J. & Raistrick, D.S. (1986) The validity of the Short Alcohol Dependence Data (SADD) Questionnaire. *British Journal of Addiction*, **81**, 217–222.

Dembo, R., Dertke, M., Schmeidler, J. & Washburn, M. (1987) Prevalence, correlates, and consequences of alcohol and other drug use among youths in a juvenile detention center. *Journal of Prison and Jail Health*, **6**, 97–127.

Dembo, R., Williams, L., Berry, E., Getreu, A., Washburn, M., Wish, E.D. & Schmeidler, J. (1990) Examination of the relationships among drug use, emotional/ psychological problems, and crime among youths entering a juvenile detention center. *International Journal of the Addictions*, **25**, 1301–1340.

Donovan, J.E. & Jessor, R. (1983) Problem drinking and the dimension of involvement with drugs. *American Journal of Public Health*, **73**, 543–552.

Donovan, D.M. & Marlatt, G.A. (Eds) (1988) *Assessment of Addictive Behaviours*. London: Hutchinson.

D'Zurilla, T.J. & Goldfried, M.R. (1971) Problem solving and behavior modification. *Journal of Abnormal Psychology*, **78**, 107–126.

D'Zurilla, T.J. & Nezu, A. (1982) Social problem solving in adults. *Advances in Cognitive–Behavioral Research and Therapy*, Vol.1. New York: Academic Press.

Elliott, D.S., Huizinga, D. & Ageton, S.A. (1985) *Explaining Delinquency and Drug Use*. Newbury Park, CA: Sage.

Farabee, D., Nelson, R. & Spence, R. (1993) Psychosocial profiles of criminal justice-

and non criminal justice-referred substance abusers in treatment. *Criminal Justice and Behavior*, **20**, 336–346.

Garland, R.J. & Dougher, M.J. (1991) Motivational interviewing in the treatment of sex offenders. In W.R. Miller & S. Rollnick (Eds), *Motivational Interviewing*. New York: The Guilford Press.

Ghodse, H. (1989) *Drugs and Addictive Behaviour: A Guide to Treatment*. Oxford: Blackwell Scientific Publications.

Goldman, M.S., Brown, S.A. & Christiansen, B.A. (1987) Expectancy theory: thinking about drinking. In H.T. Blane & K.E. Leonard (Eds), *Psychological Theories of Drinking and Alcoholism*. New York: Guilford.

Greenberg, S.W. (1982) Alcohol and crime: a methodological critique of the literature. In J.J. Collins (Ed.), *Drinking and Crime*. London: Tavistock.

Gresswell, M. & Hollin, C.R. (1992) Towards a new methodology for making sense of case material: An illustrative case involving attempted multiple murder. *Criminal Behaviour and Mental Health*, **2**, 329–341.

Haggerty, K.P., Wells, E.A., Jenson, J.M., Catalano, R.F. & Hawkins, J.A. (1989) Delinquents and drug use: A model program for community reintegration. *Adolescence*, **24**, 439–456.

Hall, S.M., Loeb, P., Coyne, K. & Cooper, J. (1981) Increasing employment in ex-heroin addicts. I: Criminal justice sample. *Behavior Therapy*, **12**, 453–460.

Hammersley, R. & Morrison, V. (1987) Effects of polydrug use on the criminal activities of heroin users. *British Journal of Addiction*, **82**, 899–906.

Hammersley, R. & Morrison, V. (1988) Crime amongst heroin, alcohol, and cannabis users. *Medicine and Law*, **7**, 185–193.

Heather, N. (1989) Brief intervention strategies. In R.K. Hester & W.R. Miller (Eds), *Handbook of Alcoholism Treatment Approaches*. New York: Pergamon.

Heather, N., Kissoon-Singh, J. & Fenton, G.W. (1990) Assisted natural recovery from alcohol problems: effects of a self-help manual with and without supplementary telephone contact. *British Journal of Addiction*, **85**, 1177–1185.

Heather, N., Robertson, I., McPherson, B., Allsop, S. & Fulton, A. (1987) Effectiveness of a controlled drinking self-help manual: one year follow-up results. *British Journal of Clinical Psychology*, **26**, 279–287.

Heather, N., Whitton, B. & Robertson, I. (1986) Evaluation of a self-help manual for media recruited problem drinkers: Six month follow-up results. *British Journal of Clinical Psychology*, **25**, 19–34.

Hester, R.K. & Miller, W.R. (1987) Self-control training. In H.T. Blane & K.E. Leonard (Eds), *Psychological Theories of Drinking and Alcoholism*. New York: Guilford.

Hillbrand, M., Foster, H.G. & Hirt, M. (1991) Alcohol abuse, violence, and neurological impairment: a forensic study. *Journal of Interpersonal Violence*, **6**, 411–422.

Hodgins, D.C. & Lightfoot, L.O. (1988) Types of male alcohol- and drug-abusing incarcerated offenders. *British Journal of Addiction*, **83**, 1201–1213.

Hodgson, R.J. (1991) Substance misuse. *Behavioural Psychotherapy*, **19**, 80–87.

Hoffman, N.G., Ninonuevo, F., Mozey, J. & Luxenberg, M.G. (1987) Comparison of court-referred DWI arrestees with other outpatients in substance abuse treatment. *Journal of Studies on Alcohol*, **48**, 591–594.

Hope, T. (1985) Drinking and disorder in the inner city. In *Implementing Crime Prevention Measures*. Home Office Research Study, No. 86. London: HMSO.

Husband, S.D. & Platt, J.J. (1993) The cognitive skills component in substance abuse treatment in correctional settings: a brief review. *Journal of Drug Issues*, **23**, 31–42.

Inciardi, J.A. (1979) Heroin use and street crime. *Crime and Delinquency*, **25**, 335–346.

Indermaur, D. & Upton, K. (1988) Alcohol and drug use patterns of prisoners in Perth. *Australian and New Zealand Journal of Criminology*, **21**, 144–167.

Izzo, R.L. & Ross, R.R. (1990) Meta-analysis of rehabilitation programmes for juvenile delinquents. *Criminal Justice and Behavior*, **17**, 134–142.

Lang, A.R. & Sibrel, P.A. (1989) Psychological perspectives on alcohol consumption and interpersonal aggression. *Criminal Justice and Behavior*, **16**, 299–324.

Laws, D.R. (Ed.) (1989) *Relapse Prevention with Sex Offenders*. New York: Guilford.

Lightfoot, L.O. & Hodgins, D. (1988) A survey of alcohol and drug problems. *International Journal of the Addictions*, **23**, 687–706.

Lightfoot, L.O. & Hodgins, D.C. (1993) Characteristics of substance-abusing offenders: implications for treatment programming. *International Journal of Offender Therapy and Comparative Criminology*, **37**, 239–250.

Maden, A., Swinton, M. & Gunn, J. (1992) A survey of pre-arrest drug use in sentenced prisoners. *British Journal of Addiction*, **87**, 27–33.

Mahoney, M.J. & Thoresen, C.E. (1974) *Self-Control: Power to the Person*. Monterey, CA: Brookes/Cole.

Marlatt, G.A. & Gordon, J.R. (Eds) (1985) *Relapse Prevention*. New York: Guilford.

Marques, J.K. & Nelson, C. (1989) Understanding and preventing relapse in sex offenders. In M. Gossop (Ed.), *Relapse and Addictive Behaviour*. London: Tavistock/Routledge.

McBride, D.C. (1981) Drugs and violence. In J.A. Inciardi (Ed.) *The Drugs-Crime Connection*. Beverly Hills, CA: Sage.

McCord, J. (1981) Alcoholism and criminality: confounding and differentiating factors. *Journal of Studies on Alcohol*, **42**, 739–748.

McDougall, C. & Boddis, S. (1991) Discrimination between anger and aggression: implications for treatment. In *Issues in Criminological and Legal Psychology*, No. 17. Leicester: British Psychological Society.

McLean, A. (1988) Screening for alcoholism in New Zealand prison inmates. *Australian and New Zealand Journal of Criminology*, **21**, 45–57.

McMurran, M. (1991) A cognitive–behavioural intervention with a sex offender. *Delinquencia*, **2**, 311–330.

McMurran, M. & Bellfield, H. (1993) Sex-related alcohol expectancies in rapists. *Criminal Behaviour and Mental Health*, **3**, 76–84.

McMurran, M. & Hollin, C.R. (1989a) Drinking and delinquency: another look at young offenders and alcohol. *British Journal of Criminology*, **29**, 386–394.

McMurran, M. & Hollin, C.R. (1989b) The Short Alcohol Dependence Data (SADD) Questionnaire: norms and reliability data for male young offenders. *British Journal of Addiction*, **84**, 315–318.

McMurran, M. & Hollin, C.R. (1993) *Young Offenders and Alcohol-Related Crime: A Practitioner's Guidebook*. Chichester: Wiley.

McMurran, M., Hollin, C.R. & Bowen, A. (1990) Consistency of alcohol self-report measures in a male young offender population. *British Journal of Addiction*, **85**, 205–208.

McMurran, M., Hollin, C.R. & Williams, M. (1995) Alcohol expectancies in male young offenders. *Journal of Adolescence*, in press.

McMurran, M. & Thomas, G. (1991) An intervention for alcohol-related offending. *Senior Nurse*, **11**, 33–36.

Miller, B.A. & Welte, J.W. (1986) Comparisons of incarcerated offenders according to use of alcohol and/or drugs prior to offence. *Criminal Justice and Behavior*, **13**, 366–392.

Miller, W.R. (1978) Behavioral treatment of problem drinkers: a comparative outcome study of three controlled drinking therapies. *Journal of Consulting and Clinical Psychology*, **46**, 74–86.

Miller, W.R. (1985) Motivational interviewing: a review with special emphasis on alcoholism. *Psychological Bulletin*, **98**, 84–107.

Miller, W.R. & Baca, L.M. (1983) Two-year follow-up of bibliotherapy and therapist directed controlled drinking training for problem drinkers. *Behavior Therapy*, **14**, 441–448.

Miller, W.R., Gribskov, C.J. & Mortell, R.L. (1981) Effectiveness of a self-control manual for problem drinkers with and without therapist contact. *International Journal of the Addictions*, **16**, 1247–1254.

Miller, W.R. & Hester, R.K. (1986) The effectiveness of alcoholism treatment: what research reveals. In W.R. Miller & N. Heather (Eds), *Treating Addictive Behaviors: Processes of Change*. New York: Plenum.

Miller, W.R., Pechachek, T.F. & Hamburg, S. (1981) Group behavior therapy for problem drinkers. *International Journal of the Addictions*, **16**, 829–839.

Miller, W.R. & Rollnick, S. (1991) *Motivational Interviewing: Preparing People to Change*. New York: Guilford.

Miller, W.R. & Sovereign, R.G. (1989) The Check-Up: a model for early intervention in addictive behaviors. In T. Loberg, W.R. Miller, P.E. Nathan & G.A. Marlatt (Eds) *Addictive Behaviors: Prevention and Early Intervention*. Amsterdam: Swets and Zeitlinger.

Miller, W.R. & Taylor, C.A. (1980) Relative effectiveness of bibliotherapy, individual, and group self-control training in the treatment of problem drinkers. *Addictive Behaviors*, **5**, 13–24.

Monti, P.M., Abrams, D.B., Kadden, R.M. & Cooney, N.L. (1989) *Treating Alcohol Dependence*. London: Cassell.

Murdoch, D., Pihl, R.O. & Ross, D. (1990) Alcohol and crimes of violence: present issues. *International Journal of the Addictions*, **25**, 1065–1081.

Nurco, D.N., Ball, J.C., Shaffer, J.W. & Hanlon, T. (1985) The criminality of narcotic addicts. *Journal of Nervous and Mental Disease*, **173**, 94–102.

Orford, J. & Keddie, A. (1986) Abstinence or controlled drinking in clinical practice: a test of the dependence and persuasion hypotheses. *British Journal of Addiction*, **81**, 495–505.

Peters, R.H. (1993) Treatment in jail and detention centers. In.J.A. Inciardi (Ed.), *Drug Treatment and Criminal Justice*. Newbury Park, CA: Sage.

Peters, R.H. & Dolente, A.S. (1990) Relapse prevention for drug dependent inmates in the Hillsborough County jail. *American Jails*, **3**, 107–110.

Peters, R.H. & Kearns, W.D. (1992) Drug abuse history and treatment needs of jail inmates. *American Journal of Drug and Alcohol Abuse*, **18**, 355–366.

Pithers, W.D., Marques, J.K., Gibat, C.C. & Marlatt, G.A. (1983) Relapse prevention with sexual aggressives: a self-control model of treatment and maintenance of change. In J.G. Greer & I.R. Stuart (Eds), *The Sexual Aggressor: Current Perspectives on Treatment*. New York: Van Nostrand.

Prochaska, J.O., DiClemente, C.C. & Norcross, J.C. (1992) In search of how people change: applications to addictive behaviors. *American Psychologist*, **47**, 1102–1114.

Ramsay, M. (1982) *City Centre Crime: The Scope for Situational Prevention*. Research and Planning Unit Paper, No. 10. London: Home Office.

Raistrick, D.S., Dunbar, G. & Davidson, R.J. (1983) Development of a questionnaire to measure alcohol dependence. *British Journal of Addiction*, **78**, 89–95.

Rice, M.E., Harris, G.T. & Cormier, C.A. (1992) An evaluation of a maximum security therapeutic community for psychopaths and other mentally disordered offenders. *Law and Human Behavior*, **16**, 399–412.

Robertson, I. & Heather, N. (1986) *Let's Drink To Your Health!* Leicester: The British Psychological Society.

Rosenberg, H. (1993) Prediction of controlled drinking by alcoholics and problem drinkers. *Psychological Bulletin*, **113**, 129–139.

Ross, R.R., Fabiano, E.A. & Ross, R.D. (1986) *Reasoning and Rehabilitation*. Ottawa: University of Ottawa.

Saunders, B. & Wilkinson, C. (1990) Motivation and addiction behaviour: a psychological perspective. *Drug and Alcohol Review*, **9**, 133–142.

Savage, S.A., Hollin, C.R. & Hayward, A.J. (1990) Self-help manuals for problem drinking: the relative effectiveness of their educational and therapeutic components. *British Journal of Clinical Psychology*, **29**, 373–382.

Selzer, M.L. (1971) The Michigan Alcoholism Screening Test: a quest for a new diagnostic instrument. *American Journal of Psychiatry*, **127**, 1653–1658.

Sisson, R.W. & Azrin, N.H. (1989) The Community Reinforcement Approach. In R.K. Hester & W.R. Miller (Eds), *Handbook of Alcoholism Treatment Approaches*. New York: Pergamon.

Skinner, M.A. (1982) The Drug Abuse Screening Test. *Addictive Behaviors*, **7**, 363–371.

Slaby, R.G. & Guerra, N.G. (1988) Cognitive mediators of aggression in adolescent offenders. *Developmental Psychology*, **24**, 580–588.

Smith, S.S. & Newman, J.P. (1990) Alcohol and drug abuse-dependence disorders in psychopathic and nonpsychopathic criminal offenders. *Journal of Abnormal Psychology*, **99**, 430–439.

Stallard, A. & Heather, N. (1989) Relapse prevention and AIDS among intravenous drug users. In M. Gossop (Ed.), *Relapse and Addictive Behaviours*. London: Tavistock/Routledge.

Stitzer, M.L. & McCaul, M.E. (1987) Criminal justice interventions with drug and alcohol abusers: the role of compulsory treatment. In E.K. Morris & C.J. Braukmann (Eds), *Behavioral Approaches to Crime and Delinquency: A Handbook of Application, Research and Concepts*. New York: Plenum.

Swadi, H. (1988) Drug and substance use among 3,333 London adolescents. *British Journal of Addiction*, **83**, 935–942.

Swadi, H. & Zeitlin, H. (1988) Peer influence and adolescent substance abuse: a promising side? *British Journal of Addiction*, **83**, 153–157.

Temple, M. & Ladouceur, P. (1986) The alcohol–crime relationship as an age-specific phenomenon: a longitudinal study. *Contemporary Drug Problems*, **13**, 89–115.

Thornton, D., Cookson, H. & Clark, D. (1990) Profiles of the youth custody population: dependencies, delinquencies and disciplinary infractions. In M. McMurran (Ed.), *Applying Psychology to Imprisonment: Young Offenders*. Issues in Criminological and Legal Psychology, No. 15. Leicester: British Psychological Society.

Tuck, M. (1989) *Drinking and Disorder: A Study of Non-Metropolitan Violence*. Home Office Research Study, No. 108. London: Home Office.

Tucker, J.A., Vuchinich, R.E. & Downey, K.K. (1992) Substance abuse. In S.M. Turner, K.S. Calhoun & H.E. Adams (Eds), *Handbook of Clinical Behavior Therapy*, 2nd edn. New York: Wiley.

Wanigaratne, S., Wallace, W., Pullin, J., Keaney, F. & Farmer, R. (1990) *Relapse Prevention for Addictive Behaviours: A Manual for Therapists*. Oxford: Blackwell.

Werch, C.E., Gorman, D.R. & Marty, P.J. (1987) Relationship between alcohol consumption and alcohol problems in young adults. *Journal of Drug Education*, **17**, 261–276.

West, D.J. & Farrington, D.P. (1977) *The Delinquent Way of Life*. London: Heinemann.

White, R. & Boyer, K. (1985) Alcoholism among the Tasmanian prison population: a research note. *Australian and New Zealand Journal of Criminology*, **18**, 109–114.

CHAPTER NINE

YOUNG OFFENDERS
Clive R. Hollin

The aim of this chapter is first to offer an overview of current psychological approaches, based on behavioural and cognitive-behavioural theory, to the treatment of delinquent behaviour. In this light, the content should be seen narrowly as an addition to existing reviews within that theoretical tradition (e.g. Garrido & Sanchis, 1991; Hollin, 1990a, 1993; Ross & Ross, 1989), and broadly as a contribution to the field of delinquency prevention (e.g. Basta & Davidson, 1988; Farrington, 1992; Gendreau, Cullen & Bonta, 1994; Mulvey, Arthur & Reppucci, 1993). Following this overview of the literature, the second aim of this chapter is to look at the issue of "what works" in the treatment of offending behaviour.

CHANGING DELINQUENT BEHAVIOUR

For the sake of review, the practice of behavioural and cognitive-behavioural intervention with young offenders can be divided into two camps – individual programmes and residential and community programmes. The former can be thought of as individual in the sense of *individualized*, in that the programme is designed for a particular young offender. On the other hand, the latter can be seen as being designed for all young offenders in a particular community or residential setting.

INDIVIDUAL PROGRAMMES

The literature on individually focused intervention for young offenders can be classified into three broad types – individual behaviour therapy, social skills training and cognitive-behaviour modification (see Hollin, 1990a).

Working with Offenders: Psychological Practice in Offender Rehabilitation.
Edited by C.R. Hollin. © 1996 John Wiley & Sons Ltd.

Individual Behaviour Therapy

In its traditional form, drawing on theories of learning and applied behaviour analysis, behaviour therapy (or behaviour modification) is widely practised with a vast range of client populations (Bellack, Hersen & Kazdin, 1982). Briefly, behaviour therapy aims to modify behaviour by changing the environment in which the behaviour occurs. This can be achieved in one of two ways: through changing the setting events – such as the physical environment or the words and actions of other people – that prompt or trigger the behaviour (i.e. *stimulus control*); or by changing the consequences for the behaviour either to increase (i.e. *reinforce*) or to decrease (i.e. *punish*) the target behaviour (Martin & Pear, 1992). The major reviews of behavioural intervention with young offenders suggest that individual behaviour therapy of this persuasion is not a popular option with this population (Blakely & Davidson, 1984; Gordon & Arbuthnot, 1987; Milan, 1987). However, there are some relevant contingency management studies and typical examples are given below.

Reinforcement

Fo & O'Donnell (1974, 1975) devised the "buddy system" in which trained adult volunteers were paired with young offenders to increase (i.e. *reinforce*) socially acceptable behaviour. A two-year follow-up (O'Donnell, Lydgate & Fo, 1979) found mixed results: serious offenders appeared to improve, while young people who had committed only minor offences showed an increased arrest rate.

Daniel (1987) devised a *stimulus satiation* programme for use with a young firesetter. This type of programme is based on the withholding of contingent reinforcement, leading to extinction of the behaviour. The programme consisted of a series of 50-minute sessions during which the young offender lit matches according to agreed rules. After eight sessions the time the young person spent striking matches per session began to decrease; after 10 sessions the young offender refused to continue with the "boring" sessions and stopped carrying matches. A six-month follow-up showed no further convictions for fire setting.

Punishment

Individually based punishment programmes are a rarity in rehabilitative programmes with young offenders. Restitution and reparation programmes, i.e. financial recompense and apology, are probably the nearest to a punishment means of changing behaviour. Blagg (1985) described the effect of personal reparation on offenders: the young offenders required to face their victims said they were "terrified" and "felt sick", although afterwards they said they felt they had benefited enormously from the experience. While restitution programmes are generally favoured by victims, there is also some support for the position that they can be effective in reducing offending (Schneider, 1986).

Social Skills Training

There is a considerable body of research on the use of social skills training with young offenders, including adolescent sex offenders (Graves, Openshaw & Adams, 1992), for which detailed reviews are available (Henderson & Hollin, 1983, 1986; Hollin, 1990b). These social skills training programmes have focused on micro-skills such as eye contact and body posture; macro-skills such as negotiating with parents and handling encounters with the police; and institutional behaviour such as avoiding fights. The effectiveness of social skills training has been assessed using measures of discrete skill performance, behaviour ratings, changes in cognition, institutional performance and recidivism. Broadly speaking, social skills training has been found to be effective as assessed by the behavioural and cognitive measures; but there is little in the way of convincing evidence that social skills training can lead to a reduction in offending.

Cognitive–Behavioural Programmes

While behaviour therapy is traditionally associated with operant theory, and social skills training with models of skill acquisition (Argyle, 1967), the advent of the cognitive–behavioural movement marks a shift in the theoretical paradigm that informs behaviour therapy. Although the exact parameters of this theoretical shift are a matter of debate (Fishman, Rotgers & Franks, 1988), it is generally agreed that a distinguishing feature of cognitive–behaviourism is the application of both social learning theory and cognitive theory to inform therapeutic methods. Thus a cognitive–behavioural style of therapy is marked by an increased emphasis on understanding the role of social factors, alongside a focus on changing affect and cognition as well as overt behaviour. As reviewed by Hollin (1990a) a range of cognitive–behavioural programmes for young offenders have been reported in the literature and a sample is presented below.

Self-control and Self-instruction

Cognitive–developmental research suggests that most children achieve self-control as covert or "inner" speech develops to govern voluntary actions (Luria, 1961). Such inner speech, as self-statements or self-talk, serves several functions including self-observation, self-evaluation and self-reinforcement. The modification of self-statements to achieve increased self-control can be attempted through *self-instructional training* (Goldstein & Kellar, 1987). Some studies have employed self-institutional training with young offenders and have found that it does increase self-control and accordingly decreases aggressive behaviour (Snyder & White, 1979).

Anger Control

A further application of self-control procedures has been in interventions specifically designed for anger control. Most closely identified with the work of Novaco (1975, 1979, 1985, 1994), there are anger control programmes specifically for adolescent populations (Feindler & Ecton, 1986). A typical anger management programme consists of three stages – cognitive preparation, skill acquisition and application training – not with the aim of eliminating anger but of lowering the frequency of aggressive behaviour through increasing control over angry arousal. There have been several studies of anger control with young offenders. A typical study by McDougall et al. (1987) with 18 institutionalized young offenders found that the anger control programme assisted in lowering the level of institutional offending. Lochman (1992) reported a three-year follow-up of aggressive young men participating in a school-based anger control programme. The results were encouraging in showing that compared to untreated controls the treated group had lower rates of substance abuse and higher levels of self-esteem and social problem-solving skills. There was no evidence, however, that the programme had a significant long-term effect on delinquent behaviour.

Role Taking

Chandler (1973) describes a programme designed to encourage male young offenders to see themselves from the perspective of other people and so to develop their own role-taking abilities. The study was a clear clinical success, enhancing the young offenders' role-taking skill. A similarly successful programme in social perspective-taking skills, carried out with female delinquents, has been reported by Chalmers & Townsend (1990).

Social Problem-solving

Spivack, Platt & Shure (1976) suggested that several cognitive problem-solving skills are necessary for successful social interaction. These cognitive skills include sensitivity to interpersonal problems; the ability to choose the desired outcome of a social exchange ("means–end thinking"); considering the likely outcomes of one's actions ("consequential thinking"); and generating different ways to achieve the desired outcome ("alternative thinking"). In social problem-solving skills training a variety of training techniques, including modelling, role play and discussion, are blended with cognitive techniques, principally self-instructional training. Several studies have provided clear evidence that social problem-solving skills training can lead young offenders to generate more solutions to social problems (e.g. Hains, 1984).

Moral Reasoning Development

A steady string of empirical studies has suggested that immature moral reasoning is a general characteristic of juvenile delinquents (Nelson, Smith & Dodd, 1990). In this light, several programmes have been designed to increase moral reasoning in young offenders. In a typical study, Gibbs et al. (1984) conducted an intervention in the form of small group discussions on a range of socio-moral dilemmas: the young offenders not only gave their views, but were required to justify their opinions and to attempt to reach a consensus on the best solution. As assessed by a measure of Kohlberg's moral judgement stages, the intervention led to a significant upward shift in moral reasoning ability.

Multimodal Programmes

Some programmes have incorporated a variety of the methods discussed above into a multimodal treatment programme. Gross et al. (1980) used a combination of social skills training, behaviour therapy and self-management training with 10 female young offenders. The programme improved self-control, reduced problem behaviour and reduced school absenteeism. There are some similar programmes, including *Aggression Replacement Training* (ART; Glick & Goldstein, 1987). ART uses three main approaches to changing behaviour: structured learning training, including social skills training and social problem-solving training; anger control training; and moral education. The outcome studies show that ART does lead to improved skills, greater self-control and improved institutional behaviour. Leeman, Gibbs & Fuller (1993) similarly found that their multicomponent programme, based on ART, was successful in both improving conduct and lowering recidivism.

The Reasoning and Rehabilitation Programme developed by Ross & Fabiano (1985) also incorporates several methods and techniques. Based on their analysis of cognitive mediators of aggression in adolescent offenders (Slaby & Guerra, 1988), Guerra & Slaby (1990) designed an intervention programme to bring about change in those cognitive factors associated with aggression. Guerra & Slaby report that the programme was successful in increasing social problem-solving skills, led to less firm belief in the legitimacy of aggression, and reduced the frequency of aggressive behaviour. However, there were no long-term gains from the programme as assessed by parole violations.

As many practitioners will testify, the key to this type of work lies in assessment (Hollin, Epps & Kendrick, 1995). The brief case outline given below provides a perfect illustration of the need for clear assessment in programme planning.

Case example

Geoff, aged 15 years, was admitted to a secure residential establishment because of a long history of unmanageable behaviour. His case notes revealed that he had experienced an early family breakdown, followed by a series of foster home placements, eventually culminating in placement in a children's home. The notes revealed that over the last two years in particular he had perpetrated an increasingly more violent series of assaults on members of staff. The assaults had resulted in several moves to ever more secure establishments with the eventual move to a highly secure placement.

Geoff's first weeks in his placement were relatively uneventful, no doubt due in part to the behavioural control system in operation. However, as Geoff settled into the routines and institutional control began to relax, he became increasingly hostile in his behaviour towards staff. Initially this was seen in displays of verbal aggression, but quickly escalated to physical assaults on staff. The immediate response by the staff was to initiate an anger management programme to help Geoff control his violence. Geoff's high scores on several anger arousal scales appeared to validate this approach. It quickly became apparent, however, that this initial response was not working: Geoff said he found the anger control sessions to be of little relevance and the violent attacks continued.

While the initial response to the problem was perfectly rational and understandable – many people who commit assaults do respond positively to anger control programmes, and there was a genuine need to act quickly – the initial strategy was clearly not working. A series of behavioural observations and interviews began to suggest a different pattern.

Careful recording of the violent incidents revealed that while the violence was mainly directed towards members of staff with whom Geoff was interacting, occasionally there would be violent incidents in which Geoff was not involved with the member of staff before the assault. Careful interviewing, with a young person not inclined to be co-operative, suggested that his anger and violence stemmed from his own idiosyncratic appraisal of situations. His view was that the staff were there to be of service to him and his peers and when, according to his own laws, he perceived them "acting out of turn", he saw it as his right to exact justice, either on his own behalf or for his peers. Thus, when he saw the words or actions of a member of staff not to be in accord with what he believed to be right and proper, he would become angry, and acting as judge, jury and executioner exact retribution.

Following this assessment, the focus of the intervention moved to counselling to challenge his rules about his "rights", problem solving to help him generate better ways of dealing with situations, training in "stop and think" strategies to help him curb his impulsive acts, and social skills training to help construct more acceptable ways of interacting with staff.

INSTITUTION AND COMMUNITY PROGRAMMES

In contrast to individually focused approaches, the distinguishing feature of this approach is on behavioural change via the social influence of an agency such as a residential establishment or a family.

First, with regard to institutions, the distinction can be drawn between those establishments, generally prisons, with an emphasis on custody and security and treatment a secondary consideration; and institutions with the focus on treatment, and security a lesser consideration, as in many residential establishments.

Secure Institutions

From the reviews of the application of behavioural techniques in secure institutions (Nietzel, 1979; Milan, 1987), clearly the token economy programme (TEP) has been the single most widespread method of behaviour change used in prisons. Simply, the TEP offers a system of reinforcing behaviour by the contingent use of tokens that can later be exchanged for reinforcers such as confectionary and extra privileges. The TEP can be used in two ways: as an aid to management control, or as a means of clinical intervention. There are several examples, mainly American, of the first use of the TEP (see Milan, 1987), and a smaller number of treatment studies (e.g. Cullen & Seddon, 1981). Few practitioners would disagree that the TEP is an effective means of changing behaviour. With young offenders, TEPs have been used successfully to improve behavioural targets such as self-maintenance, institutional discipline and academic standards. However, there are only a few follow-up studies, and, of those completed, there is little evidence to show any systematic effect on reoffending. The most recent moves are towards the adoption of formal treatment programmes, such as the Reasoning and Rehabilitation Programme (Ross & Fabiano, 1985), in juvenile prisons (Garrido & Sanchis, 1991).

Residential Establishments

The "Achievement Place" style of residential provision has generated a great deal of interest in both behavioural literature and practice. The first Achievement Place, in Kansas, proved to be a model of residential care later followed by over 200 establishments in the USA and to a lesser extent in the UK. Two notable features of the Achievement Place style are the "teaching parents" and the use of behavioural methods of change. Achievement Place itself is based on a collection of family-style homes, each run by a trained married couple, for about six young offenders per home. The couple have the role of teaching parents: they have responsibility for specific behaviour change programmes, such as skills training, together with the less-structured task of parental child care. The behaviour change system progresses from a TEP to a "merit system", with a peer manager system; alongside which individually based programmes in social, educational and self-management skills also take place (see Burchard & Lane, 1982). There are several reviews of the wealth of research output from Achievement Place, the most recent by Braukmann & Wolf (1987).

The first major outcome study of Achievement Place compared 13 Achievement Place homes with nine group homes that had not used a teaching parent approach at a one-year follow-up (Kirigin et al., 1982). It was found that during the period in which the programme was running, the young offenders at Achievement Place were at a significant advantage with regard to offending. However, this advantage was not maintained after a one-year period. At least two other outcome studies have reported similar findings (Weinrott, Jones & Howard, 1982; Braukmann & Wolf, 1987). It appears overall that the achievement place model is successful in reducing offending while in operation, but that this success does not always transfer to the community in the longer term.

Obviously residential practice continues to develop. Hagan & King (1992) describe an intensive treatment programme conducted in a correctional facility for young offenders. This programme combined a range of interventions, including individual cognitive and psychotherapy, a residential management programme, education, family therapy and an independent living programme. At a two-year follow-up, there were encouraging findings with regard to the success of the programme in reducing return to further correctional placements. Similar examples of successful residential outcomes, even with the most difficult and disadvantaged young people, are sprinkled throughout the literature (e.g. Bullock et al., 1990; Haghighi & Lopez, 1993; Epps, 1994).

School-based Intervention

One of the most widely cited programmes in the literature is the Preparation through Responsive Education Programme (PREP) described in several publications in the late 1970s (see Burchard & Lane, 1982, for a review). Based in Maryland, USA, PREP was designed for pupils recommended to the programme because of academic, social and offending problems. PREP consisted of academic tutoring, social skills training and some family work. The outcome data, from over 600 pupils, showed that the programme had a significant impact on school discipline and academic performance. However, there was little indication that the programme had an effect on offending.

Family-based Intervention

Parent Management Training

Parent management training (PMT) aims to modify, through training, the way in which parents interact with their children. Typically, this training aims to guide parents to reinforce appropriate behaviour and to use appropriate discipline for inappropriate behaviour. Some studies have been carried out looking at the effects of PMT with young offenders and their families (Bank, Patterson & Reid, 1987). The findings clearly show that PMT has beneficial effects on family communication and family relationships, with some indication of a reduction in offending. A study by Kazdin, Siegal & Bass (1992) evaluated the combined effects of problem-solving skills training and PMT targeted at children showing severe antisocial behaviour. They found that the treatments combined were highly effective in ameliorating aggression and antisocial behaviour, as well as parental stress and depression.

Functional Family Therapy

While there are similarities between PMT and functional family therapy (FFT), in the latter the emphasis is much more explicitly focused on family interaction. Several studies have used *contingency contracting* as a means of changing family interaction in cases of young offenders, with success in reducing offending (Stumphauzer, 1976; Welch, 1985). Other studies, in sympathy with a multimodal approach, have used a broader range of techniques: Henderson (1981) used behavioural, cognitive and FFT methods in a programme that was successful in reducing stealing. Similarly, Alexander & Parsons (1973) used skills training, contingency contracting and problem-solving training to improve family interaction. A series of follow-up studies showed that the families participating in the FFT had lower offending for both the young offenders themselves (Alexander et al., 1976), and for the younger siblings of the offender (Klein, Alexander & Parsons, 1977). The data from FFT studies strongly suggest that the intervention can both have a beneficial effect on family interactions, and reduce recidivism. It is increasingly evident that work with families must be an important ingredient in working with young offenders Kazdin, (e.g. 1987; Henggeler et al., 1993).

Probation

As several commentators have noted (e.g. Hudson, 1986), behavioural case-work is used by some probation officers, with social skills training proving particularly popular. In a review, Remington & Remington (1987) suggest that there is enormous scope for use of behavioural methods in probation work. Many problems faced by offenders – anxiety, depression, drug and alcohol abuse, and so on – are precisely those in which behavioural intervention has proved effective. Further, it is evident that training programmes can be successful in equipping probation officers with the skills to be effective behaviour therapists (e.g. Wood, Green & Bry, 1982). The STOP Project conducted by Mid-Glamorgan Probation Service in Wales was based on the Reasoning and Rehabilitation Programme (Ross & Fabiano, 1985; Ross & Ross, 1988, 1989). At a one-year follow-up the findings showed that those offenders (not all juveniles) who completed the STOP programme showed lower rates of reconviction than comparable offenders who had received custodial sentences (Raynor & Vanstone, 1994). Indeed, the use of intensive probation and supervision schemes, sometimes incorporating treatment elements, as an alternative to custody is currently a focus of attention (Brownlee & Joanes, 1993; Gendreau, Cullen & Bonta, 1994).

Diversionary Projects

There are several measures that have the aim of diverting young offenders from custody and so, it is argued, away from the detrimental effects of the criminal justice system. *Intermediate treatment* (IT) is one such diversionary strategy that inspired a rush of programmes and schemes. One IT scheme, Birmingham Action for Youth (BAY), used a range of behavioural methods, including a reinforcement programme and social skills training, to prepare young offenders for employment (Preston, 1982). While the young peoples' level of actual employment was low after leaving the scheme, a short-term follow-up did show some reduction in offending. Several programmes in the USA have suggested that diversionary schemes can reduce offending (e.g. Davidson et al., 1987, 1990).

This overview of the literature raises the important issues of "does treatment work?" If so, then what elements are contained in successful programmes?

DOES TREATMENT WORK?

To place what follows in context, there are two points to make. First, as Roberts (1987) notes: "In view of the millions of dollars expended each year to protect society, care for, and rehabilitate juvenile offenders, it is astonishing that so few systematic research and follow-up studies have been conducted by juvenile justice agencies" (p. 44). Secondly, not only is there a general lack of research, but, as Blakely & Davidson (1984) observe, "After twenty years of research, it is unfortunate that delinquent behavior is assessed directly in less than half of the available research" (p. 261). Thus, not only is there little in the way of systematic research, but the research that is available fails in large part to say anything about offending. It follows that any lessons that can be taken from the research are, in truth, based on a tiny sample of the rehabilitative work taking place. With this caveat in mind, there are some important points to be made in the light of recent developments in the field.

MAKING SENSE OF THE EVIDENCE

Narrative Review

In essence the problem of making sense of the evidence is very much an academic one: in the field of offender rehabilitation, for example, we are faced with many different types of intervention, conducted in different settings, with different measures of "success". As there are literally hundreds of outcome studies, how can meaningful conclusions be drawn from this literature about what works, for whom, and under what conditions?

The traditional approach to making sense of a large body of research evidence was for a reviewer to conduct a narrative or qualitative literature review. The skill of the narrative reviewer lies in gathering the relevant literature and through personal interpretation and judgement offering a view of the messages inherent in the literature. Such a narrative approach often uses the tactic of pooling the results of several hundred studies and "vote counting". For example, suppose some studies show no effect of rehabilitative efforts, while other studies, but less of them, show a positive effect of rehabilitation: by simply counting the votes, the general conclusion to be drawn is that rehabilitation with offenders does not work.

Now, as several authors note (e.g. Gendreau & Andrews, 1990; Cook et al., 1992), such an approach to understanding the messages embedded in a large empirical literature is not without its drawbacks. Not only is there a risk of author bias in the conclusions presented in the narrative, but consideration must also be given to the demands of the intellectual task of attempting to balance the effects of different studies, with different strengths, employing different methods, and conducted under different conditions and in different settings. Thus, the position is reached in which some narrative reviews of offender rehabilitation are pessimistic in concluding the nothing works (Martinson, 1974; Lipton, Martinson & Wilks, 1975); while other narrative reviews claim that there are successful treatments (e.g. Gendreau & Ross, 1979, 1987; Ross & Gendreau, 1980). The development of the statistical technique of *meta-analysis* has gone some way towards providing a means by which to produce a standardized summary of a large number of studies.

Meta-analysis

As Izzo & Ross (1990) explain, meta-analysis is

> A technique that enables a reviewer to objectively and statistically analyse the findings of each study as data points ... The procedure of meta-analysis involves collection of relevant studies, using the summary statistics from each study as units of analysis, and then analysing the aggregated data in a quantitative manner using statistical tests. (p. 135)

For example, in a typical meta-analytic study, Garrett (1985) included in her analysis 111 studies reported between 1960 and 1983, involving a total of 13 055 young offenders. The results of such a meta-analysis allow conclusions to be made about whether treatment works, and allow estimates to be made of what type of intervention works best in what setting.

There have been several meta-analytic studies of the offender treatment literature (Andrews et al., 1990; Garrett, 1985; Gottschalk et al., 1987; Izzo & Ross, 1990; Lipsey, 1992; Lösel & Köferl, 1989; Roberts & Camasso, 1991; Whitehead & Lab, 1989), with a summary provided by Gendreau & Andrews (1990). As with most research, later studies can build upon and avoid the criticisms levelled at earlier efforts, therefore the conclusions listed below are based mainly on the two most recent meta-analytic studies reported by Andrews et al. (1990) and by Lipsey (1992).

Outcome Measures

As is evident from the studies discussed above, the experimental literature involves a wide range of both qualitative and quantitative outcome measures such as cognitive variables, social skills, family functioning, academic performance and institutional behaviour. Such outcome measures make sense in judging the effectiveness of interventions in bringing about personal change, but what relevance do they have to offending? While there are studies that show differences between offenders and non-offenders on the types of measures noted above (e.g. Ross & Fabiano, 1985; Quay, 1987), it is a large theoretical assumption that these factors are functionally related to offending. It follows then, that the assumption is stretched still further if it is taken that changing the clinical target will, in turn, modify the offending (Hollin & Henderson, 1984). For example, Gaffney & McFall (1981) made the observation that: "Although the data show a relationship between a lack of competence in social situations and delinquent behavior, the research does not provide evidence that delinquency is caused by a lack of social skills" (p. 967). Indeed, Emery & Marholin (1977) suggested that less than one-third of the studies they reviewed established a case for relating referral and target behaviours.

At both a theoretical level and an individual clinical level, establishing a functional relationship between clinical measures and offending is an empirical concern. Without an empirical foundation and rigorous offence assessment with an individual offender, treatment programmes are left hoping that their targets will be the right ones. Given this, it is not surprising that the major reviews reported in the early 1980s fail to show any systematic and consistent effect of cognitive–behavioural intervention in offending (Burchard & Lane, 1982; Blakely & Davidson, 1984). However, the impact of the meta-analyses has been to allow some firmer conclusions to be made about "what works" in terms of reducing offending.

Findings

The points given below are those linked with *reduced offending* as an outcome variable. It is important to note that this says nothing about clinical or personal change. It is, however, clear that psychological, educational and behavioural treatment programmes are effective in bringing about clinical change (Lipsey & Wilson, 1993).

The initial point to note is that indiscriminate targeting of treatment programmes may be counter-productive in reducing recidivism. Andrews & Bonta (1994) suggest that the *risk principle* states that important predictors of success are that offenders assessed (by criminal history or a standardized measure) as being medium to high risk of recidivism should be selected for intensive programmes. A programme developed incorporating the risk principle, and showing signs of success in reducing recidivism, has been designed by Howell & Enns (in press).

The type of treatment programme is important: "More structured and focused treatments (e.g., behavioral, skill-orientated) and multimodal treatments seem to be more effective than the less structured and focused approaches (e.g., counseling)" (Lipsey, 1992, p. 123). On the other hand, Andrews et al. (1990) suggest that some therapeutic approaches are not suitable for general use with offenders. Specifically, they argue that "Traditional psychodynamic and non-directive client-centred therapies are to be avoided within general samples of offenders" (p. 376). This leads Andrews & Bonta (1994) to the *responsivity principle*: the need to deliver programmes in a way that is congruent with the style of service delivery to which young offenders will be likely to respond.

However, the most successful studies, while behavioural in nature, include a cognitive component in order to focus on the "attitudes, values, and beliefs that support anti-social behaviour" (Gendreau & Andrews, 1990, p. 182). Roberts & Camasso (1991) also stress the importance of working with families to reduce recidivism. The focus on offending is in keeping with the *need principle*, as Andrews & Bonta (1994) explain:

> Many offenders, especially high-risk offenders, have a variety of needs. They need places to live and work and/or they need to stop taking drugs. Some have poor self-esteem, chronic headaches or cavities in their teeth. These are all "needs". The need principle draws our attention to the distinction between *criminogenic* and *noncriminogenic* needs. Criminogenic needs are a subset of an offender's risk level. They are dynamic attributes of an offender that, when changed, are associated with changes in the probability of recidivism. Non-criminogenic needs are also dynamic and changeable, but these changes are not necessarily associated with the probability of recidivism. (p. 176)

With respect to setting, treatment programmes conducted in the community are likely to have stronger effects on delinquency than residential programmes. While residential programmes can be effective, they should be structurally linked with community-based interventions. Further, programmes that help the offender to gain real employment in the community have a significantly enhanced chance of success.

Finally, the meta-analyses strongly suggest that the most effective programmes have high "treatment integrity". In essence, this means that the programmes are conducted by trained staff, while those individuals responsible for the management and supervision of treatment are involved in all the operational phases of the programme (Hollin, 1995; Hollin, Epps & Kendrick, 1995; Lösel & Wittmann, 1989).

Given the above, Lipsey (1992) concludes that treatment can produce decreases in recidivism of 20–40% above the baseline levels from mainstream criminal sanctioning of offenders. It is fair to conclude that it is not true that "nothing works" when it comes to the treatment of offenders: intervention, particularly cognitive-behavioural intervention, can have an impact on a range of target behaviours, including criminal behaviours.

The impact of the meta-analyses has been seen in several areas. There has been a willingness to reassert the potential effectiveness of intervention and place rehabilitation of young offenders back on the political agenda (e.g. Palmer, 1991, 1992). Allied to this, there is a new firmness in both questioning sentencing practices (Andrews, 1990) and promoting effective policies (Leschied & Gendreau, 1994). Finally, efforts are being made to bridge the research–practice divide by distilling the complexities of the meta-analysis into blueprints for the design of effective programmes (Antonowicz & Ross, 1994; Coulson & Nutbrown, 1992; Gendreau, in press; Lösel, 1995).

It would be a mistake, however, to assume that there is a consensus in the field and that everyone is pulling in the same direction. There are several barriers to success that merit discussion.

BARRIERS TO SUCCESS

There are four key areas of resistance that provide barriers to success: these are client resistance, institutional resistance, resistance to treatment integrity, and social resistance.

CLIENT RESISTANCE

The concept of client resistance refers to the reluctance of young offenders to engage in rehabilitation programmes. This is a problem for practitioners to solve as shown in the development of the technique of "motivational interviewing" (Miller & Rollnick, 1991). With particular emphasis on problem drinking, Miller (1985) described a range of variables – including client characteristics, environmental factors and therapist characteristics – to explain a client's lack of motivation for engaging in a clinical programme. However, Miller also suggested that motivation to engage in treatment can be encouraged by attention to all three of these areas: "When motivation is conceptualized as a probability of behaviour occurring within an interpersonal context, however, psychological interventions can be developed and evaluated for increasing the likelihood of entering, continuing in, and complying with recovery-relevant actions" (p. 99). Perkins (1991) has outlined strategies based on both the psychology of persuasion and contingency management for engaging therapeutically with sex offenders characterized by high levels of denial. The tailoring of such techniques to working with young offenders would be a welcome development.

INSTITUTIONAL RESISTANCE

This type of resistance refers to the obstacles – be it in a community or residential setting – that impede the progress that might be made with a properly implemented treatment programme. Laws (1974) has described the barriers he faced in attempting to set up a residential behavioural programme with offenders. Essentially, the barriers were about control: control over admission to the programme, offenders leaving the programme before its completion, control over finances, control over staff training. Laws, as have others, documented professional clashes both with administrators and fellow practitioners. Overcoming such institutional resistance implies a need for greater political and organizational awareness and ability by behavioural practitioners. As Burchard & Lane (1982) comment: "With respect to resistance to change . . . behavior-modification advocates who do not recognize that much of their time will be spent trying to change the behavior of staff and policy and administrators are in for a rude awakening" (p. 616).

RESISTANCE TO TREATMENT INTEGRITY

The third barrier lies in the realization of the concept of *treatment integrity*. As the meta-analysis shows, any treatment programme, whatever its theoretical base, can only stand a chance of being successful if it is rigorously and properly implemented. Solid and effective treatment programmes do not magically appear overnight: they require planning for both content and resources; trained personnel to conduct assessments and deliver treatment; and the flexibility to cope with the varying demands and problems presented by different clients.

SOCIAL RESISTANCE

The final barrier lies in the domain of social resistance to the principle of working with young offenders. Two strands to social resistance can be identified: the first is public and political resistance; the second is academic resistance or what Gendreau (in press) terms "theorecticism", or "knowledge destruction" as Andrews & Wormith (1989) prefer.

There is a great deal of rhetoric to the effect that the public at large has no heart for rehabilitation and is more concerned with retribution and punishment. However, as Gardiner (1956) so eloquently said, "To some politicians, too, it may not be unfair to say that public opinion is 'the clamour of the ignorant mob' when they do not support the politician's view, and the 'voice of the people' when they do" (p. 68). Indeed, it is interesting that empirical studies suggest that while the public are far from being against punishment, there is a view that rehabilitation should be one of the goals of the criminal justice system (Cullen et al., 1990). As Cullen et al. note, the tenacity of a belief in the need for rehabilitation is probably pragmatic in that offenders "should be given the education, training, employment experiences, and, perhaps, counselling that will enable them to become productive citizens" (pp 15–16). It is probably true that most victims of crime simply want their property back, want not to be revictimized, want for their friends and neighbours not to suffer in the same way, and finally want the offender to be caught and not reoffend. Accepting the need for some degree of retribution, it is a matter of debate whether there would be strong public support for harsh punitive measures of doubtful effect on reoffending (Gendreau et al., 1993; Macallair, 1993; Mathlas & Mathews, 1991; Thornton et al., 1984).

Academic resistance to working with offenders is not hard to find. As Gendreau (in press) notes, there are two main tactics used in knowledge destruction (see also Andrews, 1989; Andrews & Wormith, 1989): the first is to ignore or to dismiss on spurious grounds findings that are not in accord with one's own favoured position; the second is to mount broad-scale "philosophical" arguments against rehabilitation. As an example of the first tactic, Pitts (1992) mounts the argument that the view that "something works" in rehabilitation is, basically, a right-wing government plot. Pitts argues that rehabilitation of offenders does not work because a string of studies has shown this to be true. The studies cited in support of this position span the period 1969 to 1980, and are inferred to have established as "fact" the "abandonment of the quest for effective forms of rehabilitation" (p. 135). The renewed interest in rehabilitation in the 1990s is, following Pitts' analysis, a government scheme to "rationalise expenditure on criminal justice" (p. 133). However, what about, for example, the impact of the meta-analyses, reported from 1985 onwards, and the changes they have caused in contemporary thinking about rehabilitative possibilities? Not a citation to be found: indeed, the evidence to balance the "fact" that "nothing works" is conveniently dealt with by "putting [it] to one side" (p. 133). Now, the point here is not to deny that Pitts' analysis of government policy may be correct; it may arguably be valid to a greater or lesser degree. Rather the point here is to illustrate outright knowledge destruction through selective use of the literature to support a preferred thesis.

The "philosophical" objections, which most of us have faced in conferences and seminars, generally run along the lines of statements such as "human problems are intractable", "rehabilitation is about social control not freedom" and "positive findings do not have an answer to every possible question about every possible criminal group". As Gendreau has said, faced with this level of opposition, knowledge destruction wins out every time.

CONCLUSION

Thus to conclude, there are growing grounds for optimism in the field of offender treatment. If barriers can be overcome, there is every indication that the methods are available that will allow treatment interventions to have a significant impact on recidivism. It is true that there are other challenges to be met by practitioners. Legislative changes will continue to exercise practitioners in their impact on the design of treatment programmes. Similarly, technical advances, as with the application of functional analysis to offending histories in single case analysis (Gresswell & Hollin, 1992), will continue to inform the field. Nonetheless there is now a firm base from which to design effective programmes; such an achievement is to the advantage of all concerned – the offenders and their families, the potential future victims, and the public who have to bear the costs of offending.

REFERENCES

Alexander, J.F. & Parsons, B.V. (1973) Short-term behavioral intervention with delinquent families: impact on family processes and recidivism. *Journal of Abnormal Psychology*, **81**, 223–231.
Alexander, J.F. Barton, C., Schiavo, R.S. & Parsons, B.V. (1976) Systems behavioral intervention with families of delinquents: therapist characteristics, family behavior, and outcome. *Journal of Consulting and Clinical Psychology*, **44**, 656–664.
Andrews, D.A. (1989) Recidivism is predictable and can be influenced: Using risk assessments to reduce recidivism. *Forum on Corrections Research*, **1**, 11–18.
Andrews, D.A. (1990) Some criminological sources of anti-rehabilitation bias in the Report of The Canadian Sentencing Commission. *Canadian Journal of Criminology*, **32**, 511–524.
Andrews, D.A. & Bonta, J. (1994) *The Psychology of Criminal Conduct*. Cincinnati, OH: Anderson.
Andrews, D.A. & Wormith, J.S. (1989) Personality and crime: knowledge destruction and construction in criminology. *Justice Quarterly*, **6**, 289–309.

Andrews, D.A., Zinger, I., Hoge, R.D., Bonta, J., Gendreau, P. & Cullen, F.T. (1990) Does correctional treatment work? A clinically relevant and psychologically informed meta-analysis. *Criminology*, **28**, 369–404.

Antonowicz, D.H. & Ross, R.R. (1994) Essential components of successful rehabilitation programs for offenders. *International Journal of Offender Therapy and Comparative Criminology*, **38**, 97–104.

Argyle, M. (1967) *The Psychology of Interpersonal Behaviour*. Harmondsworth, Middlesex: Penguin.

Bank, L., Patterson, G.R. & Reid, J.B. (1987). Delinquency prevention through training parents in family management. *Behavior Analyst*, 75–82.

Basta, J.M. & Davidson, W.S. (1988) Treatment of juvenile offenders: study outcomes since 1980. *Behavioral Sciences and the Law*, **6**, 355–384.

Bellack, A.S., Hersen, M. & Kazdin, A.E. (Eds) (1982) *International Handbook of Behavior Modification and Therapy*. New York: Plenum.

Blagg, H. (1985) Reparation and justice for juveniles. *British Journal of Criminology*, **25**, 267–279.

Blakely, C.H. & Davidson, W.S. (1984) Behavioral approaches to delinquency: a review. In P. Karoly & J.J. Steffan (Eds), *Adolescent Behavior Disorders: Foundations and Contemporary Concerns*. Lexington, MA: Lexington Books.

Braukmann, C.J. & Wolf, M.M. (1987) Behaviourally based group homes for juvenile offenders. In E.K. Morris & C.J. Braukmann (Eds), *Behavioral Approaches to Crime and Delinquency: A Handbook of Application, Research, and Concepts*. New York: Plenum.

Brownlee, I.D. & Joanes, D. (1993) Intensive probation for young adult offenders. *British Journal of Criminology*, **33**, 216–230.

Bullock, R., Hosie, K., Little, M. & Millham, S. (1990) Secure accommodation for very difficult adolescents: some recent research findings. *Journal of Adolescence*, **13**, 205–216.

Burchard, J.D. & Lane, T.W. (1982) Crime and delinquency. In A.S. Bellack, M. Hersen & A.E. Kazdin (Eds), *International Handbook of Behavior Modification and Therapy*. New York: Plenum.

Chalmers, J.B. & Townsend, M.A.R. (1990) The effects of training in social perspective taking on socially maladjusted girls. *Child Development*, **61**, 178–190.

Chandler, M.J. (1973) Egocentrism and anti-social behavior: the assessment and training of social perspective-taking skills. *Developmental Psychology*, **9**, 326–332.

Cook, T.D., Cooper, H., Cordray, D.S., Hartmann, H., Hedges, L.V., Light, R.J., Louis, T.A. & Mosteller, F. (Eds) (1992) *Meta-analysis for Explanation: A Casebook*. New York: Russell Sage.

Coulson, G.E. & Nutbrown, V. (1992) Properties of an ideal rehabilitative program for high-need offenders. *International Journal of Offender Therapy and Comparative Criminology*, **36**, 203–208.

Cullen, F.T., Skovron, S.E., Scott, J.E. & Burton, V.S. (1990) Public support for correctional treatment: the tenacity of rehabilitative ideology. *Criminal Justice and Behaviour*, **17**, 6–18.

Cullen, J.E. & Seddon, J.W. (1981) The application of a behavioural regime to disturbed young offenders. *Personality and Individual Differences*, **2**, 285–292.

Daniel, C.J. (1987) A stimulus satiation treatment programme with a young male firesetter. In B.J. McGurk, D.M. Thornton & M. Williams (Eds), *Applying Psychology to Imprisonment: Theory & Practice*. London: HMSO.

Davidson, W.S., Redner, R., Blakely, C.H., Mitchell, C.M. Mitchell, C.M. & Emshoff,

J.G. (1987) Diversion of juvenile offenders: an experimental comparison. *Journal of Consulting and Clinical Psychology*, **55**, 68–75.

Davidson, W.S., Redner, R., Andur, R.C. & Mitchell, C.M. (1990) *Alternative Treatments for Troubled Youth: The Case of Diversion from the Justice System.* New York: Plenum.

Emery, R.E. & Marholin, D. (1977) An applied behavior analysis of delinquency: the irrelevancy of relevant behavior. *American Psychologist*, **6**, 860–873.

Epps, K.J. (1994) Treating adolescent sex offenders in secure conditions: the experience at Glenthorne Centre. *Journal of Adolescence*, **17**, 105–122.

Farrington, D.P. (1992) Psychological contributions to the explanation, prevention and treatment of offending. In F. Lösel, D. Bender & T. Bliesener (Eds), *Psychology and Law: International Perspectives.* Berlin: De Gruyter.

Feindler, E.L. & Ecton, R.B. (1986) *Adolescent Anger Control: Cognitive–Behavioral Techniques.* New York: Pergamon.

Fishman, D.B., Rotgers, F. & Franks, C.M. (Eds) (1988) *Paradigms in Behavior Therapy: Present and Promise.* New York: Springer.

Fo, W.S.O. & O'Donnell, C.R. (1974) The buddy system: relationship and contingency conditions in a community intervention program for youth and non-professionals as behavior change agents. *Journal of Consulting and Clinical Psychology*, **42**, 163–168.

Fo, W.S.O. & O'Donnell, C.R. (1975) The buddy system: effect of community intervention on delinquent offences. *Behavior Therapy*, **6**, 522–524.

Gaffney, L.R. & McFall, R.M. (1981) A comparison of social skills in delinquent and nondelinquent adolescent girls using a behavioral role-playing inventory. *Journal of Consulting and Clinical Psychology*, **49**, 959–967.

Gardiner, G. (1956) *Capital Punishment as a Deterrent: And the Alternative.* London: Victor Gollancz.

Garrett, C.J. (1985) Effects of residential treatment on adjudicated delinquents: a meta-analysis. *Journal of Research on Crime and Delinquency*, **22**, 287–308.

Garrido, V. & Sanchis, J.R. (1991) The cognitive model in the treatment of Spanish offenders: theory and practice. *Journal of Correctional Education*, **42**, 111–118.

Gendreau, P. (1995) Offender rehabilitation: what we know and what needs to be done. *Criminal Justice and Behavior*, in press.

Gendreau, P. & Andrews, D.A. (1990) Tertiary prevention: what the meta-analyses of the offender treatment literature tells us about "what works". *Canadian Journal of Criminology*, **32**, 173–184.

Gendreau, P. & Ross, B. (1979) Effective correctional treatment: bibliotherapy for cynics. *Crime and Delinquency*, **25**, 463–489.

Gendreau, P. & Ross, R.R. (1987) Revivification of rehabilitation: evidence from the 1980s. *Justice Quarterly*, **4**, 349–407.

Gendreau, P., Cullen, F.T. & Bonta, J. (1994) Intensive rehabilitation supervision: the next generation in community corrections. *Federal Probation*, **58**, 72–78.

Gendreau, P., Paparozzi, M., Little, T. & Goddard, M. (1993) Does "punishing smarter" work? An assessment of the new generation of alternative sanctions in probation. *Forum on Corrections Research*, **5**, 31–34.

Gibbs, J.C., Arnold, K.D. Chessman, F.L. & Ahlborn, H.H. (1984) Facilitation of sociomoral reasoning in delinquents. *Journal of Consulting and Clinical Psychology*, **52**, 37–45.

Glick, B. & Goldstein, A.P. (1987) Aggression replacement training. *Journal of Counseling and Development*, **65**, 356–367.

Goldstein, A.P. & Keller, H. (1987) *Aggressive Behavior: Assessment and Intervention.* New York: Pergamon.

Gordon, D.A. & Arbuthnot, J. (1987) Individual, group and family interventions. In H.C. Quay (Ed.), *Handbook of Juvenile Delinquency*. New York: Wiley.

Gottschalk, R., Davidson, W.S., Gensheimer, L.K. & Mayer, J. (1987) Community-based interventions. In H.C. Quay (Ed.), *Handbook of Juvenile Delinquency*. New York: Wiley.

Graves, R., Openshaw, D.K. & Adams, G.R. (1992) Adolescent sex offenders and social skills training. *International Journal of Offender Therapy and Comparative Criminology*, **36**, 141–153.

Gresswell, D.M. & Hollin, C.R. (1992) Towards a new methodology for making sense of case material: an illustrative case involving attempted multiple murder. *Criminal Behaviour and Mental Health*, **2**, 329–341.

Gross, A.M., Brigham, T.A. Hopper, C. & Bologna, N.C. (1980) Self-management and social skills training: a study with pre-delinquent and delinquent youths. *Criminal Justice and Behavior*, **7**, 161–184.

Guerra, N.G. & Slaby, R.G. (1990) Cognitive mediators of aggression in adolescent offenders: 2. Intervention. *Developmental Psychology*, **26**, 269–277.

Hagan, M. & King, R.P. (1992) Recidivism rates of youth completing an intensive treatment program in a juvenile correctional facility. *International Journal of Offender Therapy and Comparative Criminology*, **36**, 349–358.

Haghighi, B. & Lopez, A. (1993) Success/failure of group home treatment programs for juveniles. *Federal Probation*, **57**, 53–58.

Hains, A.A. (1984) A preliminary attempt to teach the use of social problem-solving skills to delinquents. *Child Study Journal*, **14**, 271–285.

Henderson, J.Q. (1981) A behavioral approach to stealing: a proposal for treatment based on ten cases. *Journal of Behavior Therapy and Experimental Psychiatry*, **12**, 231–236.

Henderson, M. & Hollin, C.R. (1983) A critical review of social skills training with young offenders. *Criminal Justice and Behavior*, **10**, 316–341. ✗

Henderson, M. & Hollin, C.R. (1986) Social skills training and delinquency. In C.R. Hollin & P. Trower (Eds), *Handbook of Social Skills Training, Vol. 1: Applications Across the Life Span*. Oxford: Pergamon.

Henggeler, S.W., Melton, G.B., Smith, L.A., Schoewald, S.K. & Hanley, J.H. (1993) Family preservation using multisystemic treatment: long-term follow-up to a clinical trial with serious juvenile offenders. *Journal of Child and Family Studies*, **2**, 283–293.

Hollin, C.R. (1990a) *Cognitive-Behavioural Interventions with Young Offenders*. Elmsford, NY: Pergamon.

Hollin, C.R. (1990b) Social skills training with delinquents: a look at the evidence and some recommendations for practice. *British Journal of Social Work*, **20**, 483–493.

Hollin, C.R. (1993) Advances in the psychological treatment of delinquent behaviour. *Criminal Behaviour and Mental Health*, **3**, 142–157.

Hollin, C.R. (1995) The meaning and implications of "programme integrity". In J. McGuire (Ed.), *What Works: Effective Methods to Reduce Reoffending*. Chichester: Wiley.

Hollin, C.R. & Henderson, M. (1984) Social skills training with young offenders: false expectations and the "failure of treatment". *Behavioural Psychotherapy*, **12**, 331–341.

Hollin, C.R., Epps, K.J. & Kendrick, D.J. (1995) *Managing Behavioural Treatment: Policy and Practice with Delinquent Adolescents*. London: Routledge.

Howell, A.J. & Enns, R.A. (1995) A high risk recognition program for adolescents in conflict with the law. *Canadian Psychology*, in press.

Hudson, B.L. (1986) Community applications of social skills training. In C.R. Hollin & P. Trower (Eds), *Handbook of Social Skills Training, Vol. 1: Applications Across the Life Span.* Oxford: Pergamon.

Izzo, R.L. & Ross, R.R. (1990) Meta-analysis of rehabilitation programs for juvenile delinquents: a brief report. *Criminal Justice and Behavior,* **17,** 134–142.

Kazdin, A.E. (1987) Treatment of antisocial behavior in children: current status and future directions. *Psychological Bulletin,* **102,** 187–203.

Kazdin, A.E., Siegel, T.C. & Bass, D. (1992) Cognitive problem-solving skills training and parent management training in the treatment of antisocial behavior in children. *Journal of Consulting and Clinical Psychology,* **60,** 733–747.

Kirigin, K.A. Braukmann, C.J., Atwater, J. & Wolf, M.M. (1982) An evaluation of Achievement Place (Teaching-Family) group homes for juvenile offenders. *Journal of Applied Behavior Analysis,* **15,** 1–16.

Klein, N.C., Alexander, J.F. & Parsons, B.V. (1977) Impact of family systems intervention on recidivism and sibling delinquency: a model of primary prevention and program evaluation. *Journal of Consulting and Clinical Psychology,* **45,** 469–474.

Laws, D.R. (1974) The failure of a token economy. *Federal Probation,* **38,** 33–38.

Leeman, L.W., Gibbs, J.C. & Fuller, D. (1993) Evaluation of a multi-component group treatment program for juvenile delinquents. *Aggressive Behavior,* **19,** 281–292.

Leschied, A.W. & Gendreau, P. (1994) Doing justice in Canada: YOA policies that can promote community safety. *Canadian Journal of Criminology,* **36,** 291–303.

Lipsey, M.W. (1992) Juvenile delinquency treatment: a meta-analytic inquiry into the variability of effects. In T.D. Cook, H. Cooper D.S. Cordray, H. Hartmann, L.V. Hedges, R.J. Light, T.A. Louis & F. Mosteller (Eds), *Meta-analysis for Explanation: A Casebook.* New York: Russell Sage.

Lipsey, M.W. & Wilson, D.B. (1993) The efficacy of psychological, educational, and behavioral treatment: confirmation from meta-analysis. *American Psychologist,* **48,** 1181–1209.

Lipton, D.N., Martinson, R. & Wilks, D. (1975) *The Effectiveness of Correctional Treatment.* New York: Praeger.

Lochman, J.E. (1992) Cognitive–behavioral intervention with aggressive boys: three-year follow-up and preventive effects. *Journal of Consulting and Clinical Psychology,* **60,** 426–432.

Lösel, F. (1995) Increasing consensus in the evaluation of offender rehabilitation. Lessons from recent research syntheses. *Psychology, Crime, and Law,* **2,** 19–39.

Lösel, F. & Koferl, P. (1989) Evaluation research on correctional treatment in West Germany: a meta-analysis. In H. Wegener, F. Lösel & J. Haison (Eds), *Criminal Behaviour and the Justice System: Psychological Perspectives.* New York: Springer.

Lösel, F & Wittmann, W.W. (1989) The relationship of treatment integrity and intensity to outcome criteria. In R.F. Conner & M. Hendricks (Eds), *International Innovations in Evaluation Methodology: New Directions for Program Evaluation,* No. 42. San Francisco, CA: Jossey-Bass.

Luria, A.R. (1961) *The Role of Speech in the Regulation of Normal and Abnormal Behavior.* New York: Liveright.

Macallair, D. (1993) Reaffirming rehabilitation in juvenile justice. *Youth and Society,* **25,** 104–125.

Martin, G. & Pear, J. (1992) *Behavior Modification: What It Is and How To Do It,* 4th edn. London: Prentice-Hall.

Martinson, R. (1974) What works? Questions and answers about prison reform. *The Public Interest*, **35**, 22–54.

Mathlas, R.E. & Mathews, J.W. (1991) The boot camp program for offenders: does the shoe fit? *International Journal of Offender Therapy and Comparative Criminology*, **35**, 322–327.

McDougall, C., Barnett, R.M., Ashurst, B. & Willis, B. (1987) Cognitive control of anger. In B.J. McGurk, D.M. Thornton & M. Williams (Eds), *Applying Psychology to Imprisonment: Theory & Practice*. London: HMSO.

Milan, M.A. (1987) Basic behavioral procedures in closed institutions. In E.K. Morris & C.J. Braukmann (Eds), *Behavioral Approaches to Crime and Delinquency: A Handbook of Application, Research, and Concepts*. New York: Plenum.

Miller, W.R. (1985) Motivation for treatment: a review with special emphasis on alcoholism. *Psychological Bulletin*, **98**, 84–107.

Miller, W.R. & Rollnick, S. (1991) *Motivational Interviewing: Preparing People to Change Addictive Behavior*. New York: Guilford.

Mulvey, E.P., Arthur, M.W. & Reppucci, N.D. (1993) The prevention and treatment of juvenile delinquency: a review of the research. *Clinical Psychological Review*, **13**, 133–167.

Nelson, J.R., Smith, D.J. & Dodd, J. (1990) The moral reasoning of juvenile delinquents: a meta-analysis. *Journal of Abnormal Child Psychology*, **18**, 231–239.

Nietzel, M.T. (1979) *Crime and its Modification: A Social Learning Perspective*. New York: Pergamon.

Novaco, R.W. (1975) *Anger Control: The Development and Evaluation of an Experimental Treatment*. Lexington, MA: D.C. Heath.

Novaco, R.W. (1979) The cognitive regulation of anger and stress. In R. Kendall & S. Hollon (Eds), *Cognitive-Behavioral Interventions: Theory, Research and Practice*. New York: Academic.

Novaco, R.W. (1985) Anger and its therapeutic regulation. In M.A. Chesney & R.H. Rosenman (Eds), *Anger and Hostility in Cardiovascular and Behavioral Disorders*. New York: Hemisphere.

Novaco, R.W. (1994) Anger as a risk factor for violence among the mentally disordered. In J. Monahan & H.J. Steadman (Eds), *Violence and Mental Disorder: Developments in Risk Assessment*. Chicago, IL: University of Chicago Press.

O'Donnell, C.R., Lydgate, T. & Fo, W.S.O. (1979) The buddy system: review and follow-up. *Child Behavior Therapy*, **1**, 161–169.

Palmer, T. (1991) The effectiveness of intervention: recent trends and current issues. *Crime and Delinquency*, **37**, 330–346.

Palmer, T. (1992) *The Re-emergence of Correctional Intervention*. Newbury Park, CA: Sage.

Perkins, D. (1991) Clinical work with sex offenders in secure settings. In C.R. Hollin & K. Howells (Eds), *Clinical Approaches to Sex Offenders and their Victims*. Chichester: Wiley.

Pitts, J. (1992) The end of an era. *The Howard Journal*, **31**, 133–149.

Preston, M.A. (1982) Intermediate treatment: a new approach to community care. In M.P. Feldman (Ed.), *Developments in the Study of Criminal Behaviour, Vol. 1: The Prevention and Control of Offending*. Chichester: Wiley.

Quay, C. (Ed.) (1987) *Handbook of Juvenile Delinquency*. New York: Wiley.

Raynor, P. & Vanstone, M. (1994) *STOP: Straight Thinking on Probation, Third Interim Evaluation Report*. Bridgend, Mid-Glamorgan: Mid-Glamorgan Probation Service.

Remington, B. & Remington, M. (1987) Behavior modification in probation work: a review and evaluation. *Criminal Justice and Behavior*, **14**, 156–174.

Roberts, A.R. (1987) National survey and assessment of 66 treatment programs for juvenile offenders: model programs and pseudomodels. *Juvenile and Family Court Journal*, **38**, 39–45.

Roberts, A.R. & Camasso, M.J. (1991) Juvenile offender treatment programs and cost-benefit analysis. *Juvenile and Family Court Journal*, **42**, 37–47.

Ross, R.R. & Fabiano, E.A. (1985) *Time to Think: A Cognitive Model of Delinquency Prevention and Offender Rehabilitation*. Johnson City, TN: Institute of Social Sciences and Arts.

Ross, R.R. & Gendreau, P. (1980) *Effective Correctional Treatment*. Toronto: Butterworths.

Ross, R.R. & Ross, B.D. (1988) Delinquency prevention through cognitive training. *New Education*, **10**, 70–75.

Ross, R.R. & Ross, B.D. (1989) Delinquency prevention through cognitive training. *Educational Horizons*, Summer, 124–130.

Schneider, A.L. (1986) Restitution and recidivism rates of juvenile offenders: results from four experimental studies. *Criminology*, **24**, 533–552.

Slaby, R.G. & Guerra, N.G. (1988) Cognitive mediators of aggression in adolescent offenders: 1. Assessment. *Developmental Psychology*, **24**, 580–588.

Snyder, J.J. & White, M.J. (1979) The use of cognitive self-instruction in the treatment of behaviorally disturbed adolescents. *Behavior Therapy*, **10**, 227–235.

Spivack, G., Platt, J.J. & Shure, M.B. (1976) *The Problem-solving Approach to Adjustment: A Guide to Research and Intervention*. San Francisco, CA: Jossey–Bass.

Stumphauzer, J.S. (1976) Elimination of stealing by self-reinforcement of alternative behavior and family contracting. *Journal of Behavior Therapy and Experimental Psychiatry*, **7**, 265–268.

Thorton, D.M., Curran, L., Grayson, D. & Holloway, V. (1984) *Tougher Regimes in Detention Centres: Report of an Evaluation by the Young Offender Psychology Unit*. London: HMSO.

Weinrott, M.R., Jones, R.R. & Howard, J.R. (1982) Cost effectiveness of teaching family programs for delinquents: results of a national evaluation. *Evaluation Review*, **6**, 173–201.

Welch, G.J. (1985) Contingency contracting with a delinquent and his family. *Journal of Behaviour Therapy and Experimental Psychiatry*, **16**, 253–259.

Whitehead, J.T. & Lab, S.P. (1989) A meta-analysis of juvenile correctional treatment. *Journal of Research in Crime and Delinquency*, **26**, 276–295.

Wood, G., Green, L. & Bry, B.H. (1982) The input of behavioral training upon the knowledge and effectiveness of juvenile probation officers and volunteers. *Journal of Community Psychology*, **10**, 133–141.

WORKING WITH OFFENDERS: WHAT NEXT?

Clive R. Hollin

There is, I believe, at one level good grounds for optimism in thinking about the future of working with offenders. A clarion call of the 1990s has been to show that policies actually work: there can be few practitioners who have remained untouched by terms such as "objective", "target" and "performance indicator". While many practitioners have expressed concern at the managerialism that often surrounds this jargon, it is the case that this focus on effectiveness is to the advantage of good practice. As discussed throughout this book, there are many examples of highly effective ways of working with offenders. In some cases, as with young offenders, the evidence is very strong; in other instances, as perhaps with mentally disordered offenders, the evidence to date is not so strong. Nonetheless, there is a defensible position to the effect that when practitioners get it right, they can be highly effective in lowering rates of offending and, in the process, prevent victimization and save public money. The argument is not won and there will always be critics, but the case for working with offenders is becoming increasingly strong on grounds of effectiveness. The task for the years ahead is therefore to build on what is known about effective programmes – encompassing design of treatment programmes, and the management, support and training of practitioners – to become more effective and efficient.

Having said that, it appears that the sands are beginning to shift. In terms of criminal justice policy, both here and in the USA, a debate on basic

Working with Offenders: Psychological Practice in Offender Rehabilitation.
Edited by C.R. Hollin. © 1996 John Wiley & Sons Ltd.

philosophy is beginning to take shape. There are signals from policy makers that effectiveness in preventing offending is no longer the touchstone by which to judge the effectiveness of the system. Rather, increasingly the position appears to be taken that the criminal justice system should be a vehicle for retribution, plain and simple, so that society can see that offenders are made to suffer for their transgressions. This is seen in the "get tough" rhetoric, which talks about opening boot camps for young offenders with no other aim than to make them suffer for their crimes.

At the extremes of this retributionist movement, some American states are operating a "three strikes and out" policy, so that after three offences a life sentence is mandatory. This policy is increasing the prison population to fantastic levels, which seems to be something that the American public are at least willing to tolerate. Indeed, there are newspaper reports of a progression, if that is the right word, towards "three strikes and dead", as more states bring back the death penalty. Personally, I hope that is one American policy that drowns as it tries to cross the Atlantic.

In the face of these developments it seems likely that there will be new battles to be fought, battles in which the traditional weapons of outcome data and effectiveness may be outmoded. Time to start brushing up on moral arguments and the philosophy of punishment, I fear.

In the Preface I mentioned Robert Holdstock and Christopher Priest as the inspiration for an all British collection. For those who do not read science fiction, Holdstock and Priest are two of this country's leading science fiction authors. Their edited collection, titled *Stars of Albion*, published by Pan Books in 1979, is an anthology of the finest work of British science fiction writers.

INDEX

Index compiled by Liz Granger

Related titles of interest from Wiley...

Clinical Approaches to Working with Young Offenders

Edited by **Clive R. Hollin** and **Kevin Howells**

Examines clinical approaches used with specific groups of offenders, including adolescent sex offenders, firesetters, and alcohol and drug related crime, and reviews successful prevention programmes.

0-471-95348-2   300pp   1996   Hardback

What Works: Reducing Re-Offending

Guidelines from Research and Practice

Edited by **James McGuire**

Offers a critical review of research and practice with the focus on identifying interventions and models of offender treatment that really do work and are practical, and ways of evaluating treatment and offender services.

0-471-95053-X   264pp   1995   Hardback
0-471-95686-4   264pp   1995   Paperback

Handbook of Psychology in Legal Contexts

Edited by **Ray H.C. Bull** and **David Carson**

Highlights and emphasises both the extent to which psychologists are already assisting and informing the legal system and the potential that exists for collaboration between lawyers and psychologists.

0-471-94182-4   694pp   1995   Hardback

Young Offenders and Alcohol-Related Crime

A Practitioner's Guidebook

Mary McMurran and **Clive R. Hollin**

"The book definitely lives up to its claim to be a "Practitioner's Guidebook"... it contains some of the clearest, most user-friendly accounts of cognitive and behaviour theory and of motivational interviewing that I have come across..."   *- Probation Journal*

0-471-93839-4   208pp   1993   Paperback